P9-ART-664

PUTTING TRIALS ON TRIAL

PUTTING TRIALS ON TRIAL

Sexual Assault and the Failure of the Legal Profession

ELAINE CRAIG

McGill-Queen's University Press

Montreal & Kingston · London · Chicago

ISBN 978-0-7735-5277-7 (cloth)
ISBN 978-0-7735-5300-2 (ePDF)
ISBN 978-0-7735-5301-9 (ePUB)

Legal deposit first quarter 2018
Bibliothèque nationale du Québec

Printed in Canada on acid-free paper that is 100% ancient forest free (100% post-consumer recycled), processed chlorine free

This book has been published with the help of a grant from the Canadian Federation for the Humanities and Social Sciences, through the Awards to Scholarly Publications Program, using funds provided by the Social Sciences and Humanities Research Council of Canada.

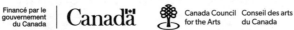

We acknowledge the support of the Canada Council for the Arts, which last year invested $153 million to bring the arts to Canadians throughout the country. Nous remercions le Conseil des arts du Canada de son soutien. L'an dernier, le Conseil a investi 153 millions de dollars pour mettre de l'art dans la vie des Canadiennes et des Canadiens de tout le pays.

Library and Archives Canada Cataloguing in Publication

Craig, Elaine, author
Putting trials on trial : sexual assault and the failure of the legal profession / Elaine Craig.

Includes bibliographical references and index.
Issued in print and electronic formats.
ISBN 978-0-7735-5277-7 (cloth). – ISBN 978-0-7735-5300-2 (ePDF). – ISBN 978-0-7735-5301-9 (ePUB)

1. Trials (Rape) – Canada. I. Title.

HV6569.C3C73 2018   345'.7102532   C2017-906267-0
                                                  C2017-906268-9

This book was designed and typeset by Peggy & Co. Design Inc. in 10.5/14 Warnock.

For Kim

Contents

Acknowledgments   ix

1   Sexual Assault and the Legal Profession   3

2   Pendulum Swings and Matriarchal Justice:
    Debunking Defence Counsel Myths   24

3   A Kinder and Gentler Approach? Interrogating
    the Heroes of the Defence Bar   61

4   The Sexual Assault Lawyer's Justice Project   100

5   The Role of the Crown in Sexual Assault Trials   135

6   Judging Sexual Assault Trials   167

7   Judicial Error in Sexual Assault Cases   191

8   We Owe a Responsibility ...   219

Notes   229

Index   301

Acknowledgments

I have great respect for the challenging work done by the legal professionals who practise in the criminal justice system. In conducting research for, and writing, this book I gained a sense of the difficulty faced by those who work in a context that forces them to confront and engage with the sexually harmful behaviour of others on a regular basis. Although a modest impact in comparison, I can relate. Days and months spent reviewing cases that detail these sexual harms, and poring over transcripts documenting other people's pain, takes a particular kind of toll. Sexual assault lawyers and judges do work that is critically important and deeply taxing.

Of course, the cost to legal professionals who work in, or study, this area of law pales in comparison to the trauma imposed upon too many of those who have relied upon our legal system to respond to violations of their sexual integrity. It seems facile, but nevertheless important, to acknowledge their ordeals.

In pursuing this project, I have benefited significantly from the generosity and support of many. There are several individuals in particular whom I would like to acknowledge.

I am indebted to the community of scholars, professionals, and experts who read parts, or all, of this work and whose insightful feedback indubitably added to the quality of this project. Thank you to Lisa Dufraimont, Elizabeth Sheehy, Constance Backhouse, Ruthann Robson, Richard Devlin, Ron MacDonald, Alice Woolley, Steve Coughlan, The Honourable Justice Thomas Cromwell, Marlane Brooks, and Jocelyn Downie. Thank you also to Justice David Cole, with whom numerous exchanges over the years have enhanced my understanding of several of the issues addressed in this book. I am deeply grateful to David Tanovich for his generous and constant support.

I would also like to acknowledge the defence lawyers and Crown attorneys who generously allowed me to interview them. These individuals were unstinting with both their time and their insights. I learned an extraordinary amount from speaking with them.

I am indebted to my generous and wise colleagues, Constance MacIntosh, Sheila Wildeman, Debra Parkes, Sonia Lawrence, and Joana Birenbaum, who, having read a draft of the full manuscript, then spent a full day workshopping the book.

Thank you to Kacie Oliver, whose meticulous and tireless research support improved this book immeasurably.

The research for this book would not have been possible without the financial support I received through an Insight Grant from the Social Sciences and Humanities Research Council of Canada. I also received support from the Schulich School of Law. Thank you to Dean Camille Cameron.

I also want to acknowledge the support and brilliance of my family, which is difficult to do in words. I am so grateful for my sons, Coltrane and Beckett: your energy and delight at the world and the people in it give me motivation and inspiration. May you inherit a society that treats women better. And most of all Kim, whose unfailing support, encouragement, good humour, and wisdom are without equal, and to whom this book is dedicated: you are my everyday light, my constant counsel and advocate, my deepest sense of connection in, and to, the world – thank you.

Parts of this book are taken from several articles I have published. This material appears throughout the book with the generous permission of previous publishers. Two paragraphs in chapter 2 and one paragraph in chapter 7 originally appeared in Elaine Craig, "Judging Sexual Assault Trials: Systemic Failure in the Case of *R v Bassam Al-Rawi*," *Canadian Bar Review* (2017, forthcoming). Passages in chapter 2, explaining section 276 of the *Criminal Code*, originally appeared in Elaine Craig, "Section 276 Misconstrued: The Failure to Properly Interpret and Apply Canada's Rape Shield Provisions," *Canadian Bar Review* 94, no. 1 (2016): 45. Passages in chapters 1, 2, and 4 are drawn from Elaine Craig, "The Ethical Identity of Sexual Assault Lawyers," *Ottawa Law Review* 47, no. 1 (2016): 73. Research originally published in Elaine Craig,

"Examining the Websites of Canada's 'Top Sex Crime Lawyers': The Ethical Parameters of Commercial Expression by the Criminal Defence Bar," UBC Law Review 48, no. 2 (2015): 257 appears in chapters 2 and 3, and passages from this article describing my methodology are included in chapter 1. Passages in chapters 1, 2, 3, 5, and 6 are drawn from Elaine Craig, "The Inhospitable Court," University of Toronto Law Journal 66, no. 2 (2016): 197, and are reprinted with permission from University of Toronto Press. Parts of chapters 2 and 4 originally appeared in Elaine Craig, "The Ethical Obligations of Defence Counsel in Sexual Assault Cases," Osgoode Hall Law Journal 51, no. 2 (2014): 427.

PUTTING TRIALS
ON TRIAL

CHAPTER 1

Sexual Assault and the Legal Profession

Imagine a society – one that purports to be a rule of law society – in which one segment of the population regularly engages in harmful acts of sexual violation against another segment of the community with almost complete legal immunity.

Canada is such a society.

Less than one percent of the sexual assaults that occur each year in Canada will result in any form of legal sanction for those who perpetrate these violations of another's sexual integrity.[1] In part, this is because most women do not report sexual assault. Indeed, over ninety percent of sexual assaults in Canada go unreported.[2] One of the main reasons women do not turn to the law to respond to their experiences of sexual violence is distrust and fear of the criminal justice process.[3] This is a stunning indictment of our legal response to sexual harm. Is this fear well-founded?

The sexual assault trial process in Canada has received significant scrutiny in the past few years as a consequence of the public attention focused on cases such as the prosecution of former Canadian Broadcasting Company radio host Jian Ghomeshi for his alleged sexual assaults on numerous women, the failings of Judge Greg Lenehan in the Halifax taxi driver case, and the judicial disciplinary proceedings against former Justice Robin Camp for his conduct in a sexual assault trial in Alberta. The current volume of public commentary, social media activity, expert opinion from legal professionals, and media coverage on issues of sexualized violence is unprecedented. Perhaps most unusually, a good deal of this attention is focused on the treatment and experiences of the women who serve our justice system as complainants in the prosecution of those accused of sexual violence.

The personal distress that the complainants in *Ghomeshi*, and in the case involving Justice Camp, reported as a consequence of their involvement in those trials was well publicized and is discussed later in this book. For now, consider how a few of the other women who performed this role in the criminal justice process in 2016 described their experience.

Following a 2016 trial in Nova Scotia, in which her former boyfriend was convicted of sexually assaulting her, the complainant reported to the CBC that her experience with the judicial system was "punishing."[4] She felt that she was treated as "less than an actual human being" throughout the two-year process. She stated that despite the conviction, she regretted having come forward.[5]

A few days after the man she accused of sexual assault was convicted, a Toronto woman described her experience with the year-long trial as follows: "The bulk of my rape trauma is not the result of the sexual assault itself but of the brutality of the legal system. This trauma is difficult to understand for those who have not lived it."[6]

In describing her experience testifying as a sexual assault complainant earlier in 2016, another Toronto woman stated: "When they say you get raped again on the stand, I initially didn't believe it to be true but it absolutely is."[7]

An Ottawa woman, who was cross-examined for almost three full days in the recent trial of the former spouse she accused of sexually assaulting her, reported: "It was shocking and horrible and traumatizing. It's not just re-traumatizing but it's a whole form of trauma itself."[8] She described requiring a bucket on the stand for the purpose of vomiting due to the level of distress she experienced during the cross-examination.

Research on sexual assault complainants who engage with the criminal justice system suggests that the damaging experiences articulated by these women are not anomalous. Numerous studies have concluded that, despite progressive law reforms aimed at protecting witnesses in sexual assault cases, for many the impact of testifying as a sexual assault complainant remains traumatizing and harmful.[9]

This problematic circumstance is compounded by the horrific reality that in some cases women are *forced* to perform this potentially traumatic role in the criminal justice process. Criminal offences, including sexual assault, are prosecuted in the name and interests of the public, not the survivor, and so just as there is no right to require that one's attacker be prosecuted, neither is there a right to refuse to participate as a witness if the Crown does decide to prosecute. As a matter of policy, some Crowns will only pursue sexual assault convictions if the complainant is a willing participant, but this is neither universally true nor legally required. This quote from a Crown attorney interviewed as part of Karen-Lee Miller's 2013 study is revealing:

> I did not want it to happen this way but it went down that I had a prostitute complainant not show up for court, and I had her arrested on the street that night where she worked so that she could come and testify. She sure as hell wasn't sticking around to file a [Victim Impact Statement] afterwards.[10]

Similarly, when asked why she continued to participate in the process given that she found it so difficult, a sexual assault complainant interviewed as part of Allyson Clarke's research stated: "Well, you see, even though I was a victim, sometimes when you're a victim you're subpoenaed to finish it. So, because of that, I had no choice. I had no choice. I had to finish it."[11] The researcher asked her whether she would have quit had that been an option. The complainant responded, "Hell yeah I would. I would have dropped out like you wouldn't believe. Because nobody deserves that. To hear those questions or to see the offender."[12]

In the following excerpt from the transcript of a 2014 sexual assault trial in Alberta, it is clear that the complainant did not want to testify. She stated eight times during her testimony in chief that she did not want to continue describing the sexual attack she had endured:

> [CROWN] Q. All right. ——, after he talked about cutting you up, what happened then?
>
> [COMPLAINANT] A. That's, like, when the sexual assault I guess happened ... He, like – he was forcing me to give him oral sex, and I didn't want to do that. And I was crying, and he was hitting me asking me why I was crying.
>
> Q. Okay. Let's stop you there.
>
> A. I don't want to talk about it.
>
> Q. ——, would you like a couple minutes just to have a drink of water?

A. Can I leave for a minute? I just want to – because there's, like, way more, and I just don't even know if I can talk about it right now because –

Q. You know what, I want you to stay there and just have a drink of water. All right.

A. I really don't want to talk about this anymore because I can't do it right now.

Q. ——, you said that he wanted you to give him oral sex. I want you to tell the Court what you mean by that, what he did.

A. I can't even talk about it.

...

Q. ——, you said he forced his something. I want you to tell the Court –

A. His penis in my face. He put it in my – he was sitting on – with his legs over top of me and he took his pants off and put his penis in my face. And I was crying. And I told him I didn't want to do that.

Q. Okay. Stop there.

A. And he kept hitting me. I don't want to talk about this.

Q. Just a minute, ——.

A. I don't want to talk about this. I want to go. I am – I cannot, like, do this right now. It's really difficult to go on from here because it's really – a lot of detail.

Q. ——, just –

A. And it's really hard right now, okay. I can't.[13]

The complainant in this trial, a twenty-two-year-old Indigenous woman, did not return to court the following day to continue testifying. As a result, she was arrested under a witness warrant, held in cells, and then forced to continue testifying in what became a five-day ordeal that left her feeling "hopeless," "depressed," and "suicidal."[14] The media has revealed other recent cases in which sexual assault complainants, in particular women from marginalized communities, have been jailed in order to compel their presence in court.[15] To summarize, there is reasonable evidence – both self-reported anecdotal evidence and qualitative and quantitative social science research – from which to conclude that sexual assault proceedings continue to traumatize complainants, including those who do not participate in this public legal process voluntarily. Despite decades of reform to the rules of evidence and the substantive law of sexual assault,[16] the trial process remains deeply harmful for many of those who allege sexual violation.

But why put sexual assault *lawyering* on trial? Is it really fair to place responsibility for the trauma of the trial on the legal profession itself? Are not defence lawyers, Crown attorneys, and trial judges simply doing their jobs within the parameters of a legal process that is unavoidably harmful to its participants, and to sexual assault complainants in particular?

It is true that certain aspects of a criminal trial make it likely that testifying as a sexual assault complainant will always be difficult for many survivors of sexual violence. Factors such as the trial's adversarial nature, and the need for complainants to recount in detail experiences and information that they are socialized to understand as deeply personal, suggest that the process will always be challenging, if not distressing. However, that the process is likely to always be difficult for complainants does not make it any less important both to recognize the ways in which lawyers and judges contribute to the trauma of the trial, and to take whatever steps are reasonably possible to make the process more humane. Some of the harm experienced by complainants is caused (and unnecessarily so) by the way that some lawyers and judges conduct sexual assault cases.

Take, for example, the issue of shame. It is very common for survivors of sexual assault to experience feelings of shame and humiliation.[17] The emotional impact of being sexually assaulted was described by one participant in a recent study by Statistics Canada as follows: "[i]t just made me feel defiled and dirty and sick and ill – like a piece of garbage."[18] Research suggests that shame is a particularly debilitating emotion – one that diminishes an individual's sense of self-worth and leads to greater reliance on unhealthy coping strategies, higher levels of post-trauma distress, and increased feelings of powerlessness.[19]

Like fear of the criminal justice system, shame is identified by survivors as one of the most common barriers to reporting their experiences of sexual violence.[20] Describing her own reluctance to disclose her rape to others, Professor Karyn Freedman writes:

> [I] was hot with shame over it ... Rape intersects with multiple taboos – sex, violence, and trauma – and its savage intrusion on our sexuality crosses the boundary into that which is most personal and private. For all these reasons, it is simply not socially acceptable for a woman to speak out about her experience as a rape survivor.[21]

Freedman also offers insight into the way in which the socially imposed inhibition about discussing one's experiences of sexual violence furthers feelings of self-blame. She explains the self-perpetuating nature of this type of shame as follows:

> Keeping our rape stories secret lowers the decibel level on the magnitude of the problem and perpetuates the idea that rape happens somewhere else, to someone else. It makes us complicit in the act of covering up the realities of sexual violence against women, which helps to preserve the myth that women have complete control over their bodies. Again, the picture of rape that falls out of this worldview turns rape into a personal problem rather than a social one. No wonder rape survivors end up blaming themselves.[22]

In other words, the shame commonly experienced by those who are sexually assaulted inhibits reporting. Lack of reporting renders sexual violence invisible, relegating it to the personal and private sphere rather than constructing it as a public, social problem. Its invisibility, in turn, promotes self-blame and discourages survivors from disclosing. Think of it as a negative feedback loop: shame inhibits reporting; lack of reporting perpetuates shame; this presumably further inhibits reporting.

What, though, is the connection between this problematic dynamic and the way in which sexual assault law is practised and adjudicated by the legal profession?

Criminal trials require sexual assault complainants to give voice publicly, over and over again, to violations of their sexual integrity about which they may experience feelings of profound shame and self-disgust. Consider this statement from a complainant in a recent Ontario trial:

> [CROWN] Q. When you went to the hospital, you said you were hurting all over. How were you – other than that, how were you feeling? Tell me about the way that you felt.
>
> [COMPLAINANT] A. I felt sick. Like I couldn't even touch myself. I couldn't even, like rubbing my hands, I felt sick. I just wanted to stand out and not touch myself. Even clothing hurt on me. I was sickened with myself. I felt nauseous and I was just so disgusted with my body.[23]

It is reasonable to conclude that testifying, even absent any aggravating factors, is likely to contribute to a sexual assault complainant's feelings of shame. Unfortunately, the way that sexual assault law is practised and adjudicated can aggravate these feelings of shame. This can occur overtly as a consequence of the strategy, tone, demeanour, or language used by legal professionals in their interactions with complainants; it can also occur in more insidious ways. To understand the latter requires recognizing the connection between gender stereotypes, women's subjugation, and the shame experienced by many survivors.

Sexualized violence is a gendered harm.[24] Given the prevailing gender hierarchies in our society, the gendered nature of sexual assault contributes to a complicated relationship between sexual victimization and self-blame (with corresponding feelings of shame). To explain further, the hierarchical manifestation of gender as a principle of social organization and control – through constructs such as the moral, mental, and physical inferiority of women, the presumptive sexual availability of women, and the notion of sexually active women as untrustworthy – makes it likely that sexual assault survivors will question their own complicity in the sexual violations they experience. They have been socialized to do so. The result of this self-blame is often shame.[25]

The relationship between sexual assault, gender hierarchy, and shame is further aggravated by the continued acceptance of, or reliance on, problematic assumptions about sexuality and sexual violence in Canadian courtrooms.[26] Again, these assumptions include discriminatory notions about women's sexual availability, and their own degree of culpability (blameworthiness) in causing the sexual violence they experience. One consequence of this continued reliance on outdated and sexist stereotypes is the reality that women who allege sexual assault will often be questioned about things such as why they failed to fight back, why they failed to scream, whether they flirted with the accused, why they went to his house alone, or whether they were wearing underwear, and if so, of what type and colour. When sexual assault complainants are forced to respond to these stereotype-infused questions in the context of alleging sexual violation, the social dynamics of shame and self-blame are reinforced. That is to say, when legal professionals invoke, reason upon, or fail to reject these gendered stereotypes, the shame experienced by sexual assault complainants is aggravated.

The vulnerability associated with performing this witness role – with providing the type of gendered testimony required of sexual assault complainants – is compounded by the inferior position of the complainant relative to other trial participants, such as the lawyers and judge. The courtroom and trial process is filled with hierarchy. Complainants (and accused individuals) play parts in the trial process that are subordinate to the roles played by legal professionals. For example, they are only permitted to answer, never ask, the questions. They must comply with, never create, the ceremonies, timing, attire, and ordering of the trial. Lawyers and judges have university educations and specialized legal training and knowledge. In many cases there will be a significant gap between the educational endowment and socio-economic status of the legal professionals involved in a trial and the complainant (as well as the accused). In addition, socio-economic status is often connected in inequitable ways to race, Indigeneity, and disability. These factors all contribute to the profound power differential between those who control the process and those who are subject to it. These attributes and performances of hierarchy at trial, in which sexual assault complainants play subordinate roles, mirror the very social dynamic (i.e. gender hierarchy and the logic of self-blame) that causes them to experience shame as a result of sexual intrusion in the first instance. In other words, the subordinate role that complainants perform in sexual assault trials may further the gendered (and often classist, racist, or able-bodied) dominance perpetuated through sexual violence itself. The result is a legal process that can be hostile to empowerment, reclamation or rehabilitation of one's sense of sexual integrity, and even psychological survival. Thus the suggestion by some complainants that the trial is nearly as traumatic as the sexual assault itself.[27]

Simply put, lawyers and judges who practise and adjudicate in ways that rely upon rape mythology cause real harm – both by shaming individual complainants and by contributing to a social context in which fear of the legal process and feelings of shame and self-blame mean that men can sexually violate women (and children) with almost complete legal impunity. Given that revisions to the rules of evidence and the law of sexual assault have legally rejected many of these gendered stereotypes about sexual violence, continued use of and reliance upon them by lawyers and judges represents one example of a harm to sexual assault survivors that is both caused by legal professionals and avoidable. In light of the reality that progressive law reforms aimed at improving the treatment of sexual assault complainants have been largely unsuccessful in increasing rates of reporting, diminishing survivors' fear of the criminal justice process, or eradicating reliance by lawyers and judges on discriminatory stereotypes, putting sexual assault lawyering on trial makes good sense.

An Outline of the Chapters

Sexual assault trials are not designed to heal complainants. They are designed to ascertain whether the state can, through a fair process, prove beyond a reasonable doubt that an accused committed the sexual offence with which he has been charged. The objective of this book is not to marry justice and healing. Given the narrow mandate and individualistic and reactive nature of the criminal trial process, such a pursuit would likely be futile. Nor is the aim to see more sexual offenders incarcerated. Instead, the ambition of this work is to identify the ways in which the legal profession unnecessarily (and in some instances unlawfully) contributes to the harms experienced by those who participate in the criminal trial process as sexual assault complainants. Yes, we have an adversarial system committed to the due process interests of the accused. The need to ensure a fair trial for any individual accused of a criminal offence is of paramount importance to the justness of our legal system. However, there are changes within the control of the legal profession that could reduce the re-victimization that is experienced by some of those who turn to, or are forced into, the criminal justice process following violations of their sexual integrity. To this end, the contributions of the legal profession to the trauma of the trial are examined in three sections in this book, corresponding to their roles: criminal defence lawyers, Crown attorneys, and trial judges.

The first part of the book (chapters 2, 3, and 4) examines the criminal defence bar. Often when complainants describe the trauma of the trial, they identify the experience of being cross-examined by defence counsel as most distressing.[28] Accused individuals have a constitutional right to full answer and defence, which in most cases means a right to confront their accusers.[29] For defence lawyers, this right of their clients translates into a duty of loyalty to cross-examine complainants in a full and thorough manner. This duty of loyalty owed by defence counsel to an accused client is frequently identified as a barrier to improving the trial experience of complainants. In part, the aim of this first section of the book is to demonstrate that defence lawyers can reduce their contributions to the trauma experienced by complainants while at the same time ensuring that neither their duty of loyalty nor their clients' right to a full and fair defence are compromised.

However, before we can consider how best to achieve this objective, there is a factual dispute that must be resolved. As was clearly evidenced in the public commentary surrounding the *Ghomeshi* trial, some members of the criminal defence bar do not accept the contention that sexual assault complainants are regularly abused, humiliated, or intimidated by criminal defence lawyers. They argue that, while complainants may experience the trial as traumatic, it is not because of the way in which they are treated by criminal defenders. In fact, some defence lawyers go even further. They assert that the pendulum has swung so far in favour of protecting sexual assault complainants that an accused individual today cannot receive a truly fair trial.[30] Chapter 2 tackles this factual debate. Relying on trial transcripts, interviews, criminal law firm websites, and reported case law, chapter 2 exposes significant evidence of defence lawyers engaging in strategies that are arguably abusive, or unnecessarily aggressive or humiliating towards sexual assault complainants.

Building on the examples of arguably problematic practices offered in chapter 2, the next chapter considers the relationship between the professional virtues celebrated by the defence bar and the treatment of sexual assault complainants. Chapter 3 asks whether the stories told about and by the legal profession's heroes, and the celebration of courtroom aggression, could be changed in ways that would discourage the mistreatment of complainants. This inquiry is pursued, in part, through case studies of four prominent criminal defence lawyers who have been highly celebrated by the legal profession. Chapter 3 shows that, despite claims to the contrary, some of the profession's most experienced criminal defence lawyers do, in fact, deploy strategies that might fairly be characterized as abusive, overly aggressive, or reliant on gendered stereotypes.

Chapter 4 explores how criminal defence lawyers themselves understand their professional role when defending someone accused of a sexual offence. Relying on interviews conducted with senior members of the criminal bar across Canada, and the published memoirs of prominent criminal lawyers, this chapter reveals a professional identity that is, in fact, inconsistent with the profession's celebration of courtroom aggression. More importantly, chapter 4 also exposes the inconsistency between the principles that defence lawyers commonly identify as fundamental to what they do, and the use of trial strategies that rely on discriminatory stereotypes or are aimed at intimidating sexual assault complainants. Revelation of this inconsistency is promising. With greater professional self-awareness, more defence lawyers may come to accept that pursuing strategies that are aimed at intimidating complainants or that rely on discriminatory stereotypes is both unethical and inconsistent with their self-understanding of their professional role in the justice system.

To be clear, this book does not advocate a diminishment of the presumption of innocence, the state's burden of proof, or the accused's right to remain silent and right to confront his accuser, nor the defence lawyer's role in protecting these rights. Nor does it suggest that defence lawyers are responsible for the social problem of sexual harm. The chapters examining the criminal defence bar are aimed at demonstrating practices by defence lawyers that I would argue are unnecessarily harmful to sexual assault complainants (and in some cases unlawful). Commitment to reducing these harms is an objective all lawyers should pursue. As Frank Addario, a highly respected criminal defence lawyer in Toronto, recently stated in reference to the work of those interested in improving the criminal trial experience for sexual assault complainants: .

> If the movement means nothing more than that gendered or rude treatment of sex assault survivors is intolerable I'll support that and so will my colleagues. If it means more education of justice system participants, including defence counsel, is needed about sexual violence and how victims behave, I'm for that too. If it means that we are no longer entitled to promote or rely on rape myths, I'm in.[31]

Indeed, Addario has identified precisely the objectives of this book (and, in particular, the next three chapters).

Chapter 5 considers the ways in which Crown attorneys either contribute to or mitigate the trauma of the trial for sexual assault complainants. Crown attorneys are duty-bound to ensure a fair process for the accused, the complainant, and the public. Chapter 5 explores the parameters of this duty in the context of sexual assault trials. With respect to sexual assault complainants, this duty includes an obligation to properly prepare them for trial, and a responsibility at trial to guard against the types of gender discrimination that distort the truth-seeking process and prevent equal access to the justice system for everyone. Relying on trial transcripts from recent sexual assault cases, this chapter offers examples both of cases in which Crown attorneys meet this duty and of those in which they arguably fail to do so.

In chapter 6 the focus is turned to trial judges. Like Crown attorneys, trial judges have a duty to protect both the trial process and its participants. This chapter examines the duty of trial judges to intervene in order to protect complainants from repetitive, overly aggressive cross-examination, and it highlights in some cases the failure to meet that duty. I also discuss a related obligation on the part of trial judges to ensure that they enforce the legal protections for sexual assault complainants achieved through law reform, such as legal limits on the use of a complainant's prior sexual history. Unfortunately, some trial judges continue to allow defence counsel to use evidence of a complainant's other sexual activity to humiliate, intimidate, or trigger discriminatory stereotypes. Chapter 6 also considers some steps that could be taken by judges to humanize the rituals and physical setting of the courtrooms in which they preside.

Chapter 7 examines the way in which judicial errors in the interpretation and application of basic legal concepts such as the definition of consent contribute to the harms experienced by sexual assault complainants. Using examples of trial judges whose reasoning in recent sexual assault cases suggests a lack of understanding of the most basic legal rule of sexual assault (the definition of consent), chapter 7 examines the particular gender-based harms to complainants caused by legal errors of this nature. The legal reasoning demonstrated in these cases raises questions about judicial appointment processes and judicial education in Canada.

The final chapter reintroduces the stories of several of the women whose cases are studied in this book. Chapter 8 focuses again on the real harms caused by the way sexual assault law is practised and adjudicated. It also highlights the resiliency and tenacity of these women, in an effort to emphasize the role they bravely (and sometimes unwillingly) perform in the public legal process that we, as a society, continue to deploy as our primary response to sexual violence.

Sexual assault lawyering as it is currently practised causes harm to many sexual assault complainants. While some of these harms may be unavoidable, there are measures that could be taken to make our courts more hospitable to women who have survived sexual violence. Promisingly, and as will be explained, the types of changes advanced in this book are not in tension with the fundamentally important, constitutionally enshrined protections for accused individuals. In other words, these changes could be achieved without having to confront the difficult (and controversial) proposition of balancing the rights of the criminally accused with those of their victims. A failure on the part of the legal profession to assume responsibility for reforms of this nature is inexcusable.

Some Notes about Choice of Language

Throughout this book, the names of the individual lawyers and judges involved in the cases discussed are used, specific law firm websites are named and examined, and the public statements of particular lawyers are scrutinized. This is a departure from the approach taken by most legal scholars. With the exception of Supreme Court of Canada jurists, it is more typical in legal writing to refer exclusively to roles (i.e. "the Crown," "the defence," and "the trial judge") and institutions (e.g. "the Court" or "the police") rather than legal actors themselves. The use of names of specific individuals is not intended to attribute individualized responsibility for the harmful treatment regularly imposed upon sexual assault complainants. To the contrary, one of the primary objectives of this book is to demonstrate that the legal profession's contributions to the harms experienced by sexual assault complainants are systemic. The profession as a whole must take responsibility for this circumstance.

The decision to use the names of specific lawyers, law firms, and judges is motivated by a desire to avoid the obfuscation and distancing that occurs when we speak only of roles and institutions rather than individuals. Dissociating legal actors from their actions reinforces an entrenched narrative about role-based morality that is, as demonstrated in this book, in need of further reflection. Lastly, when we speak only in terms of roles and institutions, the contrast between the profoundly personal exposure of the complainant that occurs during the sexual assault trial process and the faceless and nameless actors of the justice system is simply too stark. Our justice system, as a lived reality for lay participants, *is* its legal actors. Reducing them in legal scholarship to faceless roles and institutions is elitist and outdated.

In addition to the decision to name specific legal actors, three choices concerning the language used throughout this book may be controversial for some readers. First, as is apparent even from this introductory chapter, I have at times referred to "women" when discussing those subjected to sexual violence, and "men" when discussing those who sexually violate others. It is, of course, true that men are also sexually assaulted, as are male children, as well as individuals who do not identify as either male or female. It is also true that women commit sexual assault. However, sexual assault is an offence that is overwhelmingly perpetrated by men against women (and children).[32] The choice of language utilized in this book is unapologetically intended to reflect the reality that sexual violence is gendered. As was so eloquently stated by Justice Cory in *R v Osolin*, "It cannot be forgotten that a sexual assault is very different from other assaults ... Sexual assault is in the vast majority of cases gender based. It is an assault upon human dignity and constitutes a denial of any concept of equality for women."[33]

A second issue concerning language relates to the use of the term "sexual assault complainant." When referring to a woman engaged in the criminal trial process I have used the term "sexual assault complainant," and in other contexts the term "survivor." For some, the term "sexual assault complainant" problematically connotes a lack of belief in the allegations. In this book, the term "complainant" is assumed to have both legal and political meaning. Its legal connotation relates to fundamental principles of criminal justice to which all feminists should be committed: the presumption of innocence and the state's burden and standard of proof.

There is also a broader, more political element to the term "complainant," or more particularly, to the role to which the term refers. Sexual assault prosecutions are pursued in the name and interests of the public. As already noted, women who allege sexual assault have neither a right to a public prosecution, nor any standing to dictate or shape the manner in which such a prosecution will proceed. Indeed, and as also already noted, women who allege sexual assault do not even have a legal right to decide whether to participate in the public's prosecution of their alleged abuser. The minute subset of survivors who serve as complainants in the criminal law's response to sexual violence are performing a role (sometimes involuntarily) in a public process. In considering the way that sexual assault complainants are treated throughout this legal process, it is important to remain cognizant of the fact that we ask, expect, and sometimes compel these women to serve the criminal justice system in this regard.

Third, some of the content in this book is very graphic. The language used by lawyers and complainants in the cases examined is not sanitized, paraphrased, or reduced to description. This is intentional. In many instances the full texture of the treatment to which some complainants are subjected cannot be captured through description or paraphrase. To describe or paraphrase what was said to them at trial, or what was done to them to precipitate that trial, in order to make it easier to read, or less discomfiting, would betray both the objective of this work and the justification for using the stories of these women. While this makes some parts of the book difficult to read, the cost of sanitizing this content would be too great.

A Brief Word about the Methods Used

To demonstrate the ways in which legal professionals contribute to the harms experienced by sexual assault complainants, I have tried, to the extent possible, to use examples drawn from the statements and practices of lawyers and judges themselves.[34] (This seemed particularly important in chapters 2 and 3, which attempt to challenge the factual assertions, made by some vocal members of the criminal defence bar, that abusing sexual assault complainants on the stand is a thing of the past and that experienced lawyers know better than to conduct their cases in this manner.) The practices and attitudes of legal professionals in the context of sexual assault cases were studied through multiple sources of data: trial transcripts; in-depth qualitative interviews with senior lawyers; criminal law firm websites; public statements and interviews given by lawyers; lawyer memoirs; Crown policy manuals; appellate *facta*; and reported case law.

One of the primary sources of data relied upon in this book is trial transcripts. Transcripts from twenty recent sexual assault trials in

Canada were examined. Trial transcripts are extremely difficult for researchers to obtain. Securing them is time-consuming and expensive. Obtaining full transcripts of trials that have not already been transcribed is cost-prohibitive. With three exceptions, all of the transcripts relied upon here are from cases in which the transcript had already been produced, in most cases for purposes of appeal. Even when transcripts have already been produced, in some provinces it is still difficult to obtain copies of them; every province has a different, often cumbersome, administrative process for ordering copies of transcripts. Some provinces, such as Nova Scotia and Newfoundland, have no formal process for obtaining previously produced transcripts. Some of the transcripts examined for this project were obtained easily, through either formal or informal channels; obtaining others took repeated requests and months of diligent follow-up. Given the difficulty and expense of securing trial transcripts, I pursued either cases where there was some reference to the length or style of defence counsel's cross-examination of the complainant in a reported decision of the case (or in media coverage of the case), or cases in which a court of appeal, in overturning a trial decision, suggested that stereotypical thinking had informed the trial judge's reasoning.

It was important that the cases be recent. The oldest transcript relied upon is from a 2009 trial. All of the others are from trials that occurred within the last six years. There have been many changes to the rules of evidence and the substantive law of sexual assault. Using older cases would risk relying on examples of trial practices that no longer occur because of these changes.

The twenty cases for which transcripts were obtained are not relied upon to make assertions about the prevalence of the problematic practices that they arguably reveal. They are used to demonstrate the nature of these practices. They offer a more textured and detailed picture of the types of cross-examinations of complainants that trial judges consider worthy of comment in their reported decisions, and/or the treatment of complainants in cases in which Crown *facta* or appellate courts have suggested that the trial judge's reasoning was based on stereotypes.[35]

Trial transcripts are a unique type of text, in terms of both their limits and what they can reveal. As both Elizabeth Sheehy and Emma Cunliffe have noted, transcription does not produce an exact record of an event.[36] Trial transcripts omit some oral communication (such as sighing, groaning, or weeping) and fail to capture most nonverbal content (such as tone of voice, facial expression, body language, and affect).[37]

Though written transcripts are hard to obtain and do not represent an exact version of the interactions among trial participants, the trauma of a trial is still better evidenced by the transcript than by what is written about the case by a judge. The power dynamics between the various parties, the humiliating exposure of the personal, and the overall cruelty of the process can emerge clearly from a transcript's account of the words spoken, the questions asked and answered, and the emotions recorded. The microscopic level at which complainants are cross-examined is demonstrated by the transcripts in a way that simply could not be captured in a judicial decision. It becomes less possible to distance ourselves from the severity of the process that sexual assault complainants undergo when we are confronted with their own words and the words spoken to them. (This is true even though their voices are severely limited by the rigidly proscribed form of oral testimony permitted in court.)[38] That said, the same attribute that makes these transcripts a critical access point to examining the process of a sexual assault trial also poses an ethical problem. The transcripts capture the words of individuals. They record stories of trauma, violence, pain, and suffering. As lawyers, judges, and academics we examine, analyze, argue, and write about other people's painful experiences – about some of the worst moments in their lives – and we often do so without their consent. This is true whether we are working from transcripts or case law, but the dilemma seems more acute when using transcripts. Absent abandoning the attempt to study the complainants' own words (and the words spoken to them) at trial, there is not an obvious solution to this ethical issue. It is nevertheless important to be attuned to the reality that the study of these transcripts is undertaken without the consent of the complainants involved.

The same trial transcripts used in chapters 2 and 3 to illustrate arguably problematic or harmful cross-examinations are considered again in the chapters on the roles of the Crown and judiciary. Using examples from the same transcripts was intentional. It is hard to maintain that the mistreatment of sexual assault complainants is a function of a small number of problematic cross-examinations rather than a more systemic problem, when one considers the arguably parallel failure of the Crown and judiciary to perform their responsibilities in some of the same cases.

In addition to studying the words spoken by, and to, complainants at trial, statements by defence lawyers and Crown attorneys are also considered. Their words are taken from the transcripts, interviews,

Crown policy manuals, and what legal professionals have said about the law of sexual assault on their law firm websites, in social media, and through public commentary.

I conducted twenty semi-structured interviews with experienced criminal lawyers in four Canadian provinces.[39] Fifteen of the lawyers interviewed had defence practices at the time of the interview and five were working as Crown attorneys. Nine of the participants were women and the remaining eleven were men. All of the lawyers interviewed had significant practice experience in the area of sexual assault law. A transcript of each interview was created and coded.[40] The lawyers who participated in these interviews were generous with both their time and insights. The interviews were given with the stipulation that the participants would remain anonymous. The names of these lawyers do not appear in this book.[41] The names of their firms, their law firm websites, the cases they have been involved in, and any statements they have made publicly or in articles they have published also do not appear in this book.

In addition to transcripts and interviews, prominent criminal law firm websites were examined in order to ascertain how lawyers who practise in this area of law talk about sexual violence in their online marketing materials. Examination of these websites offered a window into the narratives about sexual assault that some defence lawyers construct for their clients, and perhaps also the perspectives about sexual assault held by these defence lawyers themselves. Many law firm websites are content-heavy. The richest among them include not only contact and credential information about the firm's lawyer or lawyers, but also substantive descriptions of the area of law practised by the firm, blogs discussing leading cases and contemporary legal issues, descriptions of past cases in which the lawyer secured a positive outcome for his or her client, and, at least in the criminal law context, references to the types of defences available and the kinds of trial strategies deployed by the firm.

The websites of criminal lawyers in Ontario, Alberta, British Columbia, and Manitoba were examined. The websites studied can reasonably be characterized as among the most prominent web-based advertising by criminal defence lawyers practising sexual assault law in Canada. While these websites do not exemplify the type of commercial expression present on the websites of all, or even most, criminal defence lawyers, they do reflect the type of content found on the highest-profile criminal law firm websites in these provinces at the time this study was conducted.[42]

For many of the women who serve as complainants in sexual assault cases, the experience is brutal. The trial process, which is largely designed and operated by able-bodied white people, is even worse for disabled, racialized, and Indigenous complainants.[43] The shockingly higher rate at which Indigenous women in Canada are sexually assaulted makes the traumatic reality of this process for them particularly alarming.[44] Moreover, there is at least some evidence to suggest a negative relationship between income level and rate of reporting; some research indicates that the more income a woman has, the less likely she is to report.[45] This means that women with lower incomes, and thus presumably less social status and power, may be more likely to serve the criminal justice system as sexual assault complainants.

Beyond the negative consequences for individual complainants, the potential adverse impact on reporting rates caused by the traumatic experience of complainants at trial has the potential to create broader social problems. Underreporting of a harmful criminal act, when it reaches the levels it has with respect to sexual violence in Canada, has multiple undesirable social effects. Fear of coming forward, of course, reduces the likelihood that women will access the modest benefits that are currently available for survivors – such as access to victim's compensation schemes, state-funded counselling, and health care services.

Lack of reporting, when it occurs at levels this high, also constitutes a threat to social understandings of our society as governed by the rule of law. When the overwhelming majority of women who are sexually assaulted do not report these experiences, sexual violence is more readily constructed as a series of personal and unspeakable events or isolated incidents, rather than a societal practice of systemic gender discrimination. The phenomenon of widespread, gender-based sexual harm is personalized rather than understood as a social problem, a symptom of severe societal dysfunction that demands systemic, public responses.

Consider, for example, this excerpt from a letter to the editor of the *Windsor Star* complaining that the paper had published too much coverage of a sexual assault trial taking place in Windsor, Ontario:

I can't believe the *Windsor Star* would lower itself to print, on the first page no less, this pornographic garbage.

Haven't we seen and heard enough of this? There must have been bigger and better news that should have been printed as your lead story.[46]

Setting aside the writer's troubling eroticization of the details of this sexual assault, as reported by the paper and for which the accused was ultimately convicted, her insistence that this case was not newsworthy and should be relegated to the private rather than public sphere reflects this problematic construction of sexual violence as a personal issue.

Constructing sexual violence as personal and private supports the societal disinclination to believe sexual assault survivors, and our society's corresponding tendency to interpret women who allege sexual violation as being complicit in, and thus having consented to, the sexual act at issue.[47] The connection between this construction of sexual violence as personal and private, and the victim-blaming mentality that it produces, is evident in a second letter to the *Windsor Star*, from a reader voicing a similar complaint. Reflect upon how this second letter-writer characterized what was (as had been reported by the paper) a violent sexual attack, including forced vaginal intercourse, that left the barely conscious sixteen-year-old complainant bleeding in the bathroom of a local bar:

The morbid story of the alleged sexual escapades of hockey hero Ben Johnson have now taken up a major section of the front page of my newspaper ... We should encourage our children to read newspapers but please provide them with real news ... If I want to read about kids making out in a bathroom, I will look elsewhere.[48]

Describing allegations of a brutal sexual assault on a severely intoxicated young woman as a sexual escapade or make-out session reflects precisely the type of victim-blaming, discriminatory thinking that contributes to a public discourse that shames and silences survivors of sexual violence.

A legal system in which more than nine out of every ten sexual assaults receive no legal scrutiny is a profoundly dysfunctional legal system. The criminal law and the justice system remain the state's primary response to the social problem of sexual harm. That is unlikely to change in the near future. Women who testify against those who sexually assault them perform a role in what is a public legal process. This book examines ways in which we might make the performance of that role less harmful.

To the extent that the legal profession unnecessarily contributes to the trauma of the trial, and the corresponding potential effect on rates of reporting, changes must be made. The types of changes contemplated in this book are limited to those that could be made without having to either reimagine the adversarial nature of our current process or reconcile the potential tension between protecting complainants and ensuring the constitutionally enshrined rights of the accused. In other words, these are changes that the legal profession could accept responsibility for, and make, without encountering any structural or constitutional barriers. The recommended modifications include: ways to make courtrooms more familiar, more inclusive, and less intimidating; steps that should be taken by the Crown to better support complainants throughout the process; recommendations for judges, including improved judicial education programs; and strategies to promote greater awareness and acceptance by criminal lawyers of what their ethical obligations not to abuse complainants entail.

A first step in pursuing these changes requires recognition by the legal profession that some of the ways in which sexual assault law continues to be practised in Canada today (unnecessarily) contribute to the harms experienced by those who serve the legal system as complainants. Thus the focus, in chapter 2, on refuting the claim that complainants are in fact heavily protected and not regularly subjected to arguably abusive, stereotype-infused, or intimidating treatment.

Pendulum Swings and Matriarchal Justice: Debunking Defence Counsel Myths

In a 2002 piece entitled "Regan a Victim of Matriarchal Justice," *National Post* columnist George Jonas wrote: "[t]he chances of a male accused of a sexual offence receiving a fair trial in Canada's matriarchal justice system is [sic] better than the chances of a Jew receiving a fair trial in Nazi Germany, but only just."[1] Jonas, a lifelong friend of Edward Greenspan, made this comment in an article discussing the Gerald Regan case. Greenspan was Regan's lawyer and is said by some to have made his reputation defending the former premier of Nova Scotia.[2] In the late 1990s Regan was charged with rape, attempted rape, and indecent assault involving thirteen different complainants.[3] He was tried and acquitted with respect to three of those complainants a few years before Jonas's comment was published. The Crown ultimately decided not to proceed with the many other charges against Regan, involving further women, because of the amount of time that had passed, the cost of prosecuting, and the reluctance of some of the complainants to testify.[4] Undoubtedly, the women reluctant to testify were privy to the media's coverage of the three sexual assault complainants "repeatedly driven to tears by Greenspan's incessant grilling" during Regan's first trial.[5]

In all, more than thirty different women made allegations against Gerald Regan.[6] The police had evidence from numerous complainants to support the allegation that Regan had engaged in a pattern of sexually assaulting young, primarily adolescent, women over a forty-year period.[7] Indeed, thirty-five women, most of whom did not know each other, alleged highly similar incidents in which Regan had attacked them.[8] Yet the state failed to secure a single conviction against him. Imagine describing a man accused of being a sexual predator of this magnitude, a man who incurred no criminal liability for his alleged actions, as a *victim* of matriarchal justice?

In fact, the notion that reforms to the law of sexual assault have created a criminal justice process that is grossly unfair to the accused, and unjustly skewed towards protecting complainants, is shared by many criminal defence lawyers. An article written by Toronto lawyer David Bayliss and posted on his website, entitled "The Consequences of an Allegation of Sexual Assault," captures this perspective:

> [T]he pendulum has swung from a time when allegations of sexual assault were not treated with sufficient gravity. In the justice system's efforts to correct past shortcomings, the pendulum has crashed through previously inviolable principles of criminal justice designed to protect the innocent. In many ways, the mantra of complainant sensitivity now trumps the presumption of innocence, the right to face one's accuser in court and the right to full and fair cross examination of that accuser.[9]

An examination of other prominent criminal law firm websites in Canada also reveals this perspective.[10]

Several of the lawyers I interviewed expressed a similar viewpoint. For instance, Defence Lawyer 1 commented, "it's almost become an attitude you know, 'Look, you can't be harsh or tough with a complainant.' You've got to roll over and be courteous and polite, and you know, don't raise your voice ... it seems to be everything in favour of the complainant." According to Defence Lawyer 4, "sexual assault complainants, I mean, they come in, they have their helper. They're ... practically carried into court. You know, so it's so over the top." Defence Lawyer 13 offered the following observation: "I would say the pendulum has swung too far over and the repercussions are enormous." Defence Lawyer 12 stated: "Anecdotally, my sense is trial lawyers are frustrated with sex assault cases generally ... You know, it's like, almost as if we've overcorrected and now, if a woman makes a complaint, it's very difficult to get someone acquitted ... [I]t's almost as if the burden of proof gets reversed and there's a presumption of guilt."

Related to this notion that the pendulum has swung too far in favour of complainants is an emerging narrative from some defence counsel that sexual assault complainants are not commonly bullied or attacked in court. Breese Davies, vice-president of Ontario's Criminal Lawyers' Association, expressed this perspective in a 2016 comment published in the *Toronto Star*: "Perhaps the most pernicious myth is that defence lawyers routinely, and as a matter of strategy, bully, abuse or attack complainants during cross-examination."[11] In a similar vein, many of the lawyers I interviewed expressed seemingly genuine disbelief that any lawyer would conduct, or would be permitted to conduct, a sexual assault case in this manner today. Defence Lawyer 10, for instance, made the following comments about the use of rape myths by defence lawyers: "I think most people, and I think most judges would stop it in about two seconds flat, if you, if you crossed that line. I think particularly in front of a jury, you know, the justice who is presiding would not allow that to happen. I think the Crowns would, hopefully, be on their feet in about ten seconds if lines were being crossed."

Feminism, coupled with an undue regard for "political correctness," is identified by some as the main instigator of this alleged overcorrection in favour of complainants. For example, in discussing changes to the law of sexual assault and the rules of evidence, Greenspan wrote, "Truth-testing mechanisms in our criminal justice system must not be compromised in order to service politically correct ideology ... The Supreme Court of Canada, with its victims' rights-based analysis, has injected a symmetry which just does not belong in the criminal law."[12] Bayliss, in the same online article quoted above, suggests that "[a]n overpowering environment of political correctness coupled with official directives to police officers and Crown attorneys prohibits probing questioning of sexual assault complainants."[13]

The corrosive effect of this supposed political correctness on the due process interests of those accused of sexual offences was also specifically mentioned by two of the defence lawyers interviewed for this study. Defence Lawyer 9, for example, commented, "You've gotta be politically correct ... even in court, you have to be careful with your tongue." Defence Lawyer 12 repeatedly referenced political correctness when discussing aspects of the rules limiting the use of prior sexual history evidence that she considered problematic.

This view that the criminal justice system has become too favourable to sexual assault complainants in a manner that compromises the right of the accused to a fair trial is sometimes expressed with open hostility to feminist perspectives. An almost 'us versus them' dynamic emerges from statements by some defence lawyers. For instance, in his letter attacking Justice L'Heureux-Dubé for her concurring reasons in the pivotal case of *R v Ewanchuk*,[14] Greenspan stated, "The feminist perspective has hijacked the Supreme Court of Canada and now feminists want to throw off the bench anyone who disagrees with them."[15]

The assertion that the criminal trial process, in service to a feminist agenda, unjustly favours complainants over those accused of sexual assault is difficult to understand. Certainly statistical evidence of conviction rates, charging rates, and reporting rates for sexual assault do not support this contention, either in Canada or elsewhere.[16] This raises several questions about the accuracy of these perceptions. Are defence lawyers actually precluded from asking the types of probing questions necessary to defend their clients? Can a man accused of sexual assault in Canada no longer get a fair trial? Are these constraints, supposedly imposed by a dominant culture of feminist-inspired political correctness, real? Is it a myth that complainants are regularly bullied in sexual assault trials? All of which is to ask, has the pendulum actually swung too far?

In fact, the unfortunate reality is that, in many regards, the pendulum has not swung far enough. However, in order to compellingly advance the claim that many defence lawyers in sexual assault cases contribute to the harms experienced by complainants (and do so in ways that could be stopped without requiring these lawyers to compromise their duty of loyalty to their accused clients), it may be necessary to first dispense with these defence counsel myths. The remainder of this chapter takes on these claims and concerns. Evidence from multiple sources is used in an effort to demonstrate the falsity of the following assertions: that legal reforms have unjustly limited the ability of accused individuals to conduct thorough and probing challenges to allegations of sexual violence; that an overwhelming culture of feminism and political correctness has compromised the fair trial rights of those accused of sexual offences; and that legal protections consistently insulate complainants from abusive tactics and discriminatory stereotypes about sexual violence. The remainder of the chapter is organized into three sections, each aimed at debunking one of these defence counsel myths. Arguably, the evidence relied on in this chapter does more than just debunk these myths. It also demonstrates the kinds of defence counsel practices that can and do contribute to the harms inflicted upon sexual assault complainants through the legal process.

The Right to a Full and Fair Cross-examination and the Right to Confront One's Accuser Have Not Been Compromised in Sexual Assault Trials

The trial transcripts and reported decisions from several recent sexual assault proceedings challenge the assertion that reforms to the law of sexual assault and a "mantra of complainant sensitivity"[17] prevent lawyers from performing probing and full cross-examinations. These sources also contradict the notion that sexual assault complainants are "coddle[d]" (as one prominent columnist recently suggested).[18]

In numerous recent sexual assault cases, trial judges have described the questioning of the complainant in ways that contest the assertion that defence counsel are precluded from conducting thorough and rigorous cross-examinations.[19] Consider the following examples. According to the trial judge in *R v H(JJ)*, the young complainant "wilted after three days" of "convoluted and confusing" cross-examination by defence counsel.[20] In the sentencing decision in *H(JJ)*, the Court noted that the complainant had "survived" what Justice Aitken described as "days and days of cross-examination."[21] According to the Ontario Court of Appeal in *R v G(A)*, the complainant was aggressively cross-examined for two and a half days, during which she was "admonished by defence counsel for 'making speeches'" and was accused of lying.[22] In *R v T(B)* the trial judge described the cross-examination of the complainant as "brutal."[23] Defence counsel's questioning of the complainant in *R v Gill* was characterized by the Court as "a very intense and aggressive cross-examination" in which she was "criticized for going to [an] area, when she knew that this was a place where men hung around."[24] Blaming survivors of sexual violence for their supposedly risky choices, such as attending an area of the city frequented by men, is a common defence counsel strategy – one that trades on problematic, neo-liberal assumptions about the difference between "ideal victims" and so-called "risky women."[25] In numerous other recent sexual assault cases, trial judges noted that the complainants were extensively cross-examined by defence counsel.[26]

Without the trial transcripts for each of these cases, it is not possible to ascertain whether any of these cross-examinations crossed the line from extensive, thorough, and probing to abusive, unduly repetitive, or unnecessarily rude and aggressive. What is clear is that the descriptions of the cross-examination by the courts in these reported decisions contradict the contention that accused individuals in sexual assault cases are no longer granted the right to a full and thorough cross-examination.

In other recent reported decisions, for which trial transcripts were obtained, descriptions of the cross-examinations by trial judges do suggest questioning that may have extended beyond that which could be characterized as simply probing and thorough. For example, the trial judge's description of the "long, repetitive, bullying, and painful" cross-examination of the complainant in *R v Luceno* is examined in detail in chapter 3.

The trial judge's description of a cross-examination done by David Bayliss himself in a recent sexual assault trial, *R v G(PG)*, is also worth considering. In *R v G(PG)*, the trial judge, Justice Brown, described Bayliss's two-day cross-examination of the nineteen-year-old complainant, a young woman with mental health issues, as a "prolonged and brutal attack on her character" and a "no holds barred cross-examination by a skillful and aggressive counsel."[27] Bayliss accused the complainant of being an attention-seeker and of having been, at the age of fifteen, "sexually suggestive" towards the accused.[28] The accused was the live-in boyfriend of her mother, and a father figure to the complainant, at the time that he allegedly sexually assaulted her. Bayliss questioned the complainant at length about her suicide attempts, and, according to the trial judge, ridiculed her testimony that she had tried to commit suicide seven times. He implied that her testimony that she had tried to kill herself many times was unbelievable because she had not been successful. The trial judge stated that Bayliss "virtually scoffed" at the complainant's testimony that she had attempted suicide several times.[29] The Crown attorney in *G(PG)* objected to many of Bayliss's questions on the basis that they were unfair,[30] repetitive,[31] condescending,[32] or dismissive.[33] His client was convicted of sexual assault.

G(PG) was appealed twice. On summary conviction appeal, Justice Durno described Bayliss's cross-examination as "aggressive, vigorous and thorough."[34] He also determined that some of Justice Brown's comments about the cross-examination were "ill-advised," "clearly unjustified," and "improper."[35] He noted that "from only reading and listening to the cross-examination [rather than being present in the courtroom] the characterization [of the questioning] as brutal in the sense of being savagely or coarsely cruel, harsh or merciless is not one that necessarily follows."[36] He found that Bayliss's questioning was slow-paced and that he did not interrupt the complainant. However, Justice Durno did find that at times Bayliss "appeared to be somewhat sarcastic or dismissive" towards the complainant.[37] He determined that Bayliss inappropriately made "several sarcastic, editorial comments or critiques" about the young complainant's responses,[38] and he noted that the complainant could be heard crying or sobbing while being repeatedly questioned by Bayliss about her multiple suicide attempts.[39] While Justice Durno upheld the conviction, on further appeal to the Ontario Court of Appeal it was overturned.[40] The Court of Appeal did not directly assess the trial judge's characterization of Bayliss's cross-examination, but did conclude that it was unfair of the trial judge to be highly critical of defence counsel's cross-examination in his reasons, having failed to either intervene while it was occurring, or provide defence counsel with an opportunity to address his concerns in submissions. The Court of Appeal also concluded that it was a serious error on the part of the trial judge to preclude Bayliss's cross-examination of the complainant's understanding of her psychiatric condition.[41] While the appellate courts certainly disagreed with aspects of the trial judge's treatment and characterization of Bayliss's cross-examination, they appear to have considered it to be thorough and probing.

Defence counsel's cross-examination in a recent Ontario case, *R v Finney*, certainly challenges the assertion that "previously unheard of restrictions on the right to cross-examine"[42] motivated by sensitivity to the complainant have unduly circumscribed defence counsel's ability to defend clients accused of sexual offences. Like the cross-examination in *G(PG)*, the cross-examination of the complainant in *Finney* also raises the prospect of questioning that is not only lengthy, thorough, and probing, but also potentially problematic in some regard.

The accused in *Finney* was convicted of sexual assault, choking, and unlawful confinement. Daniel Finney, whose weight was more than double that of the complainant, threw her against a wall, repeatedly forced his fingers and penis into her anus and vagina, wiped traces of fecal matter on her face, pried her mouth open with his soiled fingers and "rammed" his penis into her mouth with such force that "[i]t felt like it was going to puncture the back of [her] throat."[43] His attack lasted for more than an hour and ended only after he had ejaculated all over her face, hair, and body.[44] Finney maintained that the complainant, whom he had met for the first time that evening, had consented to and had in fact initiated all of the sexual, and physically violent, acts in which he engaged. The Ontario Court of Appeal described his lawyer Calvin Barry's cross-examination of the complainant, which spanned over 550 pages of transcript,[45] as "lengthy, at times repetitive, and often difficult to follow."[46]

Consider the following excerpt from the transcript of Barry's cross-examination of the complainant in *Finney*. In this excerpt, he questioned the complainant more than ten times as to the precise number of days it took for her body to recover enough to endure the pain of a bowel movement following a violent anal rape:

> [DEFENCE] Q. You said you waited a week from the time this [anal rape] happened before you had a bowel movement. Is that what you're telling this court today?
>
> [COMPLAINANT] A. Yeah. I didn't want to do it because it – my bottom hurt already, and I didn't want a passing of anything to hurt it more, and I didn't even like to touch myself to clean myself there.
>
> Q. Could it have been more than seven days?
>
> A. No.
>
> Q. It might have been ten days?
>
> A. No.
>
> Q. Was it eight days?
>
> A. No. No. It was like – it was approximately from five to seven days.
>
> Q. Well, you said seven days when you testified. Was it seven?
>
> CROWN: I think she indicated it was about a week, Your Honour.
>
> A. It was about a week.
>
> THE COURT: Yes, that's what I thought too. Now I want to be careful ... because I haven't gone back through my notes. But I'm going on my recollection, I don't remember her saying seven days.
>
> DEFENCE: I have, "Waited a week", in fairness.
>
> Q. Did you wait a week before you had a bowel movement? Maybe that's a fair question. Did you wait a week before you had a bowel movement? I'm just taking my best note of what you said here this week.
>
> A. Yes, I waited a week.[47]

In her direct testimony the complainant was asked by the Crown about rectal bleeding and she stated that it first occurred after her first post-rape bowel movement, which was "about a week" after the assault.[48] According to Barry, his own notes confirmed the consistency of her testimony on this point. Recall, the defence was consent: did the complainant voluntarily agree to engage in the sexual touching at issue in the allegation? The precise timing of her first post-rape bowel movement, and her consistency on this timing, were collateral to the issue of consent. Moreover, she appears to have been consistent in her testimony about the timing. Arguably, the probative value of these questions, as evidence that would challenge her credibility, was negligible. Yet, Barry was permitted to repeatedly question the complainant in this manner, on this deeply personal, collateral issue.

These examples from recent cases are not consistent with the assertion that defence lawyers today are precluded from conducting full and thorough cross-examinations of the complainants in sexual assault proceedings. Indeed, in the latter two cases, rather than the complainants being coddled or overprotected, descriptions from the court or excerpts from the trial transcripts suggest they were subjected to questioning by defence counsel that was not only thorough and probing, but also sarcastic (in the case of *G(PG)*) and overly repetitive (in the case of *Finney*).

An Overwhelming Culture of Feminism and Political Correctness Has Not Compromised the Fair Trial Rights of Those Accused of Sexual Offences

The transcripts of several recent cases also challenge the contention that defence lawyers are unduly circumscribed by feminist norms and a culture of political correctness. Indeed, the transcripts from these cases provide examples of questions and comments by defence counsel which, far from being 'politically correct,' could be argued to exhibit precisely the kinds of problematic social assumptions and discriminatory stereotypes about women and sexual violence that now decades-old law reforms, in Canada and other jurisdictions, have attempted to eradicate.

For example, later in his cross-examination in *Finney*, defence counsel appears to have insinuated to the complainant that it is not possible to force a woman to perform oral sex – "one would think that would be consensual."[49] After suggesting to the complainant that she "gave the accused oral sex," or a "blow job,"[50] and noting that there was no injury to her jaw to evidence that it had been pried open as she had testified,[51] Barry stated:

> Q. Right. And you're – and you're – you're biting down at the time to keep your mouth closed, right? Clenching your teeth?
> A. Yes.
> Q. And you have your – your lips sealed, right?
> A. Yes.
> Q. Because I'm putting it to you that – that the reason you're saying that today is that you know you're in a bit of a – I'm going to use the term "pickle" or problem here, I'm suggesting to you that, because oral sex would – one would think that would be consensual. You open your mouth, you suck, you have a – it becomes erect. You – you put a – you know, you – you seal around the penis and – and that's why you're – you're saying this about him having to pry your mouth open. You agree with me?
> A. No.
> Q. Because it was consensual.
> A. No.[52]

Barry went on to question her repeatedly about the timing of the oral sex in relation to an earlier moment when she had nipped or bitten Finney's finger after he forced it into her mouth.[53] Barry's questions seemed to be directed at ascertaining how many times, and for how long, the accused put his penis in the complainant's mouth *after* she had bitten his finger: "Okay. So, according to you ... you bite or nip his finger, and then shortly after that, he's putting his penis in the same location – where the biting happened."[54] One interpretation of this line of questioning is that it was intended to impugn her credibility based on the fact that she had not bitten Finney's penis when it was in her mouth. If she could bite his finger why couldn't she bite his penis?

The assumption that a failure on the part of the complainant to resist, or fight back, is indicative of consent is an outdated stereotype that was legally rejected by the affirmative definition of consent to sexual touching codified in the 1992 amendments to Canada's *Criminal Code* and adopted by the Supreme Court of Canada in 1998.[55]

Arguably, Barry also appears to have made use of the now legally rejected stereotype that women who fail to raise a 'hue and cry' are less believable. He cross-examined the complainant at length about her failure to scream and the timing of her disclosure (which occurred a few hours after the sexual assault). For example:

> [DEFENCE] Q. And according to you, he put up to four fingers in your rectal area, is that right?
>
> [COMPLAINANT] A. It was full.
>
> Q. So you must have been screaming at the top of your lungs.
>
> A. No.
>
> Q. Excruciating pain [begetting] a scream, and that's the – you screamed, right?
>
> A. No, I didn't. I have a pretty high pain tolerance.
>
> Q. Did he put on some lubrication? Did he pull out like a – was there a jar of Vaseline that you found the next day or anything like that?
>
> A. No.[56]

It seems reasonable to question whether the intended inference, even though she had already testified that she thought he was going to choke her to death, was that her failure to scream or cry suggests she was in fact consenting to the insertion of four of his fingers into her anus (or that Finney did not penetrate her anus in the manner she described). Later, Barry asked: "Okay. During the entire time you were in the room with Mr. Finney, you were never crying, correct?" She answered: "No, just whimpering. Whimpering and words."[57]

Arguably, defence lawyer Elizabeth Bristow's cross-examination of the complainant in *R v Ururyar* also included reliance on the legally rejected 'hue and cry' stereotype about when women who have 'actually' been raped will disclose the assault to others. The complainant and the accused were both PhD students in the same graduate program at York University when the incident occurred. After a series of questions to the complainant about the timing of her disclosure to the police (which occurred a mere two days later), Bristow asked:

> Q. But you still waited until February 2nd, you know, you called in the afternoon, I believe, to report him?

A. ... I wanted to make sure that I made an informed decision that if charges were pressed, what would that mean for my future as a PhD student at York University ... So, I waited because it was the weekend, obviously nobody was in their office or around ... I wanted to have all the information before I proceeded.

Q. So, based on what was ging [sic] to happen at school was going to be your decision on whether or not you wanted to report a violent rapist?

A. Well, I also wanted to take into consideration the impact on my career if nobody was going to do anything and the way I saw it was, I just didn't know if all my work in my PhD was going to be thrown away over this incident and I really needed time to think that through.

Q. So your career was more important than getting [a] violent rapist off the streets?

A. I'm sorry, what?

Q. You wanted to know how this was going to impact your career if you reported this to the police, so I'm suggesting to you that your career was more important than getting a violent rapist off the streets?[58]

Bristow followed her questions about the timing of disclosure with a set of questions which could be construed as rooted in the stereotypes that real victims run or try to escape, and that women who make risky choices are responsible for their own sexual victimization.[59] Bristow asserted that she was not suggesting that the incident was the complainant's fault, but then followed this assertion with questions such as the following:

- "At no point did you make any attempt to flag someone down, call a friend or do anything to get yourself away ...?"[60]
- "You didn't think it would be a wise decision to get out of there while you could?"[61]
- "You had a phone though right? ... You could have called someone?"[62]
- "Instead you chose to go home with someone who was berating you, angry and yelling at you?"[63]

The stereotype that a woman who actually does not want to have sex will escape or fight off her attacker also appears to have featured in defence counsel Patricia MacNaughton's cross-examination in *R v Adepoju*. She too repeatedly emphasized the complainant's failure to resist or escape. In *Adepoju* the complainant struggled verbally and physically for more than fifteen minutes before being subjected to non-consensual vaginal penetration:[64]

> Q. Well in fact, the night that you say my client assaulted you sexually, you just say, oh, he would stop, but you would say no, and he would stop, and then he would get after you again, but you were kissing him consensually at the beginning, weren't you?
>
> A. Once.
>
> Q. Once. And then you just said, oh, I just gave up; right?
>
> A. Yeah.
>
> Q. You never screamed, you never yelled?
>
> A. There was nobody there.
>
> Q. Well you got away from him a little bit later, after the few second sex act; correct?
>
> A. Yes.
>
> Q. You didn't bother trying to get away from him once he had your pants down like you say, did you?
>
> A. I – no, I – other than push him away, no.
>
> Q. You what?
>
> A. Other than pushing him away
>
> ...
>
> Q. You told my friend you never tried to leave because you felt it was under control; right?
>
> A. Yes.
>
> Q. And it was under your control, you didn't leave; correct?
>
> A. Yes.
>
> Q. And you could have left?
>
> A. Yeah.
>
> ...
>
> Q. And – and then eventually you stopped saying no, and you opened up your legs and the sex act occurred; correct?
>
> A. Yes.
>
> Q. You didn't scream?

A. No.

Q. You didn't cry?

A. No.

Q. You didn't go lock yourself in the bathroom?

A. No.[65]

...

Q. Well you did let him have sex with you; right?

A. Eventually, yes.

Q. Yes. You stopped saying no.

A. But I didn't say yes.

Q. You stopped saying no, and you used body language, um, complying with the sexual act; correct?

A. I – I guess I'd [sic] did.[66]

The trial judge's deeply problematic decision to acquit in *Adepoju*, discussed in chapter 7, was overturned by the Alberta Court of Appeal.

Stereotypes about the failure to fight back or to raise a hue and cry are not the only social assumptions about sexual assault arguably evidenced in the transcripts I examined. For example, the stereotype of the promiscuous party girl, ready and willing to consent to sex anywhere, with anyone, appears to have emerged in the defence of a Halifax taxi driver in a recent Nova Scotia case.[67] The complainant in *R v Al-Rawi* had spent the evening socializing and drinking with friends in a Halifax bar, and was highly intoxicated at the time of the incident. She entered the accused's taxi at 1:09 AM and was found by the police eleven minutes later, in the backseat of the accused's vehicle, unconscious and naked from the breasts down. Her legs were propped up on the bucket seats in front of her, in a straddle position with one foot on each seat. The accused was in between her legs, facing her, with his pants undone and partially lowered. She was so intoxicated that, in addition to having lost consciousness, she had lost control of her bladder and urinated on her pants and underwear.[68]

The accused's lawyer, Luke Craggs, introduced evidence that the complainant had been flirtatious with other men earlier in the evening on the night of the incident. The theory of the defence appears to have been that the complainant, when she consumes alcohol, becomes the "type of person"[69] who flirts and dances inappropriately with men in bars, and can reasonably be inferred to have entered a taxi and immediately (or almost immediately) stripped her urine-soiled clothes off, thrown them at the unknown driver, perhaps kissed or licked his face, and then propped up her legs in the straddle position minutes or seconds before passing out.

Craggs's questions and submissions throughout the trial suggest an effort not simply to portray the complainant as drunk and less inhibited on the night of the incident, but to construct an alternate personality – "Drunk Jane"[70] – devoid of *any* inhibition. In his cross-examination of the complainant, he asserted:

> DEFENCE: You don't necessarily remember the type of person you become when you're ... [drunk]?
>
> COMPLAINANT: ... I can only speculate ...
>
> DEFENCE: When you are sober you are a very together person ... you can handle real life responsibility ... But the Drunk Jane is very very different than the sober sensible person who works for —— right?
>
> COMPLAINANT: I don't know.[71]

In his cross-examination of the complainant's roommate and childhood friend, Craggs suggested that the complainant "seemed reasonable and coherent up until a certain point" and then "her demeanor totally changed? ... she went from, if I can say it, sober, sensible Jane to Drunk Jane? [Witness:] Yes."[72] In questioning the roommate's boyfriend, he again asserted that her demeanour "changed from sober, sensible Jane to drunk not sensible Jane."[73] In his closing submissions, Craggs argued:

> The staid and sensible Jane ... apparently becomes a very different person when she drinks in the quantity that she drank that night, um and that is something the court sees all the time. I've heard judges use the term "Jekyll and Hyde" personalities between the sober and the drunk person.[74]

Certainly defence counsel Naeem Rauf's 2009 closing submissions in *R v Cain* do not suggest that he felt constrained by an overwhelming culture of political correctness. His client, Joshua Cain, was charged with aggravated sexual assault, choking to overcome resistance, and threatening death. Cain admitted to choking the complainant and having sex with her, but claimed it was consensual. During his closing submissions to the jury, Rauf suggested that the complainant's failure to call her parents immediately or to leave the music event were inconsistent with her allegations of assault. She reported the alleged attack to police at approximately six o'clock the following morning. To support his assertion that her post-incident conduct was not consistent with someone who had been raped, Rauf argued:

> Look at what's on her pink T-shirt the day after she's raped she says. A picture of a penis ... Does this suggest to you a young woman who has suffered trauma? A young woman who said, I would never do that; I would never lie down on the ground. Well, for heaven's sakes. She's been raped? You would think that would sober her up, but instead, she's going around sporting a T-shirt with a picture of a penis.[75]

He returned to the T-shirt a second time during his closing submissions: "but here she is wearing a T-shirt displaying a male penis, testicles and all."[76] Rauf then suggested that "if she [was] hurt emotionally, you'd think she'd be traumatized, she'd want to go home, she'd want to be with family, somebody who could comfort her, not partying away and then dawning [sic] a T-shirt on which somebody has drawn a male penis."[77] Both the trial judge and the Alberta Court of Appeal concluded that it was far from obvious that there even was a penis drawn on her shirt.[78] Note that in fact it does not matter whether she had a penis on her shirt. The suggestion that a woman is untrustworthy, is soliciting sex, or is sexually promiscuous because she dresses in a certain way is a discriminatory stereotype. The jury's acquittal in *Cain* was overturned by the Court of Appeal in part because of Rauf's reliance on "long-discredited myths and stereotypes about women deserving to be raped because they dress provocatively."[79]

Defence counsel's conduct of the case in *R v Wagar* seemed similarly unaffected by the mantra of complainant sensitivity and this supposed feminist takeover of the judicial process.[80] In his closing submissions during Wagar's first trial (he was tried twice), Patrick Flynn asserted that the complainant had engaged in a "weekend ... of promiscuous activity"[81] and highlighted testimony that earlier in the evening she had enjoyed his client's dancing.[82] He referred to the complainant's allegations – which involved forced oral and vaginal intercourse on a bathroom counter while a party proceeded on the other side of the bathroom door – as "lovemaking" and a "romantic fling."[83] He characterized the accused's unbuttoning of his pants and "showing of his penis" as "flirtation" and suggested that the complainant (who was outweighed by the accused by nearly a hundred pounds) was "no shrinking violet" and could "take care of herself."[84]

In *R v Schmaltz*, both the trial judge and the Court of Appeal noted the following "highly objectionable"[85] line of questioning by defence counsel Kyrsia Przepiorka:

[DEFENCE] Q: After you get out of the bed, you end up in the washroom at some point. Right?

[COMPLAINANT] A: Yes.

Q: And it's fair to say that you went to the bathroom to clean yourself up. Right?

A: That was my intention when I went there, yes.

Q: And I'm going to suggest to you, by cleaning yourself up, you mean essentially to clean your vagina because it was wet. Right?

A: Because it was wet and itching. I felt disgusted, yes.

Q: You would agree with me that your vagina was wet because it was stimulated. Right?

A: I will agree that it was wet. Why was it wet? I do not agree because it was stimulated. I don't know, maybe he greased his fingers. I have no idea but it was not from stimulation, and if you look at one of my statements, I'm known to be quite dry. It's in one of my statements. Either the police – I believe the police report.

Q. I'm going to suggest that your vagina was wet because you were stimulated and enjoying yourself?

A. Well, I'm suggesting to you – and I'm not suggesting, I'm telling you that that is not the case. I was not enjoying nothing. I did not give him permission to come on that bed. That bed was put out for me, not him. He had no right to be on that bed.[86]

Przepiorka's assertion connecting the amount of moisture in a woman's vagina to her level of arousal was both unsupportable on the evidence offered at trial, and offensive. The potential degrading effect of using repetition and the assertion of unsupportable claims to cross-examine a sexual assault complainant about her vagina should be obvious.

Legal Protections for Sexual Assault Complainants Do Not Consistently Insulate Them

Some defence counsel point to Canada's rape shield laws under section 276 of the *Criminal Code* in particular as evidence that complainants are protected against discriminatory stereotypes or humiliating questions.[87] Section 276 creates exclusionary rules making evidence of a complainant's sexual activity, other than the sexual activity that forms the subject matter of the charge, presumptively inadmissible (unless introduced by the Crown).[88] Section 276 also establishes criteria to determine the circumstances in which the presumption of inadmissibility will be overcome such that the defence is allowed to introduce evidence of a complainant's other sexual activity.

The objective of section 276 is to eliminate the misuse of evidence of a complainant's sexual activity for irrelevant or misleading purposes, while ensuring that an accused's right to a fair trial is not compromised. In the main, this involves removing from the trial process any discriminatory reasoning based on gendered stereotypes about sexuality and sexual violence, and providing some protection against the use of sexual history evidence to perpetuate unnecessary incursions on the dignity and privacy interests of complainants. Two stereotypes, in particular, are categorically excluded by Canada's rape shield provisions: the discriminatory belief that women who are sexually active are less trustworthy, and the equally absurd assumption that women with sexual experience are more likely to have consented to the sex at issue in the allegation. These stereotypes are called 'the twin myths.' Section 276 also aims to eliminate other gendered stereotypes and reduce the use of a complainant's sexual history for purposes of intimidation or humiliation.

In a 2016 column published in the *Ottawa Sun*, defence lawyer Solomon Friedman advanced several claims about the treatment of complainants in sexual assault proceedings. Friedman argued:

> Let's be perfectly clear. There is no epidemic of vicious victim "whacking" at the hands of unscrupulous defence lawyers ... Sexual assault complainants are the beneficiaries of legal protections afforded to no other class of criminal law participants. First, defence counsel are prohibited from introducing evidence of a complainant's prior sexual history without first satisfying the trial judge that the evidence is not being introduced to bolster one of

the "twin myths" of sexual assault ... Those myths are outdated, discredited and discriminatory. And they have no place in our modern criminal justice system.[89]

Friedman is the law partner of Michael Edelson, the lawyer known in some Canadian circles for reportedly coining the term "whack the complainant."[90] Edelson is said to have instructed a group of criminal lawyers at a 1988 professional development session to "whack the complainant" at the preliminary inquiry for a sexual assault trial, on the assumption that if the preliminary inquiry is hard enough on her she might give up before the matter proceeds to trial.[91] The term has gained traction over the years, among both courts and academics.[92] David Tanovich, who has researched and written on the issue, defines it as follows:

> Whacking the complainant includes humiliating or prolonged cross-examination that "seek[s] to put the complainant on trial rather than the accused"; specious applications to obtain the complainant's records; and, the invoking and exploiting of stereotypical assumptions about women and consent, including assumptions about communication, dress, revenge, marriage, prior sexual history, therapy, lack of resistance and delayed disclosure.[93]

Comments from both Crown attorneys and defence lawyers I interviewed suggest that not everyone in the legal profession agrees with Friedman's assertion that complainants are not regularly whacked by defence lawyers. Crown Attorney 3, for example, indicated that some defence lawyers do precisely what Edelson advised:

> [T]here are good defence lawyers. There are bad defence lawyers ... some are going to make it very, very difficult on the complainant – especially, especially at preliminary inquiry and requiring the complainant to testify ... there are some defence lawyers who are saying "I'm going to make it hard on this person and that person will reconsider whether they truly want to go through with this."

Defence Lawyer 3 indicated that, while these are not tactics he would use himself, he believes some defence lawyers do pursue such strategies. He suggested that certain lawyers prefer superior court for sexual assault cases, because they want the opportunity to cross-examine the complainant twice (at a preliminary inquiry and at trial) in order to make the process as difficult as possible for them.

In reflecting upon Friedman's comments about the myth of whacking and the extraordinary protections offered by Canada's rape shield law, consider a section 276 application to introduce evidence of the complainant's prior sexual history that Friedman himself brought in a 2015 case in which his client was charged with sexually assaulting his two stepdaughters. In *R v T(J)* the accused was alleged to have sexually assaulted his stepdaughter AL between 2002 and 2010, when she was between six and twelve years old.[94] AL came forward with her allegations only after the accused and her mother had separated, when she was approximately fourteen years old. Shortly after the preliminary inquiry, the complainant's younger brother, DL, alleged that the complainant had engaged in one instance of sexual assault against him when she was eleven or twelve years old. AL was immediately confronted with the allegation. She admitted to the incident the same day that her brother disclosed it to school officials and his mother. AL was not charged.

The Crown alleged that the accused had sexually assaulted AL and her sister for years, beginning when they were very young, and that AL's mother knew about this abuse and blamed AL for not "closing her legs."[95] The Crown's evidence was that, given her own sexual victimization by her stepfather, from AL's eleven- or twelve-year-old perspective (when the incident with her brother occurred), sexual conduct within a family was acceptable. According to the Crown, by the time of her stepfather's trial AL had learned that her previous perception about appropriate sexual conduct was incorrect, and that both what was done to her by her stepfather and what she did to her brother were wrong.

Friedman brought an application to introduce evidence of this incident of sexual activity between the then eleven- or twelve-year-old complainant and her younger brother. There was no evidence nor submission by the defence that AL had ever denied her misconduct towards her brother (but Friedman did want to cross-examine her on why she had not voluntarily disclosed this incident at the preliminary inquiry).[96] As noted, she immediately admitted to the incident when confronted with the allegation. Nevertheless, Friedman's argument was that the evidence was relevant to impugn her credibility and to demonstrate a motive to fabricate – to suggest that she was lying about the sexual abuse by her stepfather in order to avoid sanction for her sexual behaviour with her brother. Recall that she reported this sexual abuse by her stepfather two years before her brother disclosed the incident of sexual assault by AL. In other words, Friedman's argument as to why he should be permitted to cross-examine the complainant about this humiliating and personal incident with her brother when she was a child was, in part, that it suggested she had anticipatorily fabricated allegations against her stepfather two years *before* the incident with her brother surfaced – fabricated in an effort to pre-empt criticism of her in the event that DL might someday tell someone what she had done to him. The implausibility of Friedman's theory was lost on neither the Crown nor the Court.[97]

The Crown opposed Friedman's application on the basis that the timeline contradicted his theory, that there was no evidence of fabrication, and that allowing him to cross-examine the complainant about an irrelevant sexual act that occurred when she was eleven or twelve years old would be "seriously offensive to the dignity and privacy of a young complainant like AL."[98] The Court agreed: "The defence seeks to introduce to the jury inflammatory evidence of sexual misconduct by a complainant on an unrelated matter."[99] Justice Kane even went so far as to speculate that Friedman's likely motivation for bringing this application was to discourage this young woman from testifying at trial: "Introducing such unrelated sexual misconduct evidence will discourage complainants to report and to testify which is the likely motivation of this application."[100]

If sexual assault complainants are, as Friedman argues, "the beneficiaries of legal protections afforded to no other class of criminal law participants,"[101] it is because "in no other context would the profession countenance"[102] the kinds of tactics that are deployed by some defence lawyers in some sexual assault proceedings. Bringing an application to introduce a teenaged complainant's irrelevant sexual history in order to discourage her from testifying (if the trial judge is correct that that was "the likely motivation of [his] application"[103]) is an example of precisely the type of conduct that Friedman insists is not common. While he is right that such tactics have "no place in our modern criminal justice system,"[104] some defence lawyers nevertheless continue to pursue them.

To review, section 276.1 of the *Criminal Code* requires defence counsel to file an application seeking the court's permission before attempting to introduce evidence of a complainant's other sexual activity.[105] As noted, section 276 also places limits on the purposes for which sexual history evidence can be admitted. Unfortunately, defence counsel in some cases attempt to introduce, or succeed in introducing, this type of evidence without following the rules created under the *Criminal Code.*

In *R v B(IE)*, for example, defence counsel Kevin Burke questioned the complainant as follows:

> Q. Now when you were outside having a cigarette, [was] there any activity that you engaged in while you were outside with any of your friends other than say Mr. [I.E.B – the accused].
> A. Socializing.
> Q. Other than socializing, was there any type of sexual activity?
> A. No.
> Q. Are you quite sure about that?
> A. Yes.
> Q. Any time during that evening were you kissing with anyone?
> A. No.
> Q. Inside or outside the, the tavern?
> A. Not that I recall.
> Q. So this may have occurred but you can't recall it at this time?
> A. I don't, I don't think I kissed anyone.
> Q. Well you never kissed any of your friends outside?
> A. No.[106]

Burke did not bring an application, as required by 276.1 of the *Criminal Code*, to introduce this evidence of other sexual activity.[107] Moreover, even if he had brought an application, this line of cross-examination would not properly have been permitted. The complainant's allegation was that the accused asked her to exit the rear entrance of a tavern where they had been socializing with a group of common friends. She alleged that once outside he pushed her head down by pulling her hair, thrust his penis into her mouth, and forced her to perform oral sex until he ejaculated.[108] The defence was that she consented to the oral sex and was alleging sexual assault as a consequence of post-sex regret.[109] Whether the complainant had engaged in sexual activity of any kind with other individuals prior to the incident with the accused was irrelevant to the issue of consent in this case, and would not properly have been permitted under section 276. Indeed, based on the testimony at trial and the closing submissions offered by Burke, it seems difficult not to conclude that this line of questioning was introduced to give rise to the discriminatory inference that the complainant was more likely to have consented to oral sex with the accused because she was allegedly kissing someone else in the bar earlier in the evening. Certainly the so-called mantra of complainant sensitivity and the supposed overwhelming, feminist-informed environment of political correctness and unfair bias in favour of complainants did not prevent this woman from being repeatedly forced to answer inadmissible questions about her alleged prior sexual activities.

Nor, as an aside, did political correctness and oversensitivity to the complainant prevent Burke from asking the complainant, earlier in his cross-examination, whether she had told her friends that she was "going to get fucked that night."[110] Consider this excerpt from his cross-examination of the complainant:

> [DEFENCE] Q: All right. Now did you also make a comment to any of your friends there that you had intentions to ah, I guess, have sexual relations with someone that night?
>
> [COMPLAINANT] A. No.
>
> Q. Or did you use the term you were going to get fucked that night if the, if you'll excuse my terminology?
>
> A. No.
>
> Q. Pardon me?
>
> A. No.
>
> Q. Now do you have a clear recollection of not saying that or you can't recall it?
>
> A. No, I didn't say that.
>
> Q. Now did you talk about having any relations with anyone that night?
>
> A. No.
>
> Q. There's ... you are quite sure of that?
>
> A. Yes.[111]

Asking a complainant whether she told her friends that she was "going to get fucked" that night is highly prejudicial. Even if it is not "sexual activity" for purposes of section 276, which is debatable, it raises the same types of concerns regarding both the twin myths and the mistreatment of complainants contemplated by Canada's rape shield regime.

Similar problems arose in Jody Ostapiw's defence of the accused in *R v Wright*. In *Wright* the complainant alleged that the accused engaged in non-consensual anal intercourse with her. She alleged that this occurred following an evening and night of partying with others at a bonfire, the consumption of a host of different intoxicants by both the complainant and the accused, and engagement in some consensual sexual touching between the two earlier that night. The complainant's allegation was that by early morning the alcohol, ecstasy, cocaine, and prescription drugs she had ingested throughout the night had made her nauseous and unable to move. She testified that she left the backyard party, went upstairs, and lay down on a bed with the accused following her, at which point he engaged in anal intercourse without her consent. She testified that she repeatedly asked him to stop. The accused maintained that the sexual intercourse, which he insisted was vaginal not anal, was consensual.[112]

Ostapiw's cross-examination of the complainant in *Wright* included questions that appear to have been aimed at presenting the complainant's behaviour earlier that night as risqué or promiscuous:

> [DEFENCE] Q. Okay. So you don't recall it but it wouldn't sur-
> prise you that you were dancing around the bonfire.
>
> [COMPLAINANT] A. No, not specifically, no.
>
> Q. Okay. You recall taking off your top while you were dancing around the bonfire?
>
> A. Well, I, I just confirmed for you that I don't specifically remember dancing so …
>
> Q. Okay.
>
> A. No.
>
> Q. Well, based on what you said, which is that that's something you would normally do [dance at a bonfire], would you normally when you're dancing around a bonfire also take off your top?
>
> A. Have done.
>
> Q. You just don't recall whether you did it that night.
>
> A. Correct.[113]

She raised the issue again later in her cross-examination:

> [DEFENCE] Q. … Okay. Did you have a nickname at this gathering?

A. I don't remember.

Q. Okay. You don't recall anyone calling you by a nickname?

A. No.

Q. Okay. And so if I was to suggest to you that your nickname at this party was Perky Tits you wouldn't recall that.

A. I don't recall that.

Q. No, okay. And like you told us earlier, you don't recall lifting up your top when you were dancing around the fire.

A. I don't recall that, no.[114]

The defence in *Wright* was consent. Whether the complainant was dancing topless at a party hours earlier, whether other attendees at that party were calling her "Perky Tits," and whether she had a habit of dancing topless at previous parties were not relevant to whether she consented to anal (or vaginal) intercourse with the accused several hours later.[115] Under Canada's rape shield provisions, this type of cross-examination is prohibited and should not have occurred in this case.[116] First, Ostapiw did not bring a section 276 application to introduce this evidence. Indeed, neither she, the Crown, nor the trial judge made any mention of the rape shield provisions prohibiting evidence of a complainant's sexual reputation and limiting the admission of a complainant's other sexual activity. There was no suggestion by Ostapiw that this evidence was adduced in order to impugn the credibility of the complainant on the basis of a prior inconsistent statement.[117] Second, even if she had brought an application, this evidence would not properly have been admitted. Pursuant to section 277 of the *Criminal Code*, evidence of a woman's sexual reputation (which is what this was) is never admissible in a sexual assault proceeding.[118]

As was the case in *B(IE)*, the closing submissions by the defence in *Wright* did not attempt to justify or explain the relevance of this evidence.[119] In fact, Ostapiw did not return to this evidence at any other point in the trial.[120] It seems reasonable to argue that the purpose of her questions was to trigger the discriminatory and legally impermissible inference that the complainant was more likely to have consented to anal intercourse with the accused given her supposedly risqué or promiscuous behaviour earlier that night, or the equally illegitimate inference that her purportedly promiscuous behaviour made her less worthy of belief. Given the stipulations under sections 276 and 277 of the *Criminal Code*,

Ostapiw should have refrained from asking these questions, the Crown should have objected to them, and Justice Martin should have disallowed them. Rather than being coddled, the complainant in *Wright* was not granted the protection from irrelevant and humiliating questions that Canada's rape shield provisions are intended to provide.

One issue in particular, related to section 276, has raised the ire of some defence counsel: the inclusion of evidence of other sexual activity between the complainant and the accused under Canada's rape shield provisions. Bayliss describes the concern as follows: "the most shocking example of this [pendulum swing] is the rule, first established by the Supreme Court of Canada and now encoded in the Criminal Code of Canada, that a sexual assault defendant is precluded from adducing evidence of prior sexual activity between him or herself and the accuser."[121] Several of the defence lawyers I interviewed also raised this as a problem with our current rules limiting the use of prior sexual history evidence.

It is true that section 276 places limits on the purposes for which defence counsel can introduce evidence of a complainant's sexual activities other than those forming the subject matter of the charge. It is true that these limits apply to evidence of all other sexual acts engaged in by the complainant, whether those acts were with the accused or with someone else. However, the *Criminal Code* does not, as Bayliss's statement seems to suggest, exclude all evidence of sexual activity between an accused and a complainant. Section 276 is not, as defence counsel bringing these applications undoubtedly argue, a blanket exclusion of prior sexual history evidence. Moreover, as Jennifer Koshan's recent research demonstrates, in Canada most defence counsel applications to adduce evidence of prior sexual activity between the accused and the complainant in cases involving spouses are successful, or at least partially successful.[122] While there are instances in which the complainant's sexual history with the accused is relevant and admissible under section 276 (for example, to demonstrate the manner in which consent was communicated in the past, in an effort to raise an air of reality to the defence of honest but mistaken belief in consent), there are also circumstances in which evidence of other sexual activity between the accused and the complainant is properly excluded under section 276 of the *Criminal Code*.

Consider the following example from a recent assault and sexual assault trial in British Columbia. The accused in *R v S(JS)* was alleged to have engaged in repeated acts of physical and sexual assault against his then wife. These acts included dragging her around the house, grabbing her by the throat, and punching her vagina. The sexual assault allegations involved forced anal intercourse on one occasion, and forced anal intercourse and forced fellatio on a second occasion. His defence was that his former spouse consented to the acts involved. The jury convicted him of assault and sexual assault causing bodily harm.[123] Prior to trial, his lawyer, S.R. Chamberlain, QC, brought an application to adduce evidence of the complainant's (seemingly) entire sexual history with the accused, including videos, texts, and photos.[124] In addition to his application to admit a, presumably nude, photograph of the complainant with "semen between her posterior," Chamberlain asked the trial judge to admit evidence that:

- on the couple's first date the complainant initiated sexual activity;
- during the marriage the couple had engaged in acts of fellatio, cunnilingus, and vaginal intercourse in the accused's car;
- the complainant used sex toys to stimulate herself;
- she encouraged the accused to ejaculate on different parts of her body;
- she suggested to the accused that the couple have vaginal intercourse while she was menstruating;
- she permitted the accused to photograph and videotape them as they engaged in sexual activity;
- the couple had engaged in four or five acts of consensual anal intercourse on occasions prior to the acts of allegedly forced anal intercourse;
- on two or three of those occasions the complainant was menstruating and could be said to have enjoyed the anal intercourse because of the additional lubrication her menstrual blood provided.[125]

As Crown counsel noted in opposing the application, the evidence that Chamberlain sought to introduce on behalf of his client would "badly distort the fact-finding process by humiliating the complainant and prejudicing the jurors against her, based on entirely irrelevant considerations."[126] Indeed, given the allegations and the defence of consent offered, the impetus for attempting to introduce evidence as to, for example, whether the complainant encouraged the accused to ejaculate on different parts of her body during the course of their marriage, initiated sex on their first date, used sex toys, stimulated herself during anal intercourse, or engaged in sexual activity while she was menstruating, can only have been one or both of the following two objectives: to humiliate and shame the complainant, and/or to represent her to the jury as 'the type of woman' who would consent to anything. Upon a proper application of section 276, none of this evidence should have been admitted. While the trial judge rightly excluded most of it, unfortunately Chamberlain's application was partially successful.

In *R v B(S)* the section 276 ruling by Justice Robert Stack, and the subsequent cross-examination of the complainant by defence counsel Robert Simmonds, QC, seems even worse.[127] The accused in *B(S)* was charged with multiple counts of assault and sexual assault against his former spouse over a period of several years. His defence was consent. Defence counsel brought an application to cross-examine the complainant on: (i) sexual activity between her and a third party, relying on text messages between them; (ii) anal sex between her and the accused, referring to a forty-six-minute graphic video with "extreme close-ups" of oral, vaginal, and anal penetration as well as the use of a sex toy; and (iii) other sexual activity.[128] The defence even sought to play to the jury portions of this graphic video of the complainant and the accused engaged in anal intercourse. Following a flawed pre-trial decision by Justice Stack to admit much of this evidence, Simmonds proceeded to read aloud to the jury a set of deeply personal, very graphic sexual texts between her and the third party. He did this despite the fact that the basis upon which the trial judge had admitted this evidence had not materialized.[129] He also read aloud to the jury from a highly prejudicial transcript of the sex videotape made by her and her former husband, in which the complainant repeatedly referred to herself as the accused's "ass slut" or "slut wife" during sexual role play and asked him to "stick his hard cock" in her "ass."[130] SB was acquitted and the Crown appealed.[131] The Newfoundland Court of Appeal found that the use of evidence of the complainant's other sexual activity in this case gratuitously denigrated and humiliated the complainant, and triggered the discriminatory twin myth stereotypes in front of the jury.[132] Simmonds's treatment of the complainant in *R v B(S)* will be considered in greater detail in chapter 3.

Contrary to Bayliss's assertion, cases such as *S(JS)* and *B(S)* make obvious why it is neither "shocking" nor unjust to establish a rule requiring defence counsel to demonstrate that evidence of other sexual activity between the complainant and the accused is relevant and probative, and is not being introduced simply to trigger discriminatory stereotypes or to humiliate the complainant.

In addition to reported decisions and trial transcripts, further evidence to rebut the assertion that legal reforms consistently insulate complainants from problematic strategies can be drawn from the interviews I conducted with defence lawyers and Crown attorneys. As already noted, several of the interview participants indicated that they believe some lawyers do engage in strategies that feature problematic practices such as whacking the complainant at the preliminary inquiry. Further examples are provided by statements such as this one by Defence Lawyer 12: "You know, I think in truth, to a greater or lesser extent, all the, all the rape myths still operate." She also noted that while she would like to think otherwise, she believes that "some lawyers probably do" use the prospect of an application to introduce evidence of a complainant's sexual history or to produce her psychiatric records in an effort to discourage a complainant from participating further in the criminal justice process. Similarly, Defence Lawyer 13 asserted that it is not uncommon for lawyers to use the threat of an application to introduce the complainant's sexual history, or have her counselling records produced, in order to intimidate her: "It rattles their cage. Even if you think you're going to lose, the fact that they've got to put up a fight, and think about the risk of, um, exposing, you know, their prior history or their relationship with their therapist, I think is quite intimidating. And I'm sure it's often used strategically." Defence Lawyer 13 noted that he would not use this tactic and that he did not consider it to be ethical.

Conversely, other interview subjects described using these tactics themselves and defended them as ethical. For example, in discussing the use of the complainant's prior sexual history Defence Lawyer 9 stated:

> Whether I'm right or wrong, prior sexual behaviour is usually, or can be completely irrelevant to the issue before the court. And the last thing that I want to do of course, is to embarrass the alleged victim to the point where the judge is going to have sympathy for that victim. Now, if it's somebody over the age of eighteen and

consent is an issue, then of course, my position is different. (*I: And then what's your position?*) Then I, if I can, I will go after her.

A similar example is given by Defence Lawyer 4:

> In a case where the complainants have, are, you know, either incredibly promiscuous or do have some character issues that I think will weigh against them if a judge sees that, and where I might not have a real absolute legal avenue to ask that question, right, I will do my best to find a legal avenue to ask that question. So, for example, I know that I can't ask about other sexual behaviour. However, what I can ask, according to case law, is where someone makes a direct contradiction of what they've said earlier. So I will, at the preliminary hearing, delve into and give the person room that if they're going to start saying things that contradict what they said otherwise, that deal with the times when there was other sexual behaviour, you know, I'm hopeful that they will. Because once they have, I've got it in. Right? Then I can sidestep the other rule, you know, yeah. You know, is that unethical? I mean, I don't think it's unethical at all. That's advocacy.

The assertion that legal reforms now insulate sexual assault complainants from aggressive and harsh cross-examinations, or tactics aimed at discouraging their participation in the process, is also inconsistent with the way in which some criminal lawyers market their services online. Consider Alberta lawyer Paul Gracia's website, which described the case of a fourteen-year-old girl who was allegedly sexually assaulted by three men, one of whom (the lawyer's client) was a habitual sexual offender:

> My client attended at a hotel room, where two of his friends had been taking turns engaging in repeated acts of sexual intercourse with each of two 14 year-old girls. Without saying a word, my client removed his clothing and [immediately] proceeded to have sexual intercourse with one of the girls and demand oral sex from her. He then got dressed and left. He had two prior convictions for sexual assault on his record. Then, while on release for this offence, he was accused of committing yet another sexual assault, this time upon a mentally disabled girl ... At the Preliminary Inquiry, during my

cross examination of the complainant, she became so frustrated by my questions that she effectively quit, exclaiming that she no longer desired to proceed any further. The matter was adjourned for several months. On the continuation date, the complainant refused to attend, therefore the Crown stayed all charges as against my client. The other two accused continued with their charges in relation to the other complainant. No criminal convictions.[133]

Arguably, Gracia's website tells the story of a fourteen-year-old girl who was sexually assaulted by three men, and then bullied into submission and retreat from the criminal justice system through cross-examination by the lawyer who represented one of her attackers. Presumably, this content was included on the firm's website for promotional purposes – to suggest to future clients the types of strategies Gracia is willing to deploy.

Toronto lawyer Craig Penney's website also described using strategies that could be construed as intended to intimidate a complainant or discourage her from proceeding.[134] He provided this "background" for one of his prior cases:

> Baldwin, his wife, Patricia, and her husband were friends. They socialized regularly, and went drinking together about once a week. Occasionally, they flirted with each other's spouse, and a few times they ... well, let's just say that they got to know one another a little better. This one night Baldwin, Patricia, and her husband were drinking heavily. Baldwin's wife had only a few drinks. The festivities had ended with Patricia falling asleep in her bed and with Baldwin falling asleep on the sofa. Patricia woke up to find herself having sexual intercourse with Baldwin, who she thought was her husband. The police were called.[135]

Penney's background description of this case is, in fact, a description of a sexual assault: "Patricia woke up to find herself having sexual intercourse with Baldwin."[136] Under Canadian law one cannot consent to sex while unconscious.[137] One cannot consent in advance to sex to occur while asleep.[138] By definition, a woman who "[wakes] up to find herself having sexual intercourse" is being sexually assaulted.[139] It would not matter whether she thought it was her husband, nor indeed whether it was in fact her husband.

Penney identified two main concerns with the case: that the judge would either decide Patricia was too drunk to consent or decide that Baldwin's belief that Patricia was consenting was induced by his intoxication. His concerns, the latter of which he said had "consumed [him] from day one," were well-founded.[140] Complainants who are asleep, passed out, or severely intoxicated lack the capacity to consent, and a mistaken belief in consent based on an accused's intoxication is not a defence to sexual assault.[141]

Having identified his main concerns with the facts, Penney described his strategy in the following way: "I wanted to ensure that the Trial Judge understood the context in which these allegations arose. On several occasions, Baldwin, his wife, Patricia, and her husband had crossed the line with one another. I wanted the Judge to hear this history."[142] While he noted that he was required to file a section 276 application explaining why it was relevant, he did not explain why he wanted the judge to hear this sexual history nor how it could be connected to what he rightly identified as the major issue for his client: the fact that this woman was passed out when the accused initiated sexual intercourse with her. According to his advertisement, Penney filed a section 276 application to introduce details of the sexual relationship between the two couples and four days later the Crown indicated that they had met with Patricia, reviewed Penney's materials detailing the sexual history between the four, and decided not to proceed. Penny wrote, "I wasn't privy to the conversation between Patricia and the Crown but it had taken the wind from the Crown's sails."[143]

One of two conclusions can likely be drawn. Either Patricia, faced with the humiliating prospect of having this sexual history detailed in court, indicated an unwillingness to proceed, or the Crown determined that her sexual history would be too damaging to her credibility – that because of problematic social assumptions about women and sexuality, the prospect of a conviction in the face of a complainant's supposed promiscuity and transcendence of monogamous hetero-normativity was too remote.

Key to an assessment of Penney's strategy is that on the facts of this case, as described by him, the complainant's prior sexual history would not have been relevant or admissible. Given that one cannot consent in advance to sexual intercourse to occur once they have passed out,[144] and given that a mistaken belief in consent cannot be based on an accused's intoxicated condition and requires that the accused have taken reasonable steps to ascertain consent,[145] the only plausible defence in this case was that the sexual intercourse either did not occur or that Patricia was conscious and consenting when it occurred. The fact that these two couples had engaged in sexual activity together would not be admissible to challenge the complainant's credibility about whether the sexual contact had occurred, or about whether she awoke to find the accused having intercourse with her. Nor would evidence of her prior sexual history be admissible for the purpose of inferring that because she had had sex with the accused in the past she was more likely to have consented to sex in this instance.[146] In other words, based on Penney's description of the case, there was no permissible use for this prior sexual history evidence.

Consider a seemingly similar example from a Toronto firm that advertised a case in which they say they were able to use the fact that a complainant had previously consented to sex with their client in order to convince the judge that she was lying about the nonconsensual nature of the sexual act at issue in the allegation: "we were able to prove that the complainant had sex with our client at an earlier time, and this convinced the judge that the complainant was lying about not consenting at the time and place alleged in her accusation."[147]

Again, it is an error of law for a judge to conclude that the fact that a complainant had consensual sex with the accused at an earlier time suggests or establishes, by virtue of the sexual nature of the activity, that she is lying about the allegation of nonconsensual sex at issue in the charge. Evidence of prior sexual history introduced for such purposes is expressly precluded under section 276 of the *Criminal Code*.[148] If the judge in this case actually did conclude that the complainant was lying because she had previously engaged in consensual sex with the accused, then this firm is advertising a 'past success' that is both based on an error of law and reliant for its triumph on rape myths that have been categorically rejected at law.

If these are the types of questions, comments, and strategies that occur in a legal culture supposedly inhibited by political correctness and a feminist-inspired, disproportionate concern for the complainant, it is alarming to consider what would be said and done in the absence of these perceived norms of constraint. Stated more generously, this common refrain about the undue restrictions placed upon the ability of defence counsel to properly cross-examine sexual assault complainants simply does not hold true when subjected to scrutiny. Moreover, there are too many illustrations of defence counsel in recent cases engaging in arguably aggressive tactics or seemingly stereotype-infused questioning and strategies to accept that it is a myth that sexual assault complainants regularly get whacked.

In addition, it is difficult to know how defence lawyers who insist that these types of practices do not occur would know whether this is true. As some of the lawyers I interviewed noted, criminal defence lawyers rarely see their fellow members of the defence bar cross-examine a sexual assault complainant. Defence Lawyer 10 offered this explanation when asked whether she thought some lawyers push the boundaries of what she considered to be ethical representation in sexual assault proceedings: "I suspect so. But, because of the way the courts work, I mean, I don't see what, I don't sit through other people's trials, for the most part." This same reality is described in the following way by Defence Lawyer 1: "Well, one of the problems is, being a defence lawyer, is, well, I don't want to say lonely, but you're in there by yourself. You know, it's you, your client, the Crown. There's nobody else. You know? ... And if you're a senior lawyer, you're in first and then you're out ... So you don't see anybody else."

Without studying the trial transcripts of their colleagues' sexual assault cases or conducting interview-based research with its corresponding guarantees of anonymity, criminal defence lawyers are unlikely to know the prevalence with which bullying and aggressive strategies are deployed. It seems unlikely that lawyers who do engage in these practices would broadcast such actions to their peers. Although it is true that some lawyers have advertised them on their websites!

One might point to the fact that defence lawyers do not typically have the opportunity to observe one another's courtroom practices to suggest that the interviews conducted as part of this research are of little value. There are at least two reasons not to accept this contention. First, many of the statements made by the defence lawyers I interviewed corroborate the practices and perspectives reflected in the other sources of data relied upon in this book: the trial transcripts, case law, criminal defence firm websites, and public statements of members of the defence bar. Second, unlike defence lawyers, prosecutors typically do have frequent opportunities to observe the courtroom conduct of various defence lawyers. In considering the comments of the Crown attorneys included in this book, it is worth noting that they have observed the practices of a much broader sample of defence lawyers.

It is true that we do not yet have quantitative data on the proportion of sexual assault cases that involve the types of practices discussed in this chapter. Countless sexual assault proceedings conducted every year do not result in reported decisions. Moreover, not all trial judges whose written reasons are reported would include in them a description of this type of cross-examination even if it had occurred. As such, it is not possible through case law research alone to ascertain the actual prevalence of this conduct. That said, David Tanovich's recent work documents more than twenty reported decisions in 2015 alone in which trial judges referenced or described some type of aggressive attack on the complainant.[149] While Tanovich's work cannot reveal with precision its prevalence, his work most certainly debunks the myth that whacking the complainant is mere lore. Interviews with both Crown attorneys and defence lawyers, in which they state that they either engage in these practices or (in the case of Crowns) witness others doing so, recent trial transcripts that arguably demonstrate these practices, and websites by lawyers advertising these kinds of strategies provide further evidence of this problem. Moreover, the fact that multiple sources of evidence document these practices (websites, case law, interviews, and trial transcripts) suggests that they are very far from uncommon. Regardless, it is difficult to understand a response from lawyers that essentially boils down to the claim that there is not a serious problem because this type of mistreatment of sexual assault complainants has not been empirically proven to be ubiquitous. Would these legal professionals respond in the same manner to the documentation of numerous recent cases in which lawyers had stolen from their clients?

Far from a system of matriarchal justice in which complainants are overprotected and an individual accused of sexual assault is unlikely to receive a fair trial, retired Justice Marie Corbett recently concluded that the legal system does not serve sexual assault survivors well and that ensuring due process for the accused has perhaps become the *only* function of the trial judge. In reflecting on several of the proceedings over which she presided during her tenure on the bench (including many sexual assault trials), she commented:

What was my role in righting social wrongs? "Dispensing justice" or "finding truth" are responses too wide of the mark. I was realizing that my function was narrower and more modest: as a criminal trial judge, my job was to ensure that an accused person receive a fair trial. Certainly, a fair trial is part of the goal of justice. Increasingly, I concluded that justice meant ensuring a fair trial for the accused, not necessarily redress for the victim, not necessarily the protection of others, and not necessarily the prevention of crime.[150]

Examples from the transcripts of recent sexual assault proceedings, interviews with defence lawyers, recent reported decisions, and the content on some defence lawyers' websites suggest that changes to the law of sexual assault and the rules of evidence have not sufficiently shifted the norms of defence counsel conduct in sexual assault proceedings. To be clear, feminist efforts to improve sexual assault trials are not aimed at giving complainants a "free pass," as some senior defence lawyers have suggested.[151] The objective of law reforms in this area was to level a playing field that had failed to offer survivors of sexual offences the same legal protection under the criminal law available to those subjected to other violent offences. As Constance Backhouse writes, feminists have endeavoured to create a fairer, more just legal framework for responding to sexual assault – one that eliminates "specific exceptions to the normal rules of evidence that are grounded in discriminatory, non-factually based myths about women's sexuality, credibility, and consent."[152]

It is time to debunk the myth that a feminist-inspired coup d'état has wrested the scales of justice from the grip of rightful authority. In fact, in terms of the proper application of legal reforms aimed at levelling the playing field for sexual assault complainants, the pendulum has not swung far enough. Progressive law reforms have not succeeded in preventing criminal defence practices that unfairly and unjustly traumatize sexual assault complainants.

Accepting that law reforms are unable to (fully) achieve this objective, it seems reasonable to consider whether the legal profession itself, or aspects of the culture of the legal profession, could be changed in ways that might improve the criminal trial process for sexual assault complainants. In the next chapter I explore the disjuncture between the following phenomena: the commonly articulated refrain within the profession that experienced criminal lawyers – 'the good ones' – do not abuse sexual assault complainants for strategic reasons; the profession's celebration of courtroom aggression; and the reality that some of the profession's most experienced, prominent, and celebrated criminal lawyers arguably have engaged in aspects of this type of treatment towards sexual assault complainants.

Following that, in chapter 4, consideration is given to the way in which the dominant professional identity of the criminal defence bar, identified and articulated by criminal lawyers themselves, is in fact inconsistent with the celebration of courtroom aggression as the pre-eminent marker of what it means to defend the criminally accused. More importantly, chapter 4 also demonstrates that this professional identity – this self-understanding of the defence lawyer's justice project – is actually inconsistent with trial strategies aimed at humiliating and intimidating complainants or employing discriminatory stereotypes.

CHAPTER 3

A Kinder and Gentler Approach? Interrogating the Heroes of the Defence Bar

In an online discussion regarding the high-profile sexual assault trial of Jian Ghomeshi in 2016, a senior member of the bar with expertise in legal ethics stated:

> Experienced criminal lawyers use a kinder and gentler approach to extract as much information as they possibly can, which may then be used to cross examine at trial on inconsistencies. Whacking rarely extracts much other than defensiveness and hostility. While complainants occasionally do decide they don't want to go back for another round, that is rare. The point is that whacking is not only reprehensible, and unethical ... it is generally also bad lawyering.[1]

This contention that whacking the complainant is not good lawyering and that experienced criminal lawyers know better than to pursue this strategy is offered by some lawyers in support of the claim that sexual assault complainants are not routinely subjected to aggressive and bullying tactics. Defence lawyer Breese Davies, for example, noted in a recent column that "most defence counsel see little to be gained from 'beating up' a complainant."[2] Similarly, managing partner of a Toronto criminal law firm Reid Rusonick recently asserted that "[g]ood cross-examiners don't recklessly besmirch the character of complainants (our system already protects against such behaviour and should) ... Cross-examination is rarely even attempted unless there are fairly obvious lies or serious exaggerations to be exposed."[3] The claim that whacking-type strategies are a thing of the past was addressed, and rejected, in the previous chapter. This chapter examines the assertion that good lawyers, experienced lawyers, refrain from treating complainants in this manner because of their knowledge that such practices are ineffective.

Like Davies, Rusonick, and the senior lawyer quoted in the opening paragraph, nearly every criminal defence lawyer I interviewed commented about the strategic inadvisability of cross-examining the complainant in an aggressive manner. The following explanation from Defence Lawyer 8 captures this perspective:

> In all the cases I've done, I've never had the need to beat up on a victim, on a complainant. I certainly believe you can get a lot more by making them feel comfortable, giving them an opportunity to speak, encouraging them to tell their story, and, if you think they're being outrageous or coming close to creating fiction, you simply encourage them to do so … yelling, screaming, abusing the person cows them to some extent, if they've already been abused and they climb back into their shell. So you're certainly not doing your client any good in that regard.

This commonly articulated assertion – that good lawyers know better – while likely a genuinely held belief, is inconsistent with the reality that some of our most celebrated and experienced criminal lawyers are not known for their kinder and gentler approach to the cross-examination of witnesses alleging gendered and sexualized harms. Take Marie Henein, the criminal defence lawyer involved in the Ghomeshi trial itself. Ghomeshi was represented by a very experienced lawyer, one who is exalted by her peers as the best of the best: "as fine a criminal lawyer as this country has."[4]

In an article published shortly after Ghomeshi retained Marie Henein, she was described as a lawyer who would go to war for him. The author nicknamed her "Hand Grenade Henein" and "Machete Marie."[5] Former client and fellow lawyer Michael Bryant, who served as Ontario's attorney general from 2003 to 2007, likened her to Hannibal Lecter for her supposed ability to exploit a person's deepest frailties.[6] In reference to her representation of a former client acquitted of sexual exploitation charges, Henein was described as a lawyer who not only advocates for her clients but "goes for the jugular."[7] To be clear, the much-discussed cross-examinations of the complainants in *R v Ghomeshi* did not appear from the transcripts to involve the types of practices examined in the previous chapter and later in this chapter.[8] While the trial process was profoundly traumatic for the women who testified against Ghomeshi,[9] defence counsel's conduct of the case is not to blame for their experiences. Nevertheless, it is hard to imagine anyone would suggest that Henein's approach was either kind or gentle, nor is she known for her kinder and gentler approach more broadly. Kinder and gentler, of course, is not the standard by which we should assess defence counsel cross-examinations. But as a profession, why would we in one breath suggest that good lawyers know to use a kinder, gentler tack to question sexual assault complainants, and in another venerate ruthlessness and viciousness as the markers of a true criminal defender?

Henein was mentored by Edward Greenspan, who was perhaps Canada's *most* celebrated criminal lawyer (at least in recent times), and who most certainly was not known for his kinder, gentler approach to the cross-examination of sexual assault complainants. As Constance Backhouse writes, "Greenspan's aggressive technique of cross-examining witnesses to the point of complete devastation was hailed as the hallmark of a brilliant defence counsel."[10] Greenspan's reputation as a giant of the courtroom was, she continues, built "upon virulent assaults against the credibility of women who made complaints of sexual assault and domestic violence."[11] In *R v Regan*,[12] discussed briefly in chapter 2, Greenspan's public attack on the complainants, before the trial had even started, was extraordinary.[13] For example, in an unprecedented move, he reportedly attempted to have the publication ban protecting two of the complainants lifted before the trial began. According to author Stephen Kimber, "[i]n a tone that seemed calculated to send a chill through all of the complainants," Greenspan threatened to place advertisements in newspapers across the country seeking the public's help in gathering information about the complainants' backgrounds,[14] presumably hoping to use it to discredit or intimidate them. He publicly released a nine-page open letter to the premier of Nova Scotia, in which he raised the prior sexual history and sexual reputation of one of the complainants. Using factual claims, the accuracy of which was not established, Greenspan attacked this woman's assertion that she had been a virgin when Regan allegedly raped her as a young teenager.[15]

The stories told about the heroes of the criminal defence bar often applaud their ferocity and bellicosity in the courtroom. The obituaries of some of the most prominent criminal defence lawyers in Canada are telling in this regard. As indicated, Greenspan was memorialized as an aggressive and unrelenting cross-examiner. Similarly, upon his death, renowned criminal lawyer Clyne Harradence was celebrated for being an "intellectually ferocious cross-examiner."[16] His brother Milt was said to "go to war" when he entered a courtroom.[17] Charles Dubin, who was described in one obituary as a "legal giant," was, like Marie Henein, said to have a "go for the jugular" approach to the cross-examination of witnesses.[18]

While the descriptions of these acclaimed criminal lawyers presumably refer to their practices as a whole, and not their defence of sexual offences specifically, they are offered here to make a point about the culture of the criminal defence bar: criminal lawyers receive commendation and acclaim for their aggressiveness. Indubitably, their citations for courtroom brilliance, whether offered retrospectively or *ante mortem*, do not reference an aptitude for respectful and courteous cross-examination techniques. Moreover, it would presumably be true that some of these acclaimed criminal lawyers did, like Greenspan, earn their reputations at least in part through their very aggressive defence of clients accused of sexual offences.[19] Likewise, many of the examples of arguably overly aggressive, bullying, and/or stereotype-infused treatment of sexual assault complainants examined in chapter 2 are from cases involving highly experienced criminal lawyers, some of whom have the conspicuous 'Queen's Counsel' designation behind their names, or have been otherwise recognized and honoured by their profession.

While defence lawyers may maintain that good lawyers know that antagonistic, unduly lengthy, unnecessarily repetitive, discourteous, bullying, and stereotype-infused questioning of the complainant does not work, the reality is that some of the lawyers most promoted and celebrated by the profession appear to employ, to varying degrees, some of these very tactics. Consider the following four examples.

1. Todd Brett White, the Junkyard Dog: Eddie Greenspan's "Rough and Tumble" Mentee

Like Marie Henein, Todd Brett White was also a mentee of Edward Greenspan.[20] Upon Greenspan's death, White described his mentor as "one of the greatest criminal lawyers to have ever lived."[21] White himself has become a prominent lawyer in Toronto's criminal defence bar. On his law firm's website, White states that for the fifth year in a row he has "been voted by his peers as one of the *Best Lawyers in Canada* in the area of Criminal Law."[22] According to White, "[s]election to *Best Lawyers* is based on an exhaustive and rigorous peer-review survey comprising more than three million confidential evaluations by top attorneys."[23] Promotional materials describing his practice assert that "[h]e is especially noted for his cross-examination abilities."[24] Indeed, like Greenspan, White's status as a well-known criminal lawyer appears to be premised, at least in part, on his reputation for aggressive and unrelenting cross-examinations. It is clear from the news clippings and other material included on White's website that this is a reputation that he has, if not cultivated, then certainly embraced. A prominent quote on the profile page of his website reads: "Todd White, Mr. Greenspan's partner, has been called 'Junkyard Dog' for his rough and tumble court-room style – a moniker that Mr. Greenspan once said he wished had been bestowed upon him."[25] Another article White posted on his website admiringly dubs him the "Legal JYD."[26]

Arguably, White's "rough and tumble courtroom style"[27] was on display during his cross-examination of the nineteen-year-old complainant in a 2014 sexual assault trial.[28] White's client, Giuseppe Luceno, was convicted of sexual assault and sexual interference. Luceno had sexual intercourse with the complainant, whom he met online, when she was thirteen years old. He was twenty-five at the time of the sexual assault, although online he misrepresented himself as several years younger. Given the age of consent under the *Criminal Code*, consent could not be advanced in his defence.[29] Moreover, there was no compelling evidence that he had taken any steps to ascertain the complainant's age, and thus honest but mistaken belief in consent was also not available as a defence.

Instead, Luceno's defence was that the sexual activity did not occur, and that the complainant had fabricated the allegation in conspiracy with another young woman with whom Luceno had been sexually involved. In fact, the sexual assault against the complainant was reported to the police by this other woman, years after it occurred, and without the complainant's knowledge. The trial judge in *R v L(G)*, Justice Robert Goldstein, found no evidence of a conspiracy, and significant evidence demonstrating the complainant's displeasure at having become unwillingly involved in the case.[30]

Justice Goldstein described the complainant as having been subjected to "endless days of repetitive ... cross-examination."[31] He noted that the nineteen-year-old complainant found White's "cross-examination long, repetitive, bullying, and painful, which occasionally resulted in justifiable flashes of anger and frustration on her part."[32] A review of the trial transcript reveals a cross-examination of this young woman that could fairly be characterized as excessively repetitive, unnecessarily aggressive, bullying, at times rude, confusing, and ineffective. While the tenor and tone of the cross-examination can only be gleaned, and then only partially, by reading the transcript (which spans several hundred pages) in its entirety, what follows are examples that provide some sense of White's approach to the questioning of this nineteen-year-old woman.

One of White's tactics involved repeated interruptions. Indeed, White frequently interrupted the complainant while she was attempting to answer his questions.[33] The trial judge repeatedly instructed him to stop interrupting the complainant with interventions such as:

"Sir, you've got to let her answer the question."[34]
"Hold on a minute. She's answering still, Mr. White."[35]
"You've got to stop interrupting her, okay?"[36]
"She's got to be able to answer the question. You can't interrupt her when she's answering, okay?"[37]

In fact, Justice Goldstein halted White's questioning and directed him to stop interrupting the complainant more than fifteen times during his cross-examination of this young woman.[38] While White interrupted her repeatedly, on the handful of occasions when she interrupted him, he requested or demanded that she stop.[39] Despite White's frequent interjections, the complainant did not ask him not to interrupt her while she was speaking.

Often using rapid-fire questions, White repeatedly refused the complainant's requests that she be permitted to explain her answer, or the prior testimony put to her by him.[40] More than once the trial judge instructed him to slow down.[41] For example: "you're really rapid fire, and it's not really giving her an opportunity and she's, you know, she's getting herself tripped up ... sometimes [you're] sort of going at her in a way that doesn't really give her an opportunity to respond, and I think that's causing some of the problems here."[42]

Repeatedly Justice Goldstein intervened to require that she be permitted to speak.[43] For example:

> [DEFENCE] Q. Do you recall being asked those questions and giving those answers?
> A. Can I explain now?
> Q. No. Do you recall being asked those questions and giving those answers?
> A. Yes. Can I explain now?
> Q. No.
> A. Why can't I explain?
> Q. My next question is this, I'm going to suggest to you that the officer –
> THE COURT: Sorry, Mr. White. I think she is trying to explain something, and I understand you want to control the witness and so forth –
> MR. WHITE: Okay.
> THE COURT: – but I think she should be given the opportunity to give her explanation. What's your explanation, Ms. ——— ?[44]

In addition to his frequent interruptions and refusals to her requests to explain her answers, White repeatedly asked the complainant very long questions with multiple factual assertions. Indeed, White's cross-examination of the complainant is rife with examples of compound questions, to which the complainant's yes or no responses left the finder of fact without any sense as to which of White's factual assertions she had accepted or rejected.[45] Despite the trial judge's repeated direction to him to stop using questions with multiple factual assertions,[46] White continued to do so throughout his cross-examination.[47] Notably, he persisted with this style of questioning even in the face of explicit feedback from the trial judge that such questioning was confusing both to the complainant and to the trial judge himself:

> THE COURT: Ms. ——— do you need a break? All right. We're going to take a short break. You can step down. Okay. Mr. White, I'm not trying to curtail your cross-examination in any way, but I'll be honest with you, I'm confused. So I think she's probably confused … you're asking very, very long questions with a number of facts in them.[48]

As the trial judge went on to explain, "[including multiple facts in one question] is a problem ... you don't 100 percent necessarily know what fact that the witness is answering, and I think we're seeing an example of that here."[49] Justice Goldstein directed White to stop using long questions with multiple factual assertions eight different times during his cross-examination of the complainant.[50]

The ineffectiveness of White's approach is suggested by the trial judge's assessment of the complainant's credibility in his reasons for judgment convicting the accused: "I decline to find that she is not credible simply because she answered only one of the four propositions put to her in a single question in cross-examination at the preliminary inquiry, and then answered a different proposition in a four-proposition question at the trial."[51]

The trial judge excused the complainant several times in order to advise White that his rapid-fire approach was repetitive and confusing,[52] and had become counterproductive.[53] The complainant, who had not finished high school, repeatedly expressed confusion during the cross-examination.[54] The trial judge commented on the confusion produced by White's style of questioning in his reasons for judgment: "I am also not persuaded that many of the so-called contradictions in K.S.'s evidence were contradictions at all. Rather, they were confused attempts to answer confusing questions ... I think that even a professional witness would have been confused by some of the cross-examination questions."[55]

In addition, Justice Goldstein advised White that some of his questions to the complainant were simply unfair.[56] For example, "But hold on there, Mr. White. With all due respect, I think that's a very unfair question."[57] The Crown objected more than once on the basis that White, in questioning the complainant, had misstated her previous response or testimony.[58]

Arguably, at times White's tone was sarcastic or rude.[59] In one instance Justice Goldstein directed White not to insult the complainant.[60] Upon being asked the same questions repeatedly about whether there was an inconsistency between what she testified to during the preliminary inquiry about Facebook notes and Facebook messages and what she had said in her police statement about notes, Justice Goldstein again asked White to allow her to explain her response:

THE COURT: Okay. Hold on a minute, Mr. White. She wants to explain her answer. I think she can be given the opportunity to do that.

THE WITNESS: When I said that, the notes had nothing to do with it. You keep trying to make it like they did. They had nothing to do with her. I can show you them if you like. They had absolutely nothing to do with her at all.

MR WHITE: Ma'am, no one has ever suggested that they do, okay. So get that through your head ...

THE COURT: Mr. White, first of all, you don't have to be rude to her, okay.

MR WHITE: I apologize, Your Honour.

THE COURT: That's the first thing. The second thing is, again, you're putting a whole bunch of different facts to her at once.[61]

Note that upon being admonished for his discourteous treatment of the complainant, it is the trial judge to whom the Junkyard Dog apologized, not her. Arguably, the transcript of this proceeding reveals a notable difference between his courteous and at times reverential interactions with the other legal professionals in the courtroom ("My Friend" the Crown attorney and "Your Honour" the trial judge) and his comportment towards the nineteen-year-old woman sexually assaulted by his client.

It is also worth highlighting that even if it existed, this supposed inconsistency between the complainant's various statements about Facebook notes was one that the trial judge characterized as "trivial."[62]

Having been cross-examined for days[63] – a cross-examination in which White repeatedly implied or asserted that she was lying,[64] interrupted her frequently,[65] asked her the same questions about notes dozens and dozens of times,[66] repeatedly refused to allow her to explain her answers,[67] arguably condescended to her,[68] and insulted her[69] – the complainant unsurprisingly began to express her frustration. White then attempted to use this very understandable reaction to his treatment of her as evidence of her dishonesty:

Q. So it's crystal clear, you weren't mistaken that these were post-it notes, correct?

A. Sure.

Q. You lied to his Honour when you said that you thought I –

A. No. You were confusing me.

Q. – was talking about post-it notes.

A. You were asking me the same question over and over and rewording the thing over and over again.

Q. And that's why you thought that I was talking about post-it notes?

A. You were – to me, you were talking about like post-it notes and then notes on Facebook. You weren't exactly specific about Facebook notes.

Q. I wasn't?

A. You said notes on Facebook. So I got confused and I want it to be over and done with because I didn't really want to be there and I don't want to be here.

Q. So you're just [saying] whatever you want?

A. No.

Q. You just say whatever you want to go home, right? Whatever comes to your mind, right? You didn't want to be in the police station, right?

A. I didn't, no.

Q. You didn't –

A. I didn't want to be involved –

Q. – want to be [at] that preliminary inquiry?

A. – in this, no.

Q. You didn't want to be involved in the trial?

A. No. I said that on my video as well.

Q. You just make things up.

A. No, but I don't want to be here. You think I want to rethink this over and over again for years? No.

Q. So did you make it up today when you suggested to His Honour that you thought that my questions about notes had to do with post-it notes?

A. That's what I thought. Oh, my God.[70]

Justice Goldstein intervened again, excused the complainant, and ordered White to stop questioning her about the difference between notes and Facebook notes: "Okay, Mr. White, that's it, no more about notes. I'm cutting it off. You have been at her over and over and over again about the notes."[71] Ultimately White convinced the trial judge to let him ask yet a few more questions about notes in order to "get to the punchline."[72]

Particularly striking about the Junkyard Dog's arguably aggressive and bullying cross-examination in this case was its ineffectiveness. Based on the trial judge's comments, both at trial and in his reasons for decision, White's strategy appears to have been counterproductive.[73] The complainant in *L(G)* was dragged into this proceeding involuntarily (which was not White's responsibility), accused of lying, interrupted, insulted, and forced to repeatedly respond to a series of confusing questions about what could be construed as insignificant, collateral details. Far from being a necessary by-product of the accused's fundamental right to due process, subjecting her to this treatment may have, instead, disrupted the fact-finding function of the proceeding – at least based on the trial judge's comments.

Lawyers who assert that a respectful and courteous approach to the cross-examination of a sexual assault complainant is prone to yield better results for the defence are likely correct. What could be taken as the ineffectiveness of the cross-examination of the complainant in *L(G)* appears to support this proposition. What White's cross-examination in *L(G)* does not support is the contention that experienced lawyers know better than to question sexual assault complainants using an overly aggressive, unnecessarily discourteous, or bullying style of cross-examination. Arguably, the questioning of the complainant in *L(G)*, along with several of the examples provided in chapter 2, suggest that some very experienced lawyers may in fact conduct these types of problematic and harmful cross-examinations.

White's cross-examination of the complainant did not include stereotype-infused questioning. Rape mythology did not feature in his conduct of the case in *L(G)*.

2. Naeem Rauf: Edmonton's 2014 Criminal Lawyer of the Year

Naeem Rauf is a prominent member of the criminal defence bar in Edmonton, Alberta. He has practised in Alberta for several decades. In 1994–95 he was president of the province's Criminal Trial Lawyers Association. In 2014 he was named Edmonton's criminal lawyer of the year.[74] The illustrious awards night, which boasted former member of the Supreme Court of Canada Justice Thomas Cromwell as its keynote speaker, honoured lawyers who have fought to "make the justice system fairer for all."[75]

Also in 2014, in fact the week prior to the night on which he was recognized for fighting to make the justice system fairer for all, Naeem Rauf spent approximately five days cross-examining the complainant in a sexual assault proceeding in which his client was convicted of sexual assault causing bodily harm, assault, unlawful confinement, and uttering a death threat.[76] The complainant was a nineteen-year-old Indigenous woman who had struggled with addictions and poverty. She testified that she was thrown onto the floor in the hallway of her attacker's apartment, where he forced his penis into her mouth. He slapped her repeatedly, bit her hard enough to break the skin, and threatened that if she did not stop screaming, she would be cut into little pieces by the accused, who was a butcher. Following this, the accused, Mohamed Khaery, pinned her body down, held her arms above her head, forced his penis into her mouth, and then forced his penis into her vagina. Khaery was raping her vaginally when four police officers, responding to a 911 call from his roommate, entered his bedroom, shouted at Khaery to stop thrusting and when he would not stop, physically pulled him off of the naked complainant as she screamed for help.[77]

R v Khaery, unlike many sexual assault cases, was not a so-called he-said-she-said circumstance. There were at least four eyewitnesses to the attack. In addition to the complainant's testimony, there was evidence from the roommate who called 911, physical evidence of the complainant's injuries from the Sexual Assault Response Team at the hospital where she was taken, and eyewitness evidence from the four police officers who entered the bedroom while the accused was perpetrating the sexual assault. Remarkably, the cross-examination of the complainant still stretched over five days.[78] The complainant was so distraught after Rauf's first day of cross-examination that she failed to return the next day. She was compelled back to court after being arrested and detained under a warrant issued by the trial judge. She stated numerous times that she was not mentally prepared and did not want to testify.[79] Over the five-day period of cross-examination, Rauf repeatedly accused her of lying about the entire assault and advanced a conspiracy theory between the complainant and the roommate that the trial judge characterized as "nothing more" than a "bald allegation."[80]

The trial judge described the complainant's demeanour during the cross-examination as fatigued, at times highly emotional (especially when she was required to repeatedly recount the sexual acts forced upon her), exhausted, and increasingly frustrated.[81] The complainant admitted herself to hospital midway through the week-long cross-examination. Driven to the brink of breakdown, she was afraid that she would commit suicide.[82]

The complainant's own account of her deterioration over this five-day period is telling. On the third day of cross-examination, Rauf accused her of being "completely high on drugs" the previous day in court.[83] In repeatedly denying his accusations, the complainant explained the emotional and physical toll visited upon her as a result of testifying against the man who raped her:

> I wasn't completely high on drugs ... I was not prepared for the questions. I didn't think they would affect me emotionally, having to relive that after I had completely let it go from my mind for two years ... But I wasn't prepared mentally for how – how the questions would affect me. I thought I could handle it, and by the end of the week, I was drained and just ... I couldn't cope with it mentally. I thought I was going to snap.[84]

Despite this explanation, Rauf continued to assert that she had testified while high on drugs: "you may not have been completely high on drugs, but you were high on drugs, weren't you?"[85] Insisting that she was not in fact intoxicated, the complainant admitted that after her second day of cross-examination she "[d]idn't want to come but didn't want to go sit in pink cells again for a witness warrant."[86] As noted, she had been compelled to court the previous day by a bench warrant issued by the trial judge when she failed to return after her first day of testimony. Rauf continued to assert that she had been high on drugs and that she had in fact overdosed, landing her in the hospital.[87] Repeatedly she denied his accusations.[88] Finally, he elicited testimony from her that by the third day of cross-examination her mental state had deteriorated to such an extent that she took herself to the hospital that night for fear she would kill herself:

> Q. Were you high on drugs?
> A. I told you I wasn't. I told you that twice. I said no, I wasn't.
> Q. Had you used drugs the night before?

A. No.

Q. You ended up at the hospital; is that right?

A. Yes.

Q. And that was because you were – had – were –

A. No.

Q. You had overdosed on drugs; is that right?

A. No. No, that wasn't it. I thought I was going to commit suicide ... I was having – I was feeling very hopeless. And I needed some sort of help ... So no, I wasn't there for overdosing.[89]

Despite this answer, Rauf persisted in questioning her about her visit to the hospital.[90] In response to the Crown's objection to his continued interrogation about her hospital visit, Rauf asserted that he was "entitled to ask the questions as to exactly what was going on" the previous day in court.[91] He supported his assertion of this entitlement by quoting a passage from *The Art of the Advocate*: "[w]ith evasive and dishonest witnesses, it is only by forcing them to answer the question asked that the advocate can expose their worth."[92] Recall that there were four police eyewitnesses to the sexual attack perpetrated by his client against this witness he implicitly characterized as evasive and dishonest. Recall that the trial judge described Rauf's conspiracy theory of the case as "nothing more" than a "bald allegation."[93] Moreover, the transcript appears to reveal that it was entirely clear "exactly what was going on."[94] In both her evidence in chief and her cross-examination, prior to the morning on which Rauf repeatedly accused her of being high on drugs, the complainant expressed in detail the traumatic impact of testifying about the rape as well as her strong desire not to talk about the incident.[95] For example:

Q. Ms. ——, after all this business you've described in the hallway, you ended up in the bedroom of that residence; is that right?

A. Yeah. Yes.

Q. And what was the first sexual activity in the bedroom? Was it oral sex or vaginal intercourse?

A. I'm sorry. This is just, like, all mentally just really too much, past couple of days. I'm going to try my best right now, like, that I can to answer these questions. It's just it's really, like – like, too much. I don't know if I can finish this, like complete it, with – it's just disturbing to me, like – is the – like, I just want to kill him, when I'm in here. I'm sorry. That's just me. Like psychologically, I'm not – I can't do this, these questions. I told – like, I just can't do this. I'm sorry. I just – like, the …

Q. My question –

A. I know. I'm not mentally prepared for this, to finish this, to talk about this.[96]

The transcript is rife with examples of the complainant expressing the psychological impact of testifying.[97] It is hard to imagine that there could have been any uncertainty as to the cause of the complainant's state of distress and disruption.

To summarize, Rauf's cross-examination of this distraught young complainant was at times antagonistic.[98] Throughout the trial he insinuated that she was lying,[99] and as noted, demanded to know "exactly what was going on" in spite of what seem like very clear indications as to the source of this woman's distress.[100] Unlike some of his questions and closing statements in *Cain*, discussed in chapters 2 and 5, Rauf's conduct of the case in *Khaery* did not appear to rely on discriminatory stereotypes about women and sexual violence.

Criminal lawyers should be recognized for their work to improve the circumstances of the criminally accused – a segment of society that is disproportionately composed of individuals from racialized, disabled, Indigenous, and low socio-economic status communities. The work of Rauf and so many others is much-needed and admirable. It remains equally important to recognize the many other ways in which the criminal justice system is not "fair … for all"[101] – including those who turn to it, or are forced to participate in it, following an incident of sexual violence. Lastly, it is important to acknowledge and critique the ways in which criminal lawyers, while fighting to make the process fair for some, may actually contribute to its injustices. Sexual assault complainants, like the criminally accused, are also disproportionately from racialized, disabled, Indigenous, and low socio-economic status communities.[102] Certainly this was true of the battle-weary nineteen-year-old Indigenous woman brought to the brink of collapse by the experience of testifying in *Khaery*. At a minimum, the profession should celebrate the heroes it constructs in a manner that is nuanced and cognizant of the diversity of harms and injustices caused by our adversarial system and its criminal justice actors.

3. Robert Simmonds: Queen's Counsel in St John's

Memorial University's 2013 announcement that Robert Simmonds, QC, had received an honorary doctorate of laws degree from the University described Simmonds as "one of the province's leading criminal lawyers."[103] According to his law firm biography, Simmonds, who was appointed Queen's Counsel in 2001 and was the managing partner of a St John's, Newfoundland, firm specializing in criminal law, was awarded the designation of one of the "Best Lawyers in Canada" specializing in criminal law, four years in a row, beginning in 2008.[104]

In a 2013 interview Simmonds gave for a human interest story in a St John's local paper, *The Telegram*, he was asked what motivates him. He responded, "a combination of anger, justice and the truth."[105] In describing his professional style, he noted that his voice "obviously comes across as angry," which he laughingly suggested might be "a good thing."[106] Recounting how he selected a lawyer with whom to set up his firm, Simmonds suggested with sarcasm (according to the article) that he "looked around for the most amicable, pleasant, comfortable, warm-wooly-feeling person I could find"[107] – presumably implying that he in fact sought out a law partner who possessed the opposite traits. One might ask whether his responses suggest an effort on his part to portray a professional persona marked by this notion of the hyper-aggressive criminal defence lawyer. Certainly aspects of his conduct of the case in *R v B(S)* could be construed as the opposite of amicable, pleasant, or comfortable. More specifically, his use of evidence of the complainant's prior sexual history in this case could be characterized as uncivil, unpleasant, and well beyond uncomfortable. It was also inconsistent with the protections intended by the evidentiary rules stipulated in section 276 of the *Criminal Code*.

R v B(S), discussed briefly in chapter 2, involved allegations of physical and sexual assault (including nonconsensual anal intercourse) by the former spouse of the accused. Erin Breen, who began her criminal law practice with Robert Simmonds in 2003 and one assumes may have been mentored by Simmonds,[108] brought a pre-trial application to cross-examine the complainant on sexual activity between her and a third party, relying on text messages between them; and on anal sex between the complainant and the accused, relying on texts that they exchanged and a forty-six-minute graphic video with "extreme close-ups" of oral, vaginal, and anal penetration as well as the use of a sex toy.[109] Justice Stack granted the pre-trial application to use the texts between her and the third party and to use a transcript of the videotape. He even left open the possibility that the defence might be permitted to show the jury the video itself, depending on the complainant's testimony.[110]

Consider first the evidence of sexual activity between the complainant and a third party. Justice Stack determined that the defence should be permitted to cross-examine the complainant on a series of sexually graphic texts she sent to another man, to prove that she had been dishonest when she told the police she had not cheated on her husband, the accused.[111]

During cross-examination, before introducing the texts, Simmonds drew the complainant's attention to the parts of her statements to the police in which she had asserted that she had not been unfaithful to her husband. Simmonds then asked her directly, "Have you cheated on him?"; she answered, "Yes, I have."[112] Despite her admission, Simmonds proceeded to read out to the jury a series of text messages between the complainant and this third party with whom she had been involved, including the following text:

> Oh my u have me like so horney, now, just layid here in bed thinking about you and how good I'm going to suck ur cock on the way back to the hotel. Fuck. I'm going to swallow your cum and when I get back to our hotel I want you to undress me and fuck me really hard. It will be a couple of nights you will remember. Remember for a while.
>
> ...
>
> [SIMMONDS] Q: Is this your texting to this gentleman?
> [COMPLAINANT] A: Yes, it is.[113]

Simmonds went on to cross-examine her about her assertions to the police, asking her directly whether she had lied to them about her sexual involvement with this man during her marriage:

> Q. [S]o you lied in the KGB statement, correct?
> A. Yes, I did.
> Q. Yes, you did. And, in fact, when you are carrying on this affair, you were still communicating with your husband and you were pretending that everything was fine?

A. Of course I was.

Q. January 18th, you to him, to the gentleman, (as read)

"Good morning, sexy man, hope you slept well, have safe flight back, see you Sunday."

Correct?

A. Correct. I'm not denying it.[114]

Despite the complainant's unequivocal admission that she had cheated, and her immediate and unambiguous admission that she had lied to the police about her affair, Simmonds continued to read aloud a series of deeply personal, some very graphic, sexual text messages between the complainant and this third party. Adding to her humiliation, at the trial judge's insistence, as he read out these texts Simmonds stopped recurrently to require the complainant to confirm authorship of specific messages:

SIMMONDS, Q.C.: This text I'm reading to you now, February 10, 2012, to this gentleman,

"Hoping I could come up with a good enough reason to get u back here, lol Oh the things I would like to do to you and that hot body I would pleasure u."

Is that your text?

A. Yes.

Q. Okay. February 13th, 2012,

"... Oh, my you would rock my world again Lol I should probably be good"

And then,

"I wish Ohhhhhh Baby I think we both rock each others world right about now."

Your texts back and forth to this gentleman?

A. Yes, sir.

Q. Later on, 14:51 that day, the 13th of February, 2012, you to him,

"... I can only imagine what I would do to u in one of these service rooms if I was alone with you now Anything you would want me too When I think about you I get so horny I would really love to fuck you I obviously enjoy our sex and yes I will call him now"

Now, your text?

A. Yeah.

Q. February 24th, 2012,

"You really make me crazy and make me lust for you", etcetera, etcetera, your text?

A. Yes, sir.

Q. And,

"Big strong sexy gorgeous man u are an instant orgasm for me." your text?

A. Yes, sir.[115]

Having humiliated the complainant with these texts, Simmonds then asked her: "So why did you lie to the police?"[116] She responded, "Why did I lie? Sir, my honest answer to that would be – "[117] He interrupted her with a sarcastic question: "That would be nice, your honest answer."[118] The complainant then explained that she was afraid her husband (who she alleged had physically assaulted her on numerous occasions) would find out: "I was afraid that he was going to find out somehow when I was giving statements ... I know I lied and I apologize for lying but I was really scared. I'm sorry."[119]

Simmonds read out approximately twenty-five texts between the complainant and this third party. The fact of the complainant's extramarital affair was entirely collateral in this case. Breen was explicit in her pre-trial application that "the only purpose" for which the defence was seeking to admit these texts was "purely to contradict her prior inconsistent statements" to the police.[120] At trial, Simmonds reiterated this assertion, explicitly stating that his sole purpose in seeking to cross-examine her on these texts was to show that she had lied to the police about her extramarital affair: "they are simply to show that she lied, plain and simple."[121] Again, Justice Stack granted defence counsel's pre-trial application to cross-examine her using the texts between her and this third party in order to demonstrate that she had lied to the police about her affair. Yet, Simmonds read almost all of these texts to the jury *after* the complainant had explicitly admitted that she had cheated and that she had lied to the police about cheating. The basis upon which Justice Stack had granted the application to use them did not materialize. There was no legal justification for reading out these private messages, given that she readily admitted at trial that she had cheated on her husband and testified that she had lied to the police about this sexual activity. This is why the Newfoundland Court of Appeal concluded that the use of prior sexual history evidence in this case amounted to "the gratuitous humiliation and denigration of [the] complainant."[122] According to the Court, the effect of reading out these texts was to conjure up the legally rejected (and I would add discriminatory) myth that a woman of so-called "easy virtue" is more likely to have consented to the sexual activity at issue in the allegation.[123] Far from intervening to stop this appalling treatment of the complainant, and despite the Crown's repeated efforts to have him do so, Justice Stack explicitly condoned Simmonds's conduct, including when the sexually explicit nature of the texts was drawn to his attention by Simmonds himself prior to introducing them.[124] Note that defence counsel's responsibility for the decision to read aloud these highly personal and sexually graphic texts, despite the fact that the basis upon which they were to be admitted had not materialized, is not removed simply because the trial judge also failed this complainant.

Now contemplate Simmonds's treatment of the complainant with respect to a video of the accused and the complainant engaged in sexual activities. At the pre-trial hearing, Simmonds's colleague, Breen, sought permission to play for the jury portions of a forty-six-minute video of the accused and the complainant engaged in various sexual acts, including anal intercourse.[125] The articulated justification for introducing this evidence was to impugn the complainant's credibility by challenging her assertions to the police that she was "against anal sex" or that anal sex was not her preference, but that she had engaged in it to satisfy her husband's desires.[126] At the pre-trial application Breen argued that the video should be admitted, and portions shown to the jury, in order to prove that the complainant was, in fact, a willing if not eager participant in anal intercourse with her then husband.[127] As noted, Justice Stack admitted the transcript of the video and left open the possibility that the video itself might need to be shown.

On cross-examination at trial, the complainant maintained that she had engaged in anal sex with her husband many times, that it was not her first choice of sexual acts, but that she had consented to it on many occasions because he was her husband. As the Court of Appeal concluded, there was no meaningful difference between her statements to the police about her preferences regarding anal intercourse and her participation in the video.[128] Nor was there any meaningful difference between these statements and her testimony at trial. Yet, Simmonds nevertheless proceeded to read from the transcript of the video:

[s.b.] "My little hottie, oh yeah, turn around. Don't go anywhere. Stay where are you are. Hmm yeah."

[c.m.] "What do you want, baby?"

[s.b.] "Oh".

[c.m.] "To stick that hard cock in it later".

[s.b.] "In what, baby?"

[c.m.] "In my ass".

[s.b.] "In where?"

[c.m.] "Right there" … "That big cock of yours".

[s.b.] "What do you want me to do to you tonight, baby?"

[c.m.] "I want you to fuck your slut wife, baby."

[s.b.] "Are you my slut wife, baby?"

[c.m.] "I'm your slut wife, baby, yes".

[s.b.] "What kind of slut are you, baby?"

[c.m.] "Yeah, ass slut. You're gonna make me come while your cock is in my ass?"[129]

When the complainant attempted to explain that she and the accused were role-playing in the video (she was wearing a French maid's costume), and to emphasize that she had never suggested that the anal intercourse captured in the video was non-consensual, Simmonds responded with what could be interpreted as a threat to play the video for the jury:

A. [COMPLAINANT] And what do you think the conversation might have been before that video? Would it be any likelihood that that was a conversation that we were role playing for the video?

Q. [SIMMONDS] Well, I'll tell you now –

A. Is that likely?

Q. You be very careful when you go down this road.

A. I'm just asking.

Q. Because you be very careful before you go down this road, because I got no urge, believe me to put on the sex tape of you and [s.b.].

A. Go ahead.

Q. And let the jury watch it, but they'll make a decision if you're saying that you were forced into this.

A. I never said I was forced.[130]

Repeatedly the complainant reiterated that she had consented to anal intercourse in the past in order to satisfy her then husband, but that it was not her first choice of sexual activities – which she testified is what she meant when she told the police she was "against having anal sex."[131] Simmonds nevertheless continued to read aloud from the transcript of the video:

> SIMMONDS, QC: You stated, on page three, (as read)
>   "I want you to fuck your slut wife".
> A little further down, you actually state,
>   "You gonna make me come while your cock is in my ass?"
> A little further along, "S.B." [asks]
>   "Where do you want the sperm in baby?"
>   "C.M.", "you gonna come right in my ass baby"
>   "C.M." poses, on her knees, leans forward, touches her rear
>   end and says, "right there … stick your cock up my ass."[132]

Simmonds ended this line of cross-examination with the following question: "'C.M.' when I go over the statements and put them to you, I want to ask you, is it not true that in this forty-six-minute video, you climax a number of times and, in fact, once, at least once, if not more, during the anal sex?"[133]

The Court of Appeal rejected as "naïve" or "disingenuous" the possibility that these excerpts were introduced in order to test the complainant's credibility.[134] The Court questioned whether the video had any probative value and concluded that even if it did, its probative value was outweighed by prejudice to the complainant. The Court concluded that the "entirely predictable effect was to signal to the jury that by her own words the complainant was promiscuous and, therefore, she was more likely to have consented to sex on the two occasions when she alleged that she had not."[135] This is, of course, one of the 'twin myths' explicitly excluded by section 276. Indeed, defence counsel came remarkably close to articulating this inference openly:

> Q. You tell the provincial court judge and you clearly leave
> the impression here you were against anal sex, that is not what
> this transcript, nor the video that it's made from, which goes 46
> minutes long and at the end of it two of ye [sic] sit back and relax

and appear to be having a very good time, indicates. It indicates the exact opposite of that. That not only were you into having anal sex, that you were very into having it? I'm not, the issue, it's just that that's not the impression you left with everybody.

A. As I just said five minutes ago, that I done it, it wasn't my first option, my first choice but, yes, I done it.[136]

The uses to which this evidence of the complainant's prior sexual history was put (as described by the Court of Appeal: the gratuitous humiliation and denigration of the complainant, and the invocation of legally rejected, discriminatory stereotypes) are precisely what section 276 aims to prevent. The Crown's commendable and repeated attempts to stop the denigration and humiliation of the complainant, and Justice Stack's profound failure to protect this woman, are discussed in chapter 6.

Simmonds's cross-examination of the complainant was not unduly lengthy nor overly repetitive.

4. Patrick Ducharme: "Thoughts of an Advocate"

Criminal lawyer Patrick Ducharme's biography on his Windsor, Ontario law firm website opens with the following:

PATRICK J. DUCHARME is a Fellow of the American College of
Trial Lawyers, one of the premier legal, associations in America.
    Founded in 1950, the College is composed of the best of the trial
bar from the United States and Canada. The Call to Fellowship in
the College is by special invitation only, an honour and distinction
of the highest order, bestowed upon those few, exceptional trial
lawyers ... whose art of advocacy and whose standards of ethical
conduct, professionalism, civility, and collegiality are judged
to be models to be emulated by the lawyer population at large.
Fellowship in the College is regarded as such a rare and exclusive
privilege that it can never be extended to more than 1% of the total
number of lawyers in any state or province.[137]

Like fellow member of the Ontario bar Todd White, and Newfoundland lawyer Robert Simmonds, QC, according to his website Ducharme has repeatedly been selected by his peers as one of "The Best Lawyers of Canada."[138]

Also included on his law firm website is an article, "Thoughts of an Advocate," authored by Ducharme, about one of his former clients.[139] Ducharme begins his description of this client with the statement: "Marilyn Chambers was best known as a porn star." He then suggests she had "reached legendary status for her hard-core performances."[140] Ducharme defended her against charges of indecent theatrical performance and public nudity. He recounts that

> [o]n the morning of her trial Marilyn attended my law offices dressed more like she was ready for a striptease performance than an appearance in court. I quickly summoned a couple of business-like legal secretaries to take her to a nearby women's clothing store to re-cast her image for the 10 AM start of her trial. The transformation of her appearance in 30 minutes was remarkable. She went from Porn Queen to 'business dowdy' in less than 30 minutes.[141]

Ducharme suggests that it became apparent during his client's trial that the judge was "enamored of her."[142] He narrates his perception of the judge's response to his client as follows:

> As the police constable who arrested Marilyn described in monotonous tones how she pushed her breasts together and pulled them out by their nipples, wrapped her legs around a pole onstage, then pushed her vagina against the pole, gyrating in rhythmic fashion to the music, and, flicking her sensuous tongue out at the pole simulating oral sex, the trial judge was so enthralled he appeared to hang on every word. And, when Marilyn testified the judge was leaning so far over toward her perch in the witness box that he nearly fell out of his stately judicial chair.[143]

He then appears to insinuate that the judge, who Ducharme asserts had viewed at least one of his client's "hard-core performances" prior to trial, may have acquitted this woman on the basis of his own "lust" and "admiration."[144] Certainly there was nothing in the trial judge's carefully considered statutory interpretation and constitutional analysis, citing legal authority from more than a dozen prior cases, to lend support to this arguably defamatory insinuation about his reasoning.[145] Yet, with seeming delight, Ducharme constructs an allegory of patriarchy, likening his client and her supposed performance for the judge with the dance of Salomé (the biblical femme fatale and cultural icon of dangerous female seduction). He writes: "From the time of King Herod, young, lithe, nubile dancers entertained the King and his Court with seductive dances."[146]

The intended professional lesson of Ducharme's story appears to be that he should have allowed his client to dress like a "Porn Queen" rather than a "dowdy" secretary, on the basis that any heterosexual male judge would have informed his legal reasoning based on his sexual desire for her:

> Then, having witnessed her Lincolnesque Judge fawn over her in obvious admiration, and perhaps a touch of lust, she looked at me with a look of disdain and said, "I knew I should've worn my own dress." Touché, goddess of men! ... In retrospect, I should have allowed her to wear her own clothing. She would've won the case handily in any event – at least with any red-blooded male judge.[147]

Ducharme's reflections end by noting that "[t]hroughout her career she longed for legitimacy as an actress but found her fame in the seedy, squalid world of pornography."[148] It is difficult not to conclude that Ducharme's sensationalized, sexist, and profoundly unprofessional story of this case is yet another chapter (albeit *post-mortem*) in the arduous life of this woman he tellingly refers to as "a veteran in the world of pleasing men."[149]

There is no question that Patrick Ducharme is an accomplished and well-known criminal lawyer. Presumably many younger lawyers have attempted to emulate him, and not only because of his 1% membership in the American College of Trial Lawyers. What would motivate him to write and publicly post on his law firm website an article of this nature – an article that explicitly sexualizes his former client, appears to reduce her to the title of "Porn Star," trades in sexist stereotypes about women's attire and the dichotomy between so-called virgins ("dowdy" secretaries) and whores ("porn queens"), and insults a member of the judiciary? Could such an experienced and acclaimed lawyer actually believe that there is legitimacy to this type of outdated, gender-based thinking, or that it is acceptable for a legal professional to perpetuate gendered stereotypes of this nature on his law firm website? What does public storytelling, or 'shop talk,' with this type of content, by a legal professional of this stature, reveal about the culture and practices of the criminal defence bar? Does his decision to include this content on his professional website suggest Ducharme would rely on gendered stereotypes in his legal practice? As Andrew Taslitz's work studying the connection between patriarchal stories and rape trial outcomes has demonstrated, our narratives and conceptions about sexuality and gender can inform legal strategies and proceedings.[150] One might argue that this seems to be true of Ducharme's representation of hockey player Ben Johnson in a recent sexual assault trial in Windsor, Ontario.

Ducharme's cross-examination of the complainant in *Johnson* was not overly lengthy or repetitive. His conduct of the trial included an instance in which he showed significant sensitivity towards the complainant,[151] and examples of him speaking to her respectfully.[152] However, Ducharme's defence of Johnson also appears to have included an emphasis on what the complainant was wearing, introduction of evidence of prior sexual activity for which a section 276 application was not brought, and allusions to the stereotype of the promiscuous party girl.

Johnson was convicted of sexually assaulting a severely intoxicated sixteen-year-old woman in the bathroom stall of a Windsor bar. (At the time of writing his conviction was under appeal.) The complainant testified that she had only flashes of memories from the incident in the bathroom as a consequence of her level of intoxication. She testified that, while in the bathroom stall, Johnson forced her to perform oral sex, which caused her to choke and gag, and that she was then turned around in the stall, with him behind her. She testified that he penetrated her from behind, causing her more severe pain than any she had previously experienced. She testified that her head was smacked against the bathroom stall during the forced vaginal intercourse that ensued. When she arrived at the hospital following the incident, she had bruising on her head and left breast as well as injuries to her vagina. She testified that she had been a virgin prior to the sexual assault.[153]

The complainant's friend testified that she saw Johnson leave the bathroom stall doing up his pants, and that she found the complainant in the bathroom stall vomiting, eyes rolling back in her head, with the backside of her pants covered in blood. According to this witness, the complainant was so intoxicated that she could not stand up without assistance. The Crown also introduced video footage of the complainant in a taxi following her immediate exit from the bar that showed her vomiting repeatedly. The taxi driver testified that she fell in and out of consciousness during the drive home.[154]

The physical and medical evidence introduced by the Crown included the complainant's bloodstained pants, photographs revealing a fresh laceration to her hymen, a photograph of bruising on her left breast, male DNA collected from a swab of the inside of her vagina, and blood on the underwear the accused was wearing that evening.[155]

Johnson testified that he did not have vaginal intercourse with the complainant and that she did not appear intoxicated to him. He maintained that she pulled him into the bathroom stall where they kissed, following which she initiated and performed oral sex on him. He testified that he did not touch her either while they were kissing or during the oral sex.[156]

Ducharme's cross-examination of the complainant could be construed as aimed at portraying her as anything but a virginal sixteen-year-old at the time of the offence. For example, he asked the following questions about texts she had sent to her sister while on a holiday in Mexico from which she had returned earlier on the date of the assault:

Q. But we know that you drank lots of alcohol when you were in Mexico, don't we?

A. I drank in Mexico, yes.

Q. You drank a lot of alcohol in Mexico ...

A. Yes.

Q. ... am I right?

A. Yes.

Q. In fact, you texted your sister,
'Oh my God, we went to Senor Frog's and got wasted.' Do you remember texting her that?

A. Yes.

Q. 'With all these 19 to 25 year olds.'

A. Yes.

Q. So you didn't have any difficulty drinking heavily with men quite a bit older than you, did you?

A. No, but I did not have sex with them.

Q. What you did do with one of them is you had his initials tattooed on your tit, according to the message you sent your sister?

A. It was a Sharpie marker of his initials on my right side, above
my clothing.

Q. But what you wrote to her is,

   'I have a guy's initials tattooed on my tit. I hooked up with a
   22 year old named Danny.'

That's what you texted to your sister?

A. Yes.

...

MR. DUCHARME: Q. This is a photograph that was sent to your
sister about these comments of having the boy's initials tattooed on
your tit, right?

A. Yes.[157]

Arguably, the tone, phrasing, and insinuations underlying these questions are problematic. In two of the three questions in which Ducharme
uses the word "tit" he is not directly quoting from the text sent by the
complainant to her sister. That a young woman uses a slang word in
reference to her own sexual anatomy in a text sent to her sister does
not give a legal professional licence to deploy it against her in cross-
examination. Ducharme's repeated use of the word "tit" was unnecessary
and arguably demeaning. In addition, he asked her questions about how
much she drank in Mexico and with whom. One interpretation of this
line of questioning is that it was meant to depict the complainant as a
promiscuous party girl, willing to let older men write on her breasts.
Ducharme did not bring a section 276 application to introduce this
evidence. It is also worth noting that he referred to the twenty-two-
year-old man who allegedly wrote his initials on the sixteen-year-old
complainant's breast as a "boy."

Ducharme also questioned the complainant repeatedly about her
failure to raise a hue and cry during the sexual assault:

Q. You certainly don't have any recollection of saying anything, do you?

A. I remember saying, 'It hurts.'

Q. Really.

A. Yes.

Q. And would that be loud enough that somebody that was in
the bathroom would hear it?

A. I don't know.

Q. Because you did hear people come into the bathroom, didn't you?

A. No.

Q. There were other people in the bathroom when you were giving him oral sex?

A. I don't know that.

Q. And I suggest to you, you didn't make a sound? You didn't say anything at all?

A. Like I said, I felt like I couldn't talk.

Q. Well, you say that's because of the alcohol and your ...

A. Shock.

Q. ... advanced state and shock, but it wasn't that you couldn't talk – I suggest to you it was that you didn't talk?

A. I don't know.

Q. You certainly didn't raise any complaint, right?

A. I don't know.

Q. You didn't call out to anyone?

A. I don't know.[158]

Noting her high heels and lack of underwear, Ducharme cross-examined the complainant about her dancing with another member of Johnson's hockey team prior to the sexual assault:

Q. And when you're asked to describe it yesterday, you described that [dancing] as 'obnoxious'?

A. Yes.

Q. That, at least of your own perception of yourself, is not like you at all. Is that what you're saying?

A. No.

Q. You saw that grinding of your bottom into the pelvic area of this young man as distasteful and offensive?

A. Yes.

Q. And you didn't see anything in that six minutes of grinding yourself into him – anything to do with dancing. You weren't dancing, you were just grinding, right?

A. I would describe that as dancing.

Q. I see. There were dance moves in there somewhere?

A. Yes.

...

Q. In those six minutes you positioned your private area of your bottom against his private area – his pelvic area – didn't you?

A. Yes.

Q. And you pushed yourself back against him?

A. Yes.

Q. And what was described as a little stumble or something, was simply you keeping that position in those high heels you were wearing?

A. I stumbled.

Q. You were wearing high heels?

A. Yes.

Q. And you were pushing backwards into him?

A. And I was drunk.

Q. So the fact is that it can't be easy to make that push back into him with high heels on? That can't be an easy move, is it?

A. I don't know.

Q. And while you were doing this you were wearing the thinnest, smoothest, tightest of leggings, weren't you?

A. I had leggings on.

Q. You said they were thin, right?

A. Yes.

Q. You said they were tight-fitting?

A. Yes.

Q. And they were smooth?

A. Yes.

Q. And you had no underwear, so you would be able to feel his anatomy quite easily through that thin clothing?[159]

At this point in Ducharme's questioning, Justice Munroe interjected:

THE COURT: Mr. Ducharme, where are we going with this? Is this a sexual activity that I should be doing a 276 inquiry?

MR. DUCHARME: I don't think so, Your Honour. I think this is just a challenge to her recollection of things.

THE COURT: Well, but the nature of your questions are going into – it seems to me – for a sexual purpose.

MR. DUCHARME: I'm attempting to challenge her on saying that because of alcohol she stumbled. I'm suggesting that what she did is not an easy maneuver.

THE COURT: I have no problem with that.

MR. DUCHARME: Okay.

THE COURT: I – you were drifting over to what I would consider a sexual activity and if you want to persist at that – and that's your choice – then I'm going to ask that the witness be excused and we can discuss it as far as whether or not it rises to a level that needs to be addressed under 276.

MR. DUCHARME: I appreciate what you're saying, Your Honour, but I'm not going there ...

THE COURT: All right.

MR. DUCHARME: ... and I'm just dealing with the maneuvers and I'll try to keep it exactly to that.

THE COURT: All right.

MR. DUCHARME: Q. The truth is that you blame your behaviour on alcohol?

A. Yes.[160]

It seems unreasonable to suggest, as Ducharme did, that questioning a complainant as to whether she was grinding her "private area" into the "private area" of another individual while wearing "the thinnest, smoothest, tightest of leggings" and no underwear was merely intended to challenge her recollection or degree of intoxication. He asked her whether she could feel the man's "anatomy" in what would have been her rectal or genital area through her thin clothing, noting that she was not wearing any underwear. I would argue that these questions were soliciting evidence of prior sexual activity and should have been subject to section 276.

In addition to being implausible on the face of it, Ducharme's assertion to the Court that his purpose was not to introduce evidence of other sexual activity – that he was "not going there"[161] – is difficult to accept when one considers the defence in this case. Ducharme's (arguably preposterous) theory of this case appears to have been that the complainant's hymen may have been torn or re-injured earlier in the evening while she was dancing, because she was "grinding" her private parts into the private parts of her dance partner while wearing very thin leggings and no underwear.[162] His speculation, put to the medical experts who testified,[163] was that the individual she was dancing with may have inserted his penis into her vagina, over top of her leggings, while they were on the dance floor, and that that was the cause of her injured (or re-injured) vagina.[164]

Given the nature of his questions to the complainant, it seems difficult to accept that Ducharme's dance floor theory developed only as the evidence emerged at trial.[165] Surely, despite his assertion to the contrary, his questioning of the complainant could be construed as absolutely having "go[ne] there."[166] It seems highly implausible to accept that Ducharme's detailed questions to the complainant about whether she could, through her "thinnest of leggings," feel this man's "anatomy" in her "private area" while "grinding" with him on the dance floor, were asked in an "attempt ... to challenge her on saying that because of alcohol she stumbled."[167]

The legal profession has a long tradition of mentorship. Whether we think of Edward Greenspan's mentee Todd White, or the countless newer lawyers, such as Erin Breen, who have no doubt taken their tutelage from senior practitioners such as Naeem Rauf, Robert Simmonds, QC, and Patrick Ducharme, the criminal defence bar affirms attitudes and practices in part through the heroes it constructs, and the norms and narratives transmitted via its apprenticeship-style structure. Moreover, it is reasonable to assume that there is a relationship between the conduct of legal professionals and the culture of the legal profession, including as reflected in the stories its members tell. These examples of what could be construed as overly aggressive, needlessly insensitive, insulting, or stereotype-reliant cross-examinations of sexual assault complainants by four prominent, experienced, and celebrated lawyers certainly do not cohere with the commonly articulated notions that bullying the complainant is not good lawyering and that experienced lawyers know better. While not all of these tactics were employed by all of them, and some had more examples than others, the transcripts in each of these cases appear to reveal complainants who were subjected to cross-examinations that arguably included whacking-type strategies.

The Promotion of an Aggressive Approach

Advertising on the most conspicuous criminal law firm websites in several Canadian cities similarly suggests that, despite claims to the contrary, the criminal defence bar often equates aggressive and stereotype-infused lawyering with good lawyering. On some websites, courtroom aggression appears to be celebrated as one of the markers of a great criminal defender. Indeed, although codes of professional conduct for lawyers in Canada indicate that advertising that suggests or even implies a lawyer is aggressive may contravene the rules on marketing,[168] it is not uncommon to find law firm websites that describe their lawyers' advocacy skills in this manner. While the websites of most criminal law firms do not advertise aggressive representation, an examination of those most prominent on the internet reveal many advertisements in which lawyers explicitly describe their approach to defending sexual charges as aggressive. One Ontario lawyer, for example, promises with respect to sexual assault charges: "[a]s your criminal lawyer I will represent you aggressively providing you with the best defence possible."[169] Another lawyer suggests that for seventeen years he has been "fighting aggressively" to help people charged with sexual offences.[170] Another specifically notes the need to hire a defence lawyer who is capable of aggressively cross-examining the complainant: "in many sexual assault allegations, the only evidence comes from a single complainant. It is therefore critical that your lawyer be capable of conducting a thorough and exhaustive cross-examination. Depending on a host of factors, this may call for light suggestive questioning or aggressive confrontational examination."[171]

Several of the defence lawyers interviewed, all of whom were experienced, also offered comments that contradict this notion that experienced lawyers know to be respectful and courteous towards sexual assault complainants. Some explicitly affirmed the need for an aggressive approach to the cross-examination of sexual assault complainants in particular. This is true despite their assertions as to the strategic inadvisability of whacking the complainant. Defence Lawyer 6 mentioned smelling "blood in the water" in reference to frail complainants. Several of them used words such as "battle" or "weapons" to describe aspects of their sexual assault trial practice. Defence Lawyer 2 indicated that to be truly committed as a criminal lawyer, one must be prepared to defend an accused against the power of the state "at any cost."

To summarize, assertions about the strategic inadvisability of taking an aggressive approach to the cross-examination of complainants, while common, are not consistent with the way that some lawyers market themselves, nor with the discourse employed by some lawyers to describe their conduct of a sexual assault case. Nor are claims of a respectful and humane approach consistent with the typical characterization of some of our most prominent and most celebrated criminal defence lawyers.

In fact, the stories told about, and by, the heroes of the criminal defence bar consistently reference their fierce and intimidating courtroom tactics, including, in some instances, the use of these tactics in sexual assault cases.

Explaining the Disjuncture between the Culture and the Claims

What explains this incongruity between the presumably genuinely held belief that aggressive treatment of a complainant is not good lawyering and the reification of aggressive cross-examination, including the cross-examination of sexual assault complainants, as the marker of an outstanding criminal lawyer?

One possible explanation is that in sexual assault cases defence lawyers are more inclined to believe that their client is being falsely accused than they are in cases in which their clients are charged with other *Criminal Code* offences. The belief that the complaining witness is fabricating the allegation could result in a level of hostility or aggression during their cross-examination that may not be present in other cases. While some of the defence lawyers I interviewed reported that they believe most complainants are telling the truth, others offered comments that reflect the belief that false allegations of sexual assault are common, if not ubiquitous. Defence Lawyer 4, for example, indicated that in her experience many of the complainants who testified against her clients in sexual assault cases were lying. In some interviews, lawyers connected this belief to their treatment of the complainant. For instance, Defence Lawyer 6, in discussing the analysis she uses to determine whether to elect trial by superior court (so that she can cross-examine the complainant at a preliminary inquiry), stated:

> I actually always, I really always believe my client, believe in my client's cause. I actually really feel like I'm on their side ... So I really believe that this girl is lying ... I think that is a defence mechanism I think for me ... I think I have to feel that way or else I can't do my job ... It makes my job easier ... And so, at a prelim, I might, I might feel like if I take a good enough crack at her and shake her enough, then the Crown will say (sigh) You know? And then I've done my job. Because no one likes trials ... and she may not want to go through that again.

Likewise, an examination of advertising by criminal law firms with prominent websites suggests the possibility that many defence lawyers consider the rate of false allegations of sexual assault to be quite high. In fact, the most common theme about sexual offences on the criminal law firm webpages examined, other than the issue of stigma, relates to the subject of false allegations of sexual assault. For example, one lawyer opened his website description of the offence of sexual assault with the assertion that "[t]oo many people find themselves facing these life-changing charges based on false allegations from accusers who are malicious, mistaken, manipulated, or suffering regret."[172] The websites of many of these defence lawyers made explicit reference in the opening paragraphs of their discussion of the defence of sexual offenses to false allegations, false memory syndrome, and/or motives to fabricate.[173] Some made explicit claims about the problematic frequency of false allegations of sexual assault.[174] One website, for example, asserted that "[p]eople are falsely charged with sexual assault all the time."[175] Many of them offered prospective clients a list of the reasons why women lie about rape – common among them seem to be jealousy and post-sex regret: "If the complainant is lying about whether sexual activity occurred, or whether it was consensual, we will want to get to the root of why that person has chosen to lie. Often a complainant is motivated by jealousy or anger. Sometimes s/he suffers from regret after sex and does not wish to admit that it was consensual."[176]

On the websites reviewed, advertisements that included descriptions for other types of criminal defence representation did not typically discuss motives to fabricate and did not tend to raise the issue of false allegations.[177] Perhaps tellingly, the one exception to this observation involved advertisements regarding defence services for individuals accused of domestic violence. On some websites, sections on domestic violence also featured discussion of, and reference to, false accusations.[178]

Certainly Canada's legal legacy would make it unsurprising to learn that many lawyers believe the rate of false allegation of sexual assault is high. Historic rules of evidence were underpinned by antiquated social assumptions about women and sex. For example, the rule requiring that a sexual assault complainant's allegation be corroborated was justified by the belief that false rape allegations are prevalent: "Surely the simplest, and perhaps the most important, reason not to permit conviction for rape on the uncorroborated word of the prosecutrix is that that word is very often false."[179] Regret and spite were commonly identified motives for these false allegations: "A woman may accuse an innocent man of raping her because ... having consented to intercourse she is ashamed of herself and bitter at her partner, or simply because she hates the man whom she accuses."[180] Some of the social assumptions that underpinned this discriminatory legal legacy – such as the notion that women often lie about rape upon suffering post-sex regret – are reflected in the claims made on the websites of some criminal lawyers.

Moreover, gender-based hierarchies continue to inform the political, economic, and social organization of our society. Presumably a social context in which gender hierarchy prevails would support the perpetuation of discriminatory beliefs about women and sexual assault, such as the stereotype of the vengeful scorned woman, the legally rejected social assumption that unchaste women are both untrustworthy and indiscriminate in their sexual choices, and the myth that women cannot actually be raped against their will.[181] These are, of course, the same discriminatory assumptions that inform perceptions about the rate of false allegations. Why would we think that lawyers would be immune to the effects of this social context? Regardless, presumably we can assume that lawyers believe the claims they make on their own websites. This would include their claims about the likelihood that, and the reasons why, women lie about rape.

An inclination on the part of defence lawyers to disbelieve women who allege sexual assault may also reflect a coping mechanism for legal professionals. Disbelief may help criminal lawyers to distance themselves from the vicarious trauma or secondhand emotion that professionals experience when repeatedly confronted with stories of human suffering.[182] Interviews with legal professionals in the United Kingdom who deal with asylum and refugee claimants who have experienced sexual violence in their countries of origin revealed precisely these types of psychological strategies on the part of lawyers: "in your head, you have to go in thinking I don't believe this story, because if you went in there believing that story, you couldn't really do your job."[183] Criminal lawyers, given the nature of the work they do, may be particularly susceptible to the type of stress and secondhand trauma that arises from repeated exposure to the suffering of others.[184]

To summarize, perhaps a commonly held assumption that they are representing clients subjected to false allegations of rape informs the way some lawyers approach the cross-examination of sexual assault complainants. Would not anyone be more aggressive when questioning someone they believe to be lying – even if one accepts, at an intellectual level, that bullying a sexual assault complainant is not good strategy?

A second explanation for the disjunction between the claim that experienced lawyers use a respectful and humane approach towards sexual assault complainants, and the identification and celebration of courtroom aggression as the indicia of a heroic criminal lawyer, is the possibility that the profession is not of one mind. Perhaps the incongruence can be explained by the simple fact that criminal lawyers are divided in their perspectives about what makes a good criminal lawyer in a sexual assault proceeding. Not all criminal defence lawyers consider an aggressive courtroom style to be demonstrative of professional prowess.

The lawyers I interviewed held a diversity of perspectives on this issue. Defence Lawyer 11 offered this comment:

> Certainly in the area of sexual assault, when I first started practising ... in order to win a sexual assault, all you had to do was stand there, sneer and convey your sense of outrage at this false allegation. Not call your client so he didn't screw it up, and you had an acquittal in hand ... you could not lose. No matter how stupid you are, you can't lose that case ... and a lot of people thought that's a really good lawyer because they could do that trick. Or some variation on it.

In contrast, in recommending a colleague for participation in this study, Defence Lawyer 1 stated: "He's a guy who was a strong believer in whacking the complainant with the first question. He'll spend days thinking about what his first question is. And he's a very, very good lawyer in my view. And very ethical."

In her discussion of the *post requiem* on Greenspan's courtroom style, Professor Backhouse describes a conversation she had with Austin Cooper – one of the most admired criminal lawyers in Canadian history. Cooper, who was also considered a genius at cross-examining witnesses, told Backhouse that he had long harboured lingering doubts about whether his cross-examination of a sexual assault complainant, who had wilted under his questioning, was proper.[185] He questioned the woman about her prior sexual history, her lifestyle choices, and her attire.

Professor Backhouse suggests that it may not have been coincidence that Cooper's obituary recognized his cross-examination skills *and* his civility.[186] Austin Cooper was exalted by his peers as the archetype of a truly ethical lawyer. There is likely a diversity of perspectives within the criminal defence bar as to what constitutes an outstanding criminal defence lawyer, and where to draw the line between ensuring one's client receives a full and fair defence and harming complainants in ways that are either unnecessary or in some instances unlawful.

Another possible explanation for the disjuncture between the claim that experienced lawyers know not to bully sexual assault complainants and the profession's construction of the paradigmatic criminal defence lawyer is that, beginning in law school and continuing throughout their professional development, lawyers (and in particular criminal lawyers) are socialized or even trained to value aggressive, unrelenting advocacy. Perhaps as a result, even if they consider aggressive and bullying tactics to be counterproductive, or at a minimum unnecessary, some lawyers may perform them regardless.

From the very start of their legal careers, law students are said to be trained to see themselves as a particular type of advocate. They are encouraged to set aside their personal beliefs and values in order to argue any side of any issue.[187] For the criminal defence bar, this message may be reinforced by the way in which its heroes are constructed and celebrated.

Researchers and commentators have suggested that the pedagogical approach in law schools discourages law students from relying on their own values, emotional responses, moral perspectives, and sense of self-identity to inform their legal studies.[188] Others have argued that, for criminal lawyers in particular, some degree of abstraction and distancing from the emotional content connected with their cases is a healthy, and perhaps even necessary, coping strategy.[189] Certainly, the lawyers I interviewed revealed both a preference for avoiding the emotional nature of sexual assault cases and significant challenges inherent in being able to do just that. Does the demand for this type of 'no holds barred' representation encourage or enable defence lawyers to distance themselves from their own emotional engagement with, and responses to, the human pain involved in sexual assault cases?[190] Whatever the explanation, it is clear that the culture of the defence bar, or at a minimum the language often used to celebrate its heroes, does not accord with the narrative that good lawyers – experienced lawyers – know to pursue a kinder and gentler approach when it comes to the cross-examination of sexual assault complainants.

Perhaps criminal lawyers engage in aggressive strategies even when they know intellectually that they are ineffective or unnecessary (as is, many of them say, the case with respect to the cross-examination of sexual assault complainants) because the ethical identity thrust upon them from law school forward encourages them to operate based solely on a professional identity rather than on a more integrated sense of self.

Relying on essays published by defence lawyers themselves, as well as the interviews conducted for this study, the next chapter examines the dominant professional identity of criminal defence lawyers. When this identity is examined closely, it becomes clear that the role-based morality or self-understanding of their justice project, as they articulate it, is actually inconsistent with strategies that involve humiliating or harassing sexual assault complainants, circumventing rape shield laws, or relying on discriminatory stereotypes. Promisingly, and as is discussed at the end of chapter 4, recognition of this inconsistency removes the purported tension between requiring criminal defence lawyers to revisit the professional ethics of these harmful practices and acknowledging their fundamentally important duty to resolutely represent clients accused of sexual offences.

CHAPTER 4

The Sexual Assault Lawyer's Justice Project

Does the celebration of courtroom aggression correlate with the professional identity of the criminal defence bar in a way that contributes to the problematic treatment of sexual assault complainants by some lawyers? Certainly the narrative most commonly told about the criminal defence lawyer is that of the unrelenting, unmitigated, fervent advocate – the hired gun. Is there a connection between the tendency of some defence lawyers to engage in overly aggressive or stereotype-infused strategies in sexual assault proceedings, and the dominant professional identity constructed and perpetuated by criminal defence lawyers?

At first glance the answers to these questions might seem obvious. One might assume they are connected. However, the reality is more complicated. In fact, as demonstrated later in this chapter, some of the most salient features of the professional identity articulated by defence lawyers are actually inconsistent with the harmful practices discussed in chapters 2 and 3. While the profession seems to applaud courtroom aggression, and there are undoubtedly experienced and celebrated lawyers who deploy what I would argue are 'whack the complainant'–type strategies in sexual assault trials, the primary objectives identified by criminal lawyers in their defence of clients accused of sexual offences, and the underlying principles that many of them identify as central to their understanding of their role in the criminal justice process, do not support the kinds of problematic approaches considered in chapters 2 and 3.

Hired Guns or Something More?

The metaphor of lawyer as "hired gun" is purported to be both the paramount public perception of the legal professional and the dominant self-understanding of lawyers themselves.[1] The lawyer as hired gun or zealous advocate is thought to owe his or her client uncompromising and undivided loyalty. He or she is expected to do everything possible, subject only to the law and professional codes of conduct, to win the case.[2] Under this model of professionalism, lawyers are to pursue the desired substantive ends of their clients, not justice.[3] Hired guns advocate zealously for whatever their clients want, and they do so from a detached and impersonal position in which their own moral judgments are displaced by a role morality thought to justify conduct that would be otherwise unacceptable.[4] This role-based morality requires the hired gun or "neutral partisan" to use their skills and professional expertise to pursue whatever course of action is desired by the client, provided it is not illegal.[5] This detached approach is advanced as necessary to protect the autonomy and dignity of the individual client[6] and to ensure that the lawyer's conduct of a case is based on rationality and logic.[7]

The hired gun metaphor is said to be particularly apt for criminal lawyers.[8] Indeed, some legal ethicists who encourage modification of the ethical standard for legal advocates in other contexts concede that the orthodox, adversarial ethic of the hired gun is nevertheless warranted in criminal defence work.[9] Far from being derisory, in the American criminal law context the concept of legal advocate as hired gun is celebrated by some legal ethicists as necessary for the protection of rights and the pursuit of justice.[10]

Despite its dominance, this particular image of the lawyer may not adequately capture the way criminal lawyers understand their professional role. Alice Woolley, for example, has argued that the obligations reflected in Canadian professional codes of conduct, the professional speeches of Canadian lawyers, and judicial *dicta* from Canadian judges reveal a more qualified conception of the lawyer's duty of loyalty.[11] Consistent with Woolley's observations, the hired gun or zealous advocate model of advocacy is not the most apt characterization of the responses, reflections, and comments provided by the criminal lawyers I interviewed. Indeed, these lawyers articulated different perspectives on the lawyer-client relationship and the role of a criminal defence lawyer. Certainly, as documented in chapters 2 and 3, elements of this commitment to an unmitigated duty of loyalty are reflected in some of the statements of many of the defence lawyers I interviewed. However, their responses revealed more complicated and nuanced accounts of their professional role than what is captured by the traditional notion of the zealous advocate. In particular, responses regarding their primary objectives when acting for clients accused of a sexual offence, and comments regarding the decision-making approach to the conduct of a case adopted by many of them, revealed an understanding of their role that is not necessarily consistent with the hired gun approach. The interviews revealed a group of professionals that is not unanimous on some of the key features of the role and obligations of lawyers working in this capacity – including a criminal lawyer's primary objective.

When asked what they understood to be the primary objective of a criminal defence lawyer when representing a client accused of a sexual offence, some lawyers offered answers such as "to have them found not guilty"[12] or "to get them acquitted."[13] It is true that identifying an acquittal as the primary objective of a defence lawyer seems consistent with the hired gun ethic.

However, others offered different objectives. Defence Lawyer 6 indicated that her primary objective is "to turn over every rock, explore all possible problems with the complainant's statements, and always keep an open mind when looking at a case." Defence Lawyer 5 offered the following as his primary objective: "to give the defendant a full and complete defence." Defence Lawyer 2 said that her primary objective is "to ensure that the person is not convicted unless they should be." Similarly, Defence Lawyer 7 stated: "My primary objective, in terms of representing the client, is to make sure that ah, if the case is there to be laid out, that it's proven beyond a reasonable doubt using the rule of law." Defence Lawyer 8 described his primary objective as "to try and ensure that this person doesn't get convicted for something they didn't do or that they shouldn't be convicted for and to utilize [my] skills to accomplish that end." Defence Lawyer 14 stated that "the primary objective is to make sure the Crown does their job ... to make sure that the procedures are fair, that there's adequate disclosure ... But ah, I don't think the job is to get the client off."

There is a distinction between attempting to have one's client acquitted through every means available and endeavouring to provide a full and complete defence using every means possible. Can lawyers whose primary objective is the latter truly be said to understand themselves as guns for hire – bound to use their skills "solely and unreservedly to obtain what the client wants"?[14] Presumably in the vast majority of sexual assault cases what the client wants is an acquittal[15] – not a full and fair defence.

Similarly, criminal defence lawyers who identify their primary objective as to prevent wrongful convictions or to ensure that individuals are not convicted unless they should be (thus invoking maintenance of the state's burden and standard of proof as their preeminent objective) reveal a sense of professionalism that is more nuanced or multidimensional than that captured by the unqualified and unilateral duty of the hired gun. This more broadly conceptualized objective is well reflected in Defence Lawyer 10's response: "To make sure that my client has a fair trial; make sure their defence, whatever it is, gets put forward in the best manner; do my best to ensure that justice happens. And again, my job is not to represent the public interest. So my version of justice is that my client's, you know, rights are respected and heard."

It is not that these lawyers frame their ethical identity around a notion of public duty. In fact, while many of the defence lawyers interviewed stated that they owed an ethical duty to the court,[16] none of them articulated an ethical or professional obligation to members of the public, other participants in the criminal trial process, or the public interest. Indeed, as is evidenced by the comments of Defence Lawyer 10, some of them explicitly rejected owing a duty to the public. But nor do they, when discussing their primary objectives, describe the unilaterally and narrowly driven, client-centred conception of the zealous advocate.

Noteworthy in the face of these discrepant perspectives on the primary objective of defence counsel is that the lawyers interviewed generally responded to this question as if the answer was self-evident. Lawyers who identified their primary objective as to provide a full and fair defence or to put the state to its test implied that such a goal was incontrovertible. Consider this exchange with Defence Lawyer 11:

Read the question again. It is deceptively simple. [*I: In your opinion, when acting for an individual accused of a sexual offence, what's the primary objective of the lawyer?*] To see that the Crown proves its case or the client gets acquitted. That's true of every case ...
[*I: It may seem like a really obvious question, but it actually elicits*

different types of answers ...] The lawyer's professional role, it
really is not to win. It may make you feel good to win. Like, I feel
better than when I lose. Almost always. But no ... that's not, you
can't think of your role that way. If you do, then the limits which
professionalism imposes on you are literally tacked on to your
conception of yourself and what you're doing in court ... Everybody
gets taught that.

Those who identified winning, or securing an acquittal, as their
primary objective were equally certain as to the plainness of their perspective. Defence Lawyer 4 offered this response: "well the primary goal
obviously is to have them found not guilty." Defence Lawyer 3's response
conveyed a similar viewpoint: "To win. I mean, my job is to win the case
for my client, and secure an acquittal, as long as I'm doing it within my
ethical confines, that's my job."[17]

Comments that identify as the defence lawyer's primary objective
the avoidance of wrongful convictions or the provision of a full and fair
defence (rather than the obtainment of an acquittal) do not reflect a
professional identity that is fully encapsulated by the hired gun metaphor.
The lawyers interviewed for this study did not provide comments and
make assertions consistent with a professional identity that fits neatly
within the model of unmitigated zeal and the hired gun. Nor did their
comments reflect a unified perspective on the ethical limits placed on
criminal lawyers in their conduct of a sexual assault case.

One of these discrepancies emerged in response to questions about
the cross-examination of a truthful sexual assault complainant. Some
defence lawyers readily drew a line between attacking the *reliability*
of a truthful witness (so as to test the state's evidence) and attacking
the *credibility* of a witness they believed to be truthful. Such lines do
not necessarily support the deployment of unmitigated zeal. Defence
Lawyer 11 offers this explanation:

We've always drawn the rule at that [line between a complainant
they know to be truthful and the more usual circumstance in which
they do not have actual knowledge of the witness's truthfulness].
It's probably salutary. I'm not sure it's a hugely meaningful rule. But
it, I think it makes sense that that's where you, one of the places
you draw the line. Because you, you have integrity as an officer of

the court not to abuse a witness. And it's abusive to try and use a witness to say something or to achieve a result which you know is not true.

A similar ethical limit is identified in the following statement by Defence Lawyer 10: "I wouldn't do it. I would frame it differently than that. Would it be unethical? I would frame it around certainty rather than honesty."

Contrast these statements with the response given by Defence Lawyer 12. While she noted that she would very much agonize over whether to undermine the credibility of a truthful sexual assault complainant in a case in which her client had confessed to her, she concluded that "yeah I think I would challenge her credibility ... on the belief that when the system does what it is supposed to do the right outcome prevails."

Discussions about the ethics of using a preliminary inquiry to discourage a sexual assault complainant from proceeding also revealed discrepancies. Crown Attorney 3 indicated that she does not think it is problematic for defence counsel to use the preliminary inquiry in this way:

> [W]hat bothers me is if there's a lot of delays. So, it gives the defence, you know, the statement, then the transcript from the preliminary and then the evidence at the trial, which of course is going to be different, especially if there's a long delay. And then they just hammer them on cross-examination ... Little differences don't matter, but big differences do matter. So, I don't know, I don't really have a problem with it, other than the delay.

Defence Lawyer 9 also indicated that this was an acceptable use of the preliminary inquiry.

Another example of these differing perspectives is drawn from comments concerning the use of other strategies to intimidate complainants into retreating from the criminal justice process. As discussed in chapter 2, while some of the criminal lawyers I interviewed maintained that it is unethical to use the prospect of an application to introduce a complainant's prior sexual history or to have her therapeutic records produced in order to intimidate or humiliate her, others contended that this was acceptable conduct for, and perhaps even ethically required of, defence lawyers.

To summarize, the notion of criminal lawyers as hired guns, with a commitment to pursue their client's objectives at all costs, does not seem to adequately reflect the sense of professionalism some lawyers themselves describe. The discrepancies in response between the criminal lawyers interviewed, regarding their primary objectives and the ethical limits they identify, suggest that in one important respect the role of the criminal defence lawyer is not as deeply embedded and incontestable as is perhaps assumed. To be more specific, the comments of these lawyers suggest that the metaphor of the hired gun, or zealous advocate, may not adequately capture the model of advocacy adopted by some, or many, lawyers. At the same time, criminal lawyers likely do subscribe to a role-based professional identity that focuses heavily on the part they play in the adversarial process.

A Professional Identity Based on Role

While the hired gun model of advocacy does not aptly (or at least fully) capture the self-understanding of the role of the criminal lawyer, the professional identity of criminal lawyers does, nevertheless, appear to be very much performance- or role-based. All of the defence lawyers I interviewed made statements and offered comments suggesting that they had reflected frequently upon what it means to them to "do their job." Their conclusions were notably consistent and determined. If the guiding principle underpinning the medical profession is 'first do no harm,' that of the criminal defence bar may be the role-based edict 'always stay in character.'

Consistently, the lawyers I interviewed offered statements reflecting both the importance they placed on the role-based nature of the adversarial trial process and an ingrained professional identity framed almost exclusively by their sense of the part to be played by the defence lawyer in this process. Many of their statements revealed a framework for ethical decision-making based on their assessment of this role. Unsurprisingly, they premised this role-based morality and sense of professionalism on the functioning of the adversarial system. Several of them explicitly discussed their role in the adversarial process upon which our system of justice is premised. For example, Defence Lawyer 14 commented:

[Y]ou know, the, a lot of times, as a defence lawyer, you are kind of banking on the fact that everybody else in the system will play their part too ... I feel okay about representing someone charged with a horrible sex offence and advocating very strongly ... because I want to feel confident that the Crown will be the counterbalance ... and that ultimately justice will be done when everybody plays their part.

Defence Lawyer 9's assertion that he does not, and does not need to, draw conclusions about the veracity of allegations connects the adversarial nature of our legal system to his sense of the role of the defence lawyer in this process:

So, when I approach a case, I don't approach it from the position that I'm going to show that the complainant, the allegations are false. I'd leave that up to the judge. You can't become personally involved in your cases. I mean, you just can't, because I mean, you'll have a heart attack from stress. Basically, we leave it up to the judge. And as I say, we rely on the basic principles. And then the judge has to make a decision.

One of the most consistent themes to arise from the interviews was in response to questions asking whether there was a personal toll experienced by lawyers when doing this type of work. Lawyer after lawyer, whether acting as Crown or defence, described how hard they find sexual assault cases. Both prosecutors and defence lawyers reported that sexual assault cases are significantly more stressful than any other type of case. Several lawyers I spoke with stated that they find murder trials less demanding than sexual assault trials. A number of them indicated that they would prefer never to do a sexual assault file again. Crown Attorney 3's response to a question asking about the impact of this type of work captures a sentiment that was expressed by several others: "It's so personal ... I mean, I don't know, there's not too many people in the office that say 'Oh please give me more sexual assault.' You know what I mean? 'Please give me more bank robberies.' Sure. But don't give me too many sexual assaults." Defence Lawyer 10 provided a similar comment: "I could easily never give myself another sex assault trial again ... they take a toll on everybody. They're awful for everybody."

The most common explanations as to why sexual assault cases are more taxing involved the emotional and personal nature of these files, and the caregiving role that these cases require both Crown and defence lawyers to play.[18] Defence Lawyer 14's explanation was strongly echoed by several other lawyers interviewed: "It doesn't get much more, like, these are often the most emotional of the kinds of cases that we deal with."

A role-based professional identity in which the system has clearly defined roles and each actor is expected to do her part, and only her part, may insulate criminal defence lawyers from the personal toll experienced when confronted with the pain and emotion caused by a client who has done something terrible.[19] That is to say, like the inclination to disbelieve the complainant discussed in chapter 3, a heavily entrenched, role-based professional identity may be a response to the secondary trauma that criminal defence lawyers are likely subjected to as a consequence of the type of work they do.[20]

A firmly entrenched role-based identity may also help legal professionals to reconcile their role in the further trauma some sexual assault complainants experience as a consequence of testifying against their attackers. Certainly the majority of the lawyers I interviewed were acutely aware of, and empathetic about, the enormous harm to individual complainants wreaked by sexual violence. Many also recognized the additional trauma to sexual assault complainants that results from participating in the criminal justice process. Each interview participant was asked the following question: if you or someone you cared about were sexually assaulted, would you recommend reporting it and pursuing criminal conviction? Most of the lawyers I spoke with indicated that they would have serious reservations about recommending that a loved one endure this process, and that in many circumstances they would advise them against doing so because of how difficult trials are for sexual assault complainants. Consider Defence Lawyer 11's explanation for why in most cases he would not recommend reporting and pursuing a criminal conviction: "because the system is mean, horrible, cruel, and ugly and often will acquit when it should not." If the harms and injustices imposed upon individuals who have already been subjected to significant trauma are structural, then it is the system that is to blame, not those who perform its roles. A role-based professional identity insulates criminal lawyers from the pain and trauma that they know are suffered by sexual assault survivors who participate in the trial process.

Defence Lawyer 12 explicitly recognized the trauma inflicted upon sexual assault complainants by the adversarial process: "Our adversarial system involves challenging, you know, it's not intended to be a system that's supportive ... Or reinforcing in any way." When asked about possible reforms to improve the criminal justice system's response to the problem of sexual harm, she answered: "[Y]ou know ideally, we would find a way to make the process less traumatizing for complainants. But I don't know how we do that ... I think the adversarial nature of our system is very important. And, I don't know how to respect and support complainants while remaining within an adversarial system."

As many defence lawyers would surely state, being cross-examined in court about anything would be unpleasant for most people, let alone being questioned about sex and trauma. Defence Lawyer 12 described this reality as follows: "I think there's necessarily an invasion of privacy that's involved, in our adversarial system. And so people have to get up and talk about extremely personal, private, horrifying incidents and events in a very public forum. And that's traumatic for anybody."

Defence Lawyer 11's comments in response to a question about the personal toll of practising sexual assault law demonstrates the way in which defence lawyers might rely on a notion of the adversarial system to insulate themselves from the emotional impact of a particular outcome in a case:

> You approach criminal law on the footing that you're not responsible for the outcome, that your job is to defend that person and make the Crown prove their case. If they can't do it, that's the way the world's supposed to work. But at the extremes of that proposition, there's always cases that you say 'Gee, that's not the right result. I know that's not the right result.' And you may be the only one who knows it's not the right result, for that matter.

The emphasis on their role in the adversarial system as a defining feature of how criminal lawyers understand themselves and their profession, and as a way to insulate themselves to some degree from secondary trauma, is also reflected in a recently published collection of essays by a set of prominent criminal lawyers across Canada.[21]

Lawyer John Rosen's account of representing serial rapist and murderer Paul Bernardo provides an extreme example. Rosen described the impact of agreeing to represent Bernardo as follows: "My decision ... to take Bernardo on as a client fundamentally shook my belief in my role, particularly with the surfacing of the Bernardo tapes early in that process."[22] (Bernardo and his then wife Karla Homolka videotaped themselves raping and torturing their victims before they murdered them.) Rosen noted that neither his family nor his law partner wanted him to take the retainer. The emotional trauma and professional angst he experienced upon viewing portions of the Bernardo tapes (which was necessary for his representation of the client and his professional obligation not to obstruct justice by withholding physical evidence of the crimes) is clear:

> Our intention was to get an understanding of what was depicted so we could assess my legal, professional, and ethical obligations. In truth though, the images depicted shook me to the core. At one point, I needed to stop and excuse myself for a few moments. The images were deeply disturbing ... How was I going to defend this case in the face of these tapes? What would prevent the jury from coming over the boards at me for having the gall to advance any defence for this accused? Moreover, I am a father myself – what would my own family think of me? How was I going to survive a trial with my health and reputation intact?[23]

Rosen briefly queried whether he could continue to represent Bernardo after watching these videos, and ultimately decided that a failure to do so would put in question his life's work: "what would that have said about the twenty-five years of my life, at that point in time, I had dedicated to the criminal law?"[24] He begins and ends his narrative of the case with a discussion about his role in ensuring that Paul Bernardo received a fair trial. It is clear from Rosen's conclusion that he took great pride and maintained an intense sense of professionalism in the role he played in ensuring that the adversarial system functioned as he thought it should in that case. It is equally clear that he managed his emotional response to Bernardo's actions by focusing on what he understood to be his role in that process.

Evident in many of the other stories recounted by the accomplished criminal lawyers included in this collection is the same abiding commitment to their role in the adversarial process. The narratives provided by many of these lawyers suggest that, for them, the defence of the criminally accused truly is a calling. Equally apparent, and consistent with the statements made by the lawyers I interviewed, is the emotional impact many of these lawyers experienced as a consequence of doing this work. The traumatic effect of exposure to the human-perpetrated atrocities to which these professionals are exposed was evidenced by their candid remarks. This included revelations such as being repeatedly brought to tears when confronted with the harms perpetrated by the accused in some of their cases, many of which involved sexual violence. It included being forced to reassess their own assumptions about the depths of depravity and cruelty of which the human race is capable.

The observation that criminal lawyers base their professional identity on their role in the adversarial system is not particularly revelatory. Many readers would likely have assumed this to be the case even without considering the comments and narratives offered by criminal lawyers themselves. It may be similarly unsurprising to learn that this role-based identity helps criminal lawyers manage their personal reactions to the traumas to which they are repeatedly exposed. There is nevertheless an element to this observation about defence lawyers that is important to the objective of improving the experience of those who turn to the criminal justice system to respond to the sexual harms they have suffered. It is important to understand this role-based sense of professional identity, rooted as it is in the adversarial process, because it offers criteria by which to assess the practices of sexual assault lawyers on their own terms, within the ethical framework criminal defence lawyers themselves have articulated.

On what basis do criminal lawyers justify or rationalize their role in our adversarial model of criminal justice? What principles inform and underpin their belief in this role?

An Ethical Framework Based on the Principles of Legality and Respect for Dignity

Drawing on the work of American legal ethicist David Luban,[25] Alice Woolley offers an eloquent articulation of the relationship between the role of criminal lawyers, the rule of law, and the protection of human dignity.[26] She argues that defending individuals accused of (and guilty of) horrendous criminal offences is socially important – at an objective level – because it gives meaning and protection to the rule of law and its corresponding principle of legality, and because it gives voice to, and thus protects, the dignity interests of the criminally accused. In other words, the defence of the criminally accused fulfills two important liberalist functions.

First, as Woolley and others have observed, defence lawyers safeguard the rule of law (necessary for democracy) by requiring the state to prove an individual's wrongdoing through a fair and just process before it can take liberty-infringing action against that individual.[27] Central to the concept of the rule of law is a principle of legality that insists that all government action be authorized by law. A rule of law society does not use the coercive authority of the state to incarcerate an individual unless that individual has been lawfully convicted through a fair process. Criminal lawyers defend this principle of legality by ensuring that criminal proceedings against their clients are fair – that they are conducted in a manner that complies with constitutional protections such as the presumption of innocence, the right against self-incrimination, the right to be free from unreasonable interferences with one's privacy, the right to respond to one's accuser, and the right to an impartial and unbiased adjudicator.[28]

Second, the role of the criminal defender protects the inherent dignity of the criminally accused by ensuring that they have an opportunity to tell their story – to have their version of events heard.[29] Defence lawyers ensure that the legal process through which an individual's wrongful acts become the justification for the exercise of state authority against the individual is procedurally fair by ensuring that accused individuals are able to provide their account or perspective. As Luban, referring to Alan Donagan's work, describes it: "to honor a litigant's dignity as a person requires us to hear the story she has to tell, because to ignore and exclude her treats her as though her subjectivity and the point of view it inhabits are totally insignificant."[30] The education, skills, and intellectual capacities of many individuals mean that they require help to tell their story in a legal forum.[31] For most people, to have voice in a legal process requires a legal advocate.[32]

Nearly all of the defence lawyers I spoke with identified either the principle of legality, the right of their client to tell his story, or both, as central to their understanding of their role as a criminal defender. For these lawyers, performing their role in the adversarial system means protecting these interests.

Indeed, discussions regarding the principle of legality featured in most of the interviews I conducted. Defence Lawyer 9, for example, offered the following comments: "I believe in the basic principles: the presumption of innocence, the burden of proof, proof beyond a reasonable doubt and a fair and public hearing. I believe in those things. And as long as I believe in them, I can then defend anybody." Defence Lawyer 10 stated: "I mean the *Charter* is obviously fundamental to what I do every day." She went on to state: "that whole concept of proof beyond a reasonable doubt is essential to our, you know, it's why I get up and go to work in the morning."

The primary objectives identified by several of the lawyers I interviewed, such as to put the state to its burden and standard of proof, also emphasize the significance of this principle of legality to some lawyers' sense of their role. Defence Lawyer 11's insights, already quoted, were particularly telling in this regard. Recall, he indicated that lawyers who consider winning or securing an acquittal to be their primary objective have not adequately reflected on their professional role:

Some people haven't thought through the professional nature of an obligation as opposed to your personal satisfaction ... they're not thinking what their professional role is. Their professional role, it really is not to win. It may make you feel good to win. Like I feel better than when I lose. Almost always. But no, you can't think of your role that way. If you do, then the limits which professionalism imposes on you are literally tacked on to your conception of yourself and what you're doing in court.

Some of the female defence lawyers I spoke with offered thoughtful reflections on how they reconcile their feminist identity with the work they do to defend men accused of sexually assaulting women by focusing on their role in protecting the rule of law. Defence Lawyer 12's considered comments reflect this perspective:

I think there's always kind of a weirdness or a discomfort about being a woman defence lawyer doing sex cases ... I've certainly spent time thinking about that ... sometimes I feel like I am a bit of a traitor to my feminist beliefs or ideals. Like as a woman, can I really do this? Can I really represent somebody charged

with something that is just horrifying to me? ... there are some
women who are very uncomfortable with women defence lawyers
representing men charged with sex offences and it is difficult for
us to be on the other side of that. You know? Sometimes I want to
say to those women, 'I'm not a bad person. I'm doing this because
I think it's really important for us to have a rule of law system and
that means that we have to make sure that everybody gets a good
defence' ... It's for me to provide the best defence I can ... and when
I do that, the rule of law is protected.

As noted, several of the defence counsel interviewed for this study
also discussed the importance of ensuring the right of their clients to
tell their story. Defence Lawyer 10, for example, noted:

I often suspect my client isn't telling the truth. That's not my job.
I'm not the judge. So it's the job of the judge to work through that,
you know? Like, the conversation I will have with my client behind
closed doors and the case I present in court are different things.
So, I will, in any case, I will be honest with my client that what
they're telling me might be a hard sell. But if they say 'This is what
happened,' that's what, you know, I go with.

A few of the lawyers I spoke with noted that in sexual assault cases, in
particular, the case may turn on competing narratives of what occurred
– there is the complainant's story and there is their client's story – and
that their job is to ensure that their client's version is presented. Defence
Lawyer 15, for example, stated: "I mean, in these kinds of cases in particular, there's often very little objective surrounding evidence. It's basically
just two versions of what happened."

In highlighting the "inordinate amount of stress associated with a sex
assault case," Defence Lawyer 3 discussed the way in which, in sexual
assault cases in particular, the responsibility for presenting his client's
story often falls exclusively to his cross-examination of the complainant:

I think they're pretty black and white, the sex assault cases. Either,
you have what I think is the relatively rare scenario, where you have
a complainant who's fabricating a story, for some reason, in which
case I feel the pressure more acutely, in terms of my responsibilities

in cross-examination than in almost every other case … typically I don't like to call my clients in sex assault cases … So sort of the burden to win or lose … it's all on me. I've got to cross-examine in a way that, respectfully and ethically, that will show clearly, that this person is fabricating. That's a tremendous amount of pressure.

Of note, Defence Lawyer 3 went on to describe a similar burden when he cross-examines a complainant he suspects is truthful: "On the flip side, it weighs very heavily on me that I'm cross-examining, no matter how nicely I may like to think I do my job or civilly or respectfully, that I'm cross-examining someone who's been the victim of sexual violence, in an effort to show that they're being untruthful and exposing them to what can only be further traumatization from their assault." He was not the only lawyer to identify a pressure to present their client's version of events through their cross-examination of the complainant, and to show that the complainant is lying, that is unique to sexual assault cases.

To summarize, the lawyers I spoke with offered statements that are very much consistent with the commonly articulated justifications for the role and social value of the criminal lawyer. Again, these two key principles underpinning the role of the criminal defender include the rule of law (and its corresponding principle of legality) and respect for the dignity of all individuals (including recognition of the right to be heard).

Accepting that these two principles are in fact central to the way in which criminal lawyers understand their role in the adversarial process, what is the relationship between this conception of the role of the criminal defender and the treatment of sexual assault complainants? How should these principles inform our assessment of defence counsel practices in sexual assault cases? In fact, some of the strategies that some criminal lawyers deploy in sexual assault proceedings (and potentially other types of cases) are inconsistent with the rule of law and/or protection of the right of the criminally accused to be heard. Consider two examples.

First, contemplate the role of the criminal defender in ensuring that a criminal conviction only arises following a fair process in which the accused is given a voice – a legal advocate. More specifically, consider this principle in light of the way in which some defence lawyers control the information their client is permitted to share with them. For example, some of the lawyers I interviewed indicated that they intentionally do not allow their client to tell them their side of the story. Defence Lawyer 9 described this strategy as follows:

> On the first interview I will not take a statement. I usually don't take a statement from them because I really want to find out exactly what the allegations are [by contacting the Crown or police], and then of course, I can take the position that I'm going to confront my client with the allegations, get his side of the story. Or, I may very well explain to the client that I'm, you know, 'I may not ask you whether or not you did it, but you have a right to go through a trial to see whether or not the Crown can prove its case beyond a reasonable doubt.'

Defence Lawyer 13 provided a similar comment:

> Initially, I don't even want to know if he was there. I don't even want to know if that's his right name there. I mean, I just, I don't want to know anything, until I've seen disclosure and can start to see 'Do we have an identity defence?' If we have an identity defence, I don't want to know anything from this person. But, once we start to go down that road, and knock some of those pegs out, and we're down to, you know, 'Was this a consensual act?' then I do want to know what the person's going to say. But, you know, I, to get back to the question, I spend a fair bit of time working hard at not knowing, to keep as many doors open as possible. But if I know that the complainant is telling the truth about something, I think it's highly unethical to challenge that.

Crown Attorney 3 offered a similar explanation of this approach: "So, some defence lawyers, they'll meet their client, and I've talked to defence lawyers about this. And they'll say 'I don't want to hear anything from you.'"

Lawyers must have a good-faith basis to ask a witness a question, must not knowingly mislead the court, and must not present false evidence, nor assist in dishonest action.[33] Lawyers are required to cross-examine witnesses in a manner that is consistent with the rules of evidence.[34] The strategic advantage of the wilfully blind approach to communication between the lawyer and client described by these lawyers is explained in the following statement from Crown Attorney 1:

But this ethical obligation where you have to have a good faith basis to ask a question in cross-examination comes up a lot. And I think it is particularly true of sexual assault because I get questions that are just really out there ... there are two ways to approach this right? You can, some people just don't ask their client what happened, which opens up all sorts of possibilities about what they can theorize ... They can't ask questions they know to be wrong. So, but they don't ask them initially what really happened. Third party, all those things come into play then.

The rules of professional conduct regulating criminal lawyers in Canada stipulate that "notwithstanding the lawyer's private opinion on credibility or the merits, a lawyer may properly rely on any evidence or defences, including so called technicalities, not known to be false or fraudulent."[35] However, there is a distinction between a lawyer who refrains from drawing inferences of guilt based on either the client's information or external evidence, and one who refuses to receive her client's version of the facts so that she might be liberated from certain ethical obligations. While opinion is divided, some lawyers, including some of those I interviewed, consider the latter to be unethical.[36] The ethical parameters related to issues such as the duty to cross-examine a sexual assault complainant in good faith, or the legitimacy of an application to introduce a complainant's prior sexual history, will shift depending on what a lawyer is told by his client. Lawyers who refuse to receive their client's version of events, so that they might be ethically liberated to attack the credibility of the complainant in ways they otherwise could not, or who avoid knowledge of their client's perspective so that they might attempt to introduce evidence of a complainant's prior sexual history for a purpose that would be unnecessary were they to have more information, are not giving voice to their client.

If, as Luban suggests, "human dignity requires litigants to be heard," and to be heard in a legal proceeding requires a legal advocate, then "advocacy has its limits."[37] The lawyer must tell the *client's* story. While the lawyer's version of the client's story will unavoidably be in the schematic, manipulated, highly stylized form organized through, and demanded by, the legal process, he or she cannot tell a false story.[38] Although there may be sound policy justifications not to have an ethical rule requiring lawyers to learn their client's version of events – such as enforcement issues or disruption to the lawyer/client relationship

– lawyers who refuse to hear their client's story cannot convincingly be said to be serving as their voice. They must be doing something else.

To be clear, I am not suggesting that to litigate in keeping with their aim of giving an accused voice, defence lawyers must literally *tell* their client's story. A fundamental tenet of our criminal justice process is the principle against self-incrimination – the right to remain silent. Rather, I am arguing that a lawyer who refuses to hear his client's account of what occurred cannot be said to be ensuring the accused's version of events, or perspective, is presented. Whatever he is doing, it is not ensuring his client's voice is heard.

A second example of defence counsel strategies that are inconsistent with these supposedly guiding legality and dignity principles involves strategies aimed at discouraging sexual assault complainants from willingly participating in the criminal justice process through intimidation or humiliation. Chapter 2 provided examples of law firm websites that imply strategies of humiliation that have such aims. Craig Penney's website, for instance, advertised a case in which, arguably, he insinuates that he managed to have the charges against his client dropped by bringing an application to adduce evidence of the complainant's prior sexual history. Chapter 2 also discussed cases in which trial judges described a defence lawyer's objective as to encourage a complainant into retreating from the criminal trial process. Recall, for example, Justice Kane's suggestion in response to Solomon Friedman's application to introduce evidence of the fourteen-year-old complainant's sexual history in *R v T(J)*: "Introducing such unrelated sexual misconduct evidence will discourage complainants to report and to testify which is the likely motivation of this application."[39]

Some of the lawyers I interviewed also discussed strategies of this nature. For instance, in response to a question asking whether it is ethical for a lawyer to bring applications to introduce evidence of prior sexual history or to obtain therapeutic or medical records held by a third party in order to threaten or scare off the complainant, Defence Lawyer 9 commented as follows:

> I see absolutely nothing wrong ... I see nothing wrong, from a defence point of view, as to going after prior medical records, or making an application to go after prior sexual acts, as long as the lawyer feels there's some relevancy to it. Medical records, I can

never see anything wrong, for whatever reasons. If it's to scare off the alleged victim, so she won't testify, that's fine. There's nothing wrong with that ... I approve of that tactic, because you have to remember, as a defence counsel, we owe our duty to the client, not to the alleged victim.

In discussing the prospect of other lawyers bringing an application to introduce prior sexual history evidence or to produce a complainant's counselling records in order to discourage her from continuing, Defence Lawyer 2 commented: "I'm sure they do. I don't. I would never want to file an application that was just crazy. Am I happy if that's the result? Yeah. I've certainly been told by Crowns that they've discontinued prosecutions because the complainant doesn't want it coming up."

As noted in chapter 2, some of the lawyers I interviewed indicated that either they themselves, or other lawyers, use the preliminary inquiry to attempt to discourage the complainant from continuing to participate in the process. Defence Lawyer 6, for instance, described the following approach to the cross-examination of the complainant at a preliminary inquiry:

And so, at a prelim, I might, I might feel like if I take a good enough crack at her and shake her enough, then the Crown will say, (sigh) You know? And then I've done my job. Cause no one likes trials. I mean, and I, she may not want to go through that again. You know? I've now cross-examined her at a prelim. She's going to have to go through it a year later. Does she really want to or is she [done] ... that actually doesn't happen very [often but] ... that, that's always the hope.

Likewise, Paul Gracia's website, also described in chapter 2, advertised a case in which he succeeded in having the charges against his client dropped. He wrote that the fourteen-year-old complainant refused to testify at trial after having been cross-examined by him at the preliminary inquiry: "At the preliminary Inquiry, during my cross-examination of the complainant, she became so frustrated by my questions that she effectively quit, exclaiming that she no longer desired to proceed any further."[40] Arguably, the intended implication was that his questioning had been the source of her frustration and subsequent withdrawal from the process.

Tactics of humiliation or intimidation cannot be validated by a commitment to the principle of legality and the rule of law. Certainly our constitutional right to due process does not include the right to bully witnesses into withdrawing from the process. But more than that, intimidating or humiliating a complainant into retreating from the trial process is actually inconsistent with the principle of legality. Strategies aimed at eliminating a key participant in a criminal proceeding, such that the proceeding cannot continue, undermine – rather than uphold – the rule of law. A lawyer who bases their professional identity and justification for the actions they take on their belief in the presumption of innocence, the adversarial process, and the right to a fair and public hearing is not acting in a manner consistent with their sense of professionalism when they utilize strategies that undermine the process itself.

Nor are strategies of humiliation and intimidation consistent with a commitment to the principle of human dignity. Recall that the right of the criminally accused to have a voice, to respond through their legal representative to their accusers regardless of the nature of their acts, is rooted in part in the belief that a just legal system is a legal system that protects human dignity as an inherent value. In other words, a just legal system recognizes the dignity interests of all those who come in contact with it. The dignity of sexual assault complainants who participate, or are forced to participate, in the criminal justice process is also at stake. Humiliating or bullying a sexual assault complainant into submission such that they have no voice in the proceeding denies them their dignity. Lawyers who deploy such tactics do not act in a manner consistent with a professional identity founded on a commitment to the inherent value of human dignity.

One final example of defence counsel tactics that are, in fact, inconsistent with the rule of law (and its underlying principle of legality) involves the use of particular stereotypes about rape that have been legally rejected as baseless and irrelevant. For decades feminists and other law reformers have laboured at eliminating from the law of sexual assault and the rules of evidence the baseless and discriminatory social assumptions about women in general and sexual violence in particular upon which much of the law of sexual violence was structured.[41] Reforms to the *Criminal Code*,[42] and the decisions of judges, have pursued that objective both directly and indirectly. As a result, certain social assumptions or stereotypes about sexual violence have been specifically and explicitly rejected through changes to the law in Canada. These changes to the law arose because of a recognition that certain stereotypes about women and sexual violence are irrelevant, harmful, and outrageously outdated. They are founded upon discriminatory beliefs about sex and gender, not empirical reality.

One of the clearest examples of these law reforms involves the rules limiting the admissibility of evidence of a complainant's other sexual activity. As was discussed in chapter 2, section 276 of the *Criminal Code* prohibits admission of a complainant's other sexual activity for the purposes of discrediting her solely on the basis of her lack of chastity.[43] It is also not permissible to infer that prior or subsequent sexual activity alone makes a woman more likely to have consented to the sex at issue in the allegation.[44] In other words, defence lawyers are not allowed to introduce evidence of a complainant's sexual activities for these purposes. The sexual nature of a complainant's other activity with the accused or a third party is, on its own, irrelevant to the matter of whether she consented to the sexual touching at issue or whether she is a credible witness.[45]

As was briefly explained in chapter 2, this change to the law explicitly rejected two related stereotypes about rape (the twin myths). First, it rejected the absurd and discriminatory assumption that women who are unchaste are untrustworthy. Second, it rejected the assumption that women with previous sexual experience are more likely to consent than are women who are "chaste" – the ridiculous proposition that once a woman has had sex with one man she becomes less discriminating in her sexual choices.[46] According to the Supreme Court of Canada, section 276 rejects them on the basis that they are discriminatory and baseless and as a result this type of evidence risks distorting the truth-seeking function of the trial.[47] In this sense, these limits on defence counsel's ability to introduce evidence of a complainant's other sexual activity are aimed at protecting the trial process from information that would distort its fact-finding function.

Recall that under section 276, the defence must apply to the court for permission to introduce evidence of a complainant's other sexual activities. Among other things, the court is required to deny such applications if the purpose for introducing the evidence is to trigger one of the twin myths. With respect to applications to introduce prior sexual history evidence not aimed at triggering one of the twin myths, trial judges are still required to consider factors such as the need to remove any other discriminatory beliefs or bias from the fact-finding process before admitting the evidence.[48] Given its role in protecting the integrity of the trial process, intentional attempts to circumvent the limits of section 276 are not consistent with a professional identity rooted in rule of law objectives, such as the right to a fair trial. Consider the following example.

In a 1998 continuing legal education session on conducting sexual assault trials, criminal lawyer Marie Henein made these remarks to the audience regarding what was, at the time, the newly enacted section 276:

> There is another tactical judgment call that I'd like you to keep in mind and that is that while you may not have the strongest argument to do one of these applications sometimes you bring the application, especially in front of a judge alone trial, to introduce all this otherwise inadmissible evidence and if it is excluded 'well oh well the judge has heard it.'[49]

When the audience responded with what sounded to me like nervous laughter, and another panelist asked Henein whether this was fair, she conceded that a "tactical approach" of this nature would be "a close to the line application."[50] As the audience of lawyers laughed, she went on to state:

> I am absolutely confident that the judge will be able to disabuse his or her mind of the fact that she has a very extensive and lewd prior sexual history ... obviously the argument has to have merit. I'm not suggesting that you bring frivolous arguments but do remember that, again in a judge alone [trial] a different tactical advantage may be there for you to bring this type of application.[51]

Of course, the tactical advantage she was teaching this group of legal professionals is premised on precisely the opposite assumption. It is premised on the belief that exposing the trial judge to inadmissible evidence of the complainant's "extensive" and "lewd" sexual history[52] will, in fact, inform the judge's assessment of her credibility or the likelihood that she consented to the sexual act at issue in the allegation.

Unfortunately, there is every reason to believe that from a tactical perspective Henein's 1998 advice to other lawyers was astute. Indeed, there is a significant body of empirical research that confirms the tenacity of rape myths such as the ones targeted by section 276. In a United Kingdom–based study by Jennifer Temkin, one barrister reported that "juries 'were not very good (at convicting) when somebody can be depicted as a slut.'"[53] Participant lawyers agreed that the complainant's sexual character and manner of dress influences trial outcomes.[54] Some of the barristers interviewed interpreted the victim's behaviour at the time of the incident as a key factor in whether there would be a conviction. Lawyers interviewed for Temkin's study consistently reported that sexual history is almost always relevant to consent. Moreover, the lawyers Temkin interviewed reported that a woman who has had a lot of sexual experience is more likely to have consented to the sex at issue in the charge.[55] Ruthy Lazar has done empirical work in the Canadian context that suggests similar views among some Canadian lawyers.[56]

Stereotypes, including the kind discussed here, are a form of what is called heuristic or schematic thinking. Nancy Levit observes that "one of the most significant lessons from cognitive psychology in the past quarter century is the idea that when people make judgments under conditions of uncertainty, they use shorthand methods of decision making called 'heuristics.'"[57] This lesson has important implications in legal contexts.[58] The role of schematic thinking in assessments of complainant credibility in sexual assault trials is well documented: "[d]espite the fact that legal decision making is normatively defined as data driven, [i.e.,] relying exclusively on the facts and the evidence, there is plenty of scope for schematic conceptions about rape rooted in rape myths to infiltrate."[59] Fact-finders in sexual assault trials reason based on these ways of knowing without even realizing that they do so.[60] This is, of course, the insight motivating Henein's suggested "tactical advantage."

The prosecution of sexual assault reflects a judicial process with a long and deep-seated history of discriminatory beliefs about women, and a reality that in adjudicating allegations of sexual violation (which primarily means credibility assessments), finders of fact are almost always asked to make decisions under conditions of uncertainty. This makes schematic thinking both particularly likely and uniquely problematic in sexual assault trials. When a lawyer suggests to a complainant that the reason she did not tell anyone right away is because she is fabricating the allegation to cover up consensual sex she now regrets, or points to a lack of physical injury as evidence of consent, or intentionally introduces a trial judge to inadmissible evidence demonstrating a complainant's so-called promiscuity, he or she deploys a powerful heuristic that risks triggering reasoning that is both difficult to displace and wrong at law. The persuasiveness and intransigence of these entrenched stories about sexual violence divert reasoning from a process of legal findings based on relevant evidence. In other words, these stereotypes about rape jeopardize the possibility of a fair trial.

In a 2016 interview reflecting upon the high-profile sexual assault prosecution of her client Jian Ghomeshi, Henein (like the lawyers I interviewed) articulated a professional identity rooted in her role in, and her belief in, the criminal justice process. She explained her decision to provide the interview by stating: "It was important as a person who has spent 25 years of her life in the system, to perhaps address some of the misconceptions, because it is a system I believe in and I value very much and I think we should all be proud of ... We have a very, very good system."[61] She suggested that those who have worked as legal professionals should not denigrate the legal system with public statements that undermine its fundamental principles (such as the presumption of innocence), and asserted that "we have one [of] the greatest legal systems in the world."[62] In describing the concept of justice in our system, Henein identified the same two factors I discussed earlier in this chapter – the inherent dignity of allowing the criminally accused a voice, and the rule of law as reflected in the right to a fair process: "I tell my clients ... you know what you're guaranteed, you're guaranteed an opportunity to be heard and you're guaranteed a fair trial, that is it."[63]

Lawyers who intentionally invoke empirically unfounded and legally rejected social assumptions about sex and gender distort the trial process.[64] In doing so, they act contrary to the very values they identify as fundamental to their professional role. A fair trial, the interest articulated as paramount by so many defence lawyers, is not one in which empirically unfounded, discriminatory, and legally rejected stereotypes are used to disrupt the fact-finding function of the process.[65]

Shifting Attitudes and Increasing Recognition of Ethical Obligations

As a matter of law, the limits necessary to reduce, if not eliminate, many 'whack the complainant'–type strategies already exist. There are sound statutory rules of evidence and common laws prohibiting reliance on discriminatory stereotypes about sexual assault.[66] The definition of consent is premised on the assumption that a failure to resist, scream, or run away does not indicate consent.[67] The Supreme Court of Canada has recognized legal limits on the right to full answer and defence, including specifically in sexual assault cases.[68] It is not a right to pursue any and every defence possible, nor even a right to the most favourable process imaginable.[69] As the Supreme Court of Canada stated in *R v Lyttle*, "[c]ounsel are bound by the rules of relevancy and barred from resorting to harassment, misrepresentation, repetitiousness or, more generally, from putting questions whose prejudicial effect outweighs their probative value."[70] It is true that criminal defenders have a duty to raise every argument and ask every question, no matter how distasteful. But this duty to advocate resolutely on behalf of one's client is limited by law.

Lawyers are barred from posing questions or introducing evidence that is irrelevant, that is not based on a reasonable assumption, or that is calculated to mislead.[71] The right to full answer and defence is a right to a fair trial.[72] The accused has no right to a discriminatory defence. In other words, for the most part, the law is not the problem. The challenge, as feminists have long pointed out,[73] is that it is much easier to change the law than it is to make changes to the underlying and overarching legal and social culture.

What are the factors necessary to promote an attitudinal shift in the legal profession sufficient to reduce or eliminate reliance by defence counsel on strategies that invoke discriminatory stereotypes or are unnecessarily aggressive or humiliating towards sexual assault complainants? Three factors that could encourage a shift of this nature are: (i) broad recognition within the defence bar that the practice of sexual assault law perpetuates harms to complainants; (ii) acceptance that strategies aimed at humiliating complainants or that rely on rape myths violate lawyers' professional ethics; and (iii) a more nuanced and balanced articulation of the professional virtues of those who practice criminal defence law.

The first requirement is broad acceptance, within the defence bar, that whacking the complainant continues to occur, and that experienced and celebrated lawyers may not necessarily know better than to pursue such practices. These are, of course, factual claims. I attempted to substantiate them in chapters 2 and 3 using evidence of what could be construed as overly aggressive, humiliating, or discriminatory treatment by defence lawyers of sexual assault complainants, taken from law firm websites, interviews with defence lawyers and Crown attorneys, and trial transcripts.

While some members of the defence bar publicly maintain that the practice of whacking the complainant is a myth (and that if anything the pendulum has swung too far in favour of those who allege sexual violation), not all criminal defenders hold this view. For example, as highlighted in chapter 2, some of the defence lawyers I interviewed explicitly acknowledged that these problematic strategies continue to be used. Moreover, while some of the lawyers interviewed defended them, others did not. Consider, for example, what Defence Lawyer 10 stated when asked what it means to her to be a feminist defence lawyer:

> I think it means understanding the difference between advancing
> my client's case and advancing rape myths. I mean, I'm very aware
> of rape myths when I'm defending a sex assault case. And I think
> that not only do I know them to be untrue, and don't believe
> in them, but I think that on the whole, in my client's interest,
> antagonizing a complainant in the court by furthering this sort of
> nonsense, I guess, is, is not helpful to anybody.

Broad acceptance by the defence bar that the mistreatment of sexual assault complainants regularly occurs in Canadian sexual assault proceedings will require two things. First, members of the defence bar who accept that these practices continue to be used but reject them as improper or unethical need to acknowledge this publicly in order to counter the dominant narrative currently provided by some of their more vocal colleagues. Second, those who defend the practices of defence lawyers by asserting that sexual assault complainants are not routinely abused on the stand need to become either more reflective or more forthright. Abbe Smith's recent work discussing the challenges faced by feminist defence lawyers who represent individuals accused of rape could serve as an excellent touchstone in pursuing either of these ends.[74]

Smith is a well-known American legal ethicist and criminal lawyer. She is unapologetically and unreservedly committed to defending the need for criminal lawyers to use unmitigated zeal in defending the criminally accused. She advocates a no-holds-barred approach to the cross-examination of sexual assault complainants, and offers constitutional and ethical arguments for why she thinks this is justified. Smith and I do not agree on the appropriate limits on defence counsel when cross-examining a sexual assault complainant. However, she should be commended for defending her position without trying to minimize or deny the trauma caused to survivors of sexualized violence by the trial process and criminal defence lawyers. She depicts the pain caused to complainants by the process of cross-examination. She is candid about the connection between the shame and self-blame caused by rape and the reiteration of this shame and blame caused to complainants by the defence lawyers who cross-examine them. Regardless of one's position on the ethical parameters of resolute advocacy, criminal lawyers should be honest about the impact their professional conduct has on sexual assault complainants.[75]

The second ingredient necessary to shift the culture of the legal profession involves offering much more nuanced stories about, and caricatures of, the heroes this profession constructs. The legal profession (including the legal academy) is partially responsible for the way prominent criminal lawyers are described and celebrated in both professional and public discourse. It is one thing to commend prominent criminal lawyers for their tenacious dedication to representing and advocating for the (often marginalized) individuals who find themselves subject to the prosecutorial authority of the state. It is another to celebrate these lawyers as pit bulls, merciless sociopaths ready to go for the jugular, or ferocious and unrelenting courtroom giants. The legal profession must be more conscious of, and careful about, how their professional virtues are represented. It is also important to be more explicit about the harms that criminal lawyers sometimes cause. Presumably the legal profession is sophisticated enough to construct narratives about its criminal law heroes that are laudatory without obscuring the reality of harms that are very important to recognize. Constance Backhouse's feminist reflection on the eulogies surrounding Edward Greenspan's death is an exemplar of the type of work that is needed.[76]

The third ingredient necessary to promote an attitudinal shift within the legal profession involves reframing in ethical terms the continued reliance by some defence lawyers on the types of strategies discussed in this book. There are ethical limits on defence counsel's conduct of a sexual assault case that preclude many of these strategies. These ethical obligations need to be fully embraced.

Professional codes of conduct in Canada require of lawyers that their conduct of a case be discharged by fair and honourable means, without illegality, and in a manner that respects the tribunal and promotes a fair trial.[77] In defending an individual accused of a sexual offence, this duty translates into two concrete ethical limits: an obligation not to intentionally undermine or circumvent law reforms aimed at eradicating rape mythology, and an obligation not to use tactics intended to discourage a complainant from participating in the criminal justice response to her allegations of sexual violation.

Consider the ethical duty not to undermine or circumvent legal reforms aimed at eliminating rape mythology. Lawyers have an ethical obligation to conduct their cases within the bounds of law. Within the bounds of law in this context means consistent with law reforms that have categorically precluded the admission of evidence, or use of arguments, introduced in an effort to invoke stereotypes that have been legally rejected. For example, section 276 precludes the use of sexual history evidence to invoke the stereotype that prior sexual activity makes a woman less worthy of belief. A lawyer who seeks to introduce such evidence for these purposes, even if ostensibly offering it for another reason, is not litigating within the bounds of law. Legal arguments aimed at convincing a trier of fact that a woman's failure to resist or fight back demonstrates consent are similarly offside a lawyer's duty of fidelity to law. Simply put, lawyers need to ask themselves whether the evidence they seek to admit is reliant, for its probative value, on legally rejected stereotypes. If the answer is yes, its use is unethical.

As Woolley notes, "Not all improper cross-examination can be easily controlled by the trial judge given the 'wide latitude' which lawyers have to ask questions."[78] In the interests of protecting the rights of the accused, lawyers need to be given the leeway to demonstrate the relevancy of their evidence and arguments.[79] However, as a result, by the time it becomes apparent that a lawyer does not have a good-faith/reasonable basis for pursuing a line of questioning, "it may be too late to repair the harm that arises."[80]

Recall the power of these social assumptions about gender and sexual violence to distort the trial process, outlined earlier in this chapter. The provision of wide latitude to defence counsel in their conduct of a case demands a concomitant ethical obligation on these lawyers not to trigger legally rejected stereotypes. Lawyers know the ins and outs of their cases better than do judges. In those cases in which the Crown has honoured its disclosure obligations, no party to a criminal proceeding is more informed than the defence. Defence counsel are singularly situated to ensure that these limits (these protections of the fact-finding process) are maintained. For example, it is the purpose for which evidence of sexual history is offered that determines whether it is improper. Advocates are the ones who know, or should know, whether the lines of questioning they pursue or the arguments they advance have a legitimate purpose. Certainly defence lawyers are better positioned to identify the purpose motivating a particular trial strategy than are Crown attorneys or trial judges.[81] Eliminating stereotype-infused reasoning from the trial process is not a function that the law and judges alone can adequately perform. Rulings of inadmissibility, admonishments to the jury, and sustained Crown objections may function retroactively and impotently – thus the need for clear ethical obligations on defence counsel.

When pressed to provide detail about what limits the canon of ethics imposes in sexual assault cases, the defence lawyers who participated in this study most commonly identified some version of the duty not to mislead the court. Defence Lawyer 1's comments captured a frequently articulated sentiment: "I truly believe that I am an officer of the court ... I still have my duty to my client. I'm carrying out that duty. But I'm not jerking around with the court." The duty not to mislead the court includes an obligation to refrain from knowingly relying on stereotypes (such as the hue-and-cry myth, the twin myths, and the failure-to-resist myth) that have been legally rejected as unfounded.

Now contemplate the ethical obligation not to humiliate or shame a complainant into withdrawing from the criminal trial process. Defence lawyers should question whether the strategy they are pursuing actually undermines the possibility of a fair trial by discouraging a key actor in a legal proceeding, such as the complainant, from participating in the process. For example, using a style of cross-examination in the preliminary inquiry intended to intimidate the complainant into refusing to cooperate with the Crown going forward disrupts, rather than furthers, the possibility of a fair trial. Such tactics can hardly be considered ethical lawyering.

Happily, abiding by the legal limits in place to ensure a fair sexual assault trial is not only consistent with the ethical duties imposed upon lawyers; it is also consistent with the values that many lawyers identify as central to their professional identity. Lawyers whose self-understanding of their professional role is rooted in a belief in the rule of law and the right to be heard through a fair process should have no difficulty accepting that they have an ethical obligation not to mislead the court by relying on myths and stereotypes that are legally impermissible, and an ethical duty not to undermine the possibility of a fair trial by humiliating or intimidating a key actor in the process into refusing to further participate.

But is it reasonable to expect defence lawyers to know how, and when, their conduct of a case contravenes these ethical limits? Yes. Lawyers have an ethical obligation to be competent.[82] They also have a duty not to discriminate.[83] The duty not to discriminate and the requirement of basic competency make it incumbent upon any defence counsel whose practice includes defending individuals accused of sexual assault to educate themselves on the parameters that these legal limits impose upon the conduct of a sexual assault trial.

Competency in this context requires lawyers to be mindful, reflective, and aware of the assumptions motivating a particular strategy and of the relationship between these assumptions and specific legal reforms such as the categorical rejection of certain stereotypes about rape. Competency requires lawyers to develop self-awareness of their own entrenched social assumptions – to ask themselves what heuristics they rely upon in designing and evaluating the defence of a client accused of sexual assault.

In other words, lawyers should reflect upon why they are seeking to introduce particular evidence, pursue a certain strategy, or assume a particular demeanour towards a witness. Moreover, they should under-stand this self-reflection as an ethical query that is directly connected to their professional identity, or self-understanding, of their role in our current system of justice. Similarly, legal educators should ensure that curricula include content and objectives aimed at building the capacity of law students to increase professional self-awareness. Law societies should ensure that continuing legal education pushes criminal lawyers to do the same.

Accepting the need to promote a legal culture in which the treatment of the complainant is understood as an ethical issue, one might next ask how these ethical obligations are to be instantiated. Accepting that these ethical obligations exist is one thing. What can be said on the issue of enforcement?

The relationships between ethical norms and rules, formal and informal sanctions, reputational harm, judicial regulation of lawyers, and professional disciplinary measures are complex. A purely positivist – or rule and order – approach to legal ethics, particularly in a context such as this, is unlikely to be successful. The recommendation that the legal profession embrace the ethical implications of engaging in, or allowing other legal professionals to engage in, the abusive, humiliating, and discriminatory treatment of sexual assault complainants is aimed at generating an attitudinal shift within the legal profession. Understanding and assessing the conduct of lawyers through an ethical framework is as much about setting professional norms as it is about sanctioning individual lawyers.

At the same time, law societies in Canada are charged with protecting the public. That is their mandate – to regulate lawyers in the interests of the public. The responsibility to do so includes creating policies and processes that sanction lawyers who threaten the administration of justice by distorting the trial process through the use of baseless (and discriminatory) stereotypes or humiliation and intimidation tactics. While trial judges may, with proper support from appellate courts, be best positioned to respond to, for example, unnecessarily rude, repetitive, or aggressive questioning of a complainant, there will be instances when a trial judge's interventions are unsuccessful. There will also be cases in which a trial judge should, but does not, intervene. Encouraging regulatory action to reduce the mistreatment of sexual assault complainants without creating a chilling effect on the ability of lawyers to advocate resolutely for their clients is a delicate calculation. Nevertheless, law societies bear some of the responsibility for doing this disciplinary work. It is clear that they have the authority and capacity to regulate this conduct. The failure to do so is a choice.

Consider this example. In recent years, the Law Society of Upper Canada has spent substantial time and resources prosecuting a securities litigator – Joseph Groia – for allegedly communicating with opposing lawyers in a manner that was offensive and not in keeping with the proper tone of professional communication during a high-profile securities trial.[84] Groia received a one-month suspension for being rude and improper towards the opposing lawyers. Appeals have stretched the case into a four-year-long spectacle that is now headed to the Supreme Court of Canada.[85] One corporate Bay Street firm fittingly characterized the case as follows:

> The Supreme Court may have the final word, but the lesson here? Litigation isn't a trial by combat. The duty to zealously advance our client's interests cannot compromise our duty to be civil to our "friends" and to the court. At the very least, we cannot attack opposing counsel's integrity using invective and strong language to advance our client's case, no matter how high the stakes.[86]

"At the very least" indeed ... conspicuously, and tellingly, absent from the list of parties to whom this lawyer suggests respectful treatment is owed are the non-legal professionals in the courtroom. It is disheartening to consider the prioritization that results in enormous efforts to ensure that well-educated, courtroom-experienced, powerful lawyers are polite to one another, but allows similarly empowered, educated, and experienced lawyers to treat young, typically less educated, almost certainly less experienced in a courtroom, and often visibly racialized and impoverished women with the kind of disrespect and disdain arguably demonstrated in some of the examples given in chapters 2 and 3. There are no reported cases in which the Law Society of Upper Canada has disciplined a defence lawyer for their rude, offensive, and unprofessional communications with a sexual assault complainant. Indeed, there are no reported cases of any Canadian law society having ever disciplined a defence lawyer for engaging in conduct of this nature towards a complainant in a sexual assault proceeding.[87]

Law societies are most certainly accountable for contributing to the culture of the legal profession. They are directly responsible for framing the legal profession's understanding of a lawyer's ethical obligations. The choices that law societies make about what conduct to regulate impact how the profession understands its ethical obligations and ethical limits. Prioritizations of the sort just described express particular values and are sure to have an impact on the culture of the legal profession. Again, law societies are mandated to regulate in the public interest. There is a significant public interest in requiring members of the legal profession to practise sexual assault law in a manner that promotes a fair trial process. Recall that a fair trial is one in which: (i) discriminatory stereotypes are not deployed by legal actors to distort the fact-finding function of the process; and (ii) key participants are not bullied or humiliated into withdrawing from the process.

Justice objectives such as safeguarding the rule of law through the protection of an accused's constitutional rights and advocating for those who face the coercive authority of the state are not only laudatory: they are fundamentally important. Defence lawyers – including, no doubt, all of the lawyers whose cases and public comments are highlighted in this book – do critically important work. They do work that is often undervalued both socially and, as a relative matter, monetarily. The injustice of wrongful convictions and the reality that the criminally accused are often members of severely marginalized communities make the work done by criminal defenders indispensable and admirable. Moreover, we need criminal defence lawyers to believe in the system and their role in it. Without this faith, criminal lawyers might be unwilling to represent those accused of our most heinous, stigmatized offences – sexual offences being chief among them.

However, as a matter of logic, some of the problematic strategies used to attack and discredit sexual assault complainants are, in fact, inconsistent with the profession's dominant self-understanding of this justice project. An examination of the profession's self-understanding of its role in the criminal justice process offers criteria by which to assess the practices of some sexual assault lawyers on their own terms, within the ethical framework criminal defence lawyers themselves have articulated. Criminal lawyers who assert that what motivates them, what justifies the professional actions they take, is a belief in their role in a system that guarantees everyone a fair process and the right to be heard should ensure that they are not pursuing or promoting strategies that, in fact, undermine these values.

Using an overly aggressive or abusive style of cross-examination at the preliminary inquiry, or the prospect of publicly revealing a complainant's sexual past, to intimidate or humiliate a complainant into refusing to proceed is antithetical to a professional identity rooted in a commitment to the rule of law and to preserving human dignity. Such tactics should be distinguished from the legitimate strategy of cross-examining a complainant, in micro-detail, to challenge either reliability or credibility.

Similarly, intentionally attempting to trigger a judge's stereotypical thinking about sexually active women, by bringing an application to introduce evidence of sexual history that one knows is inadmissible, distorts, rather than protects, the trial process. Despite their continued use, reliance on these types of strategies is inconsistent with what most criminal defence lawyers understand to be their justice project.

It is also important to examine the role of other legal professionals in contributing to the inhospitable conditions faced by sexual assault complainants. While there is no question that the tactics used by some defence lawyers cause suffering and distress to sexual assault complainants, criminal defenders are by no means the only members of the legal profession who bear responsibility for this failing of our criminal justice system. In the next chapter I discuss the duties of Crown prosecutors to prepare sexual assault complainants for trial, and to protect them from defence counsel strategies that are arguably discriminatory or abusive. Chapter 5 also examines failures on the part of some Crown attorneys to meet their duty to protect women from the types of 'whack the complainant' practices discussed in chapters 2 and 3. Following this, in chapters 6 and 7, I consider the duties of trial judges to protect complainants and the way in which a lack of basic legal knowledge on the part of trial judges can also contribute to the trauma of the trial for sexual assault complainants.

CHAPTER 5

The Role of the Crown in Sexual Assault Trials

Defence lawyers are, of course, not the only legal professionals involved in the conduct of a sexual assault trial, nor are they the only members of the legal profession to contribute to the way in which sexual assault law is practised and adjudicated. Crown attorneys can and do significantly impact how sexual assault complainants experience the criminal justice process.

Crown attorneys owe a special duty to ensure that the criminal justice process is fair to everyone involved.[1] Indeed, the prosecutor's "primary duty is not to seek to convict but to see that justice is done through a fair trial on the merits."[2] In prosecuting a sexual offence (or any other type of criminal offence), Crown attorneys must ensure, to the best of their abilities, a fair process for the accused, the complainant, and the public.

Ensuring a fair process includes protecting vulnerable witnesses; in this sense, Crown attorneys have a duty. Crown policies in several provinces address the need to accommodate vulnerable witnesses in a manner that facilitates their participation in the process.[3]

Sexual assault complainants are particularly vulnerable witnesses for several reasons, including: the way in which the experiences of sexual violence about which they are testifying are socially understood as deeply personal; the ongoing legacy of a legal response to sexual violence that was explicitly discriminatory; and the fact that in many instances the Crown's case turns almost exclusively on the complainant's testimony (sometimes because of circumstance, sometimes because of inadequate investigation by the police). This means sexual assault complainants are likely to be cross-examined with a vigour that is not always used with respect to other types of witnesses. Ontario's Crown Policy on sexual offences recognizes aspects of this vulnerability: "Sexual offences are unique because they involve violations of sexual integrity and autonomy ... Sensitivity to the perspective of victims, their privacy interests and, in particular, the deeply personal and degrading nature of their victimization, must underscore all aspects of prosecutorial action."[4] The Public Prosecution Service of Nova Scotia's policy on sexual offences also highlights the "heightened sensitivity to the needs and circumstances of the victim" required of Crown attorneys who prosecute sexual offences.[5]

The Crown's duty to ensure a fair process also includes working to eliminate those forms of discrimination that distort the fact-finding process, or prevent equal access to the criminal justice system. As such, while all lawyers have a duty not to discriminate,[6] Crown attorneys have a heightened obligation to oppose the use of, or reliance on, discriminatory stereotypes. This responsibility is explicitly recognized in some provinces. For example, Ontario's Crown Policy Manual stipulates that "Crown counsel, as key participants in the criminal justice system, play an important role in assisting to overcome any forms of discrimination that deny equal access to the criminal justice system. Crown counsel take a leadership role in ensuring that various forms of discrimination ... are not reflected in the criminal justice system."[7]

This aspect of the Crown's duty assumes particular meaning in the context of sexual assault proceedings. The unfortunate reality that gender-based stereotypes continue to inform social and legal thinking about sexual violence presents unique challenges for Crown attorneys when executing their duty to ensure a fair process. Recognizing this challenge, Ontario's Crown Policy Manual section on sexual offences states: "Despite recent advancements, both in the law and in social values, views about the dynamics of sexual offences are still permeated by long-entrenched myths and stereotypes. Crown counsel play an important role in combating the harmful effects that these distortions can have on the pursuit of justice."[8]

To summarize, Crown attorneys have a duty to protect the fairness of the criminal trial process and its participants. The need for protection is heightened for sexual assault complainants, given the vulnerabilities imposed upon them by systemic gender discrimination and the social construction of sexual violence as private and personal. Most obviously, Crown attorneys should ensure that the testimonial aids available to complainants are, in fact, accessed. Testimonial aids include the ability to bring a support person with them to have nearby in the courtroom while they are testifying, and the ability to testify behind a screen or in some instances by closed-circuit television.[9] But there is more. The Crown's duty includes guarding against the types of discrimination that prevent equal access to the justice system and distort the truth-seeking process. In sexual assault cases, protecting the process and complainants requires facilitating the participation of vulnerable witnesses and combatting the ongoing influence of gender-based stereotypes about sexual violence.

A Refusal to Recognize the Crown's Duty to Protect Complainants

Unfortunately, the Crown's duty to protect complainants and combat the harmful effects of rape mythology is not one that all prosecutors recognize as part of their job. For some Crown attorneys, lack of recognition of their role in combatting these discriminatory attitudes may flow from a failure to identify the criminal justice system as a key, institutionalized component of systemic discrimination and a constitutive factor in social conceptions of sexual violence. These comments by a Crown attorney interviewed as part of Rhyannon O'Heron's study of prosecutors in British Columbia capture this highly individualized conception of the criminal law and its impacts:

> [T]he police are the public face of the justice system and it's more important the complainant has a positive experience at this stage. The courtroom process has less of an impact on effecting [sic] reporting rapes and shaping societal beliefs about the criminal justice process for sexual assault victims. Ya, I don't think the courts play much of a role in shaping societal beliefs and perspectives, most people don't go to court, don't read case law, but people interact with police. It's all a very individual process so it may shape an individual but not society or culture.[10]

Others fail to account for this aspect of their role as Crown attorney because they do not perceive the criminal justice process to be infused with problematic attitudes about gender and sexuality. A second Crown attorney interviewed by O'Heron stated:

[L]ow reporting and conviction rates are [not] a reflection of myths in the justice system, they're more a reflection of personal decisions and personalities of the victims and other issues that are more individual in nature ... I don't see crowns supporting rape myths about short skirts or defence counsel doing this probably because judges would shut this down or crown would object for relevancy.[11]

Unfortunately, as the cases examined in chapters 2 and 3 arguably demonstrate, Crown attorneys and trial judges cannot always be relied upon to prevent discriminatory or abusive cross-examinations.

Alternatively, the misperception that rape mythology has been removed from the criminal justice process may reflect a Crown attorney's own stereotypical thinking. Ruthy Lazar's research on marital rape, in which she interviewed defence lawyers and prosecutors in Ontario, suggests that this is the case. For example, some of the prosecutors she interviewed assumed that prior sexual history evidence between the accused and the complainant will almost always be relevant to consent when the parties were involved in an ongoing relationship.[12] Jennifer Temkin's interviews, discussed in chapter 4, revealed similar attitudes among barristers who prosecute sexual offences in the United Kingdom.[13] Likewise, Amanda Konradi's American study of how rape survivors experience the criminal trial process revealed differences between the way prosecutors treated women who had been attacked by a stranger and those who were victimized by a known assailant.[14] Her research indicated that some prosecutors treat the former preferentially, suggesting the ongoing currency of the myth that real rape is perpetrated by strangers.

Another common assertion that may obfuscate the Crown's duty to protect sexual assault complainants is the notion that the prosecutor's 'client' is not the complainant, but rather the Crown in the name of the public. As Alice Woolley aptly states in contradiction: "It is of course true that the prosecutor's client is the Crown not the complainant. But there is a world of difference between saying that someone is not your client, and saying that you owe them no duty."[15] She goes on to argue that a prosecutor has the

same obligations he would have elsewhere not to participate in the wrongful infliction of harm on others. And where preventing the wrongful infliction of harm is not only not inconsistent with his professional duties, *but is in fact required to fulfill those duties*, it makes no sense at all to say that the lawyer has no duty to prevent such harm.[16]

Setting aside the obstacles presented by a refusal or failure on the part of some members of the legal profession to recognize the Crown's duty to protect complainants, what specifically does this duty require of Crown attorneys who prosecute sexual offences? Two components of this duty to protect both the process and its participants, including sexual assault complainants, involve appropriate interventions during the trial and proper witness preparation.

The Parameters of Crown Objections

Testifying as a complainant in a sexual assault trial is bound to be a traumatic experience for most individuals. Some of this harm is unavoidable. The adversarial process, the fundamental importance of protecting the rights of the accused, and the public nature of criminal trials require sexual assault complainants to testify in front of others, and be cross-examined in detail by an adversary, about experiences that they may have tried hard to forget. In the trial transcripts examined, several of the complainants described having attempted to forget about the sexual assault – to not remember – as a coping strategy. The complainant in *R v Khaery*,[17] for example, testified: "I was not prepared for the questions. I didn't think they would affect me emotionally, having to relive that after I had completely let it go from my mind for two years, you know. I did suffer from – you know, like, to get – to not relive that for two years, I did cover it up with a lot of drugs and alcohol so I wouldn't have to think about it."[18]

For some complainants, depending on the timing of the trial, this can mean that they are being cross-examined in detail about an incident that they have spent years trying to forget. Crown Attorney 3 offered these reflections:

No matter what you do, we have a public system, and they have to say what happened to them, in front of other people ... generally speaking sex is more of a private thing ... You know? If your house is broken into you feel violated, in terms of your safety and that kind of thing, but it's just different. So, I think it's traumatic for people for that, that they have to talk about that in public, and the length of time it takes to get through it makes it traumatic ... they can be in a completely different phase of their life by the time they have to talk about it again.

As noted, and as is frequently pointed out by both defence and Crown counsel, some of the harms arising from participation in the criminal trial process are likely unavoidable. That said, some of them are avoidable. To the best of their abilities, Crown prosecutors have a duty to prevent the latter, avoidable harms. To be clear, Crown attorneys must be careful not to interfere with the accused's *Charter* right to full answer and defence, including their right to robust and thorough cross-examination. Crowns who are too interventionist risk admonishment from trial judges for obstructing cross-examination. Strategically, Crowns must be judicious in choosing when to object for fear of inadvertently creating the perception that their witness is in need of greater protection because he or she is frail, unreliable, or unprepared. However, prosecutors are also duty-bound to ensure, to the best of their abilities, that sexual assault complainants are treated fairly. This duty requires that they object to cross-examinations that are abusive, premised on rape myths, or otherwise beyond what is permissible at law.

While the responsibility of Crown attorneys to ensure, as much as possible, a fair process and fair treatment of all participants can require Crown objections in any trial, the particularities of sexual assault create unique facets to this responsibility in sexual assault trials. The Crown's obligation to intervene in the cross-examination of a sexual assault complainant includes two features that are not present to the same degree in other types of proceedings: the need to protect complainants from unnecessarily aggressive or humiliating questioning, and the importance of preventing distortions to the fact-finding function of the trial, rooted in outdated and discriminatory stereotypes about rape.

First, and as noted, the nature of the offence requires sexual assault complainants to be cross-examined about experiences and details that are socially constructed as deeply personal, making the impact of overly aggressive or humiliating questions greater. Second, complainant witnesses in sexual assault proceedings are more likely to face overly aggressive and/or humiliating questions than are witnesses in other types of proceedings, because frequently the Crown's case rests entirely with their testimony. Third, historically, whacking the complainant was the bread and butter of defence counsel. As argued in chapters 2 and 3, the legacy of this practice may continue to inform the approach taken by some defence counsel. Fourth, discriminatory stereotypes continue to play a significant role in legal and social understandings of sexual violence. It is difficult to imagine an area of law in which both factual findings and legal reasoning are more at risk of influence by stereotypical assumptions about how people behave. Together these four factors inform the nature of the Crown's responsibility to raise objections when confronted with defence counsel tactics that threaten the fairness of the process or the fair treatment of its participants.

Some prosecutors strike the correct balance, diligently meeting their responsibility to protect the complainant and the process without unduly interfering with the accused's right to full answer and defence. However, unfortunately, Crown attorneys cannot always be relied upon to object to problematic lines of questioning or submissions. For example, not all Crown attorneys are conscientious about objecting when defence counsel attempt to introduce evidence of a complainant's other sexual activity without complying with Canada's rape shield regime. Ruthy Lazar's research on marital rape examines this failure on the part of some Crowns.[19] In discussing the effectiveness of section 276, one of the prosecutors Lazar interviewed stated, "On paper it looks really good but in reality most Crowns don't make themselves even aware of these cases, they don't even fight that issue."[20] Another of her subjects noted, "What happens is that we, first of all as Crowns we don't take the provision seriously enough."[21]

In several of the cases discussed in chapter 2, defence lawyers were permitted, without objection from the Crown, to cross-examine the complainants on sexual history evidence that should have been subject to a section 276 application. Recall that in *B(IE)* the complainant was questioned, without any objection by Crown attorney Robert Morrison, as to whether she had had any sexual contact with other individuals earlier in the evening on the date of the incident (and whether she had told her friends she was going to "get fucked" that night).[22] This occurred without any mention of section 276 or 277 of the *Criminal Code* by the Crown. The result is that the complainant in *B(IE)* was asked a series of questions that were arguably irrelevant, insulting, and unlawful.

The Crown in *Wright* similarly failed to object to questions from defence counsel, such as whether the complainant's nickname was "Perky Tits," whether she had done a strip tease earlier in the evening, and whether she had a habit of dancing topless at parties.[23] She should not have been made to answer these questions. Crown attorney Renee Lagimodiere should have objected on the basis that the defence had not brought an application pursuant to section 276 to determine the admissibility of this evidence. As in *B(IE)*, irrelevant and demeaning questions of this nature would have been properly excluded. Instead, the complainant was denied the protections of sections 276 and 277 of the *Criminal Code*.

In *R v Al-Rawi*, defence counsel introduced evidence that the complainant had flirted with men at the bar and danced provocatively with her best friend's boyfriend without bringing a section 276 application and without any objection from Crown attorney Ron Lacey.[24]

Attempts by defence counsel to introduce prior sexual history evidence without bringing an application pursuant to section 276.1 raise questions regarding a defence lawyer's ethical obligations to cross-examine in good faith and within the bounds of law.[25] However, responsibility for the failure of rape shield law reforms to eliminate stereotype-infused legal reasoning about a woman's sexual history and to prevent unnecessary attacks on the dignity and privacy of complainants lies not only with the practices of some defence lawyers, but with those of some Crown attorneys and trial judges as well.

Crown attorneys owe an obligation to complainants to resist the introduction of irrelevant evidence of their other sexual activity and to object to highly tenuous or suspect arguments asserting the relevance of such evidence. Some prosecutors meet this duty diligently. Consider this example of Crown attorney Jennifer Lofft's approach in *R v Ururyar*. Defence counsel in *Ururyar* brought a section 276 application to have evidence of the accused and complainant's prior sexual activities together introduced. Her submissions in support of the application failed to offer any clear indication as to why this evidence was relevant. This was Lofft's response:

> It's not enough to say something's relevant ... you can't just draw out your full answer and defence blanket and wrap that cloak around everything there is ... It has to be relevant to a particular

issue at the trial ... My friend says they don't want to use the evidence to show that she's less capable of belief or that she's likely to have consented on this time ... But what she didn't say was why they wanted to use it at all. What other – like, how is it relevant? How is it possibly relevant?[26]

Defence counsel in *Ururyar* suggested that because the complainant had successfully requested that the publication ban be lifted and had been publicly open about her sexual assault, the protections intended by section 276 were less relevant in this case. She argued: "it takes away a little bit of the argument in terms of her privacy interest in prior sexual conduct with Mr. Ururyar because of the fact she's gone out and spoken to the media about her case,"[27] and "[t]his is a, as I mentioned, a very different case than most sexual assault cases ... where the complainant says I don't want a publication ban, I want my name out there and has been all over the media because she does not want to hide her name."[28] In response, Lofft argued: "And that my friend puts a great deal of emphasis on the fact Ms. Gray has spoken about her ordeal, does that mean that she must lay bare her entire history? Why on earth does that make it more okay for her to have her privacy intruded upon than someone else?"[29] Defence counsel's application to admit evidence of the complainant's other sexual activity with the accused was dismissed.[30] Lofft also objected to several other questions asked of the complainant by defence counsel on the basis that they were irrelevant,[31] prohibited by the rape shield provisions,[32] unfair,[33] or disrespectful in some other regard.[34]

The Crown attorney in *R v Wagar*, Hyatt Mograbee, also objected when defence counsel attempted to introduce evidence that is subject to section 276 – questions about whether the complainant had flirted with anyone else that evening.[35] When defence counsel persisted with this line of questioning, Mograbee again raised section 276, requesting that the complainant be excused so that she could make submissions on the applicability of the rape shield provisions.[36] Once the complainant was excluded, she made every effort to explain to the trial judge why defence counsel's questions were improper:

THE COURT: Well, surely we're – we're not talking about dangerous thinking, Ms. Mograbee. We're talking about the law.

MS. MOGRABEE: Yeah. Well, the law – if you look at the –

THE COURT: The law doesn't stop people thinking.

MS. MOGRABEE: Well, the law does talk about – that particular section talks about, you know, a way of thinking that would lead a co – that would re – that would essentially cause one to conclude that a person was more likely or less likely to consent to activity.

...

THE COURT: Yeah. But it also matters whether she was – whether she was physically able to deal with it. All sorts of circumstances surround the – surround the issue.

MS. MOGRABEE: The –

THE COURT: Were there people close by that she could call on for help, did she have a telephone, all those things are permissible. And one of them would be, presumably, in the ordinary course, absent 276 and what you call antiquated thinking or con – con – contemporary thinking, would be is she morally, and by [']morally', I don't mean in terms of ethic morally but in terms of having the inner strength, or physically strong enough to rebuff men if she feels like it.

MS. MOGRABEE: I still maintain my objection, Sir. It's not relevant what she did with other men. It's relevant what she did with this accused. And this line of questioning, in my respectful submission, does fall under 276. My other objection is that it's not relevant.[37]

Not dissuaded by what might be characterized as Judge Camp's apparent disdain for section 276 of the *Criminal Code*,[38] Mograbee again objected when defence counsel made yet another attempt to introduce evidence of the complainant's sexual activity with others without bringing a section 276 application.[39]

Similarly, the Crown attorney in *R v JK*, Glynne Faulkner, immediately shut down defence counsel's improper attempt to introduce evidence of the complainant's sexual history:

Q. [DEFENCE] So if I put it to you that either during that intervening time period or some time later that evening you met with someone else and had intercourse with them –

MS. FAULKNER: I'm going to object to that because there has been no Section 276 Application made here. Any evidence of other sexual activity aside from that which comprises the alleged offence is inadmissible. She cannot be asked any questions about sexual activity other than with [JK] on ... March 14th, 2011, which became the subject matter of these charges. It's inadmissible.

THE COURT: Would you like to comment on that Section of the Code?

MR. O'BRIAN: Yes, Justice, I guess our position is that it speaks to potential defence theory and it doesn't actually relate to past sexual conduct for the purpose of either, you know – I wonder if I could have a moment to review that particular section, Justice.

MS. FAULKNER: This would have had to have been put to you. I need notice, you need an Application.

MR. O'BRIAN: I understand that.

MS. FAULKNER: To decide if any questions can be asked, any at all, even if they don't go to her believability or that, you know, she's likely to have fabricated this event. There has to be a hearing on that to ask her anything.

...

THE COURT: ... The Code requires a procedure to be followed before those questions can be asked.

MR. O'BRIAN: I'm aware of the procedure, Justice. This was not a question I anticipated on asking. I apologize.

THE COURT: Thank-you very much.

MR. O'BRIAN: ... Those are all the questions I have for you, ——. Thank-you.[40]

It is true that O'Brian's first question may have triggered discriminatory stereotypes about supposedly unchaste women before the Crown had an opportunity to object. Nevertheless, the difference between what occurred in *B(IE)*, *Wright*, and *Al-Rawi*, and what occurred in *Ururyar*, *Wagar*, and *JK* is striking.

Unfortunately, there continues to be a good deal of confusion and misunderstanding among some trial judges regarding the interpretation and application of section 276.[41] As demonstrated in *B(IE)*, *Wright*, and *Al-Rawi*, absent an objection by the Crown, not all trial judges will intervene when defence counsel attempt to introduce evidence that should be scrutinized and potentially excluded under section 276. That said, Crown attorneys who do object to the admission of evidence of the complainant's other sexual activities without a proper section 276 application by the defence are likely to have these objections upheld, or at least seriously considered.[42] For instance, in *R v Wagar*,[43] despite his seeming disdain for Canada's rape shield regime,[44] Judge Camp nevertheless upheld Mograbee's objection to admitting evidence of sexual activity that the complainant may have had with other individuals that evening following the alleged sexual assault.[45]

In addition to their duty to object when defence counsel attempts to introduce prior sexual history evidence that has not been admitted following a section 276.1 application, Crown attorneys should also be careful not to put prior sexual history at issue by eliciting irrelevant testimony from the complainant that can then be challenged on cross-examination (without triggering section 276). For example, the Crown in *R v Schmaltz*[46] (Andrea Dolan) asked the complainant whether there had been any flirting going on earlier in the evening on the date of the alleged assault.[47] The complainant's negative response to this question opened the door for defence counsel to then cross-examine her about flirting with the accused.[48] Rather than protecting the complainant from irrelevant evidence of prior sexual activity, the Crown's question resulted in the complainant having to answer a series of questions about flirting from the defence. Whether she was flirting with the accused hours before he allegedly penetrated her with his fingers while she was asleep[49] was irrelevant and the defence would presumably not have been permitted to cross-examine her about this but for the Crown's question on the issue. (Dolan also led evidence about the cut and colour of the complainant's underwear and whether she was wearing a bra, without any apparent explanation as to the relevance of these facts.)

The Crown's responsibility to protect complainants by objecting to the admission of evidence that is rooted in stereotypes about sexual violence extends beyond objecting to cross-examinations that do not comply with section 276 of the *Criminal Code*. Crown attorneys should contest any questioning that is clearly reliant on rape mythology for its probative value, or that is unnecessarily harassing, sarcastic, or contemptuous. Requiring defence counsel to justify, and the trial judge to rule on, a line of questioning that is facially discriminatory or abusive does not place an unjust burden on the accused. The criminally accused do not have a constitutional right to be defended by any means possible. They do not, for example, have a right to invoke discriminatory stereotypes in their defence.[50] Nor do they have a right to humiliate, badger, or abuse complainants.[51] Crown attorneys have a duty to object to attempts by the defence to pursue such tactics. Unfortunately, several of the trial transcripts considered in chapters 2 and 3 contain examples of questions by defence counsel that I would argue should have been, but were not, objected to by the Crown.

Defence counsel's cross-examination in *R v Finney*,[52] discussed in chapter 2, provides an example. The Crown in *Finney*, Ronald Davidson, did not object when defence counsel cross-examined the complainant repeatedly about her failure to resist forced oral penetration – to bite the accused's penis.[53] Davidson also allowed defence counsel to question her at length about her failure to raise a 'hue and cry' – to scream, vomit, or gag loud enough for his friends "just down the hall" to hear what was occurring.[54] Nor was there an objection when defence counsel suggested to the complainant that it was not possible to force a woman to perform a "blow job" – "one would think that would be consensual."[55]

Similarly, the Crown in *Schmaltz* remained silent when defence counsel put irrelevant, unfounded, and offensive questions to the complainant about the degree of moisture in her vagina during and following the alleged offence, repeatedly insisting that her "vagina was wet because it was stimulated."[56]

The transcripts also reveal many examples of Crown attorneys protecting, to the best of their abilities, both the process and its participants. A clear illustration of this is found in Mograbee's conduct of the case in *Wagar*. In addition to objections based on the rape shield provisions, Mograbee intervened to request that defence counsel allow time for the complainant to properly answer his questions before moving on[57] and to highlight defence counsel's repetitive questioning of the complainant.[58] She also objected to defence counsel's unnecessary editorializing during cross-examination:

> [DEFENCE] Q. Well, what I'm a little surprised about is this, Ms. ——, you have the – you have the – the willpower to look down and see ——.
>
> MS. MOGRABEE: I'm just going to object for a moment. And I – and I'm going to say this now because it's happened a few times. When my friend ... prefaces a question with, I'm surprised, that's not appropriate. Those are comments that counsel's making. It is

permissible for him, of course, to ask the question. He can suggest
to her, to advance his client's interest, the questions that are necessary. I'm not trying to get in the way of that, but those comments
are not acceptable. And I'm going to ask, Sir, that you direct my
friend to refrain from saying those kinds of things before he asks a
question. His opinion is not relevant in this proceeding; it's what
the evidence is. So I'm going to ask, please, that there be a direction
to that end.[59]

She was vigilant in attempting to protect the complainant from irrelevant defence questions seeking her general understanding about how
men and women respond to sexual jealousy:

> [DEFENCE] Q. ... Would you agree with me that if a man was
> interested in a – sorry, if a man was interested in a woman, the
> man thought maybe they were going to have a relationship, but at
> some point this woman turned – you know, said no to this person,
> similar to what you did with [the accused's brother] –
> A. Yeah.
> ...
> MS. MOGRABEE: I – I just find this line of questioning to be odd,
> to say the least. I know where my friend is going with this. I appre-
> ciate that. But I don't think that the line of questioning is either
> clear or relevant to what happened between her and this accused.
> ...
> MS. MOGRABEE: ... What I'm saying is the evidence relating to
> that needs to be more pointed. I don't think it's fair to – for –
> for my friend to ask questions about generally the way men and
> women would respond. I think he can ask particular questions
> about what was happening in that bathroom. And that's simply my
> objection, is that he needs to ask questions about that, what she
> saw, she heard, what he saw – what she, you know, saw and noticed
> around her. Those are all fair questions. But beyond that, I don't
> think those are fair – fair questions to ask.[60]

Throughout the proceeding, and in her closing submissions, the
Crown in *Wagar* persevered in her attempts to explain to the trial judge

the law of sexual assault, including the rape shield provisions, the legal definition of consent, the rules limiting the inferences to be drawn from delayed disclosure, and the requirement that the accused take reasonable steps to ascertain consent.[61] Her conduct of the case was exemplary. Had *Wagar* been presided over by a judge with knowledge of the law of sexual assault, or an awareness of the role that discriminatory stereotypes can play in sexual assault trials, it seems likely that the Crown's commendable efforts to protect the fairness of the process and fairer treatment of the complainant would have been more successful.

One further point concerning the Crown's role in *Wagar* should be noted. Were it not for the Crown's decision to appeal this unreported decision by Judge Camp, and to highlight for the Court of Appeal in its factum the nature of Judge Camp's errors, it is highly unlikely that his stereotype-infused statements and disgraceful treatment of the complainant in *Wagar* (which are discussed in chapter 7) would have come to light. In order to meet its duties to protect both complainants and the process, it is critical that the Crown pursue appeals and make the kinds of arguments that were advanced by appellate Crown counsel Jolaine Antonio in *Wagar*. As Lucinda Vandervort observes, "Over time and in the aggregate, failure to appeal what are arguably erroneous and regressive interpretations of the sexual assault laws allows those laws to operate differently ... than current legal standards prescribe."[62]

Wagar was tried (and acquitted) a second time.[63] Like Mograbee, the Crown attorney during his second trial (Janice Walsh) also objected successfully numerous times during cross-examination to require that the complainant be permitted to finish her answers, to prevent defence counsel from including his own commentary in his questions, to stop repetitive questioning, and to otherwise shield the complainant from questions that were irrelevant or unfair.[64] Consider the following excerpt:

> MR. FLYNN: Do you consider yourself a good person, a generous person?
> MS. WALSH: Again, objection, Your Honour.
> MR. FLYNN: I don't think – okay.
> MS. WALSH: Do you consider yourself a good person?
> MR. FLYNN: A generous person.
> THE COURT: Well, where are you going?[65]

Performance of the Crown's duty to protect the complainant from cross-examination that is unnecessarily sarcastic or arguably unfair was also exemplified in *R v G(PG)*, discussed in chapter 2.[66] Recall that both the trial judge and appellate court in *G(PG)* found that defence counsel's cross-examination of the complainant included sarcasm and unnecessary editorial critiques.[67] After asking her if she had tried to commit suicide, how many times she had tried, when these attempts occurred, and what types of attempts she had made (which were considered proper questions by both the trial and appellate judges),[68] defence counsel asked for more details on exactly how she had tried to hang herself.[69] Crown attorney Kelli Frew successfully objected on the basis that it was unfair to require the complainant to provide such details:

> Q. [DEFENCE] And, and when you say you tried to hang yourself, can you give us a little more detail?
> MS. FREW: Your Honour, I mean for the purpose for which – of why he wanted to ask these questions, I think asking the bare bones is enough. I don't think it's fair to make her explain the steps she took in attempting to do what she's indicated she did.
> MR. BAYLISS: Well, I don't, I don't know why it's unfair. I'm not sure how to respond to that.
> THE COURT: Well, I think it's a very sensitive issue and I don't think she needs to go into the details of the manner of the attempts.[70]

Frew also objected successfully when defence counsel's cross-examination of the complainant became condescending:

> Q. [DEFENCE] So it was all very convenient, wasn't it?
> MS. FREW: Your Honour, I don't know how she is supposed to answer that. First of all, the tone is getting really condescending towards her. And I mean that's not even really a question.[71]

At a later point in the cross-examination she objected on the basis that defence counsel was being dismissive of the complainant's answers.[72] Later still she objected as follows:

> MS. FREW: Your Honour, I can understand her perfectly. But I just – I'm wondering when I should stand up and say something because I feel counsel's tone and the way he's phrasing questions is

borderline abusive to this witness, and I just – I want him to show her the respect that everyone deserves in this courtroom.[73]

Like the Crown's conduct of the case in both *Wagar* trials, in *G(PG)* Crown counsel's performance of her duty to protect, to the best of her abilities, both the parties and the process was exemplary.

Crown attorneys who object to problematic questioning by defence counsel help to facilitate the trial judge's responsibility to protect the complainant. Conversely, prosecutors who fail to object in these types of circumstances shift the onus to intervene entirely onto the trial judge. It is perhaps not surprising that in *Finney* and *Schmaltz*, in which Crown attorneys failed to object when I would argue they should have, convictions at trial were appealed, in part, on the basis that the trial judge's interventions to protect the complainant created a reasonable apprehension of bias.[74] Trial judges are less susceptible to allegations of bias or impermissible interference for upholding a Crown objection than they are when they, of their own volition, intervene in a cross-examination in order to protect a complainant.[75] The trial judge's duty to intervene will be discussed further in chapter 6.

Preparing Complainants for Trial[76]

All trial participants should be prepared. As many lawyers will say, one of the most critical aspects of performing as an advocate is preparation. This includes preparing one's witnesses. As Alice Woolley notes, a "lawyer acts both negligently and incompetently if she fails to prepare witnesses for the rigours of an adversarial proceeding."[77] Sexual assault complainants, because they bear a unique vulnerability, require particular types of preparation. To be clear, this vulnerability flows not from some inherent susceptibility shared by those who experience sexual violence, but as a consequence of societal inequalities based on gender, race, disability, and class that are reiterated in the way law responds to violence against women. As Elizabeth Sheehy writes, "'Vulnerability' here is created by the nature of the offence and its legal treatment: in other words, offences of male violence against women and children are premised upon their inequality, which is in turn exacerbated by the legal processing, including the 'rules' or lack thereof with respect to the examination of witnesses."[78]

Unfortunately, sexual assault complainants are often woefully unprepared for the criminal trial process.[79] The specialized language used, the roles of particular parties, the courtroom procedures, and the trial process more generally will be unfamiliar to many sexual assault complainants. Consider, for example, the complainant in *Finney*. Her lack of familiarity with the process is evident from the transcript:

> [CROWN] Q. Okay. And do you recall whether he had a heart attack during a preliminary inquiry in this matter?
> [COMPLAINANT] A. I'm not sure what a – a preliminary inquiry is, but I was in this situation while he had his second heart attack, yes.
> Q. Oh, so you were in a situation where you were giving evidence in a court?[80]

At trial she was cross-examined at length about details from her testimony years earlier at the preliminary inquiry. Ultimately, the complainant acknowledged that she had never actually read the transcript of her preliminary inquiry testimony.[81]

Many complainants come to court unrepresented, without having completed even basic preparation such as a review of their statement to the police or their testimony at a preliminary inquiry. Even when Crown counsel has established a rapport with the complainant, the obstacles to properly preparing sexual assault complainants are substantial. Some complainants understandably do not want to revisit the sexual assault, let alone contemplate and discuss it in detail over and over again. As noted, avoidance is a common response to traumatic experiences. For some complainants, testifying about their experience(s) of sexual violation will run counter to the coping mechanisms they have developed to survive the experience. This was clearly the case for the complainant in *Khaery*. In this excerpt from the cross-examination in *Khaery*, defence counsel questioned her on details from her police statement:

> Q. MR. RAUF: – have you told us everything about the sexual activity that took place on that occasion?
> A. Yes. That I can recall.
> Q. Did you – you watched your videotape?
> A. A portion of it.

Q. Well, you spent a good portion of the morning watching your videotape statement.

A. I – no. I spent about –

...

A. – five –

Q. Sorry. Let's –

A. – minutes watching it.

Q. Let – you spent a good portion of the morning watching your videotape; is that right?

A. No.

Q. Did you say anything in your evidence in chief today about digital penetration?

A. Digital?

Q. Yes. That is, with fingers.

A. No.

Q. Okay. And did that happen?

A. I can't recall.

Q. That's what you told the nurse?

A. I – it could have happened. I don't – I can't recall at this point.

Q. Did you say anything in your videotape, the parts you watched, about digital penetration?

A. I didn't watch – like, I didn't watch up until – I watched about five minutes of it.

Q. You were given an opportunity to watch the videotape?

A. Yes.

Q. But you only watched five minutes of it?

A. Yes.

Q. Even though court didn't start until 11:30 or so?

A. I didn't want to watch it due to emotional – I couldn't watch it. I – it was too – I was – it was depressing.[82]

The reality that sexual assault complainants may have tried hard to forget, or at least not think about, the very details about which they will be required to testify makes preparation more challenging. It also makes it more important.

The likelihood that most complainants will have very little knowledge of, or experience with, courts and legal processes also informs the nature of the Crown's duty to prepare. Complainants, and other witnesses, often participate in the trial process without familiarity with the setting, the rigid procedural requirements, or the technical language used by those 'inside the institution.'[83] Consider these comments from one of the interview subjects in Cheryl Regehr's study of the treatment of victims of sexual violence in the Canadian justice system: "they used all these fancy ... I was just there listening to mumbo jumbo ... it made no sense to me."[84] It is true that the *Criminal Code* includes several witness protections for sexual assault complainants, such as the ability to testify behind a screen or with a support person in close proximity.[85] Unfortunately, despite the availability of these testimonial aids, the courtroom atmosphere remains intimidating and extremely stressful for many sexual assault complainants.[86] One advocate interviewed as part of a 2011 study of rape crisis workers described sexual assault survivors' experiences with the criminal justice system in the following way: "The whole process is so intimidating. There are people in uniforms. The victim is always put in a position where others are dominating. They [victims] sit lower. People use language they can't understand. [There are] more males than females. Often there are guns. There are many ways that it's very intimidating for people whether they are male or female."[87]

Other studies have revealed similar observations. Cheryl Regehr et al.'s 2008 study, for example, concluded that "[o]verall, the court process was viewed by participants as a foreign and intimidating process ... The language and customs of the court felt exclusionary to many participants."[88] In a 2014 study commissioned by Department of Justice Canada, in which 114 sexual assault survivors were interviewed, two of the most common recommendations offered by participants concerning how to improve the criminal justice process involved making survivors feel more safe and comfortable and providing them with greater education on the process.[89]

As Woolley notes, one of the ways in which Crown attorneys should protect complainants from the wrongful infliction of harm is through witness preparation.[90] For example, even something as basic as familiarizing complainants with the rituals of the trial is important. Rituals are a part of the trial process.[91] Indeed, trials are steeped in ritual.[92] The rituals of the trial involve acts and procedures exercised in accordance with prescribed rules or customs regarding attire, physical setting, manner of address, mode of communication, stylized language, and observance of what might be described as micro-ceremonies, such as swearing an oath or rising from one's seat when an adjudicator enters the room. A sexual assault complainant's capacity to be believed in court, to share in the production of meaning about an instance of what she alleges was unwanted sexual contact, requires her to play a part in certain rituals of the trial. Many of these rituals are hierarchical, positioning legal professionals at the top and requiring complainants to perform subordinate roles that mirror the gender-, race-, and socio-economic status–based societal hierarchies in which the problem of sexual violence is rooted.

Unfamiliarity with the trial process and its rituals may heighten the traumatic effect of the process on the complainant. Trial rituals, given their hierarchical nature and unfamiliarity, can be particularly damaging for sexual assault complainants.[93] Lack of familiarity with a particular ritual strengthens the impact it may have – it makes individuals more susceptible "to being impressed by the ritual at a basic level of identity."[94] The unfamiliarity of time and space that occurs during a lay participant's performance of their role – the removal of one's ordinary social anchors – makes some trial participants more vulnerable to this effect. In other words, the performance of ritual causes individuals to identify with their assigned roles.[95] In this sense, the rituals of the trial can be identity-forming for trial participants.

For sexual assault complainants, the impact of performing these trial rituals may be particularly dangerous. To some extent, it may be dangerous because many of the rituals of the trial, from how participants are dressed to how they are addressed, articulate hierarchy. Two of the most explicit social dominations articulated through the rituals of the sexual assault trial are class- and gender-based hierarchies. As explained in chapter 1, many women who are sexually assaulted report feelings of shame, humiliation, and powerlessness.[96] For some survivors of sexual violence, the performance of rituals in which they occupy subordinate roles may reinforce the feelings of self-blame, shame, and powerlessness experienced as a result of the sexual assault. Better preparation would not modify or eliminate problematic trial rituals, but it would make them more familiar, which could help to ensure that the performance of these rituals by sexual assault complainants is less constitutive of their sense of self or 'identity as a complainant.'

Sexual assault complainants, Konradi writes, "can and do get better at being witnesses" and their self-perceptions of improvement in this regard are "coupled with greater confidence in fulfilling the witness role."[97]

Simply put, proper preparation reduces the traumatic impact of testifying. Lack of familiarity with the process, or lack of knowledge of the questions to be posed, reduces self-confidence and increases feelings of gendered (and class- and race-based) powerlessness, and their corresponding shaming effect.

The failure to prepare sexual assault complainants also has the potential to distort the trial process. While the Crown's objective is not to secure a conviction, prosecutors are expected to vigorously pursue a legitimate result in the prosecution of an offence.[98] Given the adversarial nature of our system, they are expected to act as strong and effective advocates for the prosecution.[99] Among other things, to do so requires witness preparation. As Alice Woolley notes: "No competent advocate presents a case at trial with witnesses unprepared for the rigours of cross-examination. No ethical advocate coaches witnesses, but no competent advocate fails to prepare them."[100] The Crown is expected to act as a strong and effective advocate within the context of our adversarial system.[101] As Crown Attorney 5 noted during our interview: "it is ridiculous to suggest that Crowns shouldn't prepare their witnesses. A Crown who goes to trial without having done so isn't doing his or her job."

Indeed, competent advocacy requires the preparation of all witnesses. However, the need to prepare sexual assault complainants to testify, and to withstand the rigours of cross-examination, is even greater given the type of evidence they will be expected to provide, combined with the aversion to remembering and the impact that trauma can have on memory. Human memory at the best of times is fragmented and imperfect.[102] Researchers have demonstrated that during experiences of intense stress or fear, our executive functioning – the part of the brain responsible for focusing our attention and rational thought – is impaired.[103] As a result, "we are less able to willfully control what we pay attention to, less able to make sense of what we are experiencing, and therefore less able to recall our experience in an orderly way."[104] Once the brain's "fear circuitry" kicks in, attention to what is occurring becomes even less coherent, further fragmenting the memories that are formed.[105] Fear also impairs the brain's ability to store memories of the peripheral details, such as the layout of the room or the sequencing of events surrounding a traumatic experience.[106] The combination of this phenomenon (the impact of trauma on memory formation) with the predominant method by which defence lawyers challenge the credibility of sexual assault complainants can be profoundly disabling. The job of the defence lawyer is to demonstrate inconsistencies in the complainant's account of what occurred. This involves cross-examining complainants in infinitesimal detail regarding the incident, and questioning any inconsistencies about these details in a complainant's statements to police, nurses, doctors, counsellors, friends and family, and judges at the preliminary inquiry. Defence lawyers have a duty to perform this type of detailed cross-examination. While, as Alice Woolley explains, the frailty of human memory means Crown attorneys must be vigilant in ensuring that witness preparation does not become witness coaching,[107] it also means that proper preparation is critical. An unprepared complainant is a sitting duck.

Despite the vulnerability of sexual assault complainants, some criminal lawyers argue that Crown attorneys should not prepare or interview complainants because of the risk that they will coach their testimony or otherwise improperly influence the proceeding. In an article posted on his firm's website, defence lawyer Sean Robichaud discusses Crown preparation of complainants and the dangers of Crown interference and undue influence over the proceeding.[108] He speaks favourably of Crowns limiting their pre-trial engagement with the complainant, indicating that some Crowns will meet with the complainant in advance "out of respect and courtesy," and in order "to introduce themselves and ask basic questions."[109]

The issue of witness coaching is an important one to consider. Crowns must remain acutely conscious of this risk.[110] However, there are factors that assist Crown attorneys in this regard. First, compliance with properly drafted Crown policy manuals, which include mechanisms to encourage Crown vigilance in this regard, are of assistance. Crown policies stipulate that prosecutors are precluded from interviewing complainants alone. Nova Scotia's *Practice Note* on interviewing witnesses, for example, recommends that Crown counsel have a police officer or other appropriate third-party observer, such as another Crown attorney, present when interviewing a sexual assault complainant.[111] The purpose of requiring an observer is to preclude any allegation that a Crown prosecutor has improperly influenced the witness.

Second, prosecutors are barred from conducting investigative interviews.[112] Crown attorneys are expected to observe the separation in our system between the police investigative function and the Crown prosecutorial function.[113]

Third, Crown attorneys and the drafters of Crown policy manuals have the benefit of guidance from recommendations such as those made by the Kaufman commission into the wrongful conviction of Guy Paul Morin.[114] The Kaufman Report offers direction for prosecutors on how to prepare Crown witnesses without contaminating them as witnesses. It is true that the Crown must vigilantly maintain its objectivity.[115] It is not true that this is incompatible with careful witness preparation.

Finally, there is no reason to assume that Crown prosecutors are more at risk of dishonouring their ethical obligation not to coach witnesses than are defence lawyers. It is true that Crown attorneys, given their role in the state's criminal trial process, must be particularly careful not to coach witnesses. However, that they bear a heightened obligation to ensure that preparation does not become coaching does not suggest that they are less capable of maintaining this distinction. Moreover, and as Crown Attorney 5 stated in his interview, "it is actually much easier to coach an accused, as usually there is no other statement to test their credibility." Indeed, if we can trust defence lawyers to prepare their clients for the stand but not to coach them, why would we not similarly trust Crown counsel? For example, given the legal definition of consent to sexual touching, it is hard to imagine a more delicate and nuanced distinction than that between *preparing* one's client to offer evidence of a mistaken belief that the complainant communicated a willingness to participate through words or actions and *coaching* one's client to offer such evidence. Yet, we assume that defence lawyers can and will comply with the ethical obligation to maintain this distinction.

To suggest that the Crown's responsibility to interact with sexual assault complainants prior to trial amounts to little more than the courtesy of introducing oneself and asking some basic questions, if that is what Robichaud was suggesting, underestimates the need for, and duty of, prosecutors to engage with, and prepare, complainants. Certainly Crown policy manuals in provinces such as Ontario and Nova Scotia suggest more is expected of Crown attorneys in their pre-trial role. Ontario's Crown policy manual, for example, stipulates: "The administration of justice is best served by a trial process that strives to ensure that witnesses provide complete, honest and independent evidence. Properly conducted witness interviews can contribute significantly to that goal. While it is impossible to interview all witnesses in all cases, the effective prosecution of serious or sensitive cases often requires Crown counsel to interview witnesses."[116]

Nova Scotia's policy on interviewing witnesses opens by stating that "proper preparation for trial often requires that victims and other important witnesses be interviewed by the prosecutor. Indeed, establishing an appropriate rapport with vulnerable or sensitive witnesses may be essential to eliciting the information necessary to support a charge."[117] Nova Scotia's *Practice Note* on the prosecution of sexual offences in particular states that in sexual assault cases prosecutors *should* prepare complainants: "Prior to the commencement of the trial, or preliminary inquiry, the prosecutor should interview the victim in preparation for giving testimony and plan the presentation of evidence with a view to minimizing the stress and trauma on victims, and assisting in an accurate and complete presentation of the facts."[118]

What specifically can and should Crown attorneys do to prepare sexual assault complainants for trial? Proper preparation of complainants includes familiarizing them with the courtroom setting, the rituals, procedures, and micro-ceremonies that will occur, the specialized language that will be used, and the roles of the different legal actors participating in the process. This may involve providing them with the opportunity to visit the courtroom in which they are to testify. Preparation includes providing assistance to ensure that complainants have properly reviewed their statements to the police and any testimony given in the preliminary inquiry.[119] Appropriate supports may include offering complainants a suitable physical space for reviewing these materials, the ability to review them at home, and a follow-up meeting with the Crown attorney to ensure that their previous statements and testimony have actually been reviewed. Certainly these supports include explaining to complainants the use to which their prior statements will be put by the defence. Proper preparation also includes reviewing with them the difference between direct and cross-examination, guidance on how to be an effective witness, and a considered and thorough review of the questions (and the strategies motivating the questions) that they are likely to face on cross-examination. In some cases, proper preparation may include adjusting complainants' expectations about the process and what it is likely to achieve, and not achieve, for them.

The most detailed (publicly available) directions to Crown attorneys in Canada on the preparation of sexual assault complainants are those developed by the Public Prosecution Service of Nova Scotia. As previously noted, Nova Scotia's *Practice Note on Sexual Offences*, in fact, directs prosecutors to prepare sexual assault complainants by inter- viewing them and planning the presentation of evidence.[120]

The Nova Scotia policy advises that several interviews may be required. The policy helpfully includes a "First Interview – Checklist" and a "Second Interview – Checklist" to guide prosecutors on the con- tent of these meetings. [121] The "First Interview – Checklist" asks Crown attorneys to "explain the court process ... the disclosure process ... the importance of telling the whole truth ... day of trial expectations," and the procedures for applications to produce third-party records or prior sexual history.[122] It also directs prosecutors "to provide a copy of [the complainant's] statement to be reviewed for the next meeting." In addi- tion, the checklist recommends discussing with the complainant "why a statement is taken and what use can be made of it in court."[123]

The "Second Interview – Checklist" indicates that prosecutors should: determine whether the complainant has read their statement; discuss court procedure, appropriate demeanour, and testimonial fears; and pro- vide 'good witness' advice such as listening to the question and answering what is asked. The "Second Interview – Checklist" also advises Crown counsel to emphasize the "importance of telling the whole truth and [the] necessity of being explicit/graphic."[124] It suggests prosecutors review the questions the Crown intends to ask, and explain to the complainant the difference between leading and non-leading questions, the Crown's role regarding objections, and the role of defence counsel. It advises prosecutors to review lines of questioning that will inevitably arise in cross-examination and to provide complainants with a "heads-up" regarding inconsistencies in their evidence.[125] (It is important to note that there is a distinction between highlighting inconsistencies and advising complainants of errors in their evidence. The former is acceptable while the latter is not.[126])

While the degree to which Nova Scotia's policy on sexual offences is applied – including reliance on the checklists – is unclear, the content of the policy is thoughtful and comprehensive. Currently Nova Scotia, Ontario, and British Columbia are the only provinces that have publicly available Crown counsel policies that specifically address the prosecution of sexual offences.[127] Common features of the policies in Nova Scotia, Ontario, and British Columbia include proactively establishing and maintaining communication with the complainant, dealing expeditiously with sexual offences by giving these cases priority in scheduling, and ensuring, whenever feasible, that the same Crown attorney handles a case throughout the process by assigning carriage of the file at an early stage in the proceedings.[128] The latter aspect of these policies is aimed at limiting the number of individuals to whom the complainant must recount the details of the alleged offence and form a connection.

The policies in British Columbia and Nova Scotia also stipulate that, whenever possible, sexual assault cases should be assigned to Crown counsel who have specialized training (in British Columbia),[129] or appropriate trial experience (in Nova Scotia).[130] Ontario's 2015 strategy on sexual violence provides for an "enhanced prosecution model for sexual assault cases which includes five specialized Crown Attorney positions, and a mentorship program for Crowns new to sexual assault prosecutions."[131] Nova Scotia recently announced funding to appoint two sexual assault specialists to the Public Prosecution Service in that province.[132]

The issue of training is important. Crown attorneys who prosecute sexual assault cases must be properly trained. The need to ensure that sexual assault cases are handled by properly trained professionals was documented in Sharon Murphy et al.'s 2013 study: "Across the board, the professionals in our study discussed the need for specialized training."[133] Specialized training for Crown counsel should include substantive aspects of sexual assault law such as the rules of evidence regarding the use of prior sexual history and the production of therapeutic records. The examples of Crown counsel in some cases failing to object to the unlawful admission of prior sexual history evidence or the repetitive badgering of the complainant suggest that better and more explicit training on these aspects of their duty to protect the trial process is also warranted.

It is essential that Crown attorneys receive sufficient education, and are competent, with respect to the role that rape mythology has played, and continues to play, in the criminal law response to sexual assault. Unreported cases in which trial judges resort to gendered stereotypes about sexual violence to assess credibility or interpret and apply the law of consent – such as those discussed in chapter 7 – are often only revealed (and ultimately overturned) when knowledgeable prosecutors identify the problem and make the decision to appeal. In order to provide this systemic check and balance, Crown attorneys must possess sound knowledge of the law of sexual assault, the rules of evidence, and the relationship between these areas of law and discriminatory stereotypes.

Instruction and guidance for Crown prosecutors assigned to sexual assault cases should also include trauma-informed knowledge and skills-based training specific to sexualized violence. A trauma-informed approach includes: recognition of how traumatic experiences affect memory and behaviour; acknowledgment of the relationship between the trauma of sexual violence and societal myths and stereotypes about gender-based harm; and strategies aimed at working with survivors in a manner that facilitates trust and communication.[134] As one survivor in a 2014 Statistics Canada survey commissioned by the federal Department of Justice stated:

> I think they really, truly need to understand there needs to be better education on the side of law enforcement, or on the judicial side, as to why it is so under reported; why people feel such a sense of shame; why victims will blame themselves or feel responsible ... why people tend to get away with this and why people are reluctant to come forward.[135]

According to the same report, other survivor participants recommended that, as part of their professional development, legal professionals should spend more time with front-line workers and others who are knowledgeable about the effects of sexual assault, and should spend more individual, in-person time with complainants prior to trial.[136]

Complainants need better resources to help prepare them for trial. While some of this preparation could be done by victim witness assistants and sexual assault organizations, some of the preparatory work that sexual assault complainants require can only be provided by members of the legal profession. The most obvious additional resource in this regard would be independent, state-funded legal representation for sexual assault complainants. Lawyers acting on behalf of sexual assault complainants can provide several greatly needed services such as liaising with the police and the Crown in order to provide the complainant with updates on the case, assisting with victim impact statements, and explaining developments in the case.[137] Governments should provide the remarkably small fraction of survivors of sexual assault willing to participate in the state's response to sexual violence with this resource.[138]

Unfortunately, at this time, even the provision of state-funded legal representation for sexual assault complainants when the defence makes an application for third-party records under section 278 of the *Criminal Code* is patchy.[139] Section 278 creates rules that limit the accused's access to a complainant's medical, counselling, or other personal records. Unlike at trial, complainants actually have standing at section 278 proceedings. Despite this, with the exception of jurisdictions such as Toronto, Ontario, it is not common for complainants to receive independent legal representation to resist, or respond to, section 278 applications.[140]

In addition to providing funding for lawyers at third-party records proceedings, Ontario recently initiated a small, two-year pilot program to fund legal representation for sexual assault complainants generally.[141] Newfoundland and Nova Scotia, with the support of funding from the federal government, recently announced similar pilots.[142] Ontario's pilot program provides sexual assault complainants in Toronto, Ottawa, and Thunder Bay with up to four hours of free legal advice.[143] Whether this particular structure for delivering a program of this nature will be effective is unclear. Larry Wilson argues that, for purposes of continuity, efficiency, and competence, state-funded legal representation for sexual assault complainants should be provided through the creation of permanent Legal Counsel positions rather than through a legal aid certificate–type structure. With the exception of funding for one lawyer position at the Barbara Schlifer Clinic in Toronto, it is the latter that Ontario is currently piloting.[144]

To be clear, independent legal advice for complainants would not be used to lessen the duties of the Crown. While the provision of state-funded legal counsel to sexual assault complainants is an important step, and other provinces in Canada should follow Ontario's lead, ground-breaking initiatives of this nature should not be positioned as an alternative to the Crown's duty to communicate with complainants, establish rapport, and prepare them for trial. Certainly in most, if not all, cases this will require more than four hours of a lawyer's time. Moreover, other than in the context of a third-party records proceeding, complainants do not have standing in criminal proceedings and so actions such as protecting them against abusive or discriminatory cross-examination cannot be done by 'their lawyer' – state-funded or otherwise. Even under a comprehensive and well-resourced state-funded legal aid program for sexual assault complainants, this would remain the exclusive role of the Crown. In addition, the likelihood that every jurisdiction will adopt and resource a legal aid program to fund independent counsel for sexual assault complainants seems remote at this time. As noted, most provinces do not even adequately provide counsel for complainants whose therapeutic or other personal records are sought through defence applications, and these are processes in which complainants actually have standing. To reiterate, government-funded legal representation for sexual assault complainants, even were it to be offered comprehensively, would not displace the onus on Crown prosecutors to prepare and protect complainants.

At the same time, there are supports that Crown attorneys are unable to provide. For example, the Crown is unlikely to provide complainants with information about the process before an offence has been reported or even before a charge has been laid. Similarly, one source of distress highlighted by many sexual assault complainants is their realization, upon learning that the prosecutor does not represent their interests, that (unlike the accused) they do not have their own lawyer. As Crown Attorney 3 explained in response to a question asking why some complainants continue to report their experience of the criminal justice system as traumatic: "I think sometimes people struggle with the fact, they'll say 'So you're my lawyer.' right? And I'm like 'Well, I'm not. I represent the public. I represent the state.' So they feel ... sometimes, I think they feel like they're in it alone. You know ... 'He has a lawyer.' 'Why don't I have someone who's just there for me?' Right? So I think that is hard for them."

Providing complainants with state-funded legal advice could meet these types of needs. An independent legal advice program in each province is necessary. Complainants should have state-funded legal counsel at the point of reporting, during the investigation, and throughout the trial proceeding. While state-funded legal advice for sexual assault complainants would not replace the Crown's pre-existing and ongoing duties to prepare complainants for, and protect them at, trial, it would complement these duties in ways that could make the process more humane.

In order to ensure that Crown prosecutors meet their duties to prepare and protect complainants in sexual assault cases, every province and territory in Canada should have a comprehensive Crown policy on sexual assault. Policies should include provisions directing Crown attorneys to: proactively establish and maintain communication with the complainant, give sexual assault cases priority in scheduling, assign carriage of the case at an early stage in the proceedings in order to ensure continuity, and prepare complainants for trial.

The Crown attorneys I interviewed indicated that they find sexual offences more difficult to prosecute than any other type of case. As Crown Attorney 2 stated: "I would prefer I never have to do one ever again." Crown Attorney 1 noted, "I just really don't want sex assault files. They're just, they're emotional." Indeed, nearly every Crown attorney I interviewed echoed these sentiments. The primary reason they identified for this perspective was the difficulty and stress of dealing with complainants. As Crown Attorney 2 put it, in explaining why he would rather prosecute a murder than a sexual assault: "There's less anxiety. You don't, you don't have to deal with the deceased, who actually is the complainant, as opposed to dealing with a sexual assault complainant who has a whole host of difficulties in doing this. And we're not social workers. We're lawyers."

Yet, Crown attorneys have the ability to reduce the degree to which sexual assault complainants are re-traumatized by their participation in the trial process. In Regehr's study, the single most significant factor informing how sexual assault complainants experienced the criminal justice system was their perception of whether the prosecutor made him- or herself available to them.[145] Other researchers have made similar findings regarding the impact that supportive prosecutors have on a complainant's trial experience.[146]

Meeting with complainants, familiarizing them with the setting, procedures, and technical language used in courts, reviewing the questions the Crown will ask of them, and readying them for the types of questions that they will face on cross-examination constitute fundamentally important aspects of the role and duties of the Crown. As Vandervort argues, taking steps to address these practical matters has the potential to change both outcomes in sexual assault proceedings and the attitudes of legal professionals towards complainants and sexual assault cases.[147]

Crown attorneys owe a duty to protect both the sexual assault trial process and its participants, including sexual assault complainants. This duty includes challenging reliance on discriminatory stereotypes about sexual violence, objecting to defence counsel strategies that are contrary to rules of evidence, discriminatory, or unnecessarily humiliating to complainants, and properly preparing complainants to testify.

There are structural aspects of the trial process, such as its adversarial nature, that suggest that some of the harms that arise from serving as a sexual assault complainant are inevitable. At the same time, the secondary trauma that some sexual assault complainants are subjected to as a consequence of their participation in the criminal trial process can be alleviated and reduced. Crown prosecutors have an integral role in ensuring that such mitigation occurs.

Of course, Crown attorneys are not the sole bearers of this duty. Trial judges also play a central part in the operation of the criminal trial process and are responsible for protecting all of its participants, including sexual assault complainants. The next two chapters consider the role of trial judges in contributing to a legal process that remains traumatizing for some sexual assault complainants. Chapter 6 examines the obligations that judges owe to sexual assault complainants. Following that, chapter 7 considers the need to facilitate and support the capacity of trial judges to perform this function. This chapter also examines a more rudimentary component of the trial judge's responsibility, basic knowledge of the substantive law of sexual assault, to demonstrate the way in which failures to meet this standard expose sexual assault survivors to particular harms.

CHAPTER 6

Judging Sexual Assault Trials

The capacity of a criminal justice system to function fairly and with humanity depends a great deal on judges. Ultimately, it is judges who are responsible for maintaining standards regarding both what occurs in Canadian trials and the physical setting of our courtrooms. This chapter addresses the role that trial judges (and to some extent appellate courts) play in either preventing or contributing to the trauma of the trial for sexual assault complainants.

One of the claims sometimes made by criminal lawyers is that trial judges today simply would not allow defence lawyers to use discriminatory stereotypes, inadmissible sexual history evidence, or unnecessary aggression when cross-examining a sexual assault complainant.[1] Recall Defence Lawyer 10's statement, quoted in chapter 2: "I think most judges would stop it in about two seconds flat, if you, if you crossed that line." Certainly some trial judges do intervene to stop discriminatory or overly aggressive cross-examinations. Unfortunately, others do not.

The first two sections of this chapter address aspects of the trial judge's duty to protect complainants. The first section considers the failure of some trial judges to ensure proper application and enforcement of the legal rules created to protect sexual assault complainants. I use the example of section 276 of the *Criminal Code* – the rule limiting the use of a complainant's prior sexual history.[2] Following this is a discussion of the trial judge's duty to intervene. Like Crown attorneys, trial judges have an obligation to intervene in cross-examinations that are unduly repetitive, insulting, or unlawful. The third part of this chapter considers the ways in which judges could make the trial process less intimidating and less foreign for complainants (and others) through modest changes to the rituals of the trial and the physical setting of the courtroom.

The Duty of Trial Judges to Protect Complainants through Proper Application of the Law

The substantive law of sexual assault in Canada and the rules of evidence, when properly applied by trial judges, offer several important protections for those who serve our justice system as sexual assault complainants. These protections include the rules limiting disclosure and/or admission of a complainant's medical or counselling records under section 278.2 of the *Criminal Code*,[3] and developments in the common law such as the recognition that a lack of physical resistance does not indicate that the complainant consented. Trial judges who fail to properly apply the substantive law of sexual assault and rules of evidence, including rules such as the ones just listed, contribute to the trauma of the trial for complainants.

One of the clearest examples of this failure on the part of some trial judges involves the rape shield regime under section 276 of the *Criminal Code*. In cases such as *R v B(IE)*[4] and *R v Wright*,[5] discussed in chapter 2, sexual history evidence was improperly introduced by defence counsel without any mention of a section 276 application by anyone, including the trial judges. For instance, in *Wright*, defence counsel repeatedly questioned the complainant about sexual activity several hours prior to the alleged assault, which should have been subject to a section 276 application.[6] Indeed, a good portion of her cross-examination involved evidence of this nature:

> Q. Okay. And if I was to suggest to you that you, in fact, had vaginal sex with Nick in the park, you wouldn't agree with that?
> A. For sure no.
> Q. Okay. And you wouldn't agree that in the park Nick was lying on his back and that you were riding his penis.
> A. No.[7]

Despite defence counsel's frequent return to questions regarding sexual activity between the complainant and the accused that she suggested had taken place hours before the alleged sexual assault, not once did the trial judge, Justice Martin, intervene to require a section 276 application. Nor did Justice Martin intercede on the basis that section 277 of the *Criminal Code* categorically excludes evidence of a complainant's 'sexual reputation' when defence counsel asked the complainant whether her nickname was "Perky Tits" or when she asked her whether she had a habit of dancing topless at bonfire parties.[8]

As explained briefly in chapter 2, section 276 of the *Criminal Code* creates exclusionary rules making evidence of a complainant's sexual activity, other than the sexual activity that forms the subject matter of the charge, presumptively inadmissible.[9] The objective of section 276 is to eliminate the misuse of evidence of a complainant's sexual activity for irrelevant or misleading purposes, while also ensuring that an accused's right to a fair trial is not compromised. Essentially, this involves removing any discriminatory reasoning based on gendered stereotypes about sexuality and sexual assault. It also involves providing some protection against the use of sexual history evidence to perpetrate unnecessary incursions on the dignity and privacy interests of complainants.

The "gratuitous humiliation and denigration"[10] of the complainant in *R v B(S)*,[11] discussed in chapter 3, is a striking example of whacking a complainant with evidence of her prior sexual history. Recall that defence counsel read aloud to the jury a series of sexually explicit texts between the complainant and a third party, despite the fact that the basis upon which they were to be admitted had not materialized. He confronted the complainant with extremely graphic, sexually explicit excerpts of a transcript of a video depicting the complainant and the accused engaged in anal intercourse – evidence that had little or no probative value and considerable prejudicial effect.[12] He ensured that the jury heard the complainant call herself a "slut" in the video not once but four times.[13] He made the complainant confirm that she had reached orgasm during the video multiple times, including during anal intercourse.[14] The misuse of evidence of the complainant's prior sexual history in *R v B(S)* was an egregious violation of section 276.[15] Had the trial judge, Justice Robert Stack, performed his role properly, this would not have occurred.

To begin with, as was determined by the Newfoundland Court of Appeal,[16] Justice Stack should not have granted defence counsel's pre-trial application to introduce the videotape evidence. While he did express concern during the pre-trial motion about the impact this evidence would have on the complainant, he nevertheless admitted it. Arguably, he should also have excluded the texts between the complainant and the third party with whom she had been sexually involved, or at a minimum waited until trial to decide whether they should be admitted based on the testimony.[17] Having wrongly admitted this evidence, or wrongly admitted it at the pre-trial stage, he then failed to limit defence counsel's use of it at trial. The injustice of his failure was compounded by the fact that both the Crown and defence counsel provided opportunities for him to ensure a judicious, cautious approach to the admission of this highly prejudicial and deeply personal evidence.

Consider first defence counsel's efforts in this regard. To his credit, before he began questions leading up to the introduction of these very explicit text messages between the complainant and a third party, Robert Simmonds, QC, warned that he was about to do so and flagged for Justice Stack that the content was graphic. Despite being given this opportunity to maintain strict control over the use of these texts, Justice Stack essentially green-lighted him:

> SIMMONDS, Q.C.: My lord, I'm now going to proceed to, and this is kind of peripheral with respect to it but I'm now going to proceed to a couple of statements she made in the KGB statement and then I'm going to proceed to some text messaging which does talk about sexual activity, therefore, I believe I'm into the umbrella of 276?
>
> ...
>
> THE COURT: Yes, well, you have my Order, are you looking for further direction now or are you simply alerting me to that it's coming?
>
> SIMMONDS, Q.C.: Well, I just want to make – I don't wanna, I'm not trying to hide anything to the jury, nor am I trying to slip something in by the back door that I shouldn't, okay. So, if it becomes an issue, my lord, if you think it becomes an issue or my friend, flag it and we'll stop right there and, you know, because I'm not trying to slide something in here but this is not gonna be pleasant stuff.
>
> THE COURT: No, I understand, but you have my Order.
>
> SIMMONDS, Q.C.: Yeah, I do.
>
> THE COURT: And I've determined, A, that it's a relevant area of questioning and B, that its probative value outweighs its prejudicial effect in accordance with the written decision that I gave. So, so long as you stay within those parameters, Mr. Simmonds, I can't imagine we are going to have any difficulty, will we, Mr. Summers?[18]

Although Justice Stack suggested that the parties should "tread carefully,"[19] that is not what he actually required of them and it is not what occurred, as was demonstrated in chapter 3. Setting aside the fact that he should not have granted the pre-trial section 276 application in the first place, at the point in the trial when defence counsel raised this evidence, Justice Stack should have advised him that he would not be permitted to use the text messages between the complainant and the third party if, in cross-examination, she admitted that she had been dishonest to the police about the affair. Recall from chapter 3 that the complainant admitted that she had lied to the police about the affair the first time Simmonds asked her. Thus, the sole basis upon which the texts were admitted pre-trial did not materialize. As such, based on his own ruling, Justice Stack should not have permitted Simmonds to use them.

Crown attorney Jeff Summers provided Justice Stack with numerous opportunities to reconsider his decision to allow this sexual history evidence to be used by defence counsel. Before any of the texts were used, he stated, "what I don't want this to turn into is every single, you know, sort of salacious text message ... to be brought over, and over and over and over and over to the witness."[20] In the *voir dire* discussion responding to the Crown's concern, Simmonds offered to "go through the text messages" he planned to use.[21] Troublingly, Justice Stack responded, "I'm not concerned with the text messages."[22]

Once the cross-examination on the texts began, Summers repeatedly objected to defence counsel's use of the texts in an effort to stop the "humiliation and denigration"[23] that was occurring. For example,

MR. SUMMERS: My lord, we're getting into now, is there a question? She's already acknowledged.

THE COURT: No, no, this is a separate series of texts and he's entitled to put these to the witness and she can acknowledge that they're hers or not.

MR. SUMMERS: I think [they] address the same issue, they are the same question.

SIMMONDS, Q.C.: What would you have me do, Mr. Summers? Not go through any of this?

THE COURT: That's okay Mr. Simmonds, we've discussed this. Carry on.[24]

Justice Stack did not sustain any of the Crown's objections regarding the texts.[25]

When defence counsel, of his own volition, stopped asking the complainant to confirm that each of these texts were between her and the third party, Justice Stack insisted that this humiliating routine must continue to occur:

> Q. [SIMMONDS] ... Is that your text to the gentleman – ?
> A. I've already acknowledged that.
> THE COURT: Just so that we're clear again, you didn't because he asked you about other texts previously. So, now he's asking you about these specific texts that he just read to you and asked you whether they are yours and so you didn't acknowledge that.
> A. All of the texts that he just read out were mine.
> THE COURT: Thank you.[26]

After Simmonds put several more texts to the complainant, the Crown again appealed to Justice Stark to intervene:

> Q. [SIMMONDS] And,
>   "Big strong sexy gorgeous man u are an instant orgasm for
>   me." your text?
> A. Yes, sir.
> MR. SUMMERS: My lord, again, what is the question? What is the question ...
> SIMMONDS, Q.C.: I'm gonna stop at the next one, Mr. Summers. Are they your texts? I thought the wording was clear.
> MR. SUMMERS: With the greatest of respect she, perhaps you could just ask her, are there any texts which are not hers.
> SIMMONDS, Q.C.: No, Mr. Summers.
> MR. SUMMERS: But what is the relevance of whether – she's acknowledged that these are her texts.
>   ...
> MR. SUMMERS: I question, what is the relevance?
> THE COURT: Okay, I don't think Mr. Simmonds has to respond. The relevance is obvious that she gave statements to the police in which she said she had not cheated on "S.B." or that he thought she was cheating and "that's not me and he knows it", and these

are evidence that Mr. Simmonds is going to suggest prove to the contrary and he is asking questions each time after I suggested that he do it on the one time he missed that she adopt these as her statements and if these statements are inconsistent with her other statements he's allowed to make something of that. So, carry on, Mr. Simmonds.[27]

Again, the complainant repeatedly and unequivocally admitted at trial that she had cheated and that she had lied to the police about cheating. The basis upon which these texts were admitted pretrial did not materialize at trial. Justice Stack failed to properly apply section 276 of the *Criminal Code*, failed to uphold his own (arguably erroneous) ruling on the basis for admitting the texts, and failed to perform his role in controlling the trial process by ensuring the fair treatment of the complainant, despite being given the opportunity to do so by both Simmonds and Summers. He is as responsible for the needless, humiliating denigration of the complainant in this case as is defence counsel.

The Newfoundland Court of Appeal also failed this complainant. Although Justice Malcolm Rowe's majority decision identified Justice Stack's failure to properly apply section 276, and recognized that the introduction of this evidence to the jury had "irremediably fed" the myth that women who consent in the past are more likely to have consented to the sex at issue in the allegation, he nevertheless upheld the acquittal.[28] The jury in this trial heard evidence of the complainant texting statements to the man with whom she was having an extramarital affair, telling him that she was "going to swallow [his] cum" and asking him to "fuck [her] really hard."[29] The jury heard excerpts from the transcript of the sex tape made with the accused in which she referred to herself as an "ass slut" and told her then husband he was "gonna make [her] come while [his] cock [was] in [her] ass."[30] The jury heard her testify that she had climaxed multiple times in this video, including during anal intercourse. Imagine concluding, as Justice Rowe did, that this evidence could not "reasonably be thought"[31] to have affected the jury's conclusions regarding her allegations of non-consensual anal intercourse. Justice Rowe's majority decision to uphold the jury's acquittal reflects a stunning failure to enforce the objectives underpinning Canada's rape shield regime. His decision also profoundly underestimated the role that rape mythology plays in sexual assault trial outcomes. It was overturned in a one-paragraph oral decision by the Supreme Court of Canada shortly after Rowe was elevated to that court.[32]

Changes to the substantive law of sexual assault and the rules of evidence in Canada in the 1980s and 1990s, including revisions to our rape shield regime under section 276 of the *Criminal Code*, represent progressive improvements to the legal treatment of women who allege sexual violence, but only when they are properly applied and enforced by our judges.

The Need for Compassion and Intervention

The notion that lawyers have an ethical obligation to be civil to one another has received a great deal of public attention in Canada in the last several years because of the Law Society of Upper Canada's decision to discipline securities lawyer Joseph Groia for his allegedly provocative and offensive behaviour towards opposing counsel in a securities trial in which his client was accused of insider trading.[33] (The *Groia* case was discussed briefly in chapter 4.) Less, if any, attention has been paid to the notion that lawyers have an ethical obligation not to be offensive to women who accuse their clients of sexual assault. Recall from chapter 4 that there are no reported cases of lawyers being disciplined by law societies in Canada for whacking the complainant in a sexual assault trial.

Whether it is enforced, let us assume that there is an ethical obligation on legal professionals to be respectful to everyone in the courtroom, not just to judges and other lawyers. The responsibility to ensure that this requirement is met falls not only on law societies but on judges as well. Trial judges have the power (and duty) to control the trial process and the conduct of the lawyers who appear before them. Indeed, some legal academics and professionals argue that the responsibility to ensure respect and civility in the courtroom should lie exclusively with trial judges.[34] These commentators are concerned that imposing law society discipline upon lawyers who are offensive or disrespectful will dampen their ability to advocate properly for their clients. For example, criminal lawyer David Humphrey, commenting on the *Groia* case, argued, "What's happening in court has to be gauged by someone who's there, not by someone who later reads a transcription."[35] Presumably, those who take this position would agree that trial judges can and should intervene in circumstances where a lawyer is not treating a sexual assault complainant with respect. However, before discussing the duty of trial judges to intervene to require this of lawyers, I want to consider the obligation of judges themselves to treat complainants with civility.

There are ways in which judges can, through their demeanour, make the trial process more humane for sexual assault complainants, without threatening the constitutional rights of the accused. Trial judges should, and many do, embrace a compassionate style of interaction with complainants simply by engaging with them as human beings. The transcripts in both *R v Finney*[36] and *R v Schmaltz*,[37] examined in chapter 2, offer examples of trial judges attempting to make the process more bearable for the complainant through very basic gestures of consideration. For instance, Justice O'Connell, the trial judge in *Finney*, wished the complainant a happy birthday as he dismissed her and asked that she return for further cross-examination the following day:

> "Thank-you Ms. ——, and happy birthday, ma'am. Enjoy your day."[38]

Likewise, at one point in the cross-examination of the complainant in *Finney*, this exchange occurred between the two:

> A. Your Honour, I'm feeling a little bit overwhelmed right now. Can I have just five minutes?
> THE COURT: Yes. Just for the record the lady appears to be crying and shaking, so we are going to take a recess.[39]

Similarly, before permitting defence counsel to begin her cross-examination, the trial judge in *Schmaltz*, Judge Greaves, attempted to ensure some modicum of comfort for the complainant:

> THE COURT: Now, you make sure that you have got water and Kleenex, and all that type of stuff. If you need a break, just let us know.
> ...
> CROWN: Now, Sir, if I may, just as a point of interjection, I was wondering if the witness would be allowed to have a small break.
> THE COURT: Well, like I said, she could anytime, that is my ... invitation to her.[40]

And later in the trial:

CROWN: And, Sir, could it just be noted we did provide a chair in the witness box, if it is all right with the Court –
THE COURT: Yeah, of course. If she feels weak or otherwise strange, she is certainly welcome to comfort herself in that or any other fashion that we can work out. What else?[41]

Notably, on appeal the trial judges in both *Finney* and *Schmaltz* were accused of bias or creating an apprehension of bias.[42] In *Finney*, appellant defence counsel specifically criticized Justice O'Connell for wishing the complainant a happy birthday.[43] Both the Alberta Court of Appeal and the Ontario Court of Appeal rightly rejected the appellants' claims of bias or reasonable apprehension of bias in these cases.[44] (The appeal in *Schmaltz* was granted, but not on the grounds of bias or apprehension of bias.)

Trial judges are uniquely positioned to deviate from, and permit others to deviate from, their heavily scripted courtroom roles. They should not be accused of bias for performing basic acts of human consideration. Indeed, a more coherent and less classist conception of the lawyer's duty of civility would suggest that those charged with administering the criminal trial process – that is to say lawyers and judges – should behave in this manner towards all trial participants, not just other legal professionals, as the duty[45] tends to be interpreted and enforced by law societies today.

Moreover, appeal courts should continue to reject, and in no uncertain terms, specious arguments by appellant counsel such as the suggestion that a judge who offers a brief salutation to a woman who has spent her birthday testifying in intricate detail about being vaginally, orally, and anally raped has demonstrated 'bias' or created an apprehension of bias. Appeals of this nature, even when rejected, are sure to have a chilling effect on trial judges' willingness to treat sexual assault complainants with even this modest degree of compassion. Such practices also waste judicial resources.

In addition to these types of gestures, trial judges can make the process modestly more hospitable for complainants by preventing, to the extent possible, cross-examination that is needlessly repetitive or clearly abusive. This returns us to the discussion that opened this section of the chapter: the trial judge's duty to intervene.

The ordeal of testifying as a sexual assault complainant is aggravated by the lengthy and repetitive cross-examinations they sometimes endure. As Amanda Konradi demonstrated in her study of sexual assault complainants in the United States, complainants identify problematic interactions with defence counsel as a significant cause of distress to them.[46] The types of problematic interactions highlighted in Konradi's study include rapid-fire questioning in which complainants were not given a chance to respond, overly repetitive questioning, efforts to limit answers to one-word responses, compound questions in which they did not know which question they were supposed to respond to, and personal questions unrelated to the sexual assault which complainants felt were posed in order to humiliate them.[47] Chapters 2 and 3 provided numerous examples of cross-examinations in recent Canadian cases that can fairly be characterized (and in some instances were so characterized by trial judges) as either repetitive, difficult to follow, insulting, humiliating, rapid-fire, or highly objectionable.

In some cases, such as *R v Luceno*,[48] trial judges do intervene to protect both the process and the complainant. As revealed in chapter 3, Justice Goldstein repeatedly urged defence counsel to stop interrupting the complainant.[49] Similarly, several times during the cross-examination, including in the following instance, he insisted that defence counsel allow the complainant to explain her answer:

> THE COURT: You've got to let her finish. She's giving an answer and you're interrupting, Mr. White.
>
> MR. WHITE: Unresponsive, Your Honour. Unresponsive to my question.
>
> THE COURT: Well, you know what, I understand that, but she starts talking and she's got to be allowed to explain if she starts to give an explanation.[50]

Trial judges must balance the duty to intervene with the need to ensure that the accused's right to a thorough cross-examination is not unduly compromised. This means that there is a limit to their ability to control the conduct of lawyers in their courtrooms (which is, in part, why law societies also have a role in maintaining standards of courtroom conduct by lawyers).[51] Justice Goldstein intervened more than thirty times to direct defence counsel to stop interrupting, stop using compound questions, stop insulting the complainant, and slow down. Yet, defence counsel in *Luceno* persisted with his repetitive, confusing, rapid-fire cross-examination despite Justice Goldstein's repeated interventions. It is unlikely that further intervention would have curbed defence counsel's conduct in this case and it might have risked creating grounds for appeal. That said, it seems reasonable to assume that without Justice Goldstein's interventions there would have been even more interruptions, compound questions, and undue repetition during defence counsel's cross-examination of the complainant in this case.

Contrast Justice Goldstein's approach with what occurred in *R v Cain*,[52] also discussed in chapter 2. In *Cain*, not only did Justice Binder not intervene in defence counsel's repetitive questioning of the complainant, but when Crown attorney Gordon Hatch objected, Justice Binder failed to rule on his objection. Defence counsel repeatedly questioned the complainant on her failure to resist the accused with questions such as "Okay. I'm suggesting to you that he did do that and you didn't try to prevent him – or you didn't prevent him or even try to prevent him from doing that; do you agree with that?"[53] The cross-examination included exchanges such as:

> Q. Okay. You didn't say anything to him like "Don't" or "Stop"; is that right?
> A. Not at the very beginning, but I did tell him to stop.
> Q. In fact, not only – do you agree with my suggestion not only did you not say to him "Stop," the two of you kept going at each other; isn't that right?
> A. All I did was kiss him. That's all I did.
> Q. There was never at any time when you said "Don't"; isn't that right?[54]

Defence counsel followed this with a repetitive line of questioning about her failure to scream for help, again with no intervention from Justice Binder:

> Q. You didn't call out to her for help, did you?
> A. I had no voice.
> Q. What's that?
> A. I had no voice.
> Q. Okay. A man walked by?

A. Yes.

Q. And, in fact, you were still in the bush when he approached them?

A. Yes.

Q. Okay. [Cain] went up to them?

A. No.

Q. Okay. We'll see about that. And the man said no as well?

A. Yes.

Q. Okay. And you could hear Josh Cain, according to you, asking for a lighter –

A. Yes.

Q. – while you were in the bush?

A. Yes.

Q. Okay. And you didn't cry out to this person for help either?

A. No.

Q. Okay. And is this, again, because you didn't have any voice?

A. Because I didn't have any voice, and I needed Josh to get back to Candace.

Q. Okay. Well, if you had been knocked – or not knocked – or choked unconscious and raped, as you say –

A. Yes.

Q. – you knew there were thousands of people walking around?

A. Yes.

Q. And you didn't ask anybody for help?

A. No.

Q. Okay. Now, so you didn't ask the lady for help, you didn't ask the man for help

A. No –

Q. – is that right?

A. – I did not.

Q. Okay.[55]

At this point, Crown attorney Gordon Hatch objected. However, Justice Binder did not rule on his objection and defence counsel simply carried on with his questions:

MR. HATCH: Sir, my objection is these questions have been asked and answered a number of times, and my friend is berating the witness.

MR. RAUF: Berating the witness. With the greatest of respect, I'm asking her to confirm what she said.

Q. MR. RAUF: So Josh, at one point, turned around and asked you if you were ready to go, didn't he?[56]

Perhaps unsurprisingly given the lack of ruling on Hatch's objection, defence counsel returned to this line of questioning yet again later in his cross-examination.[57] The duty to intervene includes an obligation to rule when Crown attorneys perform their duty to protect complainants by objecting to cross-examinations that appear to be badgering or overly repetitive.

Defence lawyers must be permitted to ask exceptionally detailed questions of Crown witnesses, including sexual assault complainants – provided their questions are not motivated by an intention to trigger discriminatory and/or legally rejected stereotypes. However, there is no need for them to ask these questions repetitively, nor does the accused have a right to an overly repetitive cross-examination. Trial judges have an obligation to control the trial process.[58] This obligation includes not allowing lawyers to badger witnesses through repetitive questioning. Trial judges should be given significant deference with respect to this aspect of trial management.[59] In addition, there should be robust support from appellate courts for trial judges who do intervene to stop this type of questioning. Put otherwise, the duty of Crown counsel to protect sexual assault complainants by objecting to this type of questioning, explored in the previous chapter, should be augmented by both judicial support for such efforts, and strong appellate support for the independent responsibility of trial judges to stop cross-examinations of this nature.

Judicial interventions to reduce repetitive, abusive, or discriminatory cross-examinations do not compromise trial fairness: "Counsel are bound by the rules of relevancy and barred from resorting to harassment, misrepresentation, repetitiousness or, more generally, from putting questions whose prejudicial effect outweighs their probative value."[60] The accused's right of cross-examination is not absolute.[61] As the Supreme Court of Canada stated in *R v Shearing*: "It has been increasingly recognized in recent years, however, that cross-examination techniques in sexual assault cases that seek to put the complainant on trial rather than the accused are abusive and distort rather than enhance the search for truth."[62]

The authority of judges to manage their courtrooms represents one of the more plausible means to discourage lawyers from repetitive or unnecessarily humiliating or aggressive questioning. It is true that interventions by a trial judge can only do so much to control the courtroom conduct of lawyers, as was clearly the case in *Luceno.* That said, it is preferable for trial judges to at least attempt to rein in lawyers whose cross-examinations have crossed the line. The failure or refusal to do so leaves complainants reliant exclusively on the Crown to protect them. Some Crown attorneys meet this obligation diligently. Unfortunately, as was argued in chapter 5, others fail to perform this duty.

One way in which a cross-examination can veer into the realm of the problematic relates to a common defence strategy: the attempt to undermine credibility or reliability by demonstrating inconsistencies in a complainant's statements to the police, or at a preliminary inquiry, about even very minor details. To be clear, establishing inconsistencies in a complainant's testimony or previous statements is an important and entirely legitimate defence strategy. However, it is both common sense, and judicially recognized, that "[i]nconsistencies in the evidence of witnesses in relatively minor matters or matters of detail are, of course, normal. They are to be expected."[63] In fact, "the absence of such inconsistencies may be of even greater concern, for it may suggest collusion between witnesses in their evidence or fabrication or excessive rehearsal and regurgitation of a set story."[64] It is difficult to imagine that anyone could maintain consistency with respect to insignificant details when retelling an incident that occurred months or more likely even years prior.[65] The challenge is even greater for individuals who have attempted to manage their lives by not revisiting a trauma over and over again in their minds. While defence lawyers are expected to question complainants on inconsistencies in an effort to discredit them, persistent repetition on minute, collateral details should not be accepted by trial judges.

Trial judges are also expected to intervene to stop irrelevant questions. While it is clear that trial judges can, and should, intervene to discourage or stop irrelevant lines of questioning, judicial intervention in this context does require a more complicated assessment than is necessary with respect to questioning that is rude, unnecessarily aggressive in tone, or clearly repetitive. The accused's right to a thorough cross-examination is a fundamental and constitutionally protected component of our current

system of justice. Judicial intervention to stop irrelevant questions absolutely should occur, but it requires a careful and balanced approach
that errs in favour of not unduly circumscribing the accused's right
to cross-examine his accuser. First, defence lawyers are entitled, and
indeed ethically required, to highlight inconsistencies in a complainant's statements (including details that are peripheral to the allegation)
in an effort to discredit them. Second, defence lawyers may press the
complainant on details the relevance of which only becomes apparent
to the court, or Crown, once the defence has revealed its theory of the
case – which may not occur until closing submissions. For these reasons,
the trial judge's duty to intervene on the basis that defence counsel's
questions are irrelevant is narrow and must be exercised with significant
caution. In contrast, because abusive, unnecessarily aggressive, overly
repetitive, insulting cross-examination can often be ascertained on its
face, recommending that trial judges be vigilant in disallowing it does
not raise the same concerns.

A related point on this topic concerns the difficult issue of questions
that are ostensibly relevant on the basis of establishing inconsistencies
but are, in fact, more likely an attempt to undermine the complainant's
credibility by triggering gender-based stereotypes. Common examples include extensive cross-examination on potential inconsistencies
in minute details regarding whether the complainant was flirting, the
precise number of alcoholic drinks she consumed, or the colour and
cut of her underwear. As just explained, initially the relevancy of a line
of questioning may only be clear to defence counsel, and judges must
provide them with leeway to conduct their cases as they see fit. As is
discussed in chapter 4, the requirement that this leeway be provided
gives rise to a corresponding ethical obligation on the part of defence
lawyers not to offer evidence that is ostensibly about demonstrating
an inconsistency but is in reality motivated by an interest in triggering
legally rejected stereotypes about women and sex. At the same time,
there are cases in which it is clear that the relevance of defence counsel's
line of questioning is reliant for its probative value on rape myth, not
potential inconsistencies. In these circumstances, as with questioning
that is clearly abusive, unnecessarily repetitive, or rude, trial judges have
a duty to intervene. As the Supreme Court of Canada noted in *R v Osolin*,

> The purpose of the cross-examination must be a significant factor
> in determining if it is appropriate. Here the defence counsel in

submissions to the trial judge indicated that the cross-examination would be directed towards "what kind of person the complainant is". This on its face appears to be the very sort of improper purpose for which evidence cannot be adduced ... the trial judge was correct in refusing to permit cross-examination for that purpose.[66]

The nature of the inconsistency in a witness's statements is important. Consider again the cross-examination of the complainant in *R v Schmaltz*.[67] The complainant in *Schmaltz* alleged that she was awoken because "something was going in and out of" her.[68] She had been asleep in her daughter's apartment when she awoke to find Joshua Schmaltz inserting his fingers into her vagina. She said, "What the fuck are you doing?" and pushed at his hand while he tried to hold it there.[69] She testified that she had not met the accused prior to the date on which this occurred. The defence was that she "was a liar, a possible drug user, was drunk at the time of the assault, and consented to the sexual activity."[70]

Schmaltz was convicted of sexual assault. The defence appealed, arguing that the trial judge's interventions during the cross-examination prevented defence counsel from demonstrating inconsistencies that went to the complainant's credibility. The majority of the Alberta Court of Appeal overturned the conviction and ordered a new trial on the basis that Judge Greaves's interventions created the perception of unfairness.[71] But as Justice Paperny in dissent in *Schmaltz* highlighted, to warrant overturning Schmaltz's conviction on the basis that Judge Greaves improperly intervened, "there must be a deprivation of the right to full answer and defence; there must be an injustice, actual or reasonably perceived."[72] Trial judges go too far when their interventions convey the impression that they are on the side of the prosecution, make it impossible for defence counsel to advance their case, or prevent the accused from telling their story in their own way.[73] As Justice Paperny demonstrated, that is not what occurred in this case. Take the accused's argument that Judge Greaves improperly interfered with defence counsel's ability to cross-examine the complainant as to whether she and Schmaltz had been flirting earlier in the day. The majority of the Court of Appeal concluded that this intervention interfered with cross-examination on a potentially critical ambiguity in the complainant's statement to the police. Did she tell the police she flirted with him or not?

Under Canadian law, whether the complainant was flirting earlier in the evening is irrelevant to the issue of consent. Consent to sexual touching must be contemporaneous. It must be given at the time of sexual contact.[74] An accused cannot rely on notions of implied consent or a mistaken belief in implied consent.[75] The allegation in *Schmaltz* was that he digitally penetrated her vagina while she was asleep. He maintained that she was consenting. To characterize the presence or absence of flirting earlier in the evening as a critical ambiguity in a case in which the central issue is consent suggests a misunderstanding of the law of consent on the part of the majority of the Court of Appeal. Whether she told the police she was flirting earlier in the evening is only a critical ambiguity if you assume that flirtation earlier in the evening made it more likely she consented to the vaginal penetration later in the evening: an assumption that would be wrong at law. Indeed, far from being a critical ambiguity, upon a proper application of the law of consent, the ambiguity as to whether there was flirting was "collateral at best and irrelevant on the ultimate issue of consent."[76]

To conclude that judicial intervention to interrupt this line of questioning created the perception of an unfair trial was wrong. As the dissent in *Schmaltz* correctly noted, the accused's right to cross-examine a sexual assault complainant is circumscribed by common law rules and by provisions of the *Criminal Code*, which prohibit evidence of, among other things, a complainant's sexual history and reputation, as well as irrelevant questions directed to discredited "rape myths."[77] The problematic fact that the Crown opened the door to this line of cross-examination by asking the complainant whether there was flirting earlier in the evening (discussed in chapter 5) does not alter the low probative value of the evidence.

Appeal court judges also bear responsibility for ensuring that appropriate judicial intervention occurs in sexual assault trials. A lack of recognition by appellate courts of the duty of, and need for, trial judges to perform this role in sexual assault trials, and/or a failure by courts of appeal to allow the proper degree of deference to trial judges in this context, will undoubtedly discourage trial judges from performing this important function.

Judges Should Humanize the Courtroom Setting

Judges (and in particular chief judges and chief justices) are responsible for their courtrooms. Courtroom rituals, and even the physical setting of the courtroom itself, create an atmosphere of hierarchy that can be harmful to sexual assault complainants.[78] For example, the spatial design of a courtroom establishes particular lines of sight, rendering some participants more visible or more audible than others, and facilitating certain hierarchical lines of engagement that distinguish between the learned legal profession and the laity.[79] Judges typically sit behind an elevated bench at the front and centre of the courtroom. The courtroom is physically divided by a bar – only those ceremoniously inducted into the profession ('called to the bar') are seated in the front part of the courtroom. Others, including other professionals (such as social workers, medical professionals, courtroom support workers, articling clerks, and paralegals), are only permitted to cross this threshold under specific and invited circumstances. Unless called to testify, the public is always to remain behind 'the bar.'

While it may be important to imbue criminal trial proceedings with a sense of solemnity, the rituals, ceremony, and aesthetics currently employed to do so create a setting that is both foreign to the uninitiated and unnecessarily hierarchical. The particular gender-based harm to sexual assault complainants caused by requiring them to participate in hierarchical courtroom rituals was explained in chapter 5.

Several modest steps could be taken by the judiciary to humanize the courtroom setting without diminishing the gravity of the criminal trial process. For example, courtrooms could be modified to reduce unnecessary symbols of hierarchy and to ensure the basic comfort of vulnerable witnesses. For instance, traditionally, a witness was expected to stand while they provided testimony – thus the label 'witness stand.' While judges and jurors are seated, and lawyers sit when the other side is examining or cross-examining a witness, in some courtrooms those testifying are still expected to stand during both direct and cross-examination. In some cases this may entail standing for hours. For example, in *R v Khaery*, which was discussed in chapter 3, the complainant's request to be seated was denied, despite the trial judge having observed her obvious physical and mental exhaustion:[80]

> [COMPLAINANT] A: Can I sit down?
> THE COURT: No.
> …
> THE COURT: Ms. ——, we stand in the courtroom so that everyone can hear the evidence that's being given. You're slumped down in that witness box. It's very difficult to hear and very difficult to see.[81]

Eventually the Crown, in response to the complainant's clear distress, also requested that she be permitted to sit while testifying:

> MS. GODFREY: My Lady, I'm wondering, the Crown actually would make an application, if you consider appropriate, maybe to have the be – the witness be allowed to sit down if –
> A. I can't.
> THE COURT: Mr. Rauf? Mr. Rauf?
> MR. RAUF: Yes. I have no comment except I would respectfully ask Your Ladyship to ask her to speak loudly so we can all hear.[82]

The Crown's request was granted. However, on a subsequent day the fatigued and distressed complainant was again asked to stand while testifying.[83]

Courtrooms that position judges and/or juries in ways that do not permit them to properly observe the witness unless he or she is standing reflect hierarchy. They are designed based on an assumption that, while others may sit comfortably, it is acceptable to require a witness to stand before the court when providing their testimony.

The positioning of courtroom participants varies across provinces. In Nova Scotia, for example, witnesses sit while testifying. In British Columbia, witnesses may choose whether to sit or stand. The variance across jurisdictions suggests that the expectation in some courtrooms that witnesses stand is driven by either the physical layout of the courtrooms or tradition – neither of which are sufficient reasons to deny witnesses this basic comfort. Canadian courtrooms that are designed such that the only way for the trier of fact to properly hear and observe the witnesses requires them to remain standing should be reconfigured. Certainly, there is no inherent need to require witnesses to stand while testifying. Forcing someone to stand for hours, sometimes even days, while testifying as a complainant in a sexual assault trial is inhumane.

Related to this issue, in the transcripts examined as part of this study it was remarkably common to find trial judges repeatedly instructing sexual assault complainants to raise their voices while they were testifying, or to sit very close to the microphone. Lowering one's voice when testifying may be a common after-effect of suffering trauma. There may be cultural reasons why some witnesses testify at a lower volume.[84] Some research suggests individuals feel more confident or powerful when they speak with a lower voice.[85] Other studies show that complainants who speak quietly while recounting the details of a sexual offence in the public setting of a courtroom are perceived as more credible.[86] Regardless, sexual assault complainants should be able to testify at whatever volume is most comfortable. Simply equipping Canadian courtrooms with a proper amplification system could reduce this unnecessary stressor on survivor witnesses. Given the central role of oral testimony in trial processes based on the adversarial model, these suggested changes to the courtroom setting seem astonishingly straightforward.

For Indigenous women, who are disproportionately the victims of sexual violence in Canada,[87] the hierarchized spatial and aesthetic organization of the courtroom is compounded by the representations of imperialism and colonial power present in every criminal trial proceeding in Canada. Consider, for example, the prominent display of the Royal Coat of Arms in many Canadian courtrooms, the explicit presence of the monarchy as manifested in the role of the Crown attorney, and the fact that in Canada criminal proceedings are prosecuted in the name of the British monarchy (e.g., *Regina v John Doe*). Picture the aesthetic created each month in remote northern communities when the circuit court (composed of almost exclusively non-Indigenous lawyers and judges) flies in and plants a federal or territorial flag outside the building that will serve as courthouse for the day. Such conspicuous articulations of colonialism are both undesirable and unnecessary.

The memorialization of legal culture through judicial portraiture also contributes to an aesthetic of gender and race inequality in Canadian courts. The creation and display of judicial portraits is a longstanding ritual of the common law.[88] These visual images reflect and constitute not only the identity of the individual jurist but also that of the institution. In this way judicial portraiture contributes to the identity of the court as a state institution.[89] As official portraits, the images are intended to articulate the "qualities and characteristics of the state."[90] The hallways and courtroom walls of many Canadian courthouses are adorned with solemn-looking judges in white tabs and black robes. Many more of these formal portraits are of men than of women.[91] The overwhelming majority of these portraits are of white people.[92] One need not turn to the undoubtedly meaningful significance of even subtle differences in portraiture style and technique to observe the masculine, colonial, and Caucasian attributes of judicial portraiture as a representation of the Canadian state.

In her recently published memoir, retired Justice Marie Corbett recounts her failed attempts to have a portrait of Ontario's first woman judge of the Superior Court, Mabel Van Camp, hung in Osgoode Hall in Toronto. The rejection of her requests, made to the Chief Justice of the Ontario Superior Court and to two successive treasurers of Ontario's law society, highlights the potential for judicial portraiture to contribute to a non-inclusive courtroom aesthetic.[93]

What desirable function do prominent displays of Caucasian, imperial power perform in the courtroom? Given the role that law historically played in Canada's genocidal approach to Indigenous peoples, and the ongoing effects of this approach on First Nations in this country, it seems reasonable to assume that whatever benefit results from prominent symbolic representations of British imperialism in our courts is outweighed by the harms. Remove the Royal Coat of Arms and other symbols of colonialism from Canadian courtrooms. Similarly, take all of those old judicial portraits displayed in courtrooms across the country and donate them to museums, or perhaps create judicial portraiture galleries in a separate room in the courthouse.[94] Until the composition of the judiciary in Canada is empirically reflective of the diversity of our citizenry, its gender composition, and the constitutional status of Indigenous peoples, the ritual of judicial portraiture should be removed from conspicuous display in our halls of justice.

These changes to the aesthetic of the trial might require judges and members of the bar to revise a strongly rooted, if dubious, narrative about the nobility – the learned aristocracy – of the legal profession.[95] This would be beneficial for all sorts of reasons, not the least of which is that it is a conceptualization of lawyering that promotes elitism while failing to reflect the actual perception of lawyers held both within the profession and by the public more broadly.[96] A profession need not project the status of nobility, a historically hierarchical concept, in order to warrant respect, trust, and dignity. Indeed, today such an image might even be counterproductive to manifesting these more important attributes.

The overly formal and archaic language used in trial proceedings also adds to the foreignness and correspondingly intimidating context of the process. The effect of this outdated language is compounded by the frequent gap between the education level and socio-economic status of the legal professionals involved in the process and that of complainants (and accused individuals). Undoubtedly, and unlike the complainant, in all but a handful of cases, the trial judge, Crown attorney, and defence lawyer will have vastly greater experience and familiarity with the rituals and language of the courtroom setting. Commenting on the traditional language used to announce the charge to the jury, Justice Corbett writes:

> This outmoded, effete language always embarrassed me. Much of it, like "oyez, oyez, oyez," is incomprehensible. What institutional insecurity resists using words the public can understand? When my colleague Justice Donna Haley changed "oyez" to "Please give your attention" and updated and clarified [other phrases], the Chief Justice compelled her to stop and directed her to use the traditional language.[97]

Justice Corbett concludes that "modernizing the language in the interest of comprehension could be achieved without diminishing the power of the oath."[98]

Efforts to humanize the courtroom setting by educating and familiarizing complainants (as discussed in chapter 5), rejecting archaic and impenetrable language, and removing its physical articulation of hierarchy would contribute to a more humane and hospitable process for sexual assault complainants. Significantly, these improvements would not be in tension with the truth-seeking and justice values upon which the criminal trial process is purportedly founded. In other words, these proposed changes should not even trigger the debate concerning how to appropriately balance the due process rights of the accused with the need to protect sexual assault complainants. While the impact of these reforms on creating a more hospitable process would be modest, the resources required to achieve them are also modest. Indeed, what is hopeful about reforms of this nature is how easy they would be to accomplish – should the judiciary express the appetite for implementing them.

Judges, like defence lawyers and Crown attorneys, contribute to the way women who serve the criminal justice system as sexual assault complainants experience the trial process. Judges have a duty to ensure that the important law reforms aimed at better protecting sexual assault complainants from discriminatory or unnecessarily humiliating treatment are more than just words on paper. They also have a duty, and inherent authority, to control the processes that occur in their court-rooms. This includes a duty to intervene in cross-examinations that are overly aggressive, repetitive, or badgering. In addition, judges have the ability to make changes to the way courtrooms themselves are organized. Given that fear of the criminal justice system remains one of the main reasons survivors do not come forward, and that many complainants report experiencing the trial process as foreign and unnerving, it is incumbent upon the judiciary to do what it can to make the courtroom setting and trial process less intimidating and more inclusive.

In addition to controlling the trial process through appropriate judi-cial intervention, and humanizing the courtroom setting, this requires ensuring some minimum threshold of substantive legal knowledge on the part of trial judges. The next chapter focuses on the harms to sexual assault complainants, and survivors of sexualized violence generally, caused by allowing trial judges who do not appear to understand the most basic legal rule governing the prosecution of sexual assault to preside over sexual assault trials.

CHAPTER 7

Judicial Error in Sexual Assault Cases

"As long ago as *Magna Carta*, it was recognized that judges should have a good knowledge of the law," notes the Canadian Judicial Council's (CJC) *Ethical Principles for Judges*.[1] *Good* knowledge of the law is not the judicial virtue discussed in this chapter. Instead, this chapter addresses the expectation that all trial judges who preside over sexual assault trials possess a minimum threshold of *basic* legal knowledge. It also explores the ways in which a failure to ensure this minimum threshold of knowledge causes particular harms to sexual assault complainants – harms that are not as likely to be perpetrated by judicial deficiencies in other contexts.

Previous chapters examined how the practice of sexual assault law by criminal defence lawyers and Crown attorneys, and the failure of some trial judges to properly intervene or apply section 276 of the *Criminal Code*, can contribute to the trauma of the trial for sexual assault complainants, and discussed the duty of Crown attorneys and trial judges to take some steps to minimize this trauma. This chapter considers a particular type of judicial error. Legal errors concerning the definition of consent reflected in the trial decisions (and/or statements at trial) in three relatively recent sexual assault cases are assessed. Questions about the appointment and training of those charged with presiding over sexual assault trials are raised. Like any deficiency in judicial legal knowledge or reasoning, a failure to properly apply the substantive law of sexual assault creates legal errors, wastes judicial resources on appeal, and causes unnecessary (and harmful) legal uncertainty to accused individuals. But judicial failures to properly understand or apply the legal definition of consent cause further detriment. As will be explained, through its inevitable reliance on discriminatory stereotypes about sexual assault that hold women responsible for their own sexual victimization, legal reasoning which reflects errors of this nature causes a kind of harm to sexual assault complainants that does not occur in other types of legal proceedings.

Male Sexual Entitlement in *R v B(IE)*

In *R v B(IE)*[2] the complainant testified that she, the accused, and a few other friends were drinking at a tavern. She was celebrating having been accepted full-time into the Canadian Armed Forces. The accused, who was also in the military, was a friend of her ex-boyfriend. According to her testimony, she was drunk but could still walk. The accused approached her on the dance floor and asked her to go with him. She agreed. He led her out of the bar and into the parking lot behind the establishment. She thought he was going to tell her that she had had too much to drink and she should go home. Outside the tavern she asked him where they were going, to which he replied only: "Follow me."[3] According to her, he led her behind a dumpster in the parking lot, opened his pants, removed his penis, placed it in her hand and then grabbed her hair, pulled her head down, and inserted his penis into her mouth. After he had ejaculated, he told her "this never happened Corporal" and left.[4] She vomited and then returned to the tavern, where she found her friend and disclosed to her what had occurred. In cross-examination, she testified that she did not say yes, no, or anything else to the accused during the incident because she was in shock, was crying, and had not expected any of this to occur.[5] The defence position was that the Crown had not proven beyond a reasonable doubt that the oral sex was non-consensual.[6] The accused did not testify.

The trial judge, Justice Gerald Moir, found that the complainant was credible and that she did not, in fact, consent to oral sex with the accused. His application of this part of the legal definition of consent was correct. However, he acquitted the accused on the basis that the Crown had failed to satisfy the *mens rea* for the offence of sexual assault. To convict someone of sexual assault, the judge (or jury) must be convinced that the accused not only engaged in sexual touching without consent, but that he intended to do so or was reckless as to whether it was consensual.

Justice Moir found that there was a reasonable doubt as to whether the accused either knew that the complainant was not consenting or was reckless about her lack of consent. In other words, he had a reasonable doubt as to whether the accused had an honest but mistaken belief in consent. He reasoned as follows:

> [26] At the dance floor, Ms. [G] agrees to go outside with him for no explicit purpose. A pleasant walk with a friend, a warning about drunkenness and directions home, or other things are possibilities.
>
> [27] The situation is unchanged outside the main door. "Where are we going?" does not get a direct or honest answer. Just "follow me". He intends on sex and keeps that to himself either because he seeks no consent or he is reckless about it.
>
> [28] Then they go along the side of the tavern. Then into the dimly lit rear. Then to a dumpster. It is almost a private place. Mr. [B] opens his pants.
>
> [29] After that he is entitled to think, absent complete drunkenness, that Ms. [G] knows his intent and is going along with it. There is no evidence he saw tears, or heard cries. In all the circumstances, the absence of a protest is significant.
>
> [30] I am not satisfied beyond a reasonable doubt that Mr. [B] knew that Ms. [G] was not consenting to the sexual activity or that he was reckless about it. Consequently, I will enter an acquittal.[7]

Justice Moir concluded that the accused was "entitled to think" that the complainant was consenting because: (i) she went with the accused to a secluded parking lot; (ii) she did not protest or flee when he opened his pants and removed his penis; and (iii) there was no evidence that the accused knew she was crying when he pulled her head down by her hair and penetrated her mouth with his penis.[8] Justice Moir's decision failed to articulate and apply the affirmative definition of consent required under the common law, and failed to consider the reasonable steps requirement under section 273.2(b) of the *Criminal Code*.[9]

Contrary to Justice Moir's assertion in *B(IE)*, under Canadian law accused individuals are not "entitled to think" that women are "going along with it" because they fail to scream, fight back, or run away in response to an attack.[10] "Absence of a protest" alone is not a defence and in this case absence of protest is all there was.[11] The criminal law definition of consent to sexual touching in Canada creates an affirmative standard. This means that an accused cannot rely on a woman's passivity, or failure to resist, to establish that he had a mistaken belief in consent.[12] The defence of mistaken belief in consent must relate to a belief that the complainant communicated consent through words or actions. That is to say, the 'mistaken belief in consent' defence must be based on a belief that the complainant indicated yes, through words or actions, not a belief that the complainant did not say no. In addition, an accused cannot avail himself of this defence if he failed to take reasonable steps in the circumstances known to him at the time to ascertain consent.[13]

Instead of applying this affirmative definition of consent, Justice Moir acquitted the accused on the basis that "[t]he only outward sign that she disagreed would have been her crying ... [S]he did not walk away although she could have done. She was not compelled by a threat, and nothing, except the shock, prevented her from saying 'Don't do this' or 'I'm leaving.'"[14] In analyzing the *mens rea* element of the offence, Justice Moir's decision focused on the lack of sufficient outward signs of non-consent.[15] As Crown attorney Mark Scott argued on appeal, "How ... can luring [the complainant] further into a dimly lit alley, beside a dumpster, and exposing his penis evolve to an honest belief in [the complainant] *communicating consent* to any sexual activity?"[16] Instead, Justice Moir's assessment should have focused on whether there was any evidence of outward signs that she had agreed to perform oral sex on the accused. The criminal law definition of consent is very clear on this point and has been for quite some time: "What matters is whether the accused believed that the complainant effectively said 'yes' through her words and/or actions ... In the context of *mens rea* – specifically for the purposes of the 'honest but mistaken belief in consent' defence – 'consent' means that the complainant had affirmatively communicated by words or conduct her agreement to engage in sexual activity with the accused."[17]

Justice Moir's decision wrongly emphasized that nothing, other than shock, prevented the complainant from resisting or fleeing. Again, the 'mistaken belief in consent' defence is not established by lack of evidence that the complainant resisted, or was threatened, or was prevented from fleeing. Moreover, even if it were, complainants often describe having been overwhelmed with shock, or having frozen, during a sexual assault.[18]

Even if the law required the Crown to show that the complainant was prevented from escaping – which it does not – the paralyzing effect of shock in response to sexual violation is a well-accepted phenomenon.[19]

Regardless, it has been nearly twenty years since the Supreme Court of Canada adopted a legal definition of consent that rejects the stereotype that women who actually do not agree to the sexual contact at issue will physically resist and that those who fail to do so in fact 'wanted it'.[20] To acquit an accused of sexual assault on the basis of nothing more than an absence of protest on the part of the complainant is to set the law of sexual assault in Canada back by nearly two decades.

Now reflect specifically upon the reasonable steps requirement stipulated under section 273.2(b) of the *Criminal Code*.[21] An accused can only rely on an honest but mistaken belief in consent if he took reasonable steps under the circumstances to ascertain whether the complainant was, in fact, consenting. Under Canada's *Criminal Code*, if someone fails to take these steps, he cannot later assert that he mistakenly assumed that the complainant was consenting to the sexual acts in which he engaged.[22] Far from identifying any steps taken by the accused to ascertain consent, Justice Moir found that the accused concealed his intention to have sex with the complainant because "he either did not intend to seek consent or was reckless about obtaining consent."[23]

Recall that the complainant testified that she was crying when the accused penetrated her orally. A man who fails to observe that, and inquire as to the reason why, a drunken woman he has led into a secluded parking lot is crying prior to penetrating her with his penis has failed to take reasonable steps in the circumstances known to him at the time to ascertain that she is consenting. Again, rather than having taken any steps to ascertain consent, according to Justice Moir's finding, the accused in fact concealed his intention to have sex with the complainant.

The Nova Scotia Court of Appeal allowed the Crown's appeal on the basis that Justice Moir failed to conduct any analysis as to the 'reasonable steps' requirement for the defence of mistaken belief in consent. This alone constitutes a significant failure to appreciate, articulate, and apply the legal definition of consent. However, the Court also stated, in *obiter*, that Justice Moir's basis for acquittal was the complainant's failure to resist: "It is evident from his decision that what the judge found supportive of an acquittal was what he saw as the complainant's failure to object or resist ... It is implicit from his reasons that the judge was of the view that the absence of a protest led to an honest but mistaken belief on the part of the respondent that the complainant consented to engaging in sexual activity in question."[24]

To summarize, Justice Moir's reasoning failed to apply both the 'reasonable steps' requirement of the *Criminal Code* and the affirmative definition of consent established in *Ewanchuk*. According to the Nova Scotia Court of Appeal, he acquitted the accused because of what he considered to be the complainant's failure to object, resist, or run away.[25] The affirmation of male sexual entitlement instantiated in the reasoning in the trial decision in *B(IE)* reflects significant disregard for the sexual autonomy of women and is inconsistent with the law of consent in Canada.

No Means Keep Trying until She Gives In

In *R v Adepoju*[26] the complainant testified that she had agreed to allow the accused to move into her home as a roommate. She told the accused that going forward she wanted their relationship to be platonic, but when he arrived at her home he immediately started kissing her. She allowed the first kiss but refused further kissing. She repeatedly advised him that "she did not want to engage in any sexual activity."[27] Ignoring her repeated protestations, the accused pushed her onto a bed and repeatedly grabbed her and tried to kiss her and pull her pants and underwear off. She continued to resist verbally and physically. Ultimately the accused managed to remove her pants and underwear. He continued his attempts with her pants and underwear removed, while she "held her legs in a defensive position" and continued her efforts to make him stop.[28] After approximately fifteen to twenty minutes she stopped resisting, at which point the accused engaged in vaginal intercourse.[29]

The trial judge, Justice Kirk Sisson, accepted the complainant's testimony[30] and rejected the accused's evidence. He highlighted text messages sent by the accused in which the accused admitted to sexually assaulting the complainant: "I had to force you, you didn't wanna do it."[31] Justice Sisson's decision emphasized that the accused admitted on cross-examination to his belief that if she had previously indicated a willingness to have sex, it was okay for him to engage in sexual intercourse with her, even if he knew that she had changed her mind.[32] Nevertheless,

Justice Sisson acquitted the accused on the basis that the Crown had failed to prove lack of consent beyond a reasonable doubt. He reasoned as follows:

> Clearly the complainant initially objected to the accused's advances by words and actions, but her testimony indicates that she ceased objecting because of his persistence. There is no indication that threats or force, or like circumstances entered the equation. Taking into account all of the circumstances, the testimony of the complainant discloses more than a mere lack of consent. The sexual activity, which is the subject of this charge, commenced after the complainant stopped [saying] no, and indicated by body language that she was consenting. She testified that she gave in because of his persistence, and to get it over with. *In other words, she finally decided that she had enough and gave into him.* This was her state of mind at the time the sexual activity occurred. Consequently, the Crown has failed to prove an essential element of the offence beyond a reasonable doubt, that's lack of consent, therefore I dismiss that count.[33]

The legal analysis in *Adepoju* is reliant on the following premises: (i) forcing one's mouth (and tongue?) onto the mouth of a woman, pushing her onto a bed, groping her, and pulling her pants and underwear off do not constitute sexual assault; (ii) sexual assault occurs only when there is an act of penetration; and (iii) a woman who 'gives in' to vaginal intercourse after more than fifteen minutes of verbal and physical resistance in order to "get it over with" is consenting.[34]

The reasoning in *Adepoju* reflects substantial errors with respect to both the *actus reus* and *mens rea* elements of sexual assault. Like the trial decision in *B(IE)*, it also suggests reliance on legally rejected stereotypes about women and sexual violence.

First, Justice Sisson's reasoning reflects the assumption that sexual assault only occurs when there is penetration. He accepted the complainant's evidence that the accused kissed her, pushed her onto a bed, grabbed her, and repeatedly tried to remove her clothing. He accepted her evidence that she physically and verbally resisted these actions. Yet his verdict gave no legal effect to these factual findings. Based on his flawed analysis, these acts alone do not amount to sexual assault. As the

Crown rightly argued on appeal: "The activity preceding the intercourse was the application of sexual force – not mere 'persistence'. It alone was a sexual assault."[35]

Second, acquiescence is not consent. It would be a patently obvious error to conclude that a woman's acquiescence after fifteen to twenty minutes of verbal and physical resistance could lend an air of reality to the defence of mistaken belief in consent. Justice Sisson's conclusion was even worse. He concluded that the complainant's acquiescence gave rise to a reasonable doubt as to whether she had in fact consented.

The criminal law definition of consent to sexual touching in Canada is assessed based on the complainant's subjective state of mind at the time the sexual touching occurred.[36] In other words, whether the sexual touching was consensual, for purposes of establishing the *actus reus*, is determined based on the complainant's perspective. Justice Sisson accepted the complainant's testimony. She testified that the accused "kept trying to force himself" on her.[37] She explicitly stated that she did not, at any point during the interaction, want to engage in sexual acts with the accused.[38] She testified that he kept pulling at her clothing and trying to get on top of her. She repeatedly told him to stop and tried to push him away. She testified that after approximately fifteen to twenty minutes she "realized he wasn't going to stop."[39] She felt like she could not escape and no one would hear her if she screamed, and so she "just stopped fighting him."[40] It is unfathomable to hold any doubt (reasonable or otherwise) that a woman in these circumstances was not consenting to the sexual contact that ensued after she stopped resisting. Even someone with no legal training or criminal law knowledge should be expected to conclude that what occurred in this case did not amount to consensual intercourse.

To be legally valid, consent must be given voluntarily.[41] A complainant who, as Justice Sisson stated, "gave in" in order to "get it over with" because she had "had enough" of physically and verbally resisting the accused cannot be said to have consented.[42] Indeed, it is difficult to imagine legal reasoning in a sexual assault case that could be more inconsistent with the law of consent and less protective of women's sexual integrity than the analysis provided by Justice Sisson in *Adepoju*. The Alberta Court of Appeal determined that Justice Sisson "erred in defining sexual assault to include only sexual intercourse," erred in determining that acquiescence or submission amounts to consent, and presumably erred in failing to apply the requirement that reasonable steps be taken to ensure consent after the rejection of sexual advances.[43] The Court set aside the acquittal, entered a conviction, and remitted the matter to Justice Sisson for sentencing.[44]

"The Way of the Birds and the Bees" Rather than the Law of Consent

In *R v Wagar*[45] the complainant alleged that the accused forced her to engage in sexual intercourse and oral sex after locking her in a bathroom with him during a house party.[46] The accused, who was more than twice her size, testified that the sexual activity was consensual.[47]

In addition to statements implying disdain for the affirmative definition of consent to sexual touching required under *Ewanchuk* and for the protections against misuses of a complainant's prior sexual history provided under section 276, Justice Camp's statements at trial and his reasoning in *Wagar* involved legal errors similar to those that occurred in *Adepoju* and *B(IE)*. As in both *Adepoju* and *B(IE)*, his conduct of the case failed to articulate and apply the affirmative definition of consent established in *Ewanchuk*. Several of the questions he asked the complainant during the trial suggested a deeply flawed understanding of the definition of consent. For example, he asked her:

> Q. But when – when he was using – when he was trying to insert his penis, your bottom was down in the basin. Or am I wrong?
>
> A. My – my vagina was not in the bowl of the basin when he was having intercourse with me.
>
> Q. All right. Which then leads me to the question: Why not – why didn't you just sink your bottom down into the basin so he couldn't penetrate you?
>
> A. I was drunk.
>
> Q. And when your ankles were held together by your jeans, your skinny jeans, why couldn't you just keep your knees together?[48]

Justice Camp later stated: "She knew she was drunk ... Is [there] not an onus on her to be more careful?"[49] While Justice Camp did note that a lack of evidence of force or fear does not mean that the sex was consensual, several of his statements throughout the proceeding and in his decision nevertheless suggest that his assessment of the complainant's credibility was informed by his conclusion that she failed to resist. For example, he began his reasons for acquittal with the observation that the complainant's "version is open to question. She certainly had the ability, perhaps learnt from her experience on the streets, to tell [him] to fuck off."[50]

The trial transcript in *Wagar* provides an explicit example of a sexual assault proceeding in which it seemed to be the complainant (rather than the accused) that was put on trial, and in this case by the trial judge himself. Tellingly, Justice Camp referred to the complainant as the accused at numerous points throughout the proceeding and in his reasons for decision. For example, he stated: "the accused hasn't explained why she allowed the sex to happen if she didn't want it."[51]

Justice Camp's statements during the trial also suggested a significant lack of understanding of the reasonable steps requirement in relation to the mistaken belief in consent defence. In response to the Crown's assertion that the accused, who met the complainant for the first time on the evening of the alleged offence and who knew that the complainant was intoxicated, did not take reasonable steps to ascertain consent, Justice Camp stated:

> [W]hy must I use in any way at all the fact that they hardly knew each other? What's sauce for the goose is sauce for the gander ... You're saying that it – that it – a drunk man has a higher standard, or the fact that he knew she was drunk places a higher standard on him? ... He must be doubly careful ... She knew she was drunk ... Is [there] not an onus on her to be more careful? ... to make it clear that she's not consenting ... There's – there's no – there's no higher on – there's – there's not an equal onus on a drunk woman as on a drunk man?[52]

Justice Camp's comments appear to entirely ignore both the reasonable steps requirement under the *Criminal Code* and the affirmative definition of consent in *Ewanchuk* – the Supreme Court of Canada's leading decision on consent. As an aside, it is striking how similar Justice Camp's stereotypical statements are to those of Justice John McClung in *Ewanchuk*. Justice McClung, writing for the majority of the Alberta

Court of Appeal, characterized the actions of the accused as "clumsy passes" and "far less criminal than hormonal."[53] He emphasized her failure to fight back as relevant to consent.[54] Justice McClung's stereotype-infused decision was overturned by the Supreme Court of Canada.

As the Crown successfully argued on appeal in *Wagar*, Justice Camp's flawed understanding of the law infected his assessment of the complainant's credibility.[55] The Alberta Court of Appeal overturned Justice Camp's decision to acquit the accused and ordered a new trial.[56] The unanimous decision of the three-judge appellate panel read in part:

> [W]e are satisfied that the trial judge's comments throughout the proceedings and in his reasons gave rise to doubts about the trial judge's understanding of the law governing sexual assaults and in particular, the meaning of consent and restrictions on evidence of the complainant's sexual activity imposed by section 276 of the *Criminal Code*. We are also persuaded that sexual stereotypes and stereotypical myths, which have long since been discredited, may have found their way into the trial judge's judgment.[57]

One important distinction between Justice Camp's statements during the *Wagar* trial and those of these other jurists involves Justice Camp's seeming disdain for the law of sexual assault. For example, in one exchange with the Crown he made the following statements regarding the reasonable steps requirement under section 273.2(b) of the *Criminal Code*:[58]

> THE COURT: Are there any particular words you must use like the marriage ceremony?
> MS. MOGRABEE: Yes, he must say – oh he could say a number of different things, but he must ask if she is willing to engage in the sexual activity –
> THE COURT: He must ask to go that far?
> MS. MOGRABEE: – he has – he must ask.
> THE COURT: Where is that written?
> MS. MOGRABEE: It's in the case – all the case law that you have before you that sex – that –
> THE COURT: Are children taught this at school? Do they pass tests like driver's licenses? It seems a little extreme?

MS. MOGRABEE: The state of the law is [as] it is, Sir. It's all set out in the case law.

THE COURT: Well can you show me one of these places it says that there's ... some kind of incantation that has to be gone through? Because it's not the way of the birds and the bees.[59]

Arguably, the problems with Justice Camp's conduct of the case in *Wagar* include, but extend well beyond, lack of legal knowledge. His disdain for the law on the basis of stereotypical thinking, his disrespect towards the complainant, and his perpetuation of discriminatory stereotypes became the subject of public and professional scrutiny after a complaint to the CJC was filed on 9 November 2015 by four law professors (including the author, Alice Woolley, Jennifer Koshan, and Jocelyn Downie).[60] We argued that both during the trial proceeding and in his reasons for judgment, Justice Camp was contemptuous towards the substantive law of sexual assault and the rules of evidence. Our complaint asserted that he expressed disregard for the law of consent and then went on to assess credibility on the issue of consent in a manner that did not apply the proper legal definition. We argued that his statements regarding the rape shield provisions under section 276 of the *Criminal Code* were similarly problematic.[61]

An inquiry into Justice Camp's statements and conduct in *Wagar*, struck at the request of Alberta's attorney general, concluded that he had engaged in misconduct in this trial. The Inquiry Committee unanimously recommended his removal from office.[62] The majority of the Canadian Judicial Council accepted the Inquiry Committee's recommendation for removal, concluding that Justice Camp's statements in *Wagar* demonstrated "obvious disdain" for the law of sexual assault, and that taken as a whole the impact of his statements on the public's confidence in the judiciary required that he be removed from office.[63] He resigned shortly after the council recommended to the minister of justice that he be removed from office.[64]

Notwithstanding the unique features present in *Wagar*, there are noteworthy commonalities between these three cases. The trial decisions (and/or statements made during the trial) in all three of *Adepoju*, *B(IE)*, and *Wagar* reflect glaring, substantive legal errors. While there are aspects of sexual assault law that involve complex analysis, the legal definition of consent to sexual touching is not one of them. As Justice J.E. Topolniski recently stated in overturning an acquittal and entering a conviction in *R v R(J)*: "Consent in the context of sexual activity is not a difficult concept."[65] The decision of the trial judge in *R(J)*, Judge Michael Savaryn, included legal errors similar to those present in *Adepoju*, *B(IE)*, and *Wagar*.[66]

A stereotype-infused assessment of the complainant's credibility was also recently overturned in another Alberta case, *R v CMG*.[67] The decision of the trial judge in *CMG*, Judge Pat McIlhargey, assailed the complainant's credibility on the basis of her failure to scream or run for help.[68] At the time of writing, his decision in *CMG* was under review by the Chief Judge of the Alberta Provincial Court.[69]

In Canada, the criminal law definition of consent – which, as already noted, is well-settled and nearly twenty years old – constitutes basic legal knowledge for anyone practising sexual assault law, or adjudicating sexual assault cases. As Justice Topolniski went on to note in *R(J)*, "It is long beyond debate that in Canada 'No means No', that 'No' does not require a minimal word or gesture, and that acquiescence or ambiguous conduct do not equate to consent."[70]

The costs to both the criminal justice system and the individuals involved in a particular case that are incurred when a trial decision is overturned are significant. When a new trial is ordered, as was the case in *B(IE)*[71] and *Wagar*,[72] these costs include the expenditure of further judicial resources and the additional stress, anxiety, and insecurity imposed on both the complainant and the accused. For many complainants, the prospect of facing yet another round of cross-examination is traumatic. It is not uncommon for the Crown to decline to prosecute a second time because of a complainant's unwillingness to endure the distress and disruption of testifying at a retrial.[73] The injustice of requiring sexual assault complainants to endure a second trial – and the emotional and psychological detriment that entails – because at the first trial they were unlucky enough to have a judge who explicitly engaged in stereotypical thinking or made glaring errors with respect to basic legal concepts is significant.

Even when a Court of Appeal replaces the trial judge's verdict with its own rather than ordering a new trial, as occurred in *Adepoju*[74] and *R(J)*,[75] there are associated costs such as the emotional impact on the parties. As a general matter, we assume that these costs are outweighed by the public interest in avoiding or reversing miscarriages of justice. However, when the imposition of these burdens on both individuals and the system occurs because of a failure on the part of the trial judge to articulate and apply basic legal concepts, the calculation is different. It is not simply that these judges made legal errors. Judges make legal errors all the time. It is the type of error made, and the consequences of the type of error made, in these cases that warrants a different response. As explained in the next part of this chapter, the type of flawed legal reasoning demonstrated in these cases heightens the risk of bias and stereotype and perpetuates a particular type of harm to sexual assault survivors.

The Relationship between Stereotypical Thinking and Judicial Error

Underpinning the mistakes of law made in *B(IE)*, *Adepoju*, and *Wagar* are stereotypes about women and sexual violence. Notably, the Crown in all three of these cases argued on appeal that the trial judge's reasons revealed stereotypical thinking and/or rape mythology.[76] Indeed, in each case, the trial judge's analysis of whether there was consent, or a mistaken belief in consent, appears to have been informed by stereotypes about sexual violence.

One of the stereotypes that clearly underpinned the judicial reasoning in *B(IE)*, *Adepoju*, and *Wagar* is the belief that a woman cannot be raped against her will – that women who actually do not want to engage in sexual contact will resist physically, scream for help, or escape. The correlative assumption that flows from this stereotype is that women who are sexually assaulted have only themselves to blame. The paradox of this logic renders women who allege rape inherently and unavoidably blame-worthy: either the alleged assault was in fact consensual, as evidenced by the lack of resistance, or the complainant bears some responsibility for her failure to successfully fight her attacker off. This logic of blame is readily apparent in all three of these trial decisions. The harmful effect that such shaming can have on survivors is unquestionable. For instance, consider the complainant in *Wagar* – a young Indigenous woman who had struggled with homelessness and addictions. Reportedly, in her testimony at the CJC removal hearing for Justice Camp (who referred to her during the trial as an "amoral" person[77]), she described the impact that his questions had had on her as follows: "He made me hate myself and he made me feel like I should have done something ... that I was some kind of slut."[78]

The law of consent in Canada – including the affirmative definition of consent adopted in *Ewanchuk*[79] and the reasonable steps requirement enacted under section 273.2(b) of the *Criminal Code*[80] – is aimed, in part, at rejecting a legal approach to the issue of sexual violence that presumptively places the complainant on trial. These legal reforms reversed the presumption that women are consenting until proven otherwise. The significance of this objective cannot be overstated. The tendency to 'blame the victim' causes particular traumatic effects in the context of sexualized violence. Consider again the destructive relationship between sexual violation, gender stereotypes, and shame explained in chapter 1. Law reifies this triumvirate of trauma when its rules, its processes, or in these instances its interpreters place sexual assault complainants on trial. In other words, legal reasoning that acquits a man of sexual assault because a woman failed to sufficiently fight back amounts to an institutionalized, state-supported shaming of the complainant.

The need to ensure that trial judges understand and can apply foundational legal concepts is heightened in the context of sexual assault proceedings because of the role that discriminatory stereotypes have played, and continue to play, in this area of law. The prosecution of sexual violence occurs in a very particular legal context – one that has been burdened with a legacy of discriminatory laws informed by stereotypes about women and sexual violence.[81] Several of these discriminatory legal rules have been formally rejected through law reform. Unfortunately, as clearly demonstrated in these three cases, the social assumptions underlying them continue to inform legal reasoning.[82] In her concurring decision in *Ewanchuk*, Justice L'Heureux-Dubé wrote:

> Complainants should be able to rely on a system free from myths
> and stereotypes, and on a judiciary whose impartiality is not com-
> promised by these biased assumptions. The *Code* was amended
> in 1983 and in 1992 to eradicate reliance on those assumptions;
> they should not be permitted to resurface through the stereotypes
> reflected in the reasons of the majority of the Court of Appeal. It
> is part of the role of this Court to denounce this kind of language,
> unfortunately still used today, which not only perpetuates archaic
> myths and stereotypes about the nature of sexual assaults but also
> ignores the law.[83]

Despite law reforms, stereotypes continue to have particular cognitive traction in the context of sexual assault cases because of the nature of the decision-making that often must occur in these cases.[84] As discussed in chapter 4, researchers have found that people are more likely to rely on stereotypes when making judgments under conditions of uncertainty.[85] Sexual assault trials often require drawing conclusions about events that occurred in private, without any third-party witnesses, and that frequently feature two very different accounts of what occurred. Given the tenacity and resiliency of rape mythology, even despite legal reforms aimed specifically at eradicating these stereotypes, it is critical that trial judges charged with presiding over sexual assault trials have some minimum threshold of knowledge of what these law reforms are, and what they were intended to achieve. Unfortunately, even judges with a good understanding of the law of sexual assault can be expected to, at times, unknowingly resort to schematic or stereotype-based thinking in the face of such uncertainty. As evidenced in *B(IE)*, *Adepoju*, and *Wagar*, judicial decisions (or statements during trial) that reveal errors regarding the basic legal framework for sexual assault will almost certainly also involve reasoning based on legally discredited stereotypes about rape.

Case law research suggests that the reasoning (and/or trial statements) in these cases is not representative of the numerous sexual assault trial decisions applying the law of consent that are reported each year in Canada. That said, it is difficult to assess the extent to which the type of reasoning and statements demonstrated in these cases occurs because it is not possible to access all trial decisions. Some (unknown proportion of) sexual assault decisions go unreported each year. Moreover, trial decisions and/or statements at trial like the ones in *B(IE)*, *Adepoju*, *Wagar*, and *R(J)* should never occur. Allowing a trial judge who either does not know or does not understand the legal definition of consent to preside over sexual assault trials is like allowing a pilot who does not know how to lower the landing gear to fly the plane solo. This should never happen. That it does raises serious questions regarding Canada's judicial appointment processes, case assignment processes within the courts, and judicial education programs.

Appointment, Training, and Assessment

In a 2011 Manitoba case, Justice Robert Dewar made numerous statements suggesting an understanding of sexual assault premised largely on rape mythology. His comments were made during a sentencing decision in *R v Rhodes*.[86] Rhodes was convicted of sexually assaulting a young Indigenous woman. Justice Dewar found that he had sexually assaulted the complainant by penetrating her vagina with his fingers and his penis, anally penetrating her with his penis, and assaulting her genitals with his mouth. Despite these findings, in imposing a two-year conditional sentence to be served in the community, Justice Dewar emphasized that there was no violence knowingly imposed by the accused, and that the complainant did not run away. He characterized Rhodes's conduct as that of a "clumsy Don Juan."[87] He stated, "This is a case of misread signals and inconsiderate behavior. There is a different quality to these facts than found in many cases of serious sexual assault."[88] He pointed to the fact that the complainant was wearing a tube top without a bra, makeup, and high heels, and suggested that "sex was in the air" that evening.[89]

Several complaints were brought against Justice Dewar as a consequence of his statements in *Rhodes*. According to the CJC, Justice Dewar "offered a full and unequivocal apology to the victim for the hurt she experienced from his comments. He also is aware that his comments may have been traumatic to other women who were victims of sexual assault and expressed his sincere regret for this."[90]

In the wake of the public outcry and political criticism generated by Justice Dewar's statements, the CJC took the unusual step of publicly defending the training of the federally appointed judiciary. Executive Director Norman Sabourin stated: "Canadians rightly expect that those who serve as judges have the legal skills, competence, and temperament suited to the difficult task of deciding criminal and civil disputes."[91] Sabourin went on to assert that federally appointed judges receive extensive training upon their appointment to the bench, and noted that "[i]n their day to day work, judges must decide some of the most difficult disputes between citizens ... Thousands of decisions are rendered by the courts of law every year, after thoughtful consideration by competent and learned judges. While our system may not be perfect, on balance it works well."[92]

Trial judges cannot be expected to have practised in, let alone mastered, every substantive area of law that they will encounter in their role as judges. The judges of some courts are required to hear cases ranging across very different areas of law. In addition, novel legal issues and new areas of law continue to emerge, such that it would not be possible for trial judges to have expertise in every matter over which they preside. As well, generally speaking, our court system is structured on the assumption that those appointed to the bench possess a skill set and background that will enable them to acquire the substantive knowledge necessary to preside over matters as they come before them. For example, lawyers, as officers of the court, are ethically obligated to ensure that judges have before them any relevant and binding law of which they are aware.[93] Moreover, our system of appellate review reflects, and attempts to respond to, the reality that lower court judges will not always identify, interpret, and apply the law with exactitude.

However, regardless of a judge's pre-appointment expertise, it is reasonable to expect that he or she will understand and apply very basic legal rules directly at issue in matters that are likely to come before him or her on a regular basis. It is probably reasonable to maintain this expectation regardless of legal context. For the reasons I have just explained, regarding the relationship between lack of legal knowledge, stereotypical thinking, sexual violence, and the shaming of survivors, it is most certainly reasonable to expect that the decisions and statements of judges who preside over sexual assault cases will demonstrate this basic legal knowledge. The definition of consent to sexual touching is a legal rule of this basic nature. Sexual assault proceedings in both provincial and superior courts are far from anomalous. Indeed, sexual assault trials are an everyday occurrence in Canadian courtrooms. Judges, whether they are appointed to the criminal division of a provincial court, as was Justice Camp, or to superior court trial divisions such as the ones presided over by Justices Moir, Sisson, and Rhodes, are quite likely to find themselves handling sexual assault trials.

The trial judges in *B(IE)*, *Adepoju*, *Wagar*, and *Rhodes* have something in common. None of these judges appear to have had any criminal law expertise of note prior to being appointed to the bench. Before becoming judges, they practised business, corporate, and civil litigation. Justice Gerald Moir was an expert in insolvency law and commercial law prior to his 1997 appointment by the Liberal government to the Supreme Court of Nova Scotia.[94] Justice Kirk Sisson, who was appointed to the Alberta Court of Queen's Bench in 2006 by the Conservative government, practised in a firm that specializes in corporate and commercial law, intellectual property law, civil litigation, and real estate law.[95] Justice Dewar, also appointed by former Prime Minister Harper's government, specialized in commercial and corporate litigation, insolvency, and construction disputes before joining the trial division of the Manitoba Court of Queen's Bench in 2009.[96] Justice Robin Camp's main area of practice was commercial litigation prior to his appointment to the criminal division of the Alberta Provincial Court in 2012. He was subsequently elevated to the Federal Court by the Harper government in 2015.[97] (Justice Camp's lawyer, in his opening submissions before the CJC inquiry panel convened to consider whether Camp should be removed from office as a consequence of his actions in *Wagar*, highlighted the fact that Justice Camp "was a civil lawyer with no experience in Canadian sexual assault law prior to his appointment."[98])

Judicial appointments processes in Canada have been assessed by some as among the weakest in the world.[99] One of the main concerns is that political considerations – that is to say, political patronage – rather than merit-based factors, such as experience and expertise, play a dominant role in the selection of judges by governing parties in Canada.[100] In his public inquiry into the wrongful conviction of three men in Newfoundland, former chief justice Antonio Lamer urged ministers of justice and chief justices "to be vigilant in identifying the need for criminal law experience and expertise when vacancies [in the superior courts] occur."[101] Some members of the criminal bar have raised concerns regarding the practice of appointing lawyers with little or no criminal law experience to courts that handle primarily criminal cases. In Alberta, for example, between 1999 and 2007 the provincial government appointed twenty-eight judges to the criminal division.[102] Fifteen of those twenty-eight had no criminal law experience.[103] The criminal division of the provincial court, of course, handles exclusively criminal matters. During the same period, twenty of the twenty-four judges appointed to the Alberta Court of Queen's Bench by the federal government had little or no criminal law background. Approximately one-third of the caseload for the Alberta Court of Queen's Bench involves criminal matters.[104] The current federal government is revising the federal judicial appointments process.[105] Perhaps the new procedure will avoid some of these potential problems, at least at the federal level.

This is not to suggest that only judges with criminal law practice experience are qualified to handle criminal cases. Nor, as already explained, is it to suggest that judges can be expected to have mastered every area of law, or even every aspect of a particular area of law. Nevertheless, the prospect of judges who do not appear to understand or ably apply the legal definition of consent presiding over sexual assault trials suggests a significant failing of the appointments process, judicial education programs, case assignment, or some combination of the three. Imagine allowing a judge who does not understand the fundamental elements of a contract to preside over matters in the commercial division of a court.

If provincial and federal ministers of justice are going to appoint lawyers with no criminal law experience to courts where all, or a substantial portion, of matters are criminal, it is critical that these individuals receive adequate training and assessment. Given the harms at issue in sexual assault cases in particular, this training and assessment must occur before they are permitted to preside over sexual assault trials. Correspondingly, chief justices should develop case assignment systems that ensure that judges are never assigned to cases concerning matters about which they do not have a rudimentary understanding of the fundamentals. They should not be given such cases until they have received basic training and have been evaluated on their knowledge of the relevant basic legal rules.

The cjc recommends that superior court judges spend ten days per year on continuing education. The cjc suggests that newly appointed judges be assigned a mentor and that they develop an individualized education plan for their first four years, in collaboration with either their mentor or chief justice. The Council's position is that "[t]he education of newly-appointed judges is to be seen as a four-year process requiring 10 to 15 days of education per year, involving a mix of sitting and non-sitting time which time includes the integrated seminar for newly-appointed judges."[106]

Given these resources for, and policies about, judicial education, how do we end up with legal errors of the sort demonstrated in *B(IE)*, *Adepoju*, and *Wagar*?

One of the problems may be that, historically, judicial education has not been required of judges in Canada. According to the Office of the Commissioner for Federal Judicial Affairs, "[t]he responsibility to further their education rests with individual judges."[107] While new federally appointed judges were strongly encouraged to attend 'New Judges School' (a six-day program offered twice per year), and anecdotal evidence suggests that the majority did, attendance was not required.[108] Promisingly, the cjc very recently changed this policy, seemingly in response to public criticism and pressure from lawmakers.[109] The cjc now requires all new federally appointed judges to attend a seminar that includes "intensive, specific sessions on sexual assault law; sexual violence; and gender equality. These sessions are more than just about the law: they are designed to ensure judges are aware of the underlying factors that lead to gender inequalities."[110] The CJC should be commended for adopting this initiative and should be encouraged to extend a similar requirement to all federally appointed judges, not just those who are newly appointed. Moreover, to be effective, training and education of this nature must involve more than a one-off seminar. In the United Kingdom, in order to preside over rape trials, judges must complete the "Serious Sexual Offences Seminar" every three years.[111] The seminar aims to provide "those who try serious sexual offences with an opportunity to identify and address current legal, evidential, procedural, social, and sentencing issues. It provides an update on current law and seeks to assist judges to develop their judicial skills in relation to the trial of serious sexual offences."[112]

A good portion of sexual assault trials occur in provincial courts. Provincial courts, and the Canadian Association of Provincial Court Judges, also make training and education recommendations and offer programs to newly appointed provincial court judges. Provincially appointed judges may also avail themselves of training programs offered by the National Judicial Institute (NJI). Unfortunately, while some provinces are beginning to require sexual assault training and formal mentoring programs for provincial court judges,[113] these do not appear to be mandatory in most provinces.[114]

Those provincial courts that have not yet done so should require newly appointed judges to attend a program that offers some basic criminal law training before allowing them to preside over criminal matters. As with federally appointed judges, provincial courts should also put in place ongoing, mandatory training and education for all provincial court judges who preside over sexual assault proceedings.

Judicial independence must be safeguarded. It seems reasonable to accept that judicial independence is better protected if judges are responsible for the design and delivery of judicial education. However, a transparent system of mandatory training, provided it is designed and operated by the judiciary itself, is not presumptively in tension with judicial independence. While the details of such an enterprise would need to be developed and adopted by the judiciary itself, it is possible to offer some suggestions as to what such initiatives might entail.

For example, at both levels, this training should include education on substantive sexual assault law and the relationship between gender stereotypes and the legal process in the context of sexual assault trials. In addition to the substantive legal skills and knowledge that should be taught in mandatory seminars, the curriculum should include content on the social context surrounding and producing sexual violence. This would include content on the gendered nature of sexualized violence; the intersection of race, disability, and socio-economic status with sexual violence; the connection between common myths and stereotypes about sexual assault and victim-blaming/shaming; and programming that encourages judges to reflect upon, and challenge, their own stereotypical assumptions about gender, sexuality, and sexual violence. Examples of judges in recent sexual assault trials being overturned because of very obvious legal errors stemming from legally rejected social assumptions about sexuality, gender, and sexual assault are not difficult to find.[115] Given the problematic role that stereotypes play in sexual assault proceedings in particular, this aspect of the mandatory curriculum would likely be critical.

According to his submissions to the cjc, the training and counselling undertaken by Justice Camp in an effort to remediate the deficiencies he demonstrated in *Wagar* included instruction followed by testing of his understanding of the following topics and issues: the purpose and history of the substantive law of sexual assault, the relationship between gender and law, how sexual assault survivors respond to trauma, and stereotypes and myths about sexual violence.[116] How unfortunate that Justice Camp neither chose to, nor was required to, undertake this clearly necessary training and assessment before the costs and damage to the complainant, the accused, and the public's perception of the justice system were incurred as a result of what he himself accepted was his "disgraceful and appalling" conduct in *Wagar*.[117]

With respect to federally appointed judges, one obvious route to ensuring this basic level of legal knowledge and skill would be for the cjc to authorize the National Judicial Institute (nji) to design a mandatory curriculum for new judges, and an ongoing, recurrent program for sitting judges. The nji is one of the primary bodies responsible for delivering judicial education in Canada, particularly for federally appointed judges. The Standing Committee on the Status of Women recently recommended that the federal government provide funding to the nji "for the express purpose of developing comprehensive training on gender-based violence and sexual assault for the judiciary and those seeking to become part of the judiciary, and that the government of Canada encourage all judges to participate in this training."[118]

In the past, the NJI has offered sessions on the history of sex assault legislation, consent, credibility, evidence of sexual history, myths and stereotypes, courtroom management, disclosure and production, child witnesses, and the context and experience of complainants.[119] Moreover, with the adoption of its Social Context Education Project in 1996, Canada's NJI became a leader in providing so-called 'social context education' to judges. Although information on specific courses is not available, the NJI does provide a description of the Social Context Education Project. The project aimed to assist judges to:

- understand the nature of diversity, the impacts of disadvantage, and the particular social, cultural, and linguistic issues that shape the persons who appear before them;
- explore their own assumptions, biases, and views of the world with a view to reflecting on how these may interact with judicial process;
- learn about relevant research and community experience in order to enhance processes of judicial reasoning; and
- examine, using jurisprudential and analytical tools provided by the project, the underlying basis of legal rules and concepts to ensure that they correspond with social realities and conform to the constitutional guarantee of equality.[120]

Training of the sort formerly offered through the NJI's Social Context Education Project seems important for judges charged with the difficult responsibility of presiding over sexual assault cases. While that project came to a finish in 2004, the NJI maintains that it has an ongoing commitment to integrating relevant social context education into all of its programs.[121] Unfortunately, the NJI does not make the specific course content, syllabi, or materials for its programs publicly available, nor is there a reporting requirement making information on the number of judges who attend this program publicly available.

Regrettably, because of this lack of transparency with respect to the actual content of judicial education programs, and data on what proportion of judges attend them, it is not possible to verify this commitment to social context education or assess its likely effectiveness. It is unclear why the judiciary could not be (and permit the NJI to be) more transparent about, and accountable for, the details of their judicial education programming and the content of their curricula. There are compelling justifications for not allowing judicial education sessions to be open to the public or reported on by the media. Presumably allowing such would inhibit the ability of judges to be open with their colleagues about deficits in their legal knowledge, or could compromise their capacity to interrogate their own social assumptions about, for example, gender and race. It also seems reasonable for the judiciary not to disclose information regarding the judicial education undertaken by specific judges. What is not obvious is the justification for refusing to disclose program materials, curriculum details, or general data on the numbers of judges who attend particular courses.

To be clear, requiring judges to complete formal education sessions would not displace the professional responsibility of each individual jurist to pursue necessary continuing education to ensure their professional competence. In addition to noting that he had no experience in Canadian sexual assault law prior to appointment, Justice Camp's lawyer asserted that "[p]rior to Wagar, [Camp] received no training or judicial education on the sociology or neurobiology of sexual assault or even on the legal history of the sexual assault provisions."[122] Of course, the fact that Justice Camp may have received no training in this area is not a compelling justification for, nor a defence of, his conduct in *Wagar*. Whether judicial education on substantive sexual assault is mandatory, it is clear that any judge who sought to ensure his or her basic competence in the area could educate themselves. There is no shortage of legal writing on these issues. Justice Camp apparently chose not to sufficiently avail himself of such education. His explanation was that he "didn't know what [he] didn't know."[123] However, he also characterized his knowledge in this area of law as "non-existent."[124] It is difficult to understand how any legal professional would allow himself to be in the position of adjudicating a trial in an area of law about which he knew that he knew nothing.

It may also be problematic that there is no assessment process to ensure some minimum threshold of substantive legal knowledge as part of our judicial education system. Adam Dodek and Richard Devlin, who have written extensively on the topic of judicial education, suggest that it may be desirable to include a form of peer evaluation as part of Canada's judicial education system.[125]

It is likely that some Canadian judges would resist compulsory education with associated assessment on the grounds that it would interfere with judicial independence.[126] Dodek and Devlin suggest that concerns regarding the potential prejudice to judicial independence and impartiality posed by the prospect of evaluation of judges could be substantially reduced if such evaluations were internal and confidential. For example, they could be completed by the chief justice or associate chief justice of a court.[127] Internal and confidential evaluation would respond to some extent to the current absence of any form of competency assessment, and would do so in a manner that takes into consideration the objection based on judicial independence.

The CJC and provincial courts could also consider instituting a more formal review process for trial judges whose acquittals are successfully appealed because of the type of errors demonstrated in cases such as *B(IE)*, *Adepoju*, and *Wagar*. At the time of writing, three provincial court judges were under review by the chief judge in Alberta because of sexual assault trial decisions that demonstrated the same kinds of stereotype-infused legal reasoning discussed earlier in this chapter.[128] At least one of those cases only came under review after the chief judge was contacted and made aware of the case by the media.[129] Rather than relying on the media (which was also how Justice Dewar's comments in *Rhodes* came to light), an automatic review process by the chief judge of the provincial court, or the chief justice of the superior court in each province, triggered whenever a trial judge is overturned on the basis of stereotype-informed reasoning, would be preferable. Upon review, chief judges or chief justices – depending on the level of court at issue – could, where necessary, require judges to complete further training.

Again, the details of mandatory and assessed education programs for judges should be designed and authorized by judges themselves. The suggestions just outlined are aimed at demonstrating that programs of this nature may be both possible and consistent with the need to protect judicial independence.

In addition to mandatory sexual assault training and increased transparency regarding judicial education, judges should be required to either provide written decisions in sexual assault proceedings, or at a minimum, as Lucinda Vandervort recommends,[130] ensure that oral decisions in sexual assault cases are transcribed and reported. As is true of the trial decisions in *B(IE)*, *Adejopu*, *Wagar*, *Rhodes*, and *R(J)*, some unknown proportion of sexual assault cases do not result in reported decisions (rather, decisions are rendered orally). But for the decisions of Crown attorneys to appeal, legal errors of the sort committed in these cases are highly unlikely to come to light. Reported decisions provide a degree of transparency and public accountability not available with oral, unreported decisions. Indeed, absent the Crown's decision to appeal, or a journalist's decision to report on a trial, sexual assault cases involving oral decisions provide almost no opportunity for scrutiny by researchers, legislators, or the public. The provision of reported reasons promotes the open court principle. Given the ongoing difficulties with the criminal justice system's response to sexualized violence, there are compelling reasons to ensure that, in the sexual assault context, judicial reasoning is as assessable as possible.

In its 2008 decision in *R v REM*, the Supreme Court of Canada identified public accountability as one of the three justifications for requiring judges to provide reasons (either written or oral) in all criminal trials.[131] The degree of public accountability is greatly diminished, if not eliminated, when researchers, legislators, and the public have no way of accessing these reasons because they were issued orally and not reported.

Requiring reported decisions also has the potential to ensure more careful, thorough, and well-reasoned judgments in a sensitive and difficult area of law – an area of law in which, as noted, the legal profession and the judiciary have struggled to maintain public confidence in the administration of justice. It seems highly implausible to suggest that anyone – judge, lawyer, or academic – would apply the same degree of care in issuing a decision which is often not heard by anyone other than the parties, and a decision which will be entered in an online digital database available to everyone.

Were resources unlimited it would indeed be desirable to require written, or transcribed oral, reasons in all criminal cases. Resources, of course, are not unlimited, and so one might ask: why should we single out sexual assault trials? There are different considerations at play in the context of sexual assault cases. One of these is that, arguably, we are at a crisis point in terms of public confidence in the criminal justice system's ability to respond appropriately to allegations of sexual assault. Given this circumstance, in the sexual assault context, in particular, we should ensure that judicial reasoning is as assessable as possible. Requiring reported decisions would be the most effective way of making the process assessable and transparent. There are also other factors that make cases involving sexual violence (and gendered violence) different from other trials. These include the role that stereotyping sometimes plays in judicial reasoning involving sexual assault cases, and the nature of the potential harm to both the complainant and the accused at issue in these types of cases. These issues provide further justification for adopting sexual assault–specific rules.

Judges in Canada have a minimum of two university degrees, earn over $300,000 per year, and typically retire with generous pensions.[132] They are among the very most privileged members of our society. Individuals are entitled to assume that the judges charged with adjudicating the cases affecting them will possess some minimum threshold of legal knowledge. While trial judges must be permitted to make legal errors without such mistakes giving rise to questions regarding their competency, it is reasonable to expect them to have obtained a rudimentary understanding of any legal rule that they are charged with applying. Moreover, it is reasonable for the public to demand that judges interrogate, and attempt to eliminate from their legal reasoning, their own empirically unreliable assumptions about sexual violence. As recently noted by the Canadian Judicial Council, "Canadians expect their judges to know the law but also to possess empathy and to recognize and question any past personal attitudes and sympathies that might prevent them from acting fairly."[133] In sexual assault proceedings, this minimum threshold includes knowledge and understanding of the legal definition of consent to sexual touching.

Legal errors with respect to basic legal rules, such as the definition of consent, give rise to particular harms. First, erroneous legal reasoning of this kind significantly increases the risk that legally rejected and discriminatory stereotypes will inform and influence the outcome in sexual assault proceedings. Simply put, trial judges who do not understand, or who fail to articulate and apply, the legal definition of consent risk perpetuating the victim-blaming stereotypes about sexual violence that contribute to the shaming of women who allege sexual violation. These judges, of course, also risk coming to inappropriate legal conclusions. Second, the inhumanity of requiring sexual assault complainants to endure the trial process a second time because of a judge's failure to articulate and apply basic and well-settled legal rules cannot be overstated. It is not the same to impose this burden of a second trial on victims of, for example, fraud, or breaking and entering, or (non-domestic) assault. It is not hard to imagine that some sexual assault survivors decide to put their life on hold – to wait to start a degree, have a baby, commence therapy, or begin dating – until after the trial at which they are to testify as a complainant has finished. Our legal system is, of course, susceptible to human fallibility. But the emotional and psychological burden of a second trial imposed upon sexual assault complainants should never arise because we allowed a judge without the most basic understanding of the fundamental legal rule at issue – the definition of consent to sexual touching – to preside over a sexual assault trial.

To be clear, ensuring that basic legal rules such as the definition of consent are properly applied is not the only expectation that should be placed on the judiciary. This is a threshold requirement, the absence of which warrants restrictions on the types of cases a trial judge should be permitted to hear. There are other steps, such as the ones identified in the previous chapter, that the judiciary should take to make sexual assault trials more humane for complainants.

CHAPTER 8

We Owe a Responsibility ...

Women are more likely to be sexually assaulted during our lifetime than to, for example, obtain a university degree or be paid the same as our male counterparts.[1] Yet, less than one percent of the men who commit these crimes can expect to be sanctioned by the criminal justice system.[2] In part this is a consequence of the stunningly low rate of reporting for sexual offences.[3] One of the main reasons women give for not reporting sexual violence is fear of the legal system.[4] Given the practices of discrimination and tactics of humiliation that continue to occur in some sexual assault proceedings, this fear is well-founded.

Notwithstanding reforms to the rules of evidence and the substantive law of sexual assault, many sexual assault complainants continue to experience the criminal justice system as traumatic. But how can this be true given the existence of these progressive and protective law reforms? The reality is that legal rules, such as the *Criminal Code* definition of consent and the evidentiary rules limiting admissibility of prior sexual history, are susceptible to inadequate compliance by lawyers, or incorrect interpretation by judges, which undermine their intended protections. The same is true of the ethical rules dictated in professional codes of conduct, such as the duty not to discriminate and the requirement that lawyers have a good-faith basis for pursuing any line of cross-examination. Some lawyers simply ignore these rules. In part, it is this 'in fact' slippage between our progressive laws on the books and their application in practice that motivated this book.

The practice and adjudication of sexual assault law in Canada today continues to contribute to a legal process that is harmful to some of those who turn to, or are forced into, the criminal legal system following experiences of sexualized violence. The humiliating and abusive tactics sometimes employed by defence lawyers, the public denial of the existence of these practices by members of the criminal defence bar, the failure on the part of Crown attorneys and trial judges to meet their duties to protect complainants, and the substantive lack of understanding of some trial judges together exemplify the legal profession's disservice to the public's interest in responding humanely and effectively to sexual harm. The previous chapters were aimed at demonstrating ways in which the legal profession could mitigate the harms experienced by some sexual assault complainants as a consequence of their participation in the criminal trial process.

A common argument advanced by some members of the legal profession in response to criticisms of how the legal system treats sexual assault complainants is that improving the experience of women who turn to the criminal law following incidents of sexual violation would require changing the rules of evidence in ways that would compromise fundamental principles of justice.[5] This argument is sometimes advanced in conjunction with the contention, rejected in chapter 2, that reforms to the law of sexual assault have eradicated the practice of 'whacking the complainant.'[6] The core of the argument is that the trauma of testifying as a sexual assault complainant is caused by two entrenched, and fundamentally important, aspects of our justice system: the adversarial nature of the system and the constitutional rights of the accused. Most of the lawyers I interviewed highlighted the adversarial model in particular as a central and unavoidable cause of trauma to complainants. Defence Lawyer 10's comments are illustrative of this perspective: "I think that the criminal justice system is traumatic, probably for everybody and obviously in a completely, not a different way, but in a much more intense way [for sexual assault complainants], I mean, it's an adversarial system."

It is of course true that the adversarial nature of our legal system, and constitutional protections such as the right to full and fair cross-examination, mean that testifying as a complainant in a sexual assault trial will likely always be psychologically challenging and unpleasant. The criminal justice system is not designed to heal those who have survived sexual harm. But nor should it operate to effect a 'second rape.'[7]

As the previous chapters have demonstrated, there are measures that could be taken by the legal profession to make sexual assault trials less stressful, less traumatizing, and less inhumane. Promisingly, the

changes I propose are not in tension with, and could therefore be manifested without diminishing in any regard, the constitutional rights of the
accused. They are suggestions that do not require balancing the interests
of the complainant with the rights of the accused. Nor would these efforts
require reimagining the adversarial nature of our system. In other words,
the adversarial model and the constitutionally enshrined rights of the
accused are not an absolute bar to improving the experience of sexual
assault complainants. Indeed, some of the harms currently justified in
the name of these inviolable principles and inherent structural factors
can, and should, be addressed by the legal profession itself.

This is not to suggest that more structural changes should not be considered. Perhaps they should. However, regardless of any more ambitious
renovations to our legal system (which arguably are less achievable in
the short term), there is nothing structural (or constitutional) preventing
the legal profession from accepting responsibility for, and responding
to, some of its contributions to the brutality of the process endured
by many sexual assault complainants. Given the staggeringly low rates
of reporting, the continued prevalence of sexual violence as a social
problem, the disproportionately high number of Indigenous, disabled,
socio-economically disadvantaged, and racialized women who are
sexually victimized, and the law's ongoing legacy of discrimination in
response to sexual harm, it is incumbent upon the legal profession to
begin realizing these improvements. There are achievable gains, albeit
modest ones, to be made through corrections to the way in which sexual
assault law is practised and adjudicated.

Relying on interviews with experienced lawyers, reported case law,
commercial expression and public statements by the defence bar, and
recent trial transcripts, this book has demonstrated that, despite prominent claims to the contrary, complainants continue to be subjected to
abusive, humiliating, and discriminatory treatment when they turn to the
law to respond to violations of their sexual integrity. The book has also
revealed that the legal profession could better respond to, and remedy,
some of the factors that make sexual assault proceedings so problematic
for complainants. Perhaps most promisingly, they could do so without
placing in any jeopardy the rights of the accused.

Reforms to the way that sexual assault law is practised and adjudicated
need not, and perhaps given the marginalized status of many of the men
who are subject to the state's carceral power should not, be motivated

by a desire to see more sexual offenders incarcerated. Increasing the rate and length of incarceration for those convicted of sexual assault is presumably not the solution to the social problem of sexual harm. At the same time, the reality that almost *all* sexual assault in Canada occurs with legal impunity reflects a profound injustice. To the extent that the legal profession contributes to this legal immunity by practising in ways that unnecessarily traumatize complainants and discourage other survivors from engaging the legal system, the profession must make changes.

It would be remiss to discuss reforming the way sexual assault law is practised and adjudicated without acknowledging the relationship between the treatment and experience of sexual assault complainants in the criminal trial process and societal norms more broadly. Social assumptions about sexual violence are deeply embedded in our society and culture. Eliminating their role in the adjudication of sexual assault allegations surely involves a multi-pronged and interrelated approach aimed at changing social norms, reducing gender inequities, and educating not only lawyers and judges but also the public – the same tripartite goal feminists have targeted for decades. As Jennifer Temkin and Barbara Krahé have ably demonstrated, until social attitudes about women and gender and sexual violence change, there will continue to be a "justice gap" between progressive law reforms aimed at improving the justice system's response to sexual harm and the actual impact created by these legal reforms.[8] Lawyers and judges are, of course, products of their social context. The stereotypical thinking and sexism that inform the way we think about gender-based harms such as sexual assault continue to have a deep impact upon the way laws are interpreted and applied. To a significant degree, closing the justice gap turns on the much larger issue of changing social attitudes generally and reducing systemic gender inequality. The aims of this book are narrower.

A significant portion of this book focused on criminal defence lawyers in particular. To some extent this was necessary in order to address some of the dominant, factual claims about sexual assault trials made by some vocal members of the defence bar. Defence lawyers have been rightly criticized for employing aggressive and discriminatory strategies that discourage victims of sexual violence from coming forward, and traumatize those who do report sexual offences.[9] That said, the treatment of complainants – and the way women who serve the legal system in this capacity experience the trial process – is also informed by the professional conduct of Crown attorneys and judges. As is demonstrated by several of the cases examined in this book, it is not only defence lawyers who sometimes fail in meeting their professional obligations as related to sexual assault complainants.

To be clear, the purpose of this work is not to diminish in any regard the critically important work that defence lawyers, and the legal profession more generally, perform in the context of sexual assault cases. Not only is the work of sexual assault lawyers personally taxing and frequently thankless, members of the criminal defence bar are sometimes unfairly vilified for the legal services that they provide.[10] The most general observation gleaned from the interviews conducted with defence counsel was that the majority of these lawyers are strongly committed to a particular vision of procedural justice and very much guided by a dedication to fulfilling their understanding of their role in the criminal justice process. The lawyers I interviewed were passionate, and for the most part deeply compassionate, professionals.

Similar observations can be made by reading the memoirs of experienced lawyers, such as the ones discussed in chapter 4. It is not hyperbole to assert, as others have done,[11] that without legal advocates there can be no rule of law, no democracy, no fairness. At the same time, the legal profession must confront the brutality of the process it conducts and accept responsibility for some of the harms imposed upon those who participate in this process. Some of the lawyering that regularly occurs in sexual assault proceedings in Canada threatens and undermines the rule of law, democracy, and fairness – the principles that many defence lawyers identify as fundamental to what they do. The legal profession should not tolerate such practices.

More broadly, as a matter of social responsibility, a society that adopts the criminal trial process as a primary response to sexual violence has an obligation to ensure that the process it has chosen is conducted with compassionate recognition of the violence it effects. Sexual assault complainants bear the burden of participating in an individualized process to respond to a social problem, sexual violence, that would be better addressed through broader, systemic strategies such as wealth redistribution and greater gender and race parity in education, governance, and the labour force. We owe a responsibility to the individuals who occupy the role of sexual assault complainant. This is particularly true given that the burden of performing this role is frequently imposed upon women from communities that are marginalized by race, disability, Indigeneity, and socio-economic status. Our social responsibility to these women requires initiatives such as state-funded legal representation for sexual assault complainants and secure, robust public funding for front-line organizations such as sexual assault centres.

The focus of this book is on the harms experienced by women who participate in the criminal justice process by serving as complainants in sexual assault trials. As such, I want to end by returning to some of the stories of the women who served as complainants in some of the cases examined.

Consider again the complainant in *R v Finney*, who, having spent her birthday being cross-examined on the precise number of days following a violent anal rape it took before she could endure the pain of a bowel movement, left court at the end of the day with the knowledge that she would have to return the next day for further cross-examination.[12]

Think about the woman in *R v B(IE)* who was denied the protections of section 276 of the *Criminal Code* by the Crown attorney, trial judge, and defence lawyer – who was permitted to ask her more than once whether she had been kissing anyone else that night at the bar and whether she had told someone she was "going to get fucked that night."[13]

The young complainant in *Wright* was similarly denied the protections of Canada's rape shield laws when she was forced to answer numerous irrelevant and inadmissible questions about her supposed habit of dancing shirtless at parties, and was asked whether her nickname was "Perky Tits."[14]

Recall the young Indigenous woman in *R v Wagar*, who said the trial judge made her feel like a "slut"[15] when he asked her: "why didn't you just sink your bottom down into the basin so he couldn't penetrate you?" and "why couldn't you just keep your knees together?"[16] Like others, she then faced the gruelling prospect of enduring a second trial because the stereotype-informed statements and reasoning of the trial judge who acquitted her alleged attacker were overturned on appeal.[17]

The complainant in *R v Schmaltz* was forced to answer a series of questions about the moisture level of her vagina after the accused allegedly inserted his fingers into her while she was asleep. Repeatedly, defence counsel asserted to her that her vagina was moist because she was sexually stimulated.[18]

There is the teenaged complainant in *R v Luceno*, who, having been dragged into the criminal justice process involuntarily, was subjected to an aggressive, arguably bullying, at times rude, confusing, frustrating, and painful cross-examination by an experienced lawyer more than twice her age.[19] The cross-examination of this young woman was so disorienting, repetitive, and unclear that even the trial judge, with his bachelor's and master's degrees from the University of Toronto, law degree from McGill University, and decades as a Crown prosecutor,[20] said he found the questioning confusing.[21]

Finally, recall the young woman in *R v Adepoju*, who was forced to answer numerous questions about her failure to scream, cry, or escape. In a paradigmatic example of victim blaming, defence counsel asked her questions such as "eventually you stopped saying no, and you opened up your legs and the sex act occurred; correct?" and "Well you did let him have sex with you; right?"[22] The victim-blaming message implicit in these questions was reinforced when the trial judge wrongly acquitted the accused on the basis that the sexual intercourse was consensual because, after fifteen to twenty minutes of physical resistance, "she finally decided that she had enough and gave into him."[23]

The way in which sexual assault law is practised and adjudicated causes real harms both to individual complainants and to survivors of sexual violence more generally. The focus on these harms should not, however, obscure the strength, courage, and tenacity of many of the women who serve the criminal justice process in this capacity – their resilience emerges clearly from the transcripts of many of these trials.[24]

Recall, for example, the complainant in *R v B(S)*, a woman who did not finish high school, and who was humiliated and denigrated by a very senior member of the criminal defence bar. Imagine sitting in a courtroom in front of a jury, as she did, while a lawyer reads aloud, one by one, your deeply personal, sexually explicit texts to a lover, or reads from a videotape transcript of what you said to the accused, your former partner, during sexual role play. This woman's steadfastness, despite having been subjected to one of the worst misuses of prior sexual history evidence I have studied, is remarkable:

A. [COMPLAINANT] Again, I've made many statements, word for word is gonna be different.
Q. [DEFENCE] Word for word?
A. Absolutely.
Q. No, no, see, word for word is what you're going to use to

convict this man. Word for word is you were thrown off the mat-
tress. Word for word is you didn't like anal sex, when we got 46
minutes of it, and I don't need to go through the other quotes, do I?

    A. Anal sex, I can repeat ten different times –

    Q. Okay.

    A. – if you would like for me to, Mr. Simmonds, until you
understand what I am saying.[25]

Equally remarkable is the strength and resiliency of the many other
complainants whose cases are examined in this book.

Some of the trauma experienced by sexual assault complainants who
participate in the criminal justice process is likely unavoidable. The
criminal trial is not designed to ensure the comfort and psychological
security of those who allege criminal offences. Indeed, as suggested in
chapter 1, justice and healing may be highly unlikely to occur through
the same institutional response. The objective of this book is not to
connect these pursuits. Rather, the more modest aim of this work is
to demonstrate the ways in which the legal profession *unnecessarily*
contributes to the inhospitable, if not inhumane, conditions faced by
some of those who allege violations of their sexual integrity.

There are also numerous examples of defence lawyers, Crown attorneys, and members of the judiciary treating sexual assault complainants with compassion and respect, including in the cases examined in
this book. For instance, Justice Durno, who heard the initial appeal in
R v G(PG), took the extraordinary step of not just reading the transcript
of the cross-examination of the complainant but also listening to the
audio recording, so that he could ascertain tone, the manner in which
the questions were asked, and the complainants' reactions.[26] Had he not
done this, we would not have learned that the complainant was sobbing
while being questioned about her suicide attempts.

Justice Kirk Munroe, the trial judge in *R v Johnson*, showed compassion for the complainant at a point in her testimony where he presumably
observed her to be struggling:

[COMPLAINANT] A. Like I've said, my virginity is something
I value, and I took pride in that. I would never choose to lose my
virginity to someone I barely know in a public bar washroom.

    THE COURT: Would you like some time, ma'am?

    A. Yes, please.

THE COURT: We'll take an adjournment. You let us know when you are ready to continue. Thank you, ma'am.

A. Thank you.[27]

Crown attorney Kathy Nedelkopoulos repeatedly intervened in the cross-examination of the teenaged complainant in *R v Luceno* to protect her from what can fairly be characterized as overly aggressive questioning. To offer one example, she interceded successfully to require that the complainant be permitted a chance to respond fairly to defence counsel's rapid-fire questioning: "Objection, objection, Your Honour. By her saying she's thinking, can we allow her the moment to gather her thoughts before my friend asks her another question or suggests to her that she's making it up?"[28]

The tone of voice and pacing of questions employed by Luke Craggs during his cross-examination of the complainant in *R v Al-Rawi* were notably respectful and patient.[29]

In *R v Ghomeshi*, defence counsel Marie Henein spared the first complainant the exposure and humiliation of having a photograph of her in a string bikini (that she had sent to the accused) projected on an exhibit screen for spectators in the packed courtroom to see.[30] Similarly, in *R v Johnson*, Crown attorney Scott Kerwin and defence lawyer Patrick Ducharme agreed that "some of the sensitive photographs" of the complainant (presumably the pictures of her injured vagina taken by the Sexual Assault Nurse Examiner) did not need to be put to her, but rather could be entered through one of the expert witnesses.[31] Contrast these examples with the defence counsel's initial attempt to have a videotape of the complainant and the accused having anal intercourse shown to the jury in *R v B(S)*.[32]

There are, of course, many other examples of legal professionals treating sexual assault complainants with consideration and humanity.

The legal profession has the ability to improve the treatment of sexual assault complainants. Given this capability, why would we ever countenance practices that needlessly contribute to the trauma of the trial for the individuals who turn to the criminal law (or are forced into this legal process) to respond to their experiences of sexual violation? As a profession, if it is possible to treat the (frequently marginalized and almost certainly in this context less powerful) women who serve the criminal justice system as sexual assault complainants with greater respect and compassion, how could we make any other choice?

Notes

Chapter One

1 Holly Johnson, "Limits of a Criminal Justice Response: Trends in Police and Court Processing of Sexual Assault," in *Sexual Assault in Canada: Law, Legal Practice and Women's Activism*, edited by Elizabeth Sheehy (Ottawa: University of Ottawa Press, 2012), 613, at 631; Blair Crew, Daphne Gilbert, and Elizabeth Sheehy, "The Ghomeshi Verdict: This Is No Time for Complacency," *Policy Options* (12 April 2016), http://policyoptions.irpp.org/magazines/april-2016/the-ghomeshi-verdict-this-is-no-time-for-complacency/ ("997 of 1,000 men who commit this crime can expect to be unsanctioned").

2 See Statistics Canada, "Sexual Offences in Canada," by Rebecca Kong et al., in *Juristat* 23, no. 6, Catalogue No. 85-002-XIE (Ottawa: Statistics Canada, 25 July 2003); Statistics Canada, *Measuring Violence Against Women: Statistical Trends 2006*, by Holly Johnson, Catalogue No. 85-570-XIE (Ottawa: Statistics Canada, 2 October 2006).

3 See Canada, Department of Justice, *A Survey of Survivors of Sexual Violence in Three Canadian Cities*, by Melissa Lindsay, Catalogue No. J2-403/2014E (Ottawa: Research and Statistics Division, 2014), 13, 23 (fear of the criminal justice system identified as one of the main reasons not to report); Canada, Department of Justice Canada, *A Survey of Sexual Assault Survivors*, by Tina Hattem (Ottawa: Research and Statistics Division, October 2000), http://www.justice.gc.ca/eng/pi/rs/rep-rap/2000/rr00_4/rr00_4.pdf (38% of those interviewed cited negative perceptions of the criminal justice process as the reason they did not report). See e.g. Kathleen Daly and Brigitte Bohours, "Rape

and Attrition in the Legal Process: A Comparative Analysis of Five
Countries," *Crime and Justice* 39 (2010): 565.

4 Adina Bresage, "Bridgewater Woman Regrets Reporting Sexual Assault
after Assailant Released," CBC (29 August 2016), http://www.cbc.ca/
news/canada/nova-scotia/bridgewater-sexual-assault-appeal-1.3739312.

5 Ibid.

6 Mandi Grey, "Six Lessons I Learned from My Rape Case," *Now
Toronto* (26 July 2016), https://nowtoronto.com/news/mandi-gray-six-
lessons-i-learned-from-my-rape-case/. The trial decision to convict
in *R v Ururyar* was successfully appealed (2017 ONSC 4428). The case
is cited here as relevant to the complainant's experience of the trial
process, and not as an endorsement of the trial judge's reasoning.

7 Manisha Krishnan, "How Rape Victims' Social-Media Feeds Are Being
Used Against Them in Court," *Vice* (18 August 2016), http://www.vice.
com/en_uk/read/how-rape-complainants-are-having-their-social-
media-feeds-used-against-them-in-court.

8 "What's It Like to Testify in a Sexual Assault Trial," CBC *News*
(15 February 2016), http://www.cbc.ca/news/canada/ottawa/
sexual-assault-testify-cross-examination-1.3442279.

9 See generally Elizabeth Sheehy, ed., *Sexual Assault in Canada: Law,
Legal Practice and Women's Activism* (Ottawa: University of Ottawa
Press, 2012). See also Cheryl Regehr, Ramona Alaggia, Liz Lambert,
and Michael Saini, "Victims of Sexual Violence in the Canadian
Criminal Courts," *Victims & Offenders* 3 (2008): 99 (citing studies by
numerous researchers demonstrating negative impacts); Mary Ross,
"Restoring Rape Survivors: Justice, Advocacy, and a Call to Action,"
Annals of the New York Academy of Sciences 1087 (2006): 206, at
218–22 (summarizing research in several countries including Canada
that reveals the re-traumatization experienced by sexual assault
victims through participation in the criminal justice process); Cheryl
Regehr and Ramona Alaggia, "Perspectives of Justice for Victims of
Sexual Violence," *Victims & Offenders* 1, no. 1 (2006): 33; Sharon B.
Murphy, Victoria L. Banyard, Sarah P. Maynard, and Rebecca Dufresne,
"Advocates Speak Out on Adult Sexual Assault: A Unique Crime
Demands a Unique Response," *Journal of Aggression, Maltreatment
& Trauma* 20 (2011): 690; Amanda Konradi, *Taking the Stand: Rape
Survivors and the Prosecution of Rapists* (Westport, CT: Praeger
Publishers, 2007), 102–3; Cassia Spohn and Katharine Tellis, *Policing*

and Prosecuting Sexual Assault (Boulder, CO: Lynne Rienner Publishers, 2014), 74 (police and prosecutor interviewees identified testing as one of the primary difficulties faced by those who report).

10 Karen Lee-Miller, "Purposing and Repurposing Harms: The Victim Impact Statement and Sexual Assault," *Qualitative Health Research* 23, no. 11 (2013): 1445, at 1449.

11 Allyson Clarke, *In the Eyes of the Law: Survivor Experiences and Image Construction within Sexual Assault Cases* (Toronto: University of Toronto Graduate Department of Applied Psychology and Human Development, unpublished PhD thesis, 2014), 84.

12 Ibid., 84.

13 *R v Khaery*, Trial Transcript (23 September 2014) Edmonton 121306211Q1 (ABQB) at 13:36–15:12.

14 Ibid. at 116:18 and 117:1.

15 Janice Johnston, "'Great Unfairness': 2 More Sex Assault Cases Where Victims Were Jailed to Ensure Their Court Testimony," CBC (31 July 2017), http://www.cbc.ca/amp/1.4226601. Angela Cardinal was incarcerated for five days and forced to wear shackles in court during the preliminary hearing into the brutal sexual assault perpetrated against her (*R v Blanchard*, 2016 ABQB 706 (CanLII)).

16 For example, the requirement that juries be warned about the perils of relying on a sexual assault complainant's uncorroborated testimony was eliminated (*Criminal Law Amendment Act*, SC 1975, c 93 1974-75-76); the evidentiary rules relating to delayed disclosure were changed (*Criminal Code*, RSC 1985, c C-46, s 275; *R v DD*, 2000 SCC 43, 2 SCR 275); a new statutory approach involving a three-tiered sexual assault regime was introduced in 1982; the admissibility of evidence of prior sexual history was limited (see *Criminal Code*, RSC 1985, c C-46, s 276; *Seaboyer and The Queen, Re*, (1987) 61 OR (2d) 290, OJ No. 737); an affirmative definition of consent was adopted (see *R v Ewanchuk*, [1999] 1 SCR 330, 169 DLR (4th) 193; *Criminal Code*, RSC 1985, c C-46, ss 273, 273.2). For a brief history of sexual assault law in Canada see Janine Benedet, "Sexual Assault Cases at the Alberta Court of Appeal: The Roots of *Ewanchuk* and the Unfinished Revolution," *Alberta Law Review* 52, no. 1 (2014): 127. See also Constance Backhouse, *Carnal Crimes: Sexual Assault Law in Canada 1900–1975* (Toronto: Irwin Law, 2008). See generally Christine Boyle, *Sexual Assault* (Toronto: Carswell, 1984), on significant reforms to this area of law that were made prior to 1985.

17 Lindsay, *A Survey of Survivors of Sexual Violence*. See also Catalina M. Arata, "Coping With Rape: The Roles of Prior Sexual Abuse and Attributions of Blame," *Journal of Interpersonal Violence* 14, no. 1 (1999): 62; Heidi Zinzow and Martie Thompson, "Barriers to Reporting Sexual Victimization: Prevalence and Correlates Among Undergraduate Women," *Journal of Aggression, Maltreatment & Trauma* 20, no. 7 (2011): 711; Candice Feiring and Lynn Taska, "The Persistence of Shame Following Sexual Abuse: A Longitudinal Look at Risk and Recovery," *Child Maltreatment* 10, no. 4 (2005): 337.

18 Lindsay, *A Survey of Survivors of Sexual Violence*, 14.

19 See generally John P. Wilson, Boris Drozdek, and Silvana Turkovic, "Post-traumatic Shame and Guilt," *Trauma, Violence, & Abuse* 7, no. 2 (2006): 122, at 124; Maria Elena Vidal and Jenny Petrak, "Shame and Adult Sexual Assault: A Study with a Group of Female Survivors Recruited from an East London Population," *Sexual and Relationship Therapy* 22, no. 2 (2007): 159. See also Arata, "Coping With Rape," 63 (discussing findings in several studies that self-blame is associated with higher distress and greater reliance on maladaptive coping strategies).

20 Lindsay, *A Survey of Survivors of Sexual Violence*, 13.

21 Karyn L. Freedman, *One Hour in Paris: A True Story of Rape and Recovery* (Calgary, AB: Freehand Books, 2014), 76–7.

22 Ibid., 77.

23 *R v Finney* (28 September 2011) Lindsay C55780 (ONSC) at 305 [Finney, ONSC] at 319 line 27.

24 Women account for over 92% of police-reported sexual assaults in Canada. Male and female survivors do not show differences in their rate of reporting: Statistics Canada, "Gender Differences in Police-Reported Violent Crime in Canada," by Roxan Vaillancourt, in *Canadian Centre for Justice Statistics Profile Series*, Catalogue No. 85F0033M (Ottawa: Statistics Canada, May 2010). Men are the perpetrators of sexual assault in 99% of cases: Statistics Canada, "Measuring Violence Against Women: Statistical Trends," by Maire Sinha, in *Juristat*, Catalogue No. 85-002-X (Ottawa: Statistics Canada, 25 February 2013), 31.

25 See Karen Weiss, "Too Ashamed to Report: Deconstructing the Shame of Sexual Victimization," *Feminist Criminology* 5, no. 3 (2010): 286, at 294–9. Weiss argues that the shame of sexual victimization is culturally mediated and that cultural narratives about sex, gender, and sexual violence in fact contribute to the feelings of shame experienced by

survivors who conclude that they have not conformed to expected sex and gender norms. It is true that self-blame might also function as a coping strategy aimed at bolstering one's sense of agency and reducing feelings of powerlessness. Arguably, the two are not mutually exclusive.

26 See Melanie Randall, "Sexual Assault Law, Credibility, and 'Ideal Victims': Consent, Resistance, and Victim Blaming," *Canadian Journal of Women and the Law* 22 (2010): 397 (examining the continuing role that sex- and gender-based stereotypes play in the adjudication of sexual assault allegations); Emma Cunliffe, "Sexual Assault Cases in the Supreme Court of Canada: Losing Sight of Substantive Equality?" *Supreme Court Law Review* 57 (2012): 301 (arguing that principles of substantive gender equality have not yet infused judicial reasoning in sexual assault cases and that gender stereotypes continue to play a role in fact determination in these cases).

27 See Rebecca Campbell et al., "Preventing the 'Second Rape': Rape Survivors' Experiences with Community Service Providers," *Journal of Interpersonal Violence* 16, no. 12 (2001): 1239, at 1253–5; Lee Madigan and Nancy C. Gamble, *The Second Rape: Society's Continued Betrayal of the Victim* (New York: Lexington Books, 1991); Mary P. Koss, "Restoring Rape Survivors: Justice, Advocacy, and a Call to Action," *Annals of the New York Academy of Science* 1087 (2006): 206, at 218–22 (summarizing research in several countries including Canada that reveals the re-traumatization experienced by sexual assault victims through participation in the criminal justice process).

28 See e.g. Konradi, *Taking the Stand*, 102–3.

29 *R v Parrott*, 2001 SCC 3 at para. 51.

30 See e.g. David G. Bayliss, "The Consequences of an Allegation of Sexual Assault" (17 December 2010), http://davidgbayliss.com/consequences-allegation-sexual-assault/ (accessed 1 June 2016). I documented this sentiment on criminal law firm websites in Elaine Craig, "Examining the Websites of 'Canada's Top Sex Crime Lawyers': The Ethical Parameters of Online Commercial Expression by the Criminal Defence Bar," UBC Law Review 48, no. 2 (2015): 257.

31 Frank Addario, "Acceptance Speech for the 2016 Arthur G Martin Award" (31 October 2016), http://www.addario.ca/wp-content/uploads/2016/10/mm-speech-oct-31.pdf.

32 Statistics Canada, "Gender Differences in Police-Reported Violent Crime in Canada." Over 99% of sexual assaults are committed by males.

Females are four to six times more likely to experience sexual assault than males.

33   [1993] 4 SCR 595 at para. 165.

34   Given the methodology used in this book, I have frequently relied on the words used by lawyers, judges, or witnesses to describe a sexual assault. I am nevertheless acutely aware that the choice of language deployed by legal actors and institutions to describe specific sexual assaults can romanticize or eroticize sexual violence, or construct survivors as active participants in their own victimization. See e.g. Linda Coates and Allan Wade, "Language and Violence: Analysis of Four Discursive Operations," *Journal of Family Violence* 22 (2007): 511.

35   It is true that not all reported decisions make reference to the style or length of the cross-examination of the complainant. That many of these cases did make some such reference could suggest that these are extreme or deviant cases. However, even if these are extreme cases (and that is not conceded here), this work is methodologically defensible on the basis that there is value in selecting extreme cases to test well-formulated theories. See Robert K. Yin, *Case Study Research: Design and Methods*, 5th ed. (Thousand Oaks, CA: Sage Inc, 2014); Alan Bryman, *Quantity and Quality in Social Research* (London: Unwin Hyman, 1988); Giampietro Gobo, "Re-conceptualizing Generalization: Old Issues in a New Frame," in *The SAGE Handbook of Social Research Methods*, edited by P. Alasuutari, J. Brannen, and L. Bickman (London: Sage, 2008), 193; Jennifer Mason, *Qualitative Researching* (London: Sage Publications Ltd, 1996); Jane Ritchie and Jane Lewis, *Qualitative Research Practice: A Guide for Social Science Students and Researchers* (London: Sage, 2003); David Silverman, *Doing Qualitative Research: A Practical Handbook*, 4th ed. (London: Sage Publications Ltd, 2013). The tendency of defence lawyers to "whack the complainant" in cross-examination is a well-formulated feminist proposition. See Gillian Balfour and Elizabeth Comack, "Whacking the Complainant Hard: Law and Sexual Assault," in *The Power to Criminalize: Violence, Inequality and Law* (Winnipeg, MB: Fernwood Publishing, 2004), 110; David Tanovich, "'Whack No More': Infusing Equality into the Ethics of Defence Lawyering in Sexual Assault Cases," *Ottawa Law Review* 45, no. 3 (2015): 495; Karen Busby, "Discriminatory Uses of Personal Records in Sexual Violence Cases," *Canadian Journal of Women and the Law* 9, no. 1 (1996): 148. If in extreme cases (which, again, these are not

conceded to be) the transcripts do not reveal this type of "whacking," then the proposition might reasonably be rejected. See Gobo, *Re-conceptualizing Generalization*, at 204–5.

36 Elizabeth Sheehy, *Defending Battered Women on Trial: Lessons from the Transcripts* (Vancouver: UBC Press, 2014), 92; Emma Cunliffe, "Untold Stories or Miraculous Mirrors? The Possibilities of a Text-Based Understanding of Socio-Legal Transcript Research" (1 March 2013), http://papers.ssrn.com/sol3/papers.cfm?abstract_id=2227069.

37 Sheehy, *Defending Battered Women*, 92.

38 In recognizing the value of examining these trial transcripts it is important to also highlight the fundamental distinction between the narratives produced through the trial process and reflected in the transcripts and the lived experiences of these women. See Cunliffe, "Untold Stories," 3. Lastly, it is important to highlight the limits of language itself. I am grateful to Ruthann Robson for drawing my attention to the point that, of course, the legal process requires complainants to verbalize and narrativize their 'story' so that it is a story.

39 Purposive sampling was used, based on length of practice (ten years or more) and experience with sexual assault files. Purposive sampling refers to the notion that research participants are selected based on a known set of criteria. In this case, participants were selected by length and type of practice experience. See Jane Ritchie, Jane Lewis, and Gillian Elman, "Designing and Selecting Samples," in *Qualitative Research Practice: A Guide for Social Science Students and Researchers*, edited by Jane Ritchie and Jane Lewis (London: Sage Publications, 2003), ch. 4. In qualitative research of this nature, the size of the sample is not intended to be statistically representative of the total population. The aim is to achieve a sample large enough, and with enough diversity, to generate sufficient data from which comparisons can be made and potential explanations produced. See Jennifer Mason, *Qualitative Researching*, 2nd ed (London: Sage, 2002), 136.

40 Interview transcripts were coded and analyzed manually. An initial open coding was undertaken, in which themes were permitted to emerge freely. Following this initial phase, a list of themes was identified. These themes were ultimately organized into a coding structure involving thirty-two categories. After the coding structure was developed, thematic coding and detailed analysis were conducted anew on all interview transcripts. After both phases of manual coding and analysis

were completed, a computer-assisted qualitative data analysis program (NVIVO) was used to further identify connections and strands of similarity in the data.

41 For a more detailed description of the methodology used for the interview component of this study see Elaine Craig, "The Ethical Identity of Sexual Assault Lawyers," *Ottawa Law Review* 47, no. 1 (2016): 73.

42 Google searches using the term "sexual assault lawyer" followed by the name of a particular city were conducted for the following cities: Toronto, Brampton, Ottawa, Winnipeg, Calgary, Edmonton, Lethbridge, Vancouver, Hamilton, and Kelowna. The search results using these terms included numerous links to the websites of law firms in these and other cities. In larger cities, the majority of hits on the first two pages of Google results were links to law firm websites. In cities with a smaller population, the links to law firm websites were less dense. Regardless, for each search the first twenty law firm websites to appear in the search results were examined. A second set of Google searches was done using the term "sex crime lawyer" followed by each of the same cities. Using this search term, law firm websites appearing on the first two pages of Google results were examined. Frequently the two searches produced links to the same law firm websites. An archived version of every website discussed, as it appeared at the time, was created. For a more thorough description of the methodology used to conduct this webpage study, see Elaine Craig, "Canada's 'Top Sex Crime Lawyers.'"

43 See Janine Benedet and Isabel Grant, "Hearing the Sexual Assault Complaints of Women with Mental Disabilities: Evidentiary and Procedural Issues," *McGill Law Journal* 52 (2007): 515; Patricia Washington, "Disclosure Patterns of Black Female Sexual Assault Survivors," *Violence Against Women* 11, no. 7 (2001): 1254; Teresa Nahanee, "Sexual Assault of Inuit Females: A Comment on 'Cultural Bias,'" in *Confronting Sexual Assault: A Decade of Legal and Social Change*, edited by Julian Roberts and Renate Mohr (Toronto: University of Toronto Press, 1994), 192; Sherene Razack, *Looking White People in the Eye: Gender, Race, and Culture in Courtrooms and Classrooms* (Toronto: University of Toronto Press, 1998); Elizabeth Comack, "How the Criminal Justice System Responds to Sexual Assault Survivors: The Slippage between 'Responsibilization' and 'Blaming the Victim,'" *Canadian Journal of Women and the Law* 17, no. 2 (2005): 283.

44 Statistics Canada, *Criminal Victimization in Canada, 2014*, by Samuel
    Perreault, Catalogue No. 85-002-X (Ottawa: Statistics Canada, 23
    November 2015), 16: "[t]he differences between Aboriginal and non-
    Aboriginal people were most pronounced for break-ins and sexual
    assaults, with the rates for Aboriginals being more than double those for
    non-Aboriginals."

45 See e.g. Nathan W. Pino and Robert F. Meier, "Gender Differences in
    Rape Reporting," *Sex Roles: A Journal of Research* 40, no. 11 (1999):
    979, at 987, referenced in Bonnie S. Fisher et al., "Reporting Sexual
    Victimization to the Police and Others: Results from a National-Level
    Study of College Women," in *Current Perspectives in Forensic Psychology
    and Criminal Behavior*, edited by Curt R. Bartol and Anne M.
    Bartol (Thousand Oaks, ca: Sage Publications, 2008), 155.

46 Rosalie Gignac, "*Star* Lowers Itself with Sex Assault Story," Letter to the
    Editor, *Windsor Star* (18 July 2016), http://windsorstar.com/opinion/
    letters/star-lowers-itself-with-sex-assault-story.

47 See Lise Gotell, "Rethinking Affirmative Consent in Canadian Sexual
    Assault Law: Neoliberal Sexual Subjects and Risky Women," *Akron Law
    Review* 41 (2008): 865; Lise Gotell, "When Privacy Is Not Enough: Sexual
    Assault Complainants, Sexual History Evidence and the Disclosure of
    Personal Records," *Alberta Law Review* 43 (2006): 743.

48 H. Vandervecht, "Rape Doesn't Rate Front Page," Letter to the
    Editor, *Windsor Star* (15 July 2016), http://windsorstar.com/opinion/
    letters/rape-case-doesnt-rate-front-page.

Chapter Two

1 George Jonas, "Regan a Victim of Matriarchal Justice," *National Post* (18
   February 2002), http://www.fact.on.ca/news/news0202/np02021z.htm.

2 See e.g. Constance Backhouse, "Edward Greenspan: A Feminist
   Reflection on the Eulogies Surrounding His Death," *Canadian Journal of
   Women and the Law* 27, no. 2 (2015): 157, at 165n37.

3 *R v Regan* (1998), 174 NSR (2d) 268.

4 Stephen Kimber, "Gerald Regan Case Update," *The Coast* (25 April
   2002), http://stephenkimber.com/books/not-guilty/gerald-regan-
   case-update/.

5   John Demont, "Not Guilty: A Jury Acquits Gerald Regan of Eight Sex-Related Charges," *Maclean's* 111, no. 52 (1998): 56, http://archive. macleans.ca/issue/19981228.

6   Stephen Kimber, *"Not Guilty": The Trial of Gerald Reagan* (Toronto: Stoddart Publishing, 1999), 1.

7   *R v Regan*, 2002 SCC 12 at paras. 3–10, [2002] 1 SCR 297.

8   Kimber, *Not Guilty*, 1.

9   David G. Bayliss, "The Consequences of an Allegation of Sexual Assault" (17 December 2010), http://davidgbayliss.com/ consequences-allegation-sexual-assault/.

10   See Elaine Craig, "Examining the Websites of 'Canada's Top Sex Crime Lawyers': The Ethical Parameters of Online Commercial Expression by the Criminal Defence Bar," UBC *Law Review* 48, no. 2 (2015): 257.

11   Breese Davies, "Convicting Jian Ghomeshi Will Be Hard – for Good Reason," *Toronto Star* (2 February 2016), https://www.thestar.com/ opinion/commentary/2016/02/02/convicting-jian-ghomeshi-will-be-hard-for-good-reason.html: "Judges can and do take swift action to halt abusive cross-examinations. But they rarely have to because most defence counsel see little to be gained from 'beating up' a complainant." See also Solomon Friedman, "The Numbers Contradict Ghomeshi Case Rhetoric," *Ottawa Sun* (7 February 2016), http://www.ottawasun. com/2016/02/07/friedman-the-numbers-contradict-ghomeshi-case-rhetoric: "judges are extraordinarily diligent in protecting the dignity and rights of all who come before them, complainants and witnesses alike."

12   Edward Greenspan, "The New Truth: Victims Never Lie," *Supreme Court Law Review* 14 (2001): 89, at 90, 94.

13   Bayliss, "Consequences of an Allegation."

14   *R v Ewanchuk*, [1999] 1 SCR 330, 169 DLR (4th) 193 [*Ewanchuk* cited to SCR].

15   Edward Greenspan, "Judges Have No Right to Be Bullies," *National Post* (2 March 1999), http://www.fact.on.ca/newpaper/np99030l.htm.

16   See Statistics Canada, *Adult Criminal Court Statistics in Canada, 2010/2011*, by Mia Dauvergne, Catalogue No. 85-002-X (Ottawa: Statistics Canada, 31 May 2013), 25 (Table 4), http://www.statcan. gc.ca/pub/85-002-x/2012001/article/11646-eng.pdf. In 2010/2011, 42% of sexual assault cases completed in adult criminal court resulted in findings of guilt. In comparison, 65% of robbery cases, 55% of major assault cases, and 47% of homicide cases completed in adult court

resulted in guilty findings. See also Robyn Dolittle, "Unfounded: Why
Police Dismiss 1 in 5 Sexual Assault Cases as Baseless," *The Globe
and Mail* (3 February 2017), http://www.theglobeandmail.com/news/
investigations/unfounded-sexual-assault-canada-main/article33891309/
(showing remarkably high unfounded rates across Canada); Tina
Hattem, "Highlights from a Preliminary Study of Police Classification of
Sexual Assault Cases as Unfounded," *JustResearch* 14 (2007): 32, http://
www.justice.gc.ca/eng/rp-pr/jr/jr14/p9.html#sec55 (demonstrating
that in some provinces sexual offences allegations are more likely
to be classified as unfounded by the police than are other types of
violent offences); Statistics Canada, *Sexual Assault in Canada: 2004
and 2007*, by Shannon Brennan and Andrea Taylor Butts, Catalogue
No. 85F0033M—No. 19 (Ottawa: Statistics Canada, December 2008),
http://www.statcan.gc.ca/pub/85f0033m/85f0033m2008019-eng.pdf;
Centre for Leadership and Community Learning & Justice Institute
of British Columbia, *Police Classification of Sexual Assault Cases
as Unfounded: An Exploratory Study*, by Linda Light and Gisela
Ruebsaat, April 2007 update (original publication March 2006), http://
makingadifferencecanada.ca/pdf/LIBRARY/PDF/POLICE/police%20
classification%20of%20sexual%20assault%20cases%20as%20unfounded.
pdf (also showing that charges are less likely to be laid by the police for
reported sexual offences than for other violent crimes). See generally
Kathleen Daly and Brigitte Bouhours, "Rape and Attrition in the Legal
Process: A Comparative Analysis of Five Countries," in *Crime and
Justice: A Review of Research*, vol. 39, edited by Michael Tonry (Chicago,
IL: University of Chicago Press, 2010), 565.

17 Bayliss, "Consequences of an Allegation."
18 Christie Blatchford, "Christie Blatchford: Despite Rape Trial Acquittal,
     Innocent Accused Left to Rebuild Reputations and Good Names,"
     National Post (13 September 2013), http://news.nationalpost.com/
     full-comment/christie-blatchford-despite-rape-trial-acquittal-
     innocent-accused-left-to-rebuild-reputations-and-good-names, cited in
     Backhouse, "A Feminist Reflection," 165n37.
19 Several of these cases were brought to my attention by David
     Tanovich: "Defence 'Whacking' of Sexual Assault Complainants:
     Etiology, Prohibition, Manifestations and Responses," paper
     presented at *2016 Sexual Harassment & Violence Action Plan* (SHVAP)
     Conference (London, ON: 21 January 2016).

20   *R v H(JJ)*, 2015 ONSC 4054 at para. 87, 122 WCB (2d) 510.

21   *R v H(JJ)*, 2015 ONSC 6482 at para. 30, 125 WCB (2d) 447.

22   *R v G(A)*, 2015 ONCA 159 at para. 39, 319 CCC (3d) 441.

23   *R v T(B)*, 2012 ONSC 6799 at para. 16, 104 WCB (2d) 896.

24   *R v Gill*, 2015 BCPC 267 at para. 17, 125 WCB (2d) 112.

25   See generally Lise Gotell, "The Ideal Victim, the Hysterical Complainant, and the Disclosure of Confidential Records: The Implications of the *Charter* for Sexual Assault Law," *Osgoode Hall Law Journal* 40, no. 3 (2002): 251.

26   See e.g. *R v Zadeh*, 2015 BCPC 192 at para. 36, 123 WCB (2d) 498; *R v Peterson*, 2016 ABPC 4 at para. 12, 127 WCB (2d) 198; *R v M(L)*, 2014 ONCA 640 at para. 41, 122 OR (3d) 257; *R v I(D)*, 2014 NSSC 323 at para. 199, 116 WCB (2d) 560; *R v Slater*, 2014 ONSC 1518 at para. 24, 112 WCB (2d) 142; *R v Kelln*, 2013 ABPC 332 at para. 7, 112 WCB (2d) 194.

27   *R v G(PG)*, 2014 ONCJ 369 at paras. 42, 124, 116 WCB (2d) 319.

28   Ibid. at para. 36.

29   Ibid. at para. 39. See also *R v Griffin*, 2016 ONSC 2448 at para. 2, [2016] OJ No 1916 (appeal judge summarizing trial judge's characterization of this aspect of his cross-examination as mocking and belittling) [*Griffin* ONSC].

30   *R v G(PG)*, Trial Transcript, Volume II (26 June 2013) Burlington 10-3631 (ONCJ) at 46:21–47:3; 114:13 [*G(PG)* transcript, volume II].

31   Ibid. at 60:13. See also ibid. at 121:24.

32   Ibid. at 122:14–18.

33   *R v G(PG)*, Trial Transcript, Volume III (4 July 2013) Burlington 10-3631 (ONCJ) at 19:29.

34   *Griffin* ONSC at para. 138.

35   Ibid. at 173.

36   Ibid. at para. 153.

37   Ibid. at para. 140.

38   Ibid. at para. 142.

39   Ibid. at para. 143. With consent from both the Crown and defence, Justice Brown, the appellate judge, took the admirable but somewhat uncommon step of listening to the audio recording of the cross-examination of the complainant (at para. 136).

40   *R v PG*, 2017 ONCA 351.

41   Ibid. at paras. 36–9. There were other problems with the trial judge's decision in this case which gave rise to questions of fairness. Most

importantly, the Court of Appeal found that in his reasons for judgment he made a number of inappropriate, sarcastic, and intemperate statements about the accused and the complainant's mother (who testified for the defence).

42 Bayliss, "Consequences of an Allegation."

43 *R v Finney*, Trial Transcript, Volume II (30 September 2011) Lindsay C55780 (ONSC) at 318:16–17 [*Finney* transcript, volume II].

44 *Finney* transcript, volume II, at 389:5–18.

45 *R v Finney* (9 March 2012), Lindsay C55780 (ONSC) at 2667:14.

46 *R v Finney*, 2014 ONCA 866 at para. 2, 118 WCB (2d) 327.

47 *Finney* transcript, volume II, at 548:4–549:2.

48 Ibid. at 476:2.

49 *R v Finney*, Trial Transcript, Volume III (4 October 2011) Lindsay C55780 (ONSC) at 700:24–5 [*Finney* transcript, volume III].

50 Ibid. at 699:4–30.

51 Ibid. at 699:28.

52 Ibid. at 700:15–32.

53 Ibid. at 718 to 725.

54 Ibid. at 719:8–31.

55 *Ewanchuk* at para. 49. See generally Lucinda Vandervort, "Affirmative Sexual Consent in Canadian Law, Jurisprudence, and Legal Theory," *Columbia Journal of Gender and Law* 23, no. 2 (2012): 395.

56 *Finney* transcript, volume III at 690:5–18.

57 Ibid. at 695:17.

58 *R v Ururyar*, Trial Transcript, Volume III (1 February 2016) Toronto (ONCJ) at 20:4 to 21 [*Ururyar* transcript, volume III].

59 See e.g. ibid. at 26:13, 27:7, 27:20, 27:28, 27:30.

60 Ibid. at 27:7.

61 Ibid. at 27:20.

62 Ibid. at 27:28.

63 Ibid. at 28:7.

64 *R v Adepoju*, 2014 ABCA 100 at paras. 2, 7–8, Alta LR (6th) 387.

65 *R v Adepoju*, Trial Transcript, Volume I (30 April 2013) Red Deer 120580485Q1 (ABQB) at 87, 89–90.

66 *R v Adepoju*, Trial Transcript, Volume III (2 May 2013) Red Deer 120580485Q1 (ABQB) at 2–3.

67 *R v Al-Rawi*, Audio Trial Transcript: Oral Decision (1 March 2017) Halifax 2866665 (NSPC).

68 *R v Al-Rawi*, Audio Trial Transcript (9–10 February 2017) Halifax
    2866665 (NSPC). The officer who found her testified that Al-Rawi was
    between her legs and that he was facing towards the back of the vehicle
    – which would mean he was facing her.

69 *R v Al-Rawi*, Audio Trial Transcript: Testimony of the Complainant
    (9 February 2017) Halifax 2866665 (NSPC) at 15h:24m:42s [Testimony of
    the Complainant]. In his cross-examination, defence counsel asked the
    complainant whether, when intoxicated, she forgets where she is going
    or what she is doing. She responded that she does not know because
    she cannot always remember what happens when she is drunk. He then
    suggested that was because "you don't necessarily remember the type of
    person you become when you're ... [COMPLAINANT]: yeah I just ... I can
    only speculate."

70 Defence counsel made reference to "Drunk Jane" and contrasted
    "Drunk Jane" with "Sober Jane" more than once during the trial. See e.g
    Testimony of the Complainant, at 15h:25m:07s; *R v Al-Rawi*, Audio Trial
    Transcript: Testimony of LI (9 February 2017) Halifax 2866665 (NSPC)
    at 16h:02m:33s [Testimony of LI]; *R v Al-Rawi*, Audio Trial Transcript:
    Testimony of CO (10 February 2017) Halifax 2866665 (NSPC) at at
    10h:19m:17s [Testimony of CO]. To be clear, "Jane" is being used here
    as a pseudonym. In his cross-examinations, defence counsel used the
    complainant's real name: "Drunk ——."

71 Testimony of the Complainant, at 15h:24m:42s. It is true that the
    complainant testified in chief that she has "very poor judgment" as a
    "not sober person" (ibid. at 14h:34m:15s). When asked during cross-
    examination to clarify what she meant by this, she suggested she meant
    bad judgment about how much alcohol to consume (ibid. 15h:06m:44s).

72 Testimony of LI, at 16h:02m:14s.

73 Testimony of CO, at 10h:19m:23s.

74 *R v Al-Rawi*, Audio Trial Transcript: Defence Closing Submissions
    (10 February 2017) Halifax 2866665 (NSPC) at 13h:49m:39s [Defence
    Closing].

75 *R v Cain*, 2010 ABCA 371 at para. 22, 502 AR 322 [*Cain* CA].

76 *R v Cain*, Trial Transcript (20 November 2009), Wetaskiwin
    080971492Q1 (ABQB) at 398:11–12 [*Cain*, transcript].

77 Ibid. at 411:37–9.

78 Ibid. at 429:22; *Cain* CA at para. 30.

79 *Cain* CA at para. 30.

80 *R v Wagar*, 2015 ABCA 327, 125 WCB (2d) 471 (acquittal overturned). Wagar was tried a second time and acquitted: *R v Wagar*, 2017 ABPC 17.

81 *R v Wagar*, Trial Transcript (9 September 2014), Calgary 130288731P1 (ABPC) at 342:29.

82 Ibid. at 343:4.

83 Ibid. at 344:16, 344:41.

84 Ibid. at 345:33–6.

85 See e.g. *R v Schmaltz*, 2015 ABCA 4 at para. 47, 320 CCC (3d) 159 [*Schmaltz* ABCA].

86 *R v Schmaltz*, Trial Transcript (12 December 2013), Medicine Hat 081056319P1 (ABPC) at 85:15–35.

87 See e.g. Anne London-Weinstein, "Judges Don't Need More Coaching on Sex Assault," *Ottawa Citizen* (6 March 2017), http://ottawacitizen.com/opinion/columnists/ london-weinstein-judges-dont-need-more-coaching-on-sex-assault.

88 Casey Hill, David Tanovich, and Louis Strezos, *McWilliams' Canadian Criminal Evidence*, 5th ed., loose-leaf Release 5 (Toronto: Thomson Reuters, 2015), ch. 16, 16–18.

89 Friedman, "Ghomeshi Case Rhetoric."

90 Cristin Schmitz, "'Whack' Sex Assault Complainant at Preliminary Inquiry," *The Lawyers Weekly* (27 May 1988): 22.

91 Ibid.

92 See e.g. *R v Mills*, [1999] 3 SCR 668 at para. 90, 139 CCC (3d) 321; *R v Shearing*, 2002 SCC 58 at para. 173, [2002] 3 SCR 33 (citing *R v Mills*); see also David Tanovich, "'Whack' No More: Infusing Equality into the Ethics of Defence Lawyering in Sexual Assault Cases," *Ottawa Law Review* 45, no. 3 (2014): 495.

93 Tanovich, "'Whack' No More," 498–9.

94 *R v T(J)*, 2015 ONSC 3866 at para. 9, 122 WCB (2d) 409.

95 Ibid. at para. 21.

96 Ibid. at para. 27.

97 Ibid. at paras. 3, 31–3.

98 Ibid. at para. 3.

99 Ibid. at para. 32.

100 Ibid. at para. 52.

101 Friedman, "Ghomeshi Case Rhetoric."

102 Tanovich, "'Whack' No More," 524.

103 *R v T(J)* at para. 52.

104 Friedman, "Ghomeshi Case Rhetoric."

105 *Criminal Code*, RSC 1985, c C-46, s 276 [*Criminal Code*].

106 *R v B(IE)*, Trial Transcript (8 November 2011) Kentville 343759 (NSSC) at 35:3–18 [*B(IE)* transcript].

107 Telephone conversation with the Prothonotary for the Supreme Court of Nova Scotia (Kentville) who advised that a section 276 application was not filed in this case (11 August 2015).

108 *R v B(IE)*, 2013 NSCA 98 at para. 5, 300 CCC (3d) 481.

109 *B(IE)* transcript at 78–9.

110 Ibid. at 32:6.

111 Ibid. at 32:3–17.

112 *R v Wright*, 2013 MBCA 109 at paras. 4–12, 21, 23, 305 Man R (2d) 26 [*Wright* CA]. The accused was convicted at trial. However, his conviction was set aside on appeal, and because he had already served the bulk of his penitentiary sentence, a new trial was not ordered (at para. 54).

113 *R v Wright*, Trial Transcript, Volume 1 (28 May 2012) Winnipeg CR11-01-31550 (MBQB) at 35:13–29.

114 Ibid. at 65:30–66:9.

115 Arguably, topless dancing constitutes "sexual activity" for the purposes of section 276. See *R v Beilhartz*, 2013 ONSC 5670 at para. 27, 109 WCB (2d) 173 (a nude photograph sent by the complainant to the accused was considered "sexual activity" for the purposes of section 276).

116 *Criminal Code*, s 276.2. Furthermore, as Justice L'Heureux-Dubé stated (dissenting but not on this point, see para. 52 of the majority reasons), "[a]s to [section 277], it merely excludes evidence of sexual reputation used to impeach or support the credibility of the complainant. The notion that reputation for 'unchasteness' is relevant to credibility is insupportable and its legislative exclusion uncontentious" (*R v Seaboyer*, [1991] 2 SCR 577 at para. 212, 66 CCC (3d) 321).

117 This is not to suggest that this type of evidence should have been admissible with respect to credibility had there been a prior inconsistent statement. Rather it is to note that there was not even an attempt to introduce it under the guise of a legitimate issue. Note that the defence did not provide evidence or suggest in closing submissions that these questions were intended to impugn the complainant's credibility. There was no suggestion that she had made a prior inconsistent statement related to either of these lines of questioning. Even if that had been the intended purpose of this questioning, it would have, of course, still

been necessary to make a section 276 application prior to asking these questions. See *R v Zachariou*, 2015 ONCA 527, 123 WCB (2d) 403.

118 *Criminal Code*, s 277.

119 One of the problems that arises when trial judges fail to apply section 276 is that defence counsel are not required to justify this evidence. This is, of course, one of the intended purposes of requiring judicial consideration before this type of evidence is permitted.

120 The accused's conviction in *Wright* was set aside by the Court of Appeal. A new trial was not ordered because by the time the trial decision was overturned he had served most of his custodial sentence: *R v Wright*, (2013) 303 Man R (2d) 26, 2013 MBCA 109.

121 Bayliss, "Consequences of an Allegation."

122 Jennifer Koshan, "The Legal Treatment of Marital Rape and Women's Equality: An Analysis of the Canadian Experience" (September 2010), http://theequalityeffect.org/pdfs/maritalrapecanadexperience.pdf (her review of all reported marital rape cases in Canada between 1983 and 2013 revealed that in the majority of cases in which defence counsel applied to do so, they were permitted to lead at least some of the evidence they sought to admit).

123 *R v S(JS)*, 2015 BCSC 1369 at para. 1, 123 WCB (2d) 484.

124 *R v S(JS)*, 2014 BCSC 804 at para. 9, 120 WCB (2d) 300.

125 Ibid.

126 Ibid. at para. 23.

127 *R v B(S)*, 2014 NLTD(G) 61, 114 WCB (2d) 571 [*B(S)* NLTD].

128 Ibid. at 61 at paras. 5–11.

129 *R v B(S)*, 2016 NLCA 20 at para. 43, [2016] NJ No. 158 [*B(S)* NLCA].

130 *R v B(S)*, Trial Transcript, Volume VI (6 June 2014) St John's 201301G4957 (NLTD) at 128:5–129:17.

131 The Newfoundland Court of Appeal's majority decision not to order a new trial, following a successful Crown appeal (*B(S)* NLCA), was overturned by the Supreme Court of Canada: *R v SB*, 2017 SCC 16.

132 *B(S)* NLCA at para. 43.

133 GraciaLaw, "Sexual & Indecent Acts," http://www.gracialaw.ca/blog/result-categories/sexual-indecent-acts/ (accessed 28 April 2014). A PDF archive of this website was created on 20 November 2014 and is on file with the author.

134 A PDF archive of this website was created on 29 April 2014 and is on file with the author.

135 Craig Penney, "Sexual Assault – Oshawa Defence Lawyer," http://
torontosexualassaultlawyer.com/Craig-Penney-Lawyer-Criminal-
Attorney-Defence-Defense-Law-Crime-Sexual-Assault-Domestic-
Toronto-Mississauga-Barrie-Durham-York-Region-Ontario-
Canada-Domestic-Toronto-Attempted-Rape-Lawyer.html (accessed
29 April 2014).

136 Ibid.

137 *Ewanchuk* at para. 49.

138 *R v A(J)*, 2011 SCC 28 at para. 66, [2011] 2 SCR 440 [*A(J)*].

139 Ibid.

140 Penney, "Sexual Assault."

141 *Criminal Code*, s 273.2(a)(i).

142 Penney, "Sexual Assault."

143 Ibid.

144 *Ewanchuk* at para. 49; *A(J)* at para. 66.

145 *Criminal Code*, s 273.2(b).

146 Ibid., s 276.1(a).

147 The Criminal Law Team, "Sexual Assault Lawyers Toronto," https://
thecriminallawteam.ca/offence/sexual-assault-lawyers/. A PDF archive
of this website was created on 19 November 2014 and is on file with
the author.

148 *Criminal Code*, s 276.

149 David Tanovich, "Regulating Inductive Reasoning in Sexual Assault
Cases," in *To Ensure that Justice Is Done: Essays in Memory of
Marc Rosenberg*, edited by Ben Berger, Emma Cunliffe, and James
Stribopolous (Toronto: Carswell, 2017 [forthcoming]); Tanovich,
"Defence 'Whacking' of Sexual Assault Complainants."

150 Marie Corbett, *January: A Woman Judge's Season of Disillusion* (Holmes
Beach, FL: Broad Cove Press, 2016), 86.

151 Eric Andrew Gee, "Jian Ghomeshi's Sexual Assault Trial Fuels Debate
over Defence's Tactics," *The Globe and Mail* (4 February 2016), http://
www.theglobeandmail.com/news/toronto/jian-ghomeshis-sexual-
assault-trial-fuels-debate-over-defence-lawyering/article28548535/.
Quoting criminal lawyer Breese Davies: "We don't give a free pass to any
witness ... And just because it's about sex doesn't mean we change the
ground rules."

152 Backhouse, "A Feminist Reflection," 179.

Chapter Three

1 On file with author.

2 Breese Davies, "Convicting Jian Ghomeshi Will Be Hard – for Good Reason," *Toronto Star* (2 February 2016), https://www.thestar.com/opinion/commentary/2016/02/02/convicting-jian-ghomeshi-will-be-hard-for-good-reason.html.

3 Reid Rusonick, "In Defence of Rigorous Sexual Assault Defences," *Toronto Star* (21 February 2016), https://www.thestar.com/opinion/commentary/2016/02/21/in-defence-of-rigorous-sexual-assault-defences.html.

4 Mark Gollom, "Meet Marie Henein, the 'Fearless and Brilliant' Lawyer Defending Jian Ghomeshi," CBC *News* (27 November 2014), http://www.cbc.ca/news/canada/meet-marie-henein-the-fearless-and-brilliant-lawyer-defending-jian-ghomeshi-1.2851592.

5 Joe Warmington, "Lawyer Choice Proof Jian Ghomeshi Plans to Fight Accusations," *Toronto Sun* (5 November 2014), http://www.torontosun.com/2014/11/05/lawyer-choice-proof-jian-ghomeshi-plans-to-fight-accusations.

6 Michael Bryant, *28 Seconds: A True Story of Addiction, Tragedy, and Hope* (Toronto: Penguin Group, 2012), 211.

7 Warmington, "Lawyer Choice," 5.

8 *R v Ghomeshi*, 2016 ONCJ 155, 129 WCB (2d) 400.

9 Lucy Decouture (as told to Ruth Spencer), "Lucy Decouture on the Trauma of the Jian Ghomeshi Trial: 'After Everything I Went Through, Jian Is Free,'" *Guardian* (25 March 2016), https://www.theguardian.com/world/2016/mar/25/jian-ghomeshi-trial-lucy-de-coutere-interview.

10 Constance Backhouse, "Edward Greenspan: A Feminist Reflection on the Eulogies Surrounding His Death," *Canadian Journal of Women and the Law* 27, no. 2 (2015): 157, at 160.

11 Ibid., 165 (footnotes omitted).

12 *R v Regan*, 2002 SCC 12, [2002] 1 SCR 297.

13 Stephen Kimber, *"Not Guilty": The Trial of Gerald Regan* (Toronto: Stoddart Publishing, 1999).

14 Ibid., 249.

15 Ibid., 251–2. According to Kimber, Greenspan's assertion was not even accurate.

16   Gray's Funeral Chapel Ltd, "Obituary for J.H. Clyne Harradence," http://www.grays.ca/book-of-memories/1157322/Harradence-JH-Clyne/obituary.php (accessed 19 June 2017).

17   The Legal Archives Society of Alberta, *Milt Harradence: The Western Flair*, http://legalarchives.ca/shop/book/milt-harradence-the-western-flair/ (accessed 19 June 2017).

18   George D. Finlayson, *John J. Robinette: Peerless Mentor: An Appreciation* (Toronto: Dundurn Group, 2003), 89. Finlayson was juxtaposing Dubin's (and Arthur Martin's) aggressive approach with that of John Robinette.

19   Backhouse, "A Feminist Reflection," 165.

20   Todd Brett White, Twitter post: "Canada has lost one of its legal greats, with the passing of my mentor and former partner, Eddie Greenspan. RIP" (24 December 2014, 1:19 pm), https://twitter.com/ToddBrettWhite/status/547818784850194433?ref_src=twsrc%5Etfw.

21   Sarah Boesveld, Richard Warnica, and Barbara Schecter, "A 'Giant': Legendary Canadian Defence Lawyer Edward Greenspan Dies in Phoenix at Age 70," *National Post* (24 December 2014), http://news.nationalpost.com/news/canada/eddie-greenspan-has-died. White described Greenspan as his mentor and "former legal partner of more than 20 years."

22   Todd Brett White, "Profile," http://toddwhitelaw.com/profile (accessed 23 July 2017).

23   Ibid.

24   Todd B. White, "Todd B. White, B.A. (Hons.), LL.B." (Summer 2014), https://membernewsletters.files.wordpress.com/2014/06/todd-white-1665563-newsletter-revised.pdf.

25   White, "Profile."

26   Peter Small, "'Dogged' Defence Lawyer Barks and Bites," *Toronto Star* (8 May 2003), reprinted in Todd Brett White, "In the News," http://toddwhitelaw.com/toronto-star-toddwhite.html (of note, the *Toronto Star* article dubbing him the "Legal JYD" was not in the context of a sexual assault proceeding).

27   White, "Profile."

28   *R v L(G)*, 2014 ONSC 3403, 114 WCB (2d) 108 [*L(G)*] aff'd *R v Luceno* (2015) 331 CCC (3d) 51 (CA). Luceno's identity was subject to a publication ban at the time of trial which was subsequently lifted on appeal.

29   *Criminal Code*, RSC 1985, c C-46, s 150.1(1). The age of consent is 16. In 2008 it was raised from 14 to 16. Luceno had sexual intercourse with the

complainant, who was 13 at the time, in 2008. Under either the previous or current age of consent, the complainant in *L(G)* lacked capacity.

30 *L(G)* at paras. 59–64 ("Not only is there no evidence to support the contention, the evidence that we do have logically suggests otherwise" at para. 62).

31 Ibid. at para. 62.

32 Ibid. at para. 22.

33 See e.g. *R v Luceno*, Trial Transcript, Volume I (19 March 2014) Toronto C59248 (ONSC) at 93:6–7, 131:10–11, 133, 135, 149, 158, 159, 163, 164, 200, 202, 215 [*Luceno* transcript, volume I].

34 Ibid. at 93:6–7; see also ibid. at 131:10–11 ("You've got to let her finish answering the question").

35 Ibid. at 133:19–20.

36 Ibid. at 135:13.

37 Ibid. at 164:18–20.

38 Ibid. at 93, 131, 133, 135, 164, 182, 204–5, 226, 251, 255; *R v Luceno*, Trial Transcript, Volume II (21 March 2014) Toronto C59248 (ONSC) at 8, 11, 21, 73, 75, 127, 137 [*Luceno* transcript, volume II].

39 See e.g. *Luceno* transcript, volume I at 78, 136, 202.

40 Ibid. at 116, 122–3, 135, 142, 204, 225.

41 Ibid. at 251:8 ("Just give her a chance"); ibid. at 255:4–5 ("Just slow down a bit, Mr. White"); ibid. at 258:26; *Luceno* transcript, volume II at 122:13 ("the question comes out at rapid fire").

42 *Luceno* transcript, volume I at 258:26–259:3.

43 See e.g. ibid. at 123:8–15, 142:9–11, 204–5, 226.

44 Ibid. at 122:4–123:15.

45 See e.g. ibid. at 84, 91, 95, 125, 129, 136, 142, 148, 160, 174; *Luceno* transcript, volume II at 49, 73, 121. Justice Goldstein noted the confusion this produced in his decision: *L(G)* at para. 26.

46 *Luceno* transcript, volume I at 125, 129, 142, 160, 174; *Luceno* transcript, volume II at 49, 73, 121.

47 See e.g. *Luceno* transcript, volume I at 136, 142, 148, 160, 174; *Luceno* transcript, volume II at 49, 73, 121.

48 *Luceno* transcript, volume I at 125:8–18.

49 Ibid. at 125:30–126:3.

50 Ibid. at 125, 129, 142, 160, 174; *Luceno* transcript, volume II at 49, 73, 121.

51 *L(G)* at para. 26.

52 See e.g. *Luceno* transcript, volume I at 136:28 ("THE COURT: I mean we're going around and around on this"), 258:10 ("THE COURT: I think

we're going over the same ground a lot and I'm not finding it all that helpful, truthfully … she's getting herself tripped up …"), 281; *Luceno* transcript, volume II at 13, 89–90, 130 (trial judge referencing the repetitive nature of the cross-examination).

53 See e.g. *Luceno* transcript, volume I at 257:31–258:10–12 ("WITNESS EXCUSED … I think we're going over the same ground a lot and I'm not finding it all that helpful, truthfully"); *Luceno* transcript, volume II at 79:27–80:11 ("WITNESS EXCUSED … You've asked her the same question over and over again … You've gone over it a dozen times already and you went over it a dozen times yesterday"); *Luceno* transcript, volume II at 121:19–122:18 ("WITNESS EXCUSED … Okay. But you know what, the question comes out at rapid fire and we see it here on the transcript and we can look at it, but when she is sitting there, that doesn't necessarily mean which one's she's answering").

54 See e.g. *Luceno* transcript, volume I at 139, 210, 239, 253.

55 *L(G)* at paras. 24, 26.

56 See e.g. *Luceno* transcript, volume I at 247:11–13, and at 267:4–5 ("THE COURT: Well, I mean – okay. I mean let's try to be fair").

57 Ibid. at 247:11–13.

58 See e.g. ibid. at 254–6, 269:21.

59 *Luceno* transcript, volume II at 128:4 ("Okay. We understand that. His Honour understands it, he's very bright …"); *Luceno* transcript, volume I at 176:22 ("Are you just making this up now?"); *Luceno* transcript, volume I at 181:1 ("Q. So that's your new story. MS. NEDELKOPOULOS: Objection, Your Honour. Whether it's new or not, perhaps that's saved for submissions.").

60 *Luceno* transcript, volume I at 142:8–29.

61 Ibid. at 142:8–29.

62 *R v Luceno*, 2015 ONCA 759 at para. 28, 331 CCC (3d) 521 [*Luceno* CA].

63 The trial judge described it as "endless days of repetitive cross-examination": *L(G)* at para. 62.

64 See e.g. *Luceno* transcript, volume I at 176:23, 181:1, 182:26, 193:30–194:2, 251:4–5; *Luceno* transcript, volume II at 77:31–79:4; *L(G)* at para. 62.

65 See e.g. *Luceno* transcript, volume I at 93, 131, 133, 135, 149, 158–9, 163–4, 200, 202, 215, 283.

66 *Luceno* transcript, volume II at 80:9–11.

67 See e.g. *Luceno* transcript, volume I at 116, 122–3, 135, 142, 204, 225.

68 See e.g. ibid. at 155:1, 158:31; *Luceno* transcript, volume II at 128:3.

69 *Luceno* transcript, volume I at 142:18–19.

70 *Luceno* transcript, volume II at 77:31–79:4.

71 Ibid. at 79:25–6.

72 Ibid. at 79–85.

73 *Luceno* transcript, volume I at 259:11 ("I do think we're getting a little counterproductive"); *L(G)* at paras. 24, 26. See also *Luceno* transcript, volume I at 125:8–18; 257:31–258:10–12.

74 Criminal Trial Lawyers' Association, "About Us," http://albertactla.com/aboutus.shtml (accessed 19 June 2017).

75 Paul Simons, "An Ear for Injustice: Award-Winning Edmonton Lawyer Calls on Jim Prentice to Save Legal Aid," *Edmonton Journal* (3 October 2014), http://edmontonjournal.com/news/local-news/an-ear-for-injustice-award-winning-edmonton-lawyer-calls-on-jim-prentice-to-save-legal-aid.

76 *R v Khaery*, 2014 ABQB 676 at para. 141, 117 WCB (2d) 422 [*Khaery* ABQB].

77 *R v Khaery*, Trial Transcript (23 September 2014) Edmonton 121306211Q1 (ABQB) [*Khaery* transcript].

78 To be clear, in part, the length of the cross-examination was extended because defence counsel requested that a translator be used to translate the proceedings into the accused's first language. The trial judge noted that this made the trial even harder for the complainant – who was already visibly burdened by having to testify. The defence lawyer's justification for requiring a translator was so that he could understand what his client was saying. The accused himself indicated that he understood English and did not need a translator. *Khaery* transcript at 34:16–32.

79 Ibid.

80 *Khaery* ABQB at para. 102.

81 Ibid. at paras. 5–11.

82 *Khaery* transcript at 116:26–117:5.

83 Ibid. at 115:32–3.

84 Ibid. at 116:3–12.

85 Ibid. at 116:15–16.

86 Ibid. at 116:18–19.

87 Ibid. at 116:26–117:5.

88 Ibid.

89 Ibid. at 116:26–117:5.

90 Ibid. at 117:24–32.

91 Ibid. at 118:7–8.

92 Ibid. at 118:19–22.

93 *Khaery* ABQB at para. 102.

94 *Khaery* transcript at 118:7–8.

95 *Khaery* ABQB at para. 5.

96 *Khaery* transcript at 111:33–112:6.

97 See e.g. ibid. at 13:36–15:12, 25:3, 111:33–112:6.

98 Ibid. at 31:10, 47:32, 103:34, 106:20.

99 Ibid. at 30:8, 30:34, 31:3, 32:33.

100 Ibid. at 118:7.

101 Simons, "An Ear for Injustice."

102 Statistics Canada, *Criminal Victimization in Canada, 2014*, by Samuel
    Perreault, Catalogue No. 85-002-X (Ottawa: Statistics Canada, 23
    November 2015), 16 ("The differences between Aboriginal and non-
    Aboriginal people were most pronounced for break-ins and sexual
    assaults, with the rates for Aboriginals being more than double those for
    non-Aboriginals").

103 Memorial University of Newfoundland, "Spring Convocation
    2013: Honorary Degree Recipients Announced; Chancellor to Be
    Installed," *Gazette* (3 April 2013), https://www.mun.ca/convocation/
    honours/Gazette_April_3_honorary_pgs.pdf.

104 Sullivan Breen King Defence, "Our Team," http://www.spdefence.ca/
    our-team/ (accessed 19 June 2017).

105 Rosie Gillingham, "Bob Simmonds," *The Telegram* (18 May 2013), http://
    www.spdefence.ca/2013/06/20/robert-simmonds-qc-answers-21-
    questions/.

106 Ibid.

107 Ibid.

108 Sullivan Breen King Defence, "Our Team."

109 *R v B(S)*, 2014 NLTD(G) 61, 114 WCB (2d) 571 at paras. 5–11 [*B(S)* 2014].

110 Ibid. at para. 28.

111 The defence is not entitled to cross-examine the complainant on prior
    sexual history in an effort to create a prior inconsistent statement.
    Justice Stack's ruling was premature. The defence should only have been
    permitted to question her about this if the complainant had denied the
    affair in her testimony in chief (which a competent Crown presumably
    would not have questioned her about). See *R v Nicholson*, 1998 ABCA
    290, 129 CCC (3d) 198.

112 *R v B(S)*, Trial Transcript, Volume VI (6 June 2014) St John's
     201301G4957 (NLTD) at 50:14 [*B(S)* transcript, volume VI].

113 Ibid. at 51:8–53:26.

114 Ibid. at 54:15.

115 Ibid. at 56:9–58:6. At first, Simmonds required her to respond to each
     text of his own volition; later, after he had stopped doing this, the trial
     judge required him to do so.

116 Ibid.

117 Ibid. at 60:1.

118 Ibid. at 60:3.

119 Ibid. at 60:19.

120 *R v B(S)*, Trial Transcript, Volume II (16 May 2014) St John's
     201301G4957 (NLTD) at 16:7 [*B(S)* transcript, volume II].

121 *B(S)* transcript, volume VI at 42:8.

122 *R v B(S)*, 2016 NLCA 20 at para. 43, [2016] NJ No. 158 [*B(S)* NLCA]. The
     Newfoundland Court of Appeal's decision not to order a new trial was
     overturned by the Supreme Court of Canada: *R v BS* (2017), SCC 16.

123 *B(S)* NLCA at para. 44.

124 *B(S)* transcript, volume VI at 37:17–39:9 and 59:5. To his credit, before he
     introduced this evidence, defence counsel did flag for the trial judge that
     it was graphic and would be unpleasant. See chapter 6 for a discussion
     of the trial judge's failure to properly apply section 276.

125 *R v B(S)*, Trial Transcript, Volume I (15 May 2014) St John's 201301G4957
     (NLTD) at 12:12 [*B(S)* transcript, volume I]: "the application as it stands
     now is to actually admit the video as an exhibit."

126 *B(S)* transcript, volume II at 32:7; 35:5; 39; 41:5.

127 Ibid. at 35:5; 39; 41:5.

128 *B(S)* NLCA at paras. 53, 55.

129 *B(S)* transcript, volume VI at 128:5–129:17.

130 Ibid. at 129:20–8.

131 Ibid at 129:28–133:14.

132 Ibid. at 134.

133 Ibid. at 137.

134 *B(S)* NLCA at para. 60.

135 Ibid. at para. 60.

136 *B(S)* transcript, volume VI at 130:9.

137 Ducharme Fox Lawyers, "Patrick Ducharme," http://www.ducharmefox.
     com/patrick-ducharme (accessed 11 August 2016).

138 Ibid.

139 Patrick Ducharme, "Thoughts of an Advocate," *Ducharme Fox Lawyers*, http://www.ducharmefox.com/Article/Details/thoughts-of-an-advocate (accessed 11 August 2016), PDF on file with the author.

140 Ibid.

141 Ibid.

142 Ibid.

143 Ibid.

144 Ibid.

145 *R v Traynor*, [1987] OJ No. 1943 (QL).

146 Ducharme, "Thoughts of an Advocate." See Peter Wagner, "Oscar Wilde's 'Impression du Matin' – An Intermediary Reading," in *Icons – Texts – Iconotexts: Essays on Ekphrasis and Intermediality*, edited by Peter Wagner (Berlin: Walter de Gruyter, 1996), 300.

147 Ducharme, "Thoughts of an Advocate."

148 Ibid.

149 Ibid.

150 Andrew E. Taslitz, *Rape and the Culture of the Courtroom* (New York: New York University Press, 1999), Part I.

151 *R v Johnson*, Trial Transcript, (20 June 2016) Windsor CR-14-00003172-0000 (ONCJ) at 90:30 [*Johnson* transcript June 20]: During her examination in chief Ducharme consented to the Crown's decision not to put to the complainant photographs of her vagina taken by the Sexual Assault Nurse Examiner.

152 E.g. *R v Johnson*, Trial Transcript, (21 June 2016) Windsor CR-14-00003172-0000 (ONCJ) at 4:3 [*Johnson* transcript June 21]: Following a misunderstanding based on the way he worded a question directed to the complainant, he stated: "Oh, I'm sorry. Okay, you're right. I didn't mean to suggest ..."

153 *Johnson* transcript June 20 (examination in chief).

154 Sarah Sacheli, "Ben Johnson's Alleged Rape Victim Unable to Stand, Keep Eyes Open, Trial Hears," *Windsor Star* (21 June 2016), http://windsorstar.com/news/local-news/ben-johnsons-alleged-rape-victim-unable-to-stand-keep-eyes-open-trial-hears.

155 *R v Johnson*, Trial Transcript, (29 June 2016) Windsor CR-14-00003172-0000 (ONCJ) (evidence in chief of sexual assault nurse examiner); *R v Johnson*, Trial Transcript, (30 June 2016) Windsor CR-14-00003172-0000 (ONCJ) (cross-examination of sexual assault nurse examiner); *R v Johnson*, Trial Transcript, (19 July 2016) Windsor

CR-14-00003172-0000 (ONCJ) [*Johnson* transcript July 10] (defence closing submissions).

156 *Johnson* transcript July 10.

157 *Johnson* transcript June 21 at 4:13–5:7.

158 Ibid. at 42:22–43:17.

159 Ibid. at 15:3–16:18.

160 Ibid. at 16:20–17:15.

161 Ibid. at 17:11.

162 *Johnson* transcript July 19 at 18:28–19:7.

163 *R v Johnson*, Trial Transcript, (28 June 2016) Windsor CR-14-00003172-0000 (ONCJ) (evidence of medical expert Dr. William Mundle) at 54:17; *Johnson* transcript June 30 (cross-examination of sexual assault nurse examiner).

164 *Johnson* transcript July 19 at 18:28–19:7.

165 It is true that the Crown asked questions about the possibility that she was penetrated vaginally on the dance floor, thus causing an injury to her hymen, during direct examination of the Crown's expert witnesses. In his cross-examination of Dr Mundle, Ducharme refers to this implausible theory as a hypothetical presented by the Crown. However, it seems reasonable to conclude that the Crown raised this issue with these expert witnesses in anticipation of Ducharme's theory of the case, based on Ducharme's cross-examination of the complainant about this issue. Defence counsel's closing submissions (which speculated that her grinding on the dance floor may have been the cause of the injury or re-injury to her hymen) support my speculation that he asked the complainant these questions about her clothing, the dancing, and whether she could feel this man's genital anatomy in her genital or anal region not to challenge her recollection or level of intoxication but to suggest sexual activity on the dance floor that might have caused injury or re-injury to her hymen (*Johnson* transcript July 19 at 18:28–19:7).

166 *Johnson* transcript June 21 at 17:11.

167 Ibid. at 16:29.

168 See e.g. Federation of Law Societies of Canada, *Model Code of Professional Conduct* (Ottawa: Federation of Law Societies of Canada, 2014), http://flsc.ca/wp-content/uploads/2014/12/conduct1. pdf: "Examples of marketing that may contravene this rule include: ... (d) suggesting or implying the lawyer is aggressive" (ch. 4.2-1, commentary [1](d)).

169 Leora Shemesh, "Sexual Assault Charges," http://www.leorashemesh. com/practice-area/sexual-assault/ (accessed 24 June 2014). See also Brian Crothers's website: Crothers Law Firm, "Brian Crothers, a Mississauga Criminal Lawyer, Understands the Law," http://www. crotherslaw.com/index.php (accessed 24 June 2014): "Brian Crothers is an Aggressive Criminal Lawyer."

170 Aitan M. Lerner, "New Market Aggravated Sexual Assault Law Firm," http://www.alernerlaw.com/criminal-law-overview/new-market-sex-offences-law-firm/new-market-aggravated-sexual-assault-law-firm/ (accessed 28 April 2014): "For over 17 years, I have been fighting aggressively to help people charged with sex offences in Ontario protect their rights and their freedom."

171 Adler Bytensky Prutschi Shikman, "Sexual Assault," http://crimlawcanada. com/practice-areas/sexual-assault/ (accessed 24 June 2014).

172 Craig Penney, "Proven Results Matter – Sexual Assault Lawyer," http:// torontosexualassaultlawyer.com (accessed 12 August 2016).

173 See e.g. Neuberger & Partners LLP, "Sexual Assault and Related Offences," http://www.nrlawyers.com/Sexual-Assault-Domestic-Assault-Assault-and-Other-Violent-Crimes/Sexual-Assault-and-Offences.shtml (accessed 12 August 2016) (referencing "fabricated or false allegations"); Anthony Demarco, "Toronto Sexual Assault Lawyer Anthony Demarco," http://www.anthonydemarco.ca/Criminal-Defence-Overview/Sexual-Assault.shtml (accessed 12 August 2016) (referencing potential effect on complainant's credibility because of false memory syndrome and compulsive lying); Robb MacDonald, "Charged With Sexual Assault? Let Top Toronto Lawyer Robb MacDonald Help," http:// www.lawintoronto.com/sexual-assault-lawyer-toronto/ (accessed 12 August 2016) (referencing a case in which the complainant may have had a motive to fabricate); Tushar K. Pain, "Sexual Assault: The False Allegation," http://torontocriminaldefence.com/criminal-defence-articles/sexual-assault%C2%A0-the-false-allegation-criminal-defence-articles-by-tushar-k-pain/ (accessed 12 August 2016) (referencing the stress of facing false allegations); Mass Tsang LLP, "Assault Lawyer in Toronto," http://www.masstsang.com/services/assault-lawyer-in-toronto/ (accessed 12 August 2016) (referencing false allegations); Paul Lewandowski, "False Accusations," http://www.paullewandowski. com/results/trials/false-accusations.php (accessed 12 August 2016) (referencing false allegations); Dan Manning, "Sexual Assault," http://

www.danmanning.ca/sexual-assault/ (accessed 12 August 2016) (referencing the need to investigate the motive to fabricate).

174 Dean D. Paquette & Associate, "Sexual Offences," http://www. deanpaquettecriminallaw.calls.net/Sexual-Offences/ (accessed 12 August 2016) ("they are often the result of false allegations"); Susan Karpa, "Sexual Offences," http://www.susankarpa.com/criminal-law/ sexual-offences/ (accessed 12 August 2016) (referencing frequency of false allegations).

175 Karpa, "Sexual Offences."

176 The Defence Group Criminal Law, "Sexual Assault Defence Lawyer," http://www.defencegroup.ca/practice-areas/sexual-assault-defence-lawyer/ (accessed 12 August 2016). See also Pain, "Sexual Assault": "People do make up false charges and the motives to do so are wide and varied: jealousy, revenge, attention, and cover up are but a few examples"; Randy Norris, "Sexual Offences," http://www. mississaugacriminaldefencelawyers.com/index.php?page=sexual_ offences (accessed 12 August 2016), discussing *R v S* (May 2013) and *R v D* (February 2012).

177 See e.g. Norris, "Sexual Offences," which contains a description for defence of assault, child pornography, driving offences, theft, fraud, robbery and weapon offences, or drug offences. On the page discussing offences against the police, there is reference to police not telling the truth. See also Mass Tsang LLP, "Assault Lawyer" (compare the description of assault without reference to fabricated claims and the reference to false allegations in sexual assault cases); Neuberger & Partners LLP, "Toronto Violent Crimes and Assault Lawyers," http:// www.nrlawyers.com/Assault-and-Violent-Crimes/ (accessed 12 August 2016) (compare the description of assault without reference to fabricated claims and the reference to false allegations in sexual assault cases in Neuberger & Partners LLP, "Sexual Assault and Related Offences").

178 See e.g. Dean D. Paquette & Associate, "Domestic Violence and Violent Offences," http://www.deanpaquettecriminallaw.calls.net/Domestic-Violence-Violent-Offences/ (accessed 12 August 2016): "A domestic violence complaint can certainly result from a real act of violence involving spouses or two people who are in a relationship, but they are also often false accusations."

179 Anonymous, "Corroborating Charges of Rape," *Columbia Law Review* 67, no. 6 (1967): 1137, at 1138.

180 Ibid.

181 For a discussion of the role of these stereotypes in the development of the law, see e.g. Susan Estrich, *Real Rape* (Cambridge, MA: Harvard University Press, 1987); Carol Smart, *Feminism and the Power of Law* (London: Routledge, 1989).

182 See e.g. Peter G. Jaffe et al., "Vicarious Trauma in Judges: The Personal Challenge of Dispensing Justice," *Juvenile & Family Court Journal* 54, no. 4 (2003): 1 (finding that 63% of judges interviewed reported symptoms of work-related vicarious trauma, including sleep difficulties, anxiety, depression, overeating, anger, and cynicism, after dealing with cases of rape, domestic violence, and child abuse); Evan R. Seamone, "Sex Crime Litigation as Hazardous Duty: Practical Tools for Trauma-Exposed Prosecutors, Defense Counsel, and Paralegals," *Ohio State Journal of Criminal Law* 11, no. 2 (2014): 487 (examining secondary trauma experienced by military lawyers who prosecute and defend American military personnel accused of sexual offences).

183 Helen Baillot, Sharon Cowan, and Vanessa E. Munro, "Second-hand Emotion? Exploring the Contagion and Impact of Trauma and Distress in the Asylum Law Context," *Journal of Law and Society* 40, no. 4 (2013): 509, at 531 (noting the comments of one case officer).

184 See Lila Petar Vrklevski and John Franklin, "Vicarious Trauma: The Impact on Solicitors of Exposure to Traumatic Material," *Traumatology* 14, no. 1 (2008): 106 (finding that criminal lawyers reported significantly higher levels of subjective distress, vicarious trauma, depression, and stress).

185 Backhouse, "A Feminist Reflection," 163–4.

186 Ibid., 164.

187 See generally Judith Wegner, "Reframing Legal Education's Wicked Problems," *Rutgers Law Review* 61, no. 4 (2009): 867; Benjamin Madison and Larry O. Natt, "The Emperor Has No Clothes, but Does Anyone Really Care? How Law Schools Are Failing to Develop Students' Professional Identity and Practical Judgment," *Regent University Law Review* 17, no. 2 (2015): 339; Kath Hall, Molly Townes O'Brian, and Stephen Tang, "Developing a Professional Identity in Law School: A View from Australia," *Phoenix Law Review* 4, no. 1 (2010): 19, at 39 (discussing the reinforcement of rational thinking that occurs in law school); Joseph Allegretti, "Have Brief Case Will Travel: An Essay on the Lawyer as Hired Gun," *Creighton Law Review* 24, no. 3 (1991): 747, at 749.

188 See e.g. William Sullivan et al., *Educating Lawyers: Preparation for the Profession of Law* (San Francisco, CA: Carnegie Foundation, Jossey-Bass, 2007); Wegner, "Reframing Legal Education's Wicked Problems"; Madison and Natt, "The Emperor Has No Clothes"; Orrin K. Ames, "Concerns About the Lack of Professionalism: Root Causes Rather than Symptoms Must Be Addressed," *American Journal of Trial Advocacy* 28, no. 3 (2005): 531 (arguing that the process of teaching students to approach every issue with analytical logic to the exclusion of moral considerations creates in law students cynicism, neutrality, and moral ambiguity); Gerald Hess, "Heads and Hearts: The Teaching and Learning Environment in Law School," *Journal of Legal Education* 52, no. 1–2 (2002): 75 (law school curriculums' traditional focus on analytical skills rather than interpersonal skills and the development of relationships leads to feelings of alienation among students); Jean Stefancic and Richard Delgado, *How Lawyers Lose Their Way: A Profession Fails Its Creative Minds* (Durham, NC: Duke University Press, 2005) (arguing that unhappiness among lawyers is a function of the way they are taught in law school to privilege rationality over emotion and formality over values so as to 'think like a lawyer'); Anonymous, "Making Docile Lawyers: An Essay on the Pacification of Law Students," *Harvard Law Review* 111, no. 7 (1998): 2027 (describing the demoralizing impact of law school on law students); Kennon Sheldon and Lawrence Krieger, "Does Legal Education Have Undermining Effects on Law Students? Evaluating Changes in Goals, Values and Well-Being," *Behavioral Science and the Law* 22, no. 2 (2004): 261 (showing declines in self-determination, intrinsic valuing, and general well-being of students over the course of their legal education); Daisy Hurst Floyd, "Lost Opportunity: Legal Education and the Development of Professional Identity," *Hamline Law Review* 30 (2007): 555 (examining the professional identity of those who graduate from law school); A. Benjamin Spencer, "The Law School Critique in Historical Perspective," *Washington and Lee Law Review* 69 (2012): 1949.

189 See e.g. Susan Bandes, "Repression and Denial in Criminal Law," *Buffalo Criminal Law Review* 9, no. 2 (2006): 339, at 348 (arguing that criminal lawyers may need to distance themselves from the pain their clients may have caused, and that this strategy is only maladaptive for those lawyers who do so without self-awareness and reflection).

190 Ibid., 383: "the question of how one becomes, and remains, a zealous lawyer, what emotional strategies are involved, and what emotional costs are entailed, has received little attention."

Chapter Four

1 Joseph Allegretti, "Have Brief Case Will Travel: An Essay on the Lawyer as Hired Gun," *Creighton Law Review* 24, no. 3 (1990): 747 ("Among the metaphors that shape how lawyers view themselves, and are viewed by others, none exercises a more powerful hold than the metaphor of the hired gun," at 749); Jack Camp, "Thoughts on Professionalism in the Twenty-First Century," *Tulane Law Review* 81, no. 5–6 (2007): 1377 (arguing that "[t]oday, lawyers often view the duty to represent the client zealously as the paramount objective of the profession" and that this attitude "creates a lawyer who is little more than a hired gun," at 1381 [footnotes omitted]).

2 Monroe H. Freedman, "The Lawyer as a Hired Gun," in *Lawyers' Ethics: Contemporary Dilemmas*, edited by Allan Gerson (New Brunswick, NJ: Transaction Inc, 1980), 63.

3 Allegretti, "Have Brief Case," 754: "They are taught that the job of the lawyer is to represent clients zealously, not to seek justice."

4 See generally Monroe H. Freedman and Abbe Smith, *Understanding Lawyers' Ethics*, 4th ed. (Newark, NJ: Mathew Bender & Company, 2010).

5 Deborah L. Rhode, *In the Interests of Justice: Reforming the Legal Profession* (New York: Oxford University Press, 2000), 53–8.

6 Stephen L. Pepper, "The Lawyer's Amoral Ethical Role: A Defense, A Problem, and Some Possibilities," *American Bar Foundation Research Journal* 11, no. 4 (1986): 613 (arguing that a lawyer who refuses to act according to the client's wishes on the basis of his or her own moral judgment "substitute[s the] lawyers' beliefs for individual autonomy and diversity," at 617).

7 Freedman, "The Lawyer as a Hired Gun."

8 Allegretti, "Have Brief Case," 770 (noting that the metaphor applies to criminal defence lawyers in particular); Richard O. Brooks, "Ethical Legal Identity and Professional Responsibility," *Georgetown Journal of Legal Ethics* 4, no. 2 (1990): 317, at 329 (asserting that 'the hired gun' is a common metaphor for lawyers and in particular criminal defence lawyers).

9 Richard Wasserstrom, "Lawyers as Professionals: Some Moral Issues," *Human Rights* 5, no. 1 (1975): 1, at 12 (arguing that the immoral conduct of criminal defence lawyers specifically is justifiable in a way that similar conduct would not be for lawyers generally); Carrie Menkel-Meadow,

"The Limits of Adversarial Ethics," in *Ethics in Practice: Lawyers' Roles, Responsibilities, and Regulation*, edited by Deborah L. Rhode (New York: Oxford University Press, 2000), 123 (identifying criminal defence work as an area where the adversarial model may be justified); Deborah Rhode, "Ethical Perspectives on Legal Practice," *Stanford Law Review* 37, no. 2 (1985): 589, at 605 (arguing that the professional norms appropriate in criminal defence work are not necessarily appropriate in other contexts); David Luban, "Are Criminal Defenders Different?" *Michigan Law Review* 91, no. 7 (1993): 1729 (noting that criminal defenders, in particular public defenders, do face challenges that those who represent other types of clients do not); see also William Simon, "The Ethics of Criminal Defense," *Michigan Law Review* 91, no. 7 (1993): 1703 (critiquing legal ethicists who exclude criminal lawyers from their critique of zealous advocacy).

10 See e.g. Monroe Freedman, "In Praise of Overzealous Representation—Lying to Judges, Deceiving Third Parties, and Other Ethical Conduct," *Hofstra Law Review* 34, no. 3 (2006): 771; Abbe Smith, "The Difference in Criminal Defense and the Difference It Makes," *Washington University Journal of Law & Policy* 11 (2003): 83.

11 Alice Woolley, "Integrity in Zealousness: Comparing the Standard Conceptions of the Canadian and American Lawyer," *Canadian Journal of Law & Jurisprudence* 9, no. 1 (1996): 61.

12 Interview with Defence Lawyer 4: "Well the primary goal obviously is to have them found not guilty." Defence Lawyer 1 said: "Well, it's to see if I can have a finding of not guilty."

13 When asked what she considered to be the primary objective of a defence lawyer in a sexual assault case, Crown Attorney 3 answered: "Just to get them acquitted. Because I think that's always their objective, has to be their objective, really."

14 Allegretti, "Have Brief Case," 749.

15 See Randolph Braccialarghe, "Why Were Perry Mason's Clients Always Innocent? The Criminal Lawyer's Moral Dilemma – The Criminal Defendant Who Tells His Lawyer He Is Guilty," *Valparaiso University Law Review* 39, no. 1 (2004): 65, at 70: "It would be an unusual client whose first, if occasionally unrealistic, objective were something other than an acquittal" (69).

16 For example, Defence Lawyer 1 stated that his most important ethical obligation was "[t]o provide a full and fair defence, whilst always remembering that I'm an officer of the court."

17 A similar perspective is taken by some American lawyers. See e.g. Alan
   Dershowitz's comments in Craig M. Bradley and Joseph L. Hoffman,
   "Public Perception, Justice, and the Search for Truth in Criminal Cases,"
   Southern California Law Review 69, no. 4 (1996): 1267 ("Basically, I
   have one job when I take on a criminal case—to help my client get the
   lowest possible sentence or get acquitted," at 1297). In fact, it is not
   axiomatic that an acquittal should be a defence lawyer's paramount goal.
   See Federation of Law Societies of Canada, *Model Code of Professional
   Conduct* (Ottawa: Federation of Law Societies of Canada, 2014), ch 5.1-1,
   commentary [9]: http://flsc.ca/wp-content/uploads/2014/12/conduct1.
   pdf. According to this code, a criminal defence lawyer's "duty is to
   protect the client as far as possible from being convicted, except ... upon
   legal evidence sufficient to support a conviction for the offence with
   which the client is charged."

18 A less common but still evident theme in explanations for why sexual
   assault cases are disproportionately taxing on lawyers is that the
   stakes in these cases are higher. The higher stakes identified include
   registry on the sex offender list, inability to travel to the United States
   if convicted, and the high stigma attached to sexual offence charges.
   The risk of incarceration was identified by only one lawyer. For the
   most part, even those lawyers who identified these other explanations
   offered the intensely emotional and personal nature of these files as a
   first explanation.

19 Susan Bandes, "Repression and Denial in Criminal Lawyering," *Buffalo
   Criminal Law Review* 9, no. 2 (2006): 339, at 346.

20 See e.g. Lila Petar Vrklevski and John Franklin, "Vicarious Trauma: The
   Impact on Solicitors of Exposure to Traumatic Material," *Traumatology*
   14, no. 1 (2008): 106 (finding that criminal lawyers reported significantly
   higher levels of subjective distress, vicarious trauma, depression,
   and stress).

21 C.D. Evans and Lorene Shyba, eds., *Tough Crimes: True Cases by Top
   Canadian Criminal Lawyers* (Calgary, AB: Durance Vile Publications,
   2014).

22 John Rosen, "Defending Paul Bernardo: Am I the Devil's Advocate?" in
   Tough Crimes: True Cases by Top Canadian Criminal Lawyers, edited by
   C.D. Evans and Lorene Shyba (Calgary, AB: Durance Vile Publications,
   2014), 67, at 68.

23 Ibid., 84. Rosen was Bernardo's second lawyer. His first lawyer was charged with obstructing justice for concealing these tapes.

24 Ibid.

25 See e.g. David Luban, *Legal Ethics and Human Dignity* (New York: Cambridge University Press, 2007).

26 Alice Woolley, "Not Only in America: The Necessity of Representing 'Those People' in a Free and Democratic Society," in *How Can You Represent Those People?* edited by Abbe Smith and Monroe Freedman (New York: Palgrave Macmillan, 2013), 199.

27 Alice Woolley, *Understanding Lawyers' Ethics in Canada*, 2nd ed. (Toronto: Lexis Nexis, 2016), ch. 2, 34.

28 Woolley, "Not Only in America."

29 Woolley, *Understanding Lawyers' Ethics*, 57.

30 Luban, *Legal Ethics and Human Dignity*, 71, referring to Alan Donagan, "Justifying Legal Practice in the Adversary System," in *The Good Lawyer: Lawyers' Roles and Lawyers' Ethics*, edited by David Luban (Totowa, NJ: Rowman & Allanheld, 1983), 123, at 130, 133.

31 Luban, *Legal Ethics and Human Dignity*, 69.

32 Woolley, *Understanding Lawyers' Ethics in Canada*, 57.

33 See Federation of Law Societies of Canada, *Model Code of Professional Conduct*, ch. 3.2-7, ch. 5.1-2; see also Michel Proulx and David Layton, *Ethics and Canadian Criminal Law* (Toronto: Irwin Law, 2001). But see Monroe H. Freedman, "Professional Responsibility of the Criminal Defense Lawyer: The Three Hardest Questions," *Michigan Law Review* 64, no. 8 (1996): 1469.

34 Woolley, *Understanding Lawyers' Ethics*, ch. 8.

35 See e.g. Federation of Law Societies of Canada, *Model Code of Professional Conduct*, ch. 5.1-1, commentary [9].

36 See Proulx and Layton, *Ethics*, 38, 48.

37 Luban, *Legal Ethics and Human Dignity*, 69–70.

38 Ibid.; Federation of Law Societies of Canada, *Model Code of Professional Conduct*, ch. 5.1-1, commentary [9]; ch 5.1-2.

39 *R v T(J)*, 2015 ONSC 3866 at para. 52, 122 WCB (2d) 409: "Introducing such unrelated sexual misconduct evidence will discourage complainants to report and to testify which is the likely motivation of this application."

40 GraciaLaw, "Sexual & Indecent Acts," http://www.gracialaw.ca/blog/
result-categories/sexual-indecent-acts/ (accessed 28 April 2014). A PDF
archive of this website was created on 20 November 2014 and is on file
with the author.

41 See Christine Boyle, *Sexual Assault* (Toronto: Carswell, 1984), for a
comprehensive discussion of the early reforms and their relationship
to the rejection of the stereotypical attitudes about women that
underpinned the criminal law in Canada.

42 *Criminal Code*, RSC 1985, c C-46 [*Criminal Code*].

43 Ibid., s 276; *R v Seaboyer*, [1991] 2 SCR 577 at para. 28, 66 CCC (3d) 321.

44 *Criminal Code*, s 276.1(a).

45 *Seaboyer* at para. 28.

46 This is not to suggest that evidence of sexual activity is always
inadmissible, or even always inadmissible as relevant to consent.
Evidence of prior sexual activity remains admissible if it is relied upon
to give rise to an inference other than one of these two outdated social
assumptions and it meets the criteria under sections 276.2 and 276.3 of
the *Criminal Code*.

47 *R v Darrach*, 2000 SCC 46, [2000] 2 SCR 443 at paras. 33–4.

48 *Criminal Code*, s 276.3(d). For an analysis explaining the proper
interpretation of section 276, see Elaine Craig, "Section 276
Misconstrued: The Failure to Properly Interpret and Apply Canada's
Rape Shield Provisions," *Canadian Bar Review* 94 (2016): 1.

49 Law Society of Upper Canada Archives, "Law Society of Upper Canada
– Conducting Sexual Offence Trials – Part One" (21 February 2014),
https://www.youtube.com/watch?v=3AiohQek2zc, at 01h:04m:53s.

50 Ibid. at 01h:05m:32s.

51 Ibid. at 01h:05m:19s.

52 Ibid. at 01h:05m:26s.

53 Jennifer Temkin, "Prosecuting and Defending Rape: Perspectives from
the Bar," *Journal of Law and Society* 27, no. 2 (2000): 219, at 225.

54 Ibid., 233–4.

55 Ibid., 231, 234–5.

56 Ruthy Lazar, "Negotiating Sex – The Legal Construct of Consent in
Cases of Wife Rape in Ontario, Canada," *Canadian Journal of Women
and the Law* 22, no. 2 (2010): 329, at 340; see also Jennifer Koshan, "The
Legal Treatment of Marital Rape and Women's Equality: An Analysis of
the Canadian Experience" (September 2010), http://theequalityeffect.
org/pdfs/maritalrapecanadexperience.pdf.

57 Nancy Levit, "Confronting Conventional Thinking: The Heuristics Problem in Feminist Legal Theory," *Cardozo Law Review* 28, no. 1 (2006): 391, at 391.

58 See e.g. Kristin A. Lane, Jerry Kang, and Mahzarin R. Banaji, "Implicit Social Cognition and Law," *Annual Review of Law and Social Science* 3 (2007): 427 (examining the relationship between equal protection laws and implicit social cognition); Anders Kaye, "Schematic Psychology and Criminal Responsibility," *St John's Law Review* 83, no. 2 (2009): 565 (discussing, with respect to the issue of criminal responsibility, how "schematic blind spots and biases impair our 'moral sensitivity'— and especially our sensitivity to morally significant facts about our circumstances—more often and more profoundly than we realize," at 569).

59 Barbara Krahé et al., "Prospective Lawyers' Rape Stereotypes and Schematic Decision Making about Rape Cases," *Psychology, Crime & Law* 14, no. 5 (2008): 461, at 464. See also a 2005 study commissioned by Amnesty International (surveying 1,000 members of the general public in the United Kingdom) wherein twenty-six percent of participants thought a woman was totally or partially to blame if she was dressed provocatively. Twenty-two percent thought that a woman was totally or partially to blame if it was known that she had had several sexual partners. Amnesty International, "UK: New Poll Finds a Third of People Believe Women Who Flirt Partially Responsible for Being Raped" (21 November 2005), https://www.amnesty.org.uk/press-releases/ uk-new-poll-finds-third-people-believe-women-who-flirt-partially-responsible-being. See also Shannon Sampert, "Let Me Tell You a Story: English-Canadian Newspapers and Sexual Assault Myths," *Canadian Journal of Women and the Law* 22, no. 2 (2010): 301 (examining media discourse about sexual assault, the author demonstrates the prevalence of stereotypes about sexual assault in English-Canadian newspapers); Marc Klippenstine and Regina Schuller, "Perceptions of Sexual Assault: Expectancies Regarding the Emotional Response of a Rape Victim Over Time," *Psychology, Crime & Law* 18, no. 1 (2012): 79 (showing that participants' perceptions of sexual assault complainants were negatively influenced where the complainants' post-assault behaviour did not comply with how participants expected victims of sexual assault to act); Allyson K. Clarke and Karen L. Lawson, "Women's Judgments of a Sexual Assault Scenario: The Role of Prejudicial Attitudes and Victim Weight," *Violence Victims* 24, no. 2 (2009): 248 (demonstrating that

attributions of victim fault were positively associated with adherence
to rape myths and were higher toward thin victims than overweight
victims); Marian M. Morry and Erica Winkler, "Student Acceptance
and Expectation of Sexual Assault," *Canadian Journal of Behavioural
Science* 33, no. 3 (2001): 188 (demonstrating that attributions of victim
fault were positively associated with adherence to rape myths); Jennifer
Temkin and Barbara Krahé, *Sexual Assault and the Justice Gap: A
Question of Attitude* (Oxford, UK: Hart, 2008); Stacey Futter and
Walter R. Mebane Jr, "The Effects of Rape Law Reform on Rape Case
Processing," *Berkeley Women's Law Journal* 16 (2001): 72 (reviewing
a number of empirical studies demonstrating the limited impact
of rape law reform in the American context); Ashley A. Wenger
and Brian H. Bornstein, "The Effects of Victim's Substance Use and
Relationship Closeness on Mock Juror's Judgments in an Acquaintance
Rape Case," *Sex Roles* 54, no. 7 (2006): 547 (concluding that less rape
myth acceptance meant higher victim credibility assessments by
participants); Louise Ellison and Vanessa E. Munro, "Jury Deliberation
and Complainant Credibility in Rape Trials," in *Rethinking Rape
Law: International and Comparative Perspectives*, edited by Clare
McGlynn and Vanessa E. Munro (New York: Routledge, 2010), 281;
Sarah Ben-David and Ofra Schneider, "Rape Perceptions, Gender Role
Attitudes, and Victim-Perpetrator Acquaintance," *Sex Roles* 53, no. 5
(2005): 385 (demonstrating significant negative correlations between
gender-role attitudes and four measures of rape perception); Janice
Du Mont, Karen-Lee Miller, and Terri Myhr, "The Role of 'Real Rape'
and 'Real Victim' Stereotypes in the Police Reporting Practices of
Sexually Assaulted Women," *Violence Against Women* 9, no. 4 (2003):
466 (showing that women were more likely to report a sexual assault
to the police in cases that involved the use of physical force and the
occurrence of physical injury); Janice Du Mont and Terri Myhr, "So Few
Convictions: The Role of Client-Related Characteristics in the Legal
Processing of Sexual Assaults," *Violence Against Women* 6, no. 10 (2000):
1109 (showing that cases where the women did not physically resist were
less likely to result in a charge); Emma Cunliffe, "Judging Fast and Slow:
Using Decision Making Theory to Explore Judicial Fact Determination,"
International Journal of Evidence & Proof 18 (2014): 139 (examining the
role of heuristics in judicial decision-making).

60 Krahé et al., "Lawyers' Rape Stereotypes," 464: "In combination, these studies provide evidence of schematic processing of information about rape cases that is incompatible with the normative prescription of data-driven information processing as a basis for decision making in this context."

61 "Jian Ghomeshi's Lawyer, Marie Henein, Speaks to Peter Mansbridge," *The National* (29 March 2016), http://www.cbc.ca/news/thenational/ jian-ghomeshi-s-lawyer-marie-henein-speaks-to-peter-mansbridge-1.3511752, at 00h:00m:56s, 00h:13m:06s.

62 Ibid. at 00h:04m:19s.

63 Ibid. at 00h:05m:43s.

64 Levit, "Confronting Conventional Thinking," 393 (footnotes omitted): "Given the egocentric biases that researchers have documented, coupled with the tendencies toward stereotypic classifications, when decision makers use simplifying heuristics, they are likely to make mistakes in the direction of their pre-existing biases. The combined effects of these proclivities mean that decision makers are anchored in conventional patterns of thinking and that those patterns contain perceptual biases." Levit summarizes the 1970s research of cognitive psychologists Amos Tversky and Daniel Kahneman: "decision making often involves an abundance of information, time pressures, and an array of possible alternatives, people intuitively and unconsciously use cognitive shortcuts or 'heuristics' to make decisions about probabilities. These simplifying heuristics lead to some predictable patterns of decisional errors" (396).

65 I am not alleging, and have no evidence, that Henein has ever followed her 1998 advice. I have quoted from her statements in 1998 and 2016 in an effort to demonstrate their contradictions, not to imply that she has herself engaged in this tactic.

66 See e.g. *Criminal Code*, s 276.1; *R v Darrach*, 2000 SCC 46 at paras. 33–4, [2000] 2 SCR 443 (excluding evidence the probative value of which is based on the stereotypes that women who are sexually active are less believable and women who have consented to sex on other occasions are more likely to have consented to the sex at issue in the allegation).

67 *R v Ewanchuk*, [1999] 1 SCR 330 at paras. 49, 51, 169 DLR (4th) 193; *Criminal Code*, s 273.2(b) (precluding the application of honest but mistaken belief in consent where the "accused did not take reasonable steps ... to ascertain that the complainant was consenting").

68 *R v Lyons*, [1987] 2 SCR 309, 37 CCC (3d) 1 [*Lyons* cited to SCR];
    R v Mills, [1999] 3 SCR 668, 139 CCC (3d) 321 [*Mills* cited to SCR];
    R v Seaboyer, [1991] 2 SCR 577, 66 CCC (3d) 321.

69 *Lyons* at para. 114.

70 *Lyttle* at para. 44.

71 Ibid. at para. 48.

72 *Mills* at para. 94.

73 See e.g. Susan Brownmiller, *Against Our Will: Men, Women and Rape*
    (New York: Simon and Schuster, 1975); Lise Gotell, "The Discursive
    Disappearance of Sexualized Violence: Feminist Law Reform, Judicial
    Resistance, and Neo-Liberal Sexual Citizenship," in *Reaction and
    Resistance: Feminism, Law, and Social Change*, edited by Dorothy E.
    Chunn, Susan B. Boyd, and Hester Lessard (Vancouver, BC: University
    of British Columbia Press, 2007), 127; Carol Smart, *Feminism and the
    Power of Law* (London: Routledge, 1989); Temkin and Krahé, *Sexual
    Assault and the Justice Gap.*

74 Abbe Smith, "Representing Rapists: The Cruelty of Cross Examination
    and Other Challenges for a Feminist Criminal Defense Lawyer,"
    American Criminal Law Review 53, no. 2 (2016): 255.

75 This discussion of Abbe Smith's article "Representing Rapists" (ibid.)
    is drawn from Elaine Craig, "A Brave and Honest Examination of the
    Complexity of a Feminist Defence Ethos," in online journal *Jotwell
    Equality Section* (5 May 2016), http://jotwell.com/?p=6068.

76 Constance Backhouse, "Edward Greenspan: A Feminist Reflection on
    the Eulogies Surrounding His Death," *Canadian Journal of Women and
    the Law* 27, no. 2 (2015): 157.

77 See e.g. Federation of Law Societies of Canada, *Moral Code of
    Professional Conduct*, ch. 5.1-1, commentary [1].

78 Woolley, *Understanding Lawyers' Ethics in Canada*, 396.

79 *Griffin* at para. 110: "Counsel is often in a better position than the trial
    judge to determine what areas of a witness' testimony must be explored
    or tested." See also *R v T(SG)*, [2010] 1 SCR 688 at para. 36, 255 CCC (3d)
    1 [*T(SG)* cited to SCR].

80 Woolley, *Understanding Lawyers' Ethics in Canada*, 396.

81 *T(SG)* at para. 36.

82 See e.g. Federation of Law Societies of Canada, *Moral Code of
    Professional Conduct*, ch. 3.1-2.

83 Ibid., ch. 6.3-5. See also David Tanovich, "'Whack' No More: Infusing Equality into the Ethics of Defence Lawyering in Sexual Assault Cases," *Ottawa Law Review* 45, no. 3 (2013–2014): 495.

84 *Groia v Law Society of Upper Canada*, 2014 ONLSAP 41, [2013] LSDD No 186; *Groia v Law Society of Upper Canada*, 2016 ONCA 471, 1 Admin LR (6th) 175 (leave granted).

85 Ibid.; Alex Robinson, "Groia Eyes Supreme Court after Losing Appeal," *Law Times* (20 June 2016), http://www.lawtimesnews.com/201606205483/headline-news/groia-eyes-supreme-court-after-losing-appeal.

86 Ranjan Agarwal, "How Rude! Incivility and the Groia Appeal," *Bennett Jones Thought Network* (16 June 2016), http://blog.bennettjones.com/2016/06/16/how-rude-incivility-and-the-groia-appeal/.

87 The closest a law society has come, in reported decisions, involved a British Columbia lawyer who was disciplined for multiple reasons, one of which involved statements he made about a young sexual assault complainant to her parents – including calling her unchaste and suggesting that if she persisted with her allegations she would be subject to a long and vigorous cross-examination – in order to discourage the complainant from proceeding. See *Johnstone v Law Soc of BC*, 1987 CanLII 2585 (BC CA).

Chapter Five

1 See e.g. *Boucher v The Queen*, [1955] SCR 16; Ontario, Ministry of the Attorney General, *Role of the Crown – Preamble to the Crown Policy Manual*, October 2015 update (Toronto: Ministry of the Attorney General, 21 March 2005), 1, https://www.attorneygeneral.jus.gov.on.ca/english/crim/cpm/2005/CPMPreamble.pdf.

2 Federation of Law Societies of Canada, *Model Code of Professional Conduct* (Ottawa: Federation of Law Societies of Canada, 2014), ch. 5.1-3, commentary [1], http://flsc.ca/wp-content/uploads/2014/12/conduct1.pdf.

3 See e.g. Ontario, Ministry of the Attorney General, *Crown Policy Manual: Witnesses*, October 2015 update (Toronto: Ministry of the Attorney General, 21 March 2005), 1, https://www.attorneygeneral.jus.gov.on.ca/english/crim/cpm/2005/Witnesses.pdf; Nova Scotia,

Public Prosecution Service, *Interviewing Witnesses (Other than Experts or the Police)*, January 2006 update (Halifax: Director of Public Prosecutions, 27 September 2005), 1, http://novascotia.ca/pps/publications/ca_manual/ProsecutionPolicies/InterviewingWitnesses.pdf; Saskatchewan, Public Prosecutions Division, *Witnesses – Aids to Facilitate Testimony* (Regina: Justice and Attorney General), http://www.justice.gov.sk.ca/pp-Witnesses-Aids; Saskatchewan, Public Prosecutions Division, *Witnesses – Notification of Victims and Victim's Next-of-Kin* (Regina: Justice and Attorney General), http://www.justice.gov.sk.ca/pp-Witnesses-Notification; Saskatchewan, Public Prosecutions Division, *Witnesses – Persons with Special Needs* (Regina: Justice and Attorney General), http://www.justice.gov.sk.ca/pp-Witnesses-SpecialNeeds.

4   Ontario, Ministry of the Attorney General, *Crown Policy Manual: Sexual Offences*, October 2015 update (Toronto: Ministry of the Attorney General, 21 March 2005), https://www.attorneygeneral.jus.gov.on.ca/english/crim/cpm/2005/SexualOffences.pdf.

5   Nova Scotia, Public Prosecutions Service, *Sexual Offences – Practice Note*, February 2008 update (Halifax: Director of Public Prosecutions, 29 January 2004), 1, https://novascotia.ca/pps/publications/ca_manual/ProsecutionPolicies/SexualOffences-PracticeNote.pdf.

6   Federation of Law Societies of Canada, *Model Code of Professional Conduct*, ch. 6.3-5; see also David Tanovich, "'Whack' No More: Infusing Equality into the Ethics of Defence Lawyering in Sexual Assault Cases," *Ottawa Law Review* 45, no. 3 (2013–14): 495.

7   Ontario, *Role of the Crown*, 3.

8   Ontario, *Crown Policy Manual: Sexual Offences*, 1.

9   *Criminal Code*, RSC 1985, c C-46, ss 486.1(1), 486.2.

10 Rhyannon O'Heron, "Challenges of Women's Equality in the Courts" (5 November 2012), 38, http://www.wavaw.ca/campaigns/challenges-of-womens-equality-in-the-courts/.

11 Ibid.

12 Ruthy Lazar, "Negotiating Sex: The Construct of Consent in Cases of Wife Rape in Ontario, Canada," *Canadian Journal of Women and the Law* 22, no. 2 (2010): 329, at 346.

13 Jennifer Temkin, "Prosecuting and Defending Rape: Perspectives from the Bar," *Journal of Law and Society* 27, no. 2 (2000): 219.

14 Amanda Konradi, *Taking the Stand: Rape Survivors and the Prosecution of Rapists* (Westport, CT: Praeger Publishers, 2007), 6.

15 Alice Woolley, "What Ought Crown Counsel to Do in Prosecuting Sexual Assault Charges? Some Post-Ghomeshi Reflections," *ABlawg* (29 March 2016), http://ablawg.ca/2016/03/29/what-ought-crown-counsel-to-do-in-prosecuting-sexual-assault-charges-some-post-ghomeshi-reflections/.

16 Ibid. (emphasis in original).

17 *R v Khaery*, 2014 ABQB 676, 117 WCB (2d) 422.

18 *R v Khaery*, Trial Transcript (23 September 2014) Edmonton 121306211Q1 (ABQB) at 116:4–8 [*Khaery* transcript].

19 Lazar, "Negotiating Sex."

20 Ibid., 345.

21 Ibid.

22 *R v B(IE)*, Trial Transcript (8 November 2011) Kentville 343759 (NSSC) at 35:3–18 [*B(IE)* transcript].

23 *R v Wright*, Trial Transcript, Volume 1 (28 May 2012) Winnipeg CR11-01-31550 (MBQB) at 35:13–29, 57:8–30, 65:30–66:9.

24 *R v Al-Rawi*, Audio Trial Transcript (9–10 February 2017) Halifax 2866665 (NSPC).

25 Elaine Craig, "The Ethical Obligations of Defence Counsel in Sexual Assault Cases," *Osgoode Hall Law Journal* 51, no. 2 (2014): 427.

26 *R v Ururyar*, Trial Transcript, Volume I (1 February 2016) Toronto (ONCJ) at 42–3.

27 Ibid. at 10.

28 Ibid. at 29.

29 Ibid. at 44.

30 Ibid. at 66.

31 *R v Ururyar*, Trial Transcript, Volume II (2 February 2016) Toronto (ONCJ) at 112.

32 Ibid. at 97.

33 Ibid. at 21.

34 Ibid. at 112.

35 Ibid. at 56:18–22.

36 Ibid. at 57:9.

37 Ibid. at 60:38–63:28.

38 Ibid. at 59:9–17, 60:30–9, 63:3–7, 217:2–4.

39 Ibid. at 215:3–216:25.

40 *R v JK*, Trial Transcript, Volume II (12 June 2012) St John's 201101G7057 (SCNFLD) at 61:3–62:8.

41 Elaine Craig, "Section 276 Misconstrued: The Failure to Properly
    Interpret and Apply Canada's Rape Shield Provisions," *Canadian Bar
    Review* 94 (2016): 1.

42 See e.g. *Khaery* transcript at 72:34–9; *R v Wagar*, Trial Transcript (9
    September 2014), Calgary 130288731P1 (ABPC) at 217:16–17 [*Wagar I*
    transcript]; *R v Ururyar*, Trial Transcript, Volume I (1 February 2016)
    Toronto (ONCJ) at 42–3; *R v JK*, Trial Transcript, Volume II (12 June
    2012) St John's 201101G7057 (SCNFLD).

43 *R v Wagar*, 2015 ABCA 327, 125 WCB (2d) 471.

44 Several statements made during the proceeding by Judge Camp suggest
    disdain for the rape shield provisions. He commented that "for better or
    worse" section 276 prevents the accused from asking certain questions
    (*Wagar I* transcript at 58:29–30). He stated that both he and the framers
    of the legislation recognize that section 276 "hamstring[s] the defence"
    (at 58:39). He described the rape shield law as "very, very incursive
    legislation" which prevented the accused from asking otherwise
    permissible questions because of "contemporary thinking" (at 63:6–7).
    He suggested that no one would argue that "the rape shield law always
    worked ... fairly" (at 217:2–4).

45 *Wagar I* transcript at 217:16–17.

46 *R v Schmaltz*, 2015 ABCA 4, 320 CCC (3d) [*Schmaltz* CA].

47 *R v Schmaltz*, Trial Transcript (12 December 2013), Medicine Hat
    081056319P1 (ABPC) at 43:15–32 [*Schmaltz* transcript].

48 Ibid. at 86–9.

49 *Schmaltz* CA at para. 71.

50 *R v Osolin*, [1993] 4 SCR 595 at HN: "Cross examination for the purpose
    of showing consent or impugning credibility which relies upon
    groundless rape myths and fantasized stereotypes is improper and
    should not be permitted."

51 *R v Lyttle*, [2004] SCJ No 8, [2004] 1 SCR 193 at para. 44. See Alice
    Woolley, *Understanding Lawyers' Ethics in Canada*, 2nd ed. (Toronto:
    Lexis Nexis, 2016), 391: "codes of conduct and case law prohibit the layer
    from acting in a way that is "sarcastic, personally abusive and derisive."
    The lawyer must not "needlessly abuse, hector, or harass" a witness, and
    should be "courteous and civil."

52 *R v Finney*, 2014 ONCA 866, 118 WCB (2d) 327 [*Finney* CA].

53 *R v Finney*, Trial Transcript, Volume III (4 October 2011) Lindsay
    C55780 (ONSC) at 699:4–702:2.

54 Ibid. at 701:18–702:2.

55 Ibid.

56 *Schmaltz* transcript at 85:25.

57 *Wagar I* transcript at 54:14–17.

58 Ibid. at 80:17–20: "MS. MOGRABEE: Your Honour, I'm just going to rise for a moment, if I may. She's repeated herself a few times that she doesn't remember times, and that was her answer to that question. So I'm not sure what repeating the question is going to accomplish, but …"

59 Ibid. at 91:27–40.

60 Ibid. at 100:20–101:21.

61 E.g. ibid. at 60:38–63:28, 100:20–101:21, 384:27–385:9.

62 Lucinda Vandervort, "Lawful Subversion of the Criminal Justice Process? Judicial, Prosecutorial, and Police Discretion in *Edmondson, Kindrat,* and *Brown*," in *Sexual Assault in Canada: Law, Legal Practice and Women's Activism*, edited by Elizabeth Sheehy (Ottawa: University of Ottawa Press, 2012), 111, at 119.

63 *R v Wagar* (2017) ABPC 17.

64 See e.g. *R v Wagar*, Trial Transcript, Volume II (7 November 2016) Calgary (ABPC) 130288731P1 at 112:2, 115:4, 132:19, 138:2, 140:24, 144:34 [*Wagar II* transcript].

65 Ibid. at 132:29.

66 *R v G(PG)*, Trial Transcript, Volume II (26 June 2013) Burlington 10-3631 (ONCJ) at 31:9 [*G(PG)* transcript, volume II].

67 *G(PG)* ONCJ at para. 39. See also *R v Griffin*, 2016 ONSC 2448 at para. 2, [2016] OJ No 1916 [*Griffin* ONSC] (appeal judge summarizing trial judge's characterization of the cross-examination). Note that the publication ban in *R v G(PG)* was lifted on appeal. The summary conviction appeal judge, Justice Durno, did not agree with the trial judge's overall characterization of the cross-examination, although he did accept that the defense made several inappropriate, sarcastic comments in response to the complainant's answers (at para. 142). For further discussion of the case, see chapter 2.

68 On appeal, Justice Durno noted that it was not improper for Bayliss to ask questions about her statements asserting that she had attempted suicide multiple times, and noted that the trial judge had also allowed questioning on this issue (ibid. at para. 131).

69 *G(PG)* transcript, volume II at 46:7–21.

70 Ibid. at 46:21–47:3. The accused successfully appealed the trial decision

in this case, in part on the basis of reasonable apprehension of bias. The trial judge's ruling on this objection was not appealed (*Griffin* ONSC at para. 144).

71   Ibid. at 122:14–18.

72   *R v G(PG)*, Trial Transcript, Volume III (4 July 2013) Burlington 10-3631 (ONCJ) at 19:29.

73   Ibid. at 29:5–12.

74   *Finney* CA at paras. 2–4, 118 WCB (2d) 327; *Schmaltz* CA at paras. 2–3.

75   See *Schmaltz* CA at para. 60 (the trial judge's conviction was overturned by the majority on the basis that his interventions had created the appearance of an unfair trial). See also *Finney* CA at paras. 2–4, wherein the accused argued on appeal (unsuccessfully) that the trial judge had created a reasonable apprehension of bias.

76   Parts of this section were previously published in Elaine Craig, "The Inhospitable Court," *University of Toronto Law Journal* 66, no. 2 (2016): 197.

77   Woolley, *Understanding Lawyers' Ethics*, 365.

78   Elizabeth Sheehy, "Equality without Democratic Values? Why Feminists Oppose the Criminal Procedure Reforms," *Canadian Woman Studies* 19, no. 1/2 (1999): 6, at 19.

79   Amanda Konradi, "Too Little Too Late: Prosecutors' Pre-Court Preparation of Rape Survivors," *Law & Social Inquiry* 22 (1997): 1; Temkin, "Prosecuting and Defending Rape," 222–3 (noting that many of the prosecutors she interviewed in the United States preferred to have no contact with the complainant prior to trial).

80   *Finney* transcript, volume II at 307:9–15.

81   Ibid. at 483:8–484:18.

82   *Khaery* transcript at 31:38–32:40.

83   Konradi, "Too Little Too Late"; Temkin, "Prosecuting and Defending Rape," 222.

84   Cheryl Regehr et al., "Victims of Sexual Violence in the Canadian Criminal Courts," *Victims & Offenders* 3, no. 1 (2008): 99, at 106.

85   *Criminal Code*, ss 486.2, 486.1.

86   Judith Daylen, Wendy van Tongeren Harvey, and Dennis O'Toole, *Trauma, Trials and Transformation: Guiding Sexual Assault Victims through the Legal System and Beyond* (Toronto: Irwin Law, 2006), 129.

87   Sharon B. Murphy et al., "Advocates Speak Out on Adult Sexual Assault: A Unique Crime Demands a Unique Response," *Journal of Aggression, Maltreatment & Trauma* 20, no. 6 (2011): 690, at 700.

88 Cheryl Regehr et al., "Victims of Sexual Violence in Canadian Criminal Courts," *Victims & Offenders* 3, no. 1 (2008): 99, at 106.

89 Canada, Department of Justice, *A Survey of Survivors of Sexual Violence in Three Canadian Cities*, by Melissa Lindsay, Catalogue No. J2-403/2014E (Ottawa: Research and Statistics Division, 2014), 7, 23.

90 Woolley, "What the Crown Ought to Do."

91 See e.g. Christopher Tomlins, "Pursuing Justice, Cultivating Power: The Evolving Role of the Supreme Court in the American Polity," *Researching Law* 17, no. 1 (2006): 1 (asserting that courtroom rituals do more than simply set the tone or create an atmosphere, but are important in their own right); Oscar Chase and Jonathan Thong, "Judging Judges: The Effect of Courtroom Ceremony on Participant Evaluation of Process Fairness-Related Factors," *Yale Journal of Law & the Humanities* 24, no. 1 (2012): 221 (arguing that the ritualistic conventions of the courtroom have a substantive impact on litigants' perceptions of the fairness of the process).

92 Lorin Geitner, "Social Architecture and the Law: Law Through the Lens of Religion" (10 May 2013), http://ssrn.com/abstract=2265600: "Proceedings in the courtroom can be just as ritualistic as what you will find in religious ceremonies: from the judge sitting in state in robes, to heightened expectations of the behavior of people in the gallery, to the formal modes of address, and highly articulated steps of a proceeding" (4). Indeed, trials themselves might be characterized as ritual.

93 Geoffrey Miller, "The Legal Function of Ritual," *Chicago-Kent Law Review* 80, no. 3 (2005): 1181, at 1191: "By creating a radically unfamiliar social environment, unstructured by ordinary relationships of social status, ritual opens participants to the possibility of basic change in personal identity." See generally Catherine Bell, *Ritual: Perspectives and Dimensions* (New York: Oxford University Press, 1997).

94 Miller, "The Legal Function of Ritual," 1191.

95 Ibid.

96 Marie Elena Vidal and Jenny Petrak, "Shame and Adult Sexual Assault: A Study with a Group of Female Survivors Recruited from an East London Population," *Sexual and Relationship Therapy* 22 (2007): 159 (75% of women who were sexually assaulted reported feeling ashamed of themselves as a result of the sexual violence they experienced); Richard B. Felson and Paul-Philippe Paré, "The Reporting of Domestic Violence and Sexual Assault by Non-Strangers to the Police," *Journal of Marriage and Family* 67, no. 3 (2005): 597 (victims of sexual assault are

more likely to experience feelings of embarrassment and shame than victims of other violent offences); Karen G. Weiss, "Too Ashamed to Report: Deconstructing the Shame of Sexual Victimization," *Feminist Criminology* 5, no. 3 (2010): 286 (women who are sexually abused describe feeling powerless, alone, and that they are of little worth). See also Candice Feiring and Lynn S. Taska, "The Persistence of Shame Following Sexual Abuse: A Longitudinal Look at Risk and Recovery," *Child Maltreatment* 10, no. 4 (2005): 337 (examining the persistence of feelings of shame in youth who are sexually abused).

97   Konradi, *Taking the Stand*, 6.

98   *Boucher* at para. 26, 110 CCC 263 (the role of the Crown is not to secure a conviction but to present all "credible evidence relevant" to the allegation. This evidence should be presented firmly and effectively, but also fairly); *R v Cook*, [1997] 1 SCR 1113, 114 CCC (3d) 481 at para. 21 [*Cook*] (while the Crown is not to act solely in an adversarial manner, our judicial system is founded on the adversarial process and the Crown is expected to serve "as a strong advocate within this adversarial process").

99   *Cook* at para. 21.

100   Woolley, "What the Crown Ought to Do."

101   *Cook* at para. 21.

102   For an illuminative discussion of the frailties of human memory in the context of witness preparation see Woolley, *Understanding Lawyers' Ethics*, ch. 8.

103   James Hopper and David Lisak, "Why Rape and Trauma Survivors Have Fragmented and Incomplete Memories," TIME *Magazine* (9 December 2014), http://time.com/3625414/rape-trauma-brain-memory/; see also Daylen, Harvey, and O'Toole, *Trauma, Trials, and Transformation*, 109.

104   Hopper and Lisak, "Memories."

105   Ibid.

106   Ibid.

107   Woolley, *Understanding Lawyers' Ethics*, 375, 382.

108   See e.g. Sean Robichaud, "In Defence of the Crown: The Case of Ghomeshi," *Robichaud Law* (16 February 2016), https://robichaudlaw.ca/in-defence-of-the-crown-in-ghomeshi.

109   Ibid.

110   Woolley, *Understanding Lawyers' Ethics*, 382.

111   Nova Scotia, *Interviewing Witnesses*, 1, noting that interviews with a witness who is "the sole observer" (as complainants often are) of a

serious crime (as sexual assault is) "should be conducted in the presence of an appropriate third party."

112 See e.g. ibid., 2.

113 See e.g. Ontario, Ministry of the Attorney General, *Crown Policy Manual: Police: Relationship with Crown Counsel*, October 2015 update (Toronto: Ministry of the Attorney General, 21 March 2005), https://www.attorneygeneral.jus.gov.on.ca/english/crim/cpm/2005/PoliceRelationshipWithCrown.pdf.

114 Kaufman Report.

115 *R v Regan*, 2002 SCC 12 at paras. 66–70.

116 Ontario, *Crown Policy Manual: Witnesses*, 1.

117 Nova Scotia, *Interviewing Witnesses*, 1.

118 Nova Scotia, *Sexual Offences – Practice Note*, 2.

119 See *R v Muise*, [1974] NSJ No 298 (NSSCAD), cited in Woolley, *Understanding Lawyers' Ethics*, 368 (holding that witnesses could be given copies of their preliminary inquiry evidence).

120 Nova Scotia, *Sexual Offences – Practice Note*, 2.

121 Ibid., 14–16.

122 Ibid.

123 Ibid., 14.

124 Ibid., 15.

125 Ibid.

126 Ontario, Ministry of the Attorney General, *The Commission on Proceedings Involving Guy Paul Morin*, vol. II (Toronto: Ministry of the Attorney General, 1998), Recommendation 107. See also *R v Spence*, 2011 ONSC 2406 at para. 26.

127 Some provinces, such as Saskatchewan and New Brunswick, do not appear to have sexual assault policies. Other provinces, such as Manitoba, do not make all of their Crown policies publicly available and so it is unknown whether such policies exist in those provinces.

128 Nova Scotia, *Sexual Offences – Practice Note*; Ontario, *Crown Policy Manual: Sexual Offences*; British Columbia, Criminal Justice Branch, *Crown Counsel Policy Manual: Sexual Offences Against Adults* (Victoria: Ministry of Justice, 23 July 2015), http://www2.gov.bc.ca/assets/gov/law-crime-and-justice/criminal-justice/prosecution-service/crown-counsel-policy-manual/sex-1-sexual-offences-against-adults.pdf.

129 British Columbia, *Sexual Offences Against Adults*, 1.

130 Nova Scotia, *Sexual Offences – Practice Note*, 2.

131   See Ontario, Minister Responsible for Women's Issues, *It's Never Okay: An Action Plan to Stop Sexual Violence and Harassment* (Toronto: Ontario Women's Directorate, March 2015), 21, https://dr6j45jk9xcmk. cloudfront.net/documents/4593/actionplan-itsneverokay.pdf.

132   Jean Laroche, "Nova Scotia to Hire 2 Special Prosecutors to Handle Sexual Assault Cases," CBC (7 March 2017), http://www.cbc.ca/news/ canada/nova-scotia/bassam-al-rawi-cab-driver-sexual-assault-protest-gregory-lenehan-1.4013845. This development in Nova Scotia suggests a recognition of the need for properly trained prosecutors in this area of law. Whether designating sexual assault specialists will be sufficient to meet this need will presumably depend upon the number of sexual assault cases that continue to be prosecuted by non-specialists and whether this initiative is wrongly relied on to avoid proper training and education for these lawyers.

133   Sharon B. Murphy, Victoria L. Banyard, and Erin Dudley Fennessey, "Exploring Stakeholders' Perceptions of Adult Female Sexual Assault Case Attrition," *Psychology of Violence* 3, no. 2 (2013): 172, at 178.

134   See e.g. Office on Violence Against Women, "The Importance of Understanding Trauma-Informed Care and Self-Care For Victim Service Providers," *The United States Department of Justice* (30 July 2014), https://www.justice.gov/ovw/blog/importance-understanding-trauma-informed-care-and-self-care-victim-service-providers; National Center on Domestic Violence, Trauma & Mental Health and National Resource Center on Domestic Violence, "Trauma-Informed Domestic Violence Services: Understanding the Framework and Approach (Part 1 of 3)," *National Online Resource Center on Violence Against Women* (April 2013), http://www.vawnet.org/special-collections/DVTraumaInformed-Overview.php.

135   Canada, Department of Justice, *A Survey of Survivors of Sexual Violence*, 25.

136   Ibid.

137   Further assistance could be provided if sexual assault complainants were granted a broader right to have a lawyer represent them in the criminal proceeding. This would include protecting the complainant during cross-examination by objecting to questions that are irrelevant or unnecessarily humiliating. Sexual assault complainants do have a right to be represented when the defence has made a section 278 application for production and disclosure of third-party records (see *Criminal Code*, ss 278.4(2.1), 278.6(3)). Granting broader standing to sexual assault

complainants would represent a more fundamental change to the current process – the pros and cons of which are beyond the scope of this discussion.

138 See generally Larry C. Wilson, "Independent Legal Representation for Victims of Sexual Assault: A Model for Delivery of Legal Services," *Windsor Yearbook of Access to Justice* 23, no. 2 (2005): 249.

139 *Criminal Code*, s 278; see also Canada, Department of Justice, *Bill C-46: Records Applications Post-Mills, A Caselaw Review* (January 2015 update), s 4.8, "Independent Counsel," http://www.justice. gc.ca/eng/rp-pr/csj-sjc/ccs-ajc/rr06_vic2/p4_8.html. While other provinces include reference to state funding for complainants in these circumstances in their Victim's Rights legislation, as a practical matter they have not actually created programs to provide this funding. See e.g. *Victims of Crime Act*, RSBC 1996, c 478, s 3. For a thorough discussion of this issue see Larry Wilson, "Victims of Sexual Assault: Who Represents Them in Criminal Proceedings?" (Windsor, ON: Unpublished paper delivered at the Eleventh Colloquium on the Legal Profession, Ron W. Ianni Law Building, University of Windsor, 24 October 2008), http://www.lsuc.on.ca/media/eleventh_colloquium_wilson.pdf.

140 See Canada, Department of Justice, *Bill C-46: Records Applications Post-Mills*, http://www.justice.gc.ca/eng/rp-pr/csj-sjc/ccs-ajc/rr06_vic2/p4_8.html#f180.

141 See Ontario, Minister Responsible for Women's Issues, *It's Never Okay*.

142 See e.g. Justice and Public Safety, "Minister Announces Support for Victims of Sexual Assault" (25 April 2017), http://www.releases.gov.nl.ca/releases/2017/just/0425n01.aspx.

143 Ministry of the Attorney General, "Independent Legal Advice for Sexual Assault Survivors Pilot Program," https://www.attorneygeneral.jus.gov.on.ca/english/ovss/ila.php (accessed 23 July 1017).

144 Wilson, "Independent Legal Representation," 288.

145 Regehr et al., "Victims," 109.

146 Murphy et al., "Advocates Speak Out," 703.

147 Vandervort, "Lawful Subversion," 131. Vandervort also suggests other changes or shifts in the Crown's approach that could improve the criminal justice system's response to allegations of sexual assault. These include better use of videotaped statements, an emphasis on proceeding summarily whenever feasible in order to avoid preliminary inquiries and to ensure judge-alone trials, and requests by the Crown that oral decisions be transcribed and reported.

Chapter Six

1   See e.g. Reid Rusonick, "In Defence of Rigorous Sexual Assault Defences," *Toronto Star* (21 February 2016), https://www.thestar.com/opinion/commentary/2016/02/21/in-defence-of-rigorous-sexual-assault-defences.html; Breese Davies, "Convicting Jian Ghomeshi Will Be Hard – for Good Reason," *Toronto Star* (2 February 2016), https://www.thestar.com/opinion/commentary/2016/02/02/convicting-jian-ghomeshi-will-be-hard-for-good-reason.html.

2   *Criminal Code*, RSC 1985, c C-64, s 276 [*Criminal Code*].

3   Ibid.

4   *R v B(IE)*, 2013 NSCA 98, 300 CCC (3d) 481.

5   *R v Wright*, 2013 MBCA 109, 305 Man R (2d) 26.

6   *R v Wright*, Trial Transcript, Volume 1 (28 May 2012) Winnipeg CR11-01-31550 (MBQB) at 68:29, 69:19, 76:22.

7   Ibid. at 60:7–13.

8   Ibid. at 35:13–29, 65:30–66:9.

9   *Criminal Code*, s 276.

10 *R v B(S)*, 2016 NLCA 20 at para. 43, 336 CCC (3d) 38 [*B(S)* CA].

11 *R v B(S)*, 2014 NLTD(G) 61, 114 WCB (2d) 571.

12 *B(S)* CA at paras. 53–6.

13 *R v B(S)*, Trial Transcript, Volume VI (6 June 2014) St John's 201301G4957 (NLTD) at 129, 134 [*B(S)* transcript].

14 Ibid. at 137.

15 I conducted a comprehensive review of recent section 276 cases in Elaine Craig, "Section 276 Misconstrued: The Failure to Properly Interpret and Apply Canada's Rape Shield Provisions," *Canadian Bar Review* 94 (2016): 1.

16 *R v B(S)* CA at para. 61.

17 Janine Benedet, Case Comment, *R v B(S)*, 2014 NLTD(G) 61.

18 *B(S)* transcript at 37:17–39:9.

19 Ibid. at 39:14.

20 Ibid. at 42:18.

21 Ibid. at 45:8.

22 Ibid. at 45:10.

23 *B(S)* CA at para. 43.

24 Ibid. at 55:11–18.

25 See e.g. *B(S)* transcript at 55:11–18, 58:1–59:12.

26 Ibid. at 56:1–56:8.

27 Ibid. at 58:1–59:12.

28 *B(S)* CA at para. 88.

29 *B(S)* transcript at 52:21–2.

30 Ibid. at 129:14–17.

31 The test for overturning a jury acquittal was articulated by the Supreme Court of Canada in *R v Graveline*, [2006] 1 SCR 609 at para. 14: "It is the duty of the Crown in order to obtain a new trial to satisfy the appellate court that the error (or errors) of the trial judge might reasonably be thought, in the concrete reality of the case at hand, to have had a material bearing on the acquittal." Justice Rowe concluded, at paragraph 88, that the complainant's credibility was gravely undermined at trial and thus the necessary nexus between the admission of this prior sexual history evidence and the verdict was not demonstrated. Chief Justice Greene dissented from this aspect of Justice Rowe's decision.

32 *R v B(S)*, 2017 SCC 16, 136 WCB (2d) 161.

33 *Groia v Law Society of Upper Canada*, 2016 ONCA 471, 1 Admin LR (6th) 175 (leave granted).

34 Yamri Taddese, "Trial Judges Better Suited to Regulating Civility: Panel," *Law Times* (17 December 2012), http://www.lawtimesnews.com/201212172119/headline-news/trial-judges-better-suited-to-regulating-civility-panel.

35 Ibid.

36 *R v Finney*, 2014 ONCA 866, 118 WCB (2d) 327 [*Finney* CA].

37 *R v Schmaltz*, 2015 ABCA 4, 320 CCC (3d) 159 [*Schmaltz* CA].

38 *R v Finney*, Trial Transcript, Volume II (30 September 2011) Lindsay C55780 (ONSC) at 643:20.

39 *R v Finney*, Trial Transcript, Volume III (4 October 2011) Lindsay C55780 (ONSC) at 681:9.

40 *R v Schmaltz*, Trial Transcript (12 December 2013), Medicine Hat 081056319P1 (ABPC) at 51:34.

41 Ibid. at 79:9.

42 *Finney* CA at para. 3; *Schmaltz* CA at para. 12.

43 *R v Finney*, 2014 ONCA 866, 118 WCB (2d) 327 (Factum of the Appellant at paras. 2, 61).

44 *Finney* CA at para. 3; *Schmaltz* CA at paras. 58–9.

45 See e.g. Federation of Law Societies of Canada, *Model Code of Professional Conduct* (Ottawa: Federation of Law Societies of Canada,

2014), http://flsc.ca/wp-content/uploads/2014/12/conduct1.pdf:
"A lawyer must be courteous and civil and act in good faith with all
persons with whom the lawyer has dealings in the course of his or her
practice" (ch 7.2-1); "A lawyer must be courteous and civil and act in
good faith to the tribunal and all persons with whom the lawyer has
dealings" (ch 5.1-5). For further examination of the duty of civility, see
the discussion in chapter 4 of *Groia v Law Society of Upper Canada*
2014 ONLSAP 41, [2013] LSDD No. 186 and *Groia v Law Society of
Upper Canada*, 2016 ONCA 471, 1 Admin LR (6th) 175 (leave granted).

46 Amanda Konradi, *Taking the Stand: Rape Survivors and the Prosecution
of Rapists* (Westport, CT: Praeger Publishers, 2007), 102–3.

47 Ibid., 103.

48 *R v Luceno*, 2015 ONCA 759, 331 CCC (3d) 521.

49 *R v Luceno*, Trial Transcript, Volume I (19 March 2014) Toronto C59248
(ONSC) at 93:6–12.

50 Ibid. at 204:9–17.

51 Law societies have been reluctant to enter this regulatory sphere, and
have been criticized when they do discipline the courtroom conduct of
lawyers. The criticism seems to be rooted in the sense that judges are
better positioned to regulate courtroom conduct and that interference
by law societies risks creating a chilling effect on the willingness
and ability of lawyers to advocate resolutely for their clients. See e.g.
Taddese, "Trial Judges Better Suited." This article includes comments
from former Supreme Court of Canada Justice Ian Binnie about the
Law Society of Upper Canada's decision to discipline lawyer Joe Groia
for uncivil conduct. Justice Binnie commented that judges and not law
societies should be regulating courtroom conduct. See also Edward
Greenspan and L. David Roebuck, "The Horrible Crime of Incivility,"
The Globe and Mail (2 August 2011), http://www.theglobeandmail.com/
opinion/the-horrible-crime-of-incivility/article589082/.

52 *R v Cain*, 2010 ABCA 371, 502 AR 322.

53 *R v Cain*, Trial Transcript (20 November 2009), Wetaskiwin
080971492Q1 (ABQB) at 143:31.

54 Ibid. at 144:27.

55 Ibid. at 147:14.

56 Ibid. at 148:21.

57 Ibid. at 155:2–10.

58 See e.g. *R v Griffin*, 2016 ONSC 2448 at para. 114, 130 WCB (2d) 252.

59 Ibid. See also *R v Hamilton*, 2011 ONCA 399 at para. 48, 271 CCC (3d)
    208 at para. 48 [*Hamilton*].

60 *R v Lyttle*, 2004 SCC 5 at para. 44, [2004] 1 SCR 193 [*Lyttle*]. See also
    Hamilton.

61 *Lyttle*: "Counsel are bound by the rules of relevancy and barred from
    resorting to harassment, misrepresentation, repetitiousness or, more
    generally, from putting questions whose prejudicial effect outweighs
    their probative value" (at para. 44).

62 *R v Shearing*, 2002 SCC 58 at para. 76, [2002] 3 SCR 33.

63 *R v Kench*, 2014 ONSC 2206 at para. 32, 113 WCB (2d) 84.

64 Ibid.

65 Ibid.

66 *R v Osolin*, [1993] 4 SCR 595 at para. 44, 86 CCC (3d) 481.

67 *R v Schmaltz*, Trial Transcript (12 December 2013), Medicine Hat
    081056319P1 (ABPC) at 73:8–79, 97:6–99 [*Schmaltz* transcript].

68 Ibid. at 34:15. The description of the assault offered here is based on the
    complainant's testimony at trial.

69 Ibid. at 36:15.

70 *Schmaltz* CA at para. 86.

71 Ibid. at para. 60.

72 Ibid. at para. 64. As David Tanovich notes (in an email to the author,
    17 April 2017), the actual problem with Judge Greaves's conduct of the
    trial in *Schmaltz* was that he failed to intervene to stop defence counsel's
    clearly offensive questions, such as ones about the degree of moisture in
    the complainant's vagina, and was arguably too interventionist on more
    minor problems with the cross-examination, such as defence counsel's
    questions about alcohol and marijuana consumption.

73 *Hamilton* at para. 31.

74 *R v A(J)*, [2011] 2 SCR 440 at para. 23, 335 DLR (4th) 108.

75 *R v Ewanchuk*, [1999] 1 SCR 330, 169 DLR (4th) 193 ("There is no defence
    of implied consent to sexual assault in Canadian law" at para. 31).

76 *Schmaltz* CA at para. 82.

77 Ibid. at para. 63.

78 For a discussion of the history of court architecture, see Linda Mulcahy,
    Legal Architecture: Justice, Due Process and the Place of Law (New York:
    Routledge, 2011). For an examination of the many forms of sovereignty
    expressed in a courtroom design, see Katherine Fischer Taylor, *In the
    Theatre of Criminal Justice: The Palais de Justice in Second Empire Paris*
    (Princeton, NJ: Princeton University Press, 1993).

79 See David Tait, "Popular Sovereignty and the Justice Process: Towards a Comparative Methodology for Observing Courtroom Rituals," *Contemporary Justice Review* 4 (2001): 201 (comparing expressions of sovereignty through the spatial design of the trial in civil and common law jurisdictions).

80 The complainant's exhaustion and distress were readily apparent to the Court. Justice Crighton's decision actually opened with an unusually detailed description of how fatigued the complainant was during her testimony and how truly taxing the trial was for the complainant (*R v Khaery*, 2014 ABQB 676 at paras. 4–13, 117 WCB (2d) 422).

81 *R v Khaery*, Trial Transcript (23 September 2014) Edmonton 121306211Q1 (ABQB) at 7:24–40.

82 Ibid. at 15:3–12.

83 Ibid. at 139:29.

84 Lisa Frohmann, "Discrediting Victims' Allegations of Sexual Assault: Prosecutorial Accounts of Case Rejections," *Social Problems* 38, no. 2 (1991): 213, at 221.

85 See generally Mariëlle Stel et al., "Lowering the Pitch of Your Voice Makes You Feel More Powerful and Think More Abstractly," *Social Psychological and Personality Science* 3, no. 4 (2012): 497.

86 Frohmann, "Discrediting Victims' Allegations," 221.

87 Statistics Canada, *Criminal Victimization in Canada, 2014*, by Samuel Perreault, Catalogue No. 85-002-X (Ottawa: Statistics Canada, 23 November 2015): "The differences between Aboriginal and non-Aboriginal people were most pronounced for break-ins and sexual assaults, with the rates for Aboriginals being more than double those for non-Aboriginals" (16). See also John Borrows, "Aboriginal and Treaty Rights and Violence Against Women," *Osgoode Hall Law Journal* 50, no. 3 (2013): 699 (noting the disproportionately high rates at which Aboriginal women are sexually victimized, at 700).

88 Leslie Moran, "Judging Pictures: A Case Study of Portraits of the Chief Justices, Supreme Court of New South Wales," *International Journal of Law in Context* 5, no. 3 (2009): 295 (noting that legal historians have traced the tradition as far back as the fourteenth century, at 298).

89 Ibid., 298.

90 Ibid., 299, referencing Marianna Jenkins, *The State Portrait: Its Origin and Evolution* (New York: College Art Association of America, 1947), 1.

91 Historically, judicial appointments in Canada were almost all white
    men. This means more judicial portraits of white men. See Rosemary
    Cairns Way, "Deliberate Disregard: Judicial Appointments under
    the Harper Government," *Supreme Court Law Review* 67 (2014): 43
    (discussing the overrepresentation of white male judges in the federally
    appointed judiciary and demonstrating the failure of the Harper
    government to appoint a complement of judges that reflects gender
    parity and racial diversity). The Trudeau government is developing
    a more transparent appointments process with a greater emphasis
    on diversity: Sean Fine, "Liberals Overhaul Judicial Appointment
    Process to Boost Diversity," *The Globe and Mail* (20 October 2016),
    https://www.theglobeandmail.com/news/national/liberals-to-unveil-
    new-judicial-appointment-process-undo-changes-made-by-harper/
    article32454733/.

92 Ibid., 62 (finding that the vast majority of judicial appointments are
    Caucasian).

93 Marie Corbett, *January: A Woman Judge's Season of Disillusion* (Holmes
    Beach, FL: Broad Cove Press, 2016), 293.

94 I am grateful to Constance Backhouse for this latter suggestion and
    for proposing that such judicial portraiture galleries should include
    navigational aids to provide viewers with context and the ability to
    interpret the imagery displayed.

95 See Anthony T. Kronman, *The Lost Lawyer: Failing Ideals of the Legal
    Profession* (Cambridge, MA: Belknap Press of Harvard University
    Press, 1993) (bemoaning the disappearance of the "lawyer-statesman");
    Jennifer M. Granholm, "Nobility in the Practice of Law," *Michigan Bar
    Journal* 78, no. 12 (1999): 1397 (advancing suggestions for how the legal
    profession might once again become noble).

96 See e.g. Kara Anne Nagorney, "A Noble Profession? A Discussion of
    Civility Among Lawyers," *Georgetown Journal of Legal Ethics* 12, no. 4
    (1999): 815 (noting data confirming that lawyers find the behaviour of
    others quite inappropriate, and survey data indicating a decline in the
    public's perception of law as a prestigious profession).

97 Corbett, *January*, 172.

98 Ibid., 171.

Chapter Seven

1 Canada, Canadian Judicial Council, *Ethical Principles for Judges*, Catalogue No. JU11-4/2004E-PDF (Ottawa: Canadian Judicial Council, 2011), 19 (footnotes omitted), https://www.cjc-ccm.gc.ca/cmslib/general/news_pub_judicialconduct_Principles_en.pdf.

2 *R v B(IE)*, 2013 NSCA 98, 300 CCC (3d) 481 [*B(IE)* CA].

3 *R v B(IE)*, 2011 NSSC 424 (unreported) at para. 27 [*B(IE)* NSSC].

4 Ibid. at para. 15.

5 *R v B(IE)*, Trial Transcript (8 November 2011) Kentville 343759 (NSSC) at 9, 17–21, 36–40 [*B(IE)* transcript].

6 Ibid. at 81:9–13.

7 *B(IE)* NSSC at paras. 26–30; see also *B(IE)* CA at para. 7 (appeal judge citing this excerpt from the trial judge's unreported decision).

8 *B(IE)* NSSC.

9 *Criminal Code*, RSC 1985, c C-46, s 273.2(b) [*Criminal Code*]. For a discussion of the affirmative definition of consent in the Supreme Court of Canada's most recent case see Karen Busby, "Every Breath You Take: Erotic Asphyxiation, Vengeful Wives, and Other Enduring Myths in Spousal Sexual Assault Prosecutions," *Canadian Journal of Women and the Law* 24, no. 2 (2012): 328.

10 *B(IE)* NSSC at para. 29.

11 *B(IE)* transcript.

12 *R v Ewanchuk*, [1999] 1 SCR 330 at paras. 49, 51, 169 DLR (4th) 193 [*Ewanchuk* SCC].

13 *Criminal Code*, s 273.2(b).

14 *B(IE)* NSSC at para. 17 and *B(IE)* CA at para. 35 (Court of Appeal concluding lack of resistance grounded his acquittal).

15 *B(IE)* NSSC, and *B(IE)* CA at para. 35.

16 *R v B(IE)*, 2013 NSCA 98, 334 NSR (2d) 83 (Factum of the Appellant at para. 37).

17 *Ewanchuk* SCC at paras. 47–9.

18 See e.g. Jessica Stern, *Denial: A Memoir of Terror* (New York: Ecco, 2010), 16–23 (describing her state during her and her sister's rape as being "hypnotized into passivity").

19 See e.g. Grace Galliano et al., "Victim Reactions During Rape/Sexual Assault: A Preliminary Study of the Immobility Response and Its Correlates," *Journal of Interpersonal Violence* 8, no. 1 (1993): 109; Brian

P. Marx et al., "Tonic Immobility as an Evolved Predator Defense: Implications for Sexual Assault Survivors," *Clinical Psychology: Science and Practice* 15, no. 1 (2008): 74; Christine A. Gidycz, Amy Van Wynsberghe, and Katie M. Edwards, "Prediction of Women's Utilization of Resistance Strategies in a Sexual Assault Situation," *Journal of Interpersonal Violence* 23, no. 5 (2008): 571, at 578 (39% of the sexual assault victims in this study "reported some degree of immobility" during the assault); Katie M. Edwards et al., "In Their Own Words: A Content-Analytic Study of College Women's Resistance to Sexual Assault," *Journal of Interpersonal Violence* 29, no. 14 (2014): 2527, at 2354 (18% of the sexual assault victims in this study reported "freez[ing]/ turn[ing] cold/tens[ing] up" during the assault).

20 *Ewanchuk* SCC at paras. 47–51.

21 *Criminal Code*, s 273.2(b). For a scholarly consideration of the 'reasonable steps' requirement in the context of intoxicated or unconscious women see Elizabeth Sheehy, "Judges and the Reasonable Steps Requirement: The Judicial Stance on Perpetration Against Unconscious Women," in *Sexual Assault in Canada: Law, Legal Practice and Women's Activism*, edited by Elizabeth Sheehy (Ottawa: University of Ottawa Press, 2012), 483; Elizabeth Sheehy, "From Women's Duty to Resist to Men's Duty to Ask: How Far Have We Come?" *Canadian Woman Studies* 20 (2000): 98.

22 Ibid.

23 *B(IE)* NSSC at para. 27.

24 *B(IE)* CA at para. 35.

25 Ibid. at para. 35.

26 *R v Adepoju*, 2014 ABCA 100, 8 Alta LR (6th) 387 [*Adepoju* CA].

27 Ibid. at para. 2.

28 Ibid. at para. 7.

29 Ibid. at paras. 2, 7–8.

30 Ibid. at para. 7 ("The trial judge accepted the complainant's testimony that she objected to further sexual contact after the first kiss by the respondent").

31 Ibid. at para. 3.

32 Ibid. at para. 3 ("The trial judge acknowledged and believed the text messages sent by the respondent admitting that he had used force to have sexual intercourse with the complainant").

33 Ibid. at para. 8 (quoting Justice Sisson).

34 Ibid. at paras. 9, 12–13.

35 *R v Adepoju*, 2014 ABCA 100 (Factum of the Appellant at para. 3).

36 *Ewanchuk* SCC at para. 26.

37 *R v Adepoju*, Trial Transcript, Volume I (30 April 2013) Red Deer 1205 80485Q1 (ABQB) at 39:48 [*Adepoju* transcript].

38 Ibid. at 37:18–19, 39:28.

39 Ibid. at 35:41.

40 Ibid. at 34:34–5.

41 *Criminal Code*, s 273.1(1): "*consent* means ... the voluntary agreement of the complainant to engage in the sexual activity in question" (emphasis in original).

42 *Adepoju* transcript at 3:13–14.

43 *Adepoju* CA at paras. 9, 12–13.

44 Ibid. at para. 13.

45 *R v Wagar*, 2015 ABCA 327, 125 WCB (2d) 471 [*Wagar* CA].

46 *R v Wagar*, Trial Transcript (9 September 2014) Calgary 130288731P1 (ABPC) at 17–28 [*Wagar* transcript].

47 Ibid. at 26:40–1, 27:10, 290:12, 290:15, 290:36–7, 297:5–6.

48 Ibid. at 119:10–11, 119:14–15.

49 Ibid. at 326:8, 326:12.

50 Ibid. at 450:29.

51 Ibid. at 437:9.

52 Ibid. at 323:35–7, 325:27–9, 325:37, 326:8, 326:12, 326:17–18, 326:23–4.

53 *R v Ewanchuk*, 1998 ABCA 52 at paras. 5, 20, 21, 57 Alta LR (3d) 235.

54 Ibid. at paras. 20–1.

55 *R v Wagar*, 2015 ABCA 327, 125 WCB (2d) 471 (Factum of the Appellant at paras. 2–3) [*Wagar*, appellant factum]. *Wagar* transcript at 450:29: "The accused's [sic] version is open to question. She certainly had the ability, perhaps learnt from her experience on the streets, to tell me to fuck off."

56 Wagar's second trial also resulted in an acquittal: *R v Wagar*, 2017 ABPC 17, 47 Alta LR (6th) 356.

57 *Wagar* CA at para. 4.

58 *Criminal Code*, s 273.2(b).

59 *Wagar* transcript at 384:27–385:9.

60 The author was one of the four law professors to file the original complaint with the Canadian Judicial Council. The other three complainants were Professors Alice Woolley, Jocelyn Downie, and

Jennifer Koshan. For the complaint, see Kathleen Harris and Alison Crawford, "Federal Court Judge under Review for Berating Sexual Assault Complainant," CBC *News* (9 November 2015), http://www.cbc.ca/news/politics/canada-judge-judical-review-robin-camp-1.3311574.

61 Ibid. Aspects of the legal analysis included in our complaint, in particular analysis of transcript excerpts highlighting Justice Camp's misstatements of law during the trial, have been repeated in this section of chapter 7.

62 Canadian Judicial Council, "Report and Recommendation of the Inquiry Committee to the Canadian Judicial Council" (29 November 2016), http://www.cjc-ccm.gc.ca/cmslib/general/Camp_Docs/2016-11-29%20CJC%20Camp%20Inquiry%20Committee%20Report.pdf. The Inquiry Committee found that he had expressed antipathy and disdain towards section 276 of the *Criminal Code*. The Committee did not find evidence that he willfully refused to apply the law (at para. 83).

63 Canadian Judicial Council, *In the Matter of S 63 of the Judges Act, RS c J-1: Canadian Judicial Council Inquiry into the Conduct of the Honourable Robin Camp: Report to the Minister of Justice* (Ottawa: Canadian Judicial Council, 8 March 2017).

64 Sean Fine, "Judge in Knees Together Trial Resigns after Council Recommends He Be Fired," *The Globe and Mail* (9 March 2017), http://www.theglobeandmail.com/news/national/judicial-council-recommends-justice-robin-camp-be-fired/article34249312/.

65 *R v R(J)*, 2016 ABQB 414 at para. 15, [2016] AJ No 751 [*R(J)*].

66 Ibid. at paras. 19–33.

67 *R v G(CM)*, 2016 ABQB 368, 41 Atla LR (6th) 374 [*G(CM)*].

68 Ibid. at para. 14.

69 Sean Fine, "Third Alberta Judge Faces Review over Handling of Sex-Assault Case," *The Globe and Mail* (15 Sept 2016), http://www.theglobeandmail.com/news/national/third-alberta-judge-faces-review-over-handling-of-sex-assault-case/article31892370/.

70 *G(CM)* at para. 16.

71 *B(IE)* CA at para. 3.

72 *Wagar* CA at para. 5.

73 For recent examples, see the cases of Lyle Howe (Blair Rhodes, "Halifax Defence Lawyer Lyle Howe Has Sexual Assault Charge Dropped," CBC *News* [18 February 2016], http://www.cbc.ca/news/canada/nova-scotia/lyle-howe-sexual-assault-charges-dropped-1.3453328)

and of Stephen Taweel (Blair Rhodes, "P.E.I. Businessman Stephen Nicholas Taweel Won't Face Sex Assault Retrial," CBC *News* [9 May 2016], http://www.cbc.ca/news/canada/nova-scotia/stephen-nicholas-taweel-pei-sexual-assault-1.3573281).

74 *Adepoju* CA at para. 13.

75 *R(J)* at para. 37.

76 *Adepoju* appellant factum at paras. 51, 52; *Wagar* appellant factum at para. 3; *R v B(IE)* appellant factum at para. 40. See also *R v Rhodes*, discussed below: *R v Rhodes*, 2011 MBCA 98, 281 CCC (3d) 29 at para. 9 ("the Crown asserted that the trial judge engaged in inappropriate stereotyping") [*Rhodes* CA].

77 *Wagar* transcript at 357:31.

78 Bill Graveland, "He Made Me Hate Myself: Sex Assault Complainant Testifies at Judge's Hearing," *Toronto Star* (6 Sept 2016), https://www.thestar.com/news/canada/2016/09/06/alleged-sex-assault-victim-to-testify-at-hearing-of-knees-together-judge.html.

79 *Ewanchuk* SCC at paras. 47–9.

80 *Criminal Code*, s 273.2(b).

81 See generally Christine Boyle, *Sexual Assault* (Toronto: Carswell, 1984).

82 See generally Susan Erlich, "Perpetuating – and Resisting – Rape Myths in Trial Discourse," in *Sexual Assault in Canada: Law, Legal Practice and Women's Activism*, edited by Elizabeth Sheehy (Ottawa: University of Ottawa Press, 2012), 389; Lise Gotell, "When Privacy Is Not Enough: Sexual Assault Complainants, Sexual History Evidence and the Disclosure of Confidential Records," *Alberta Law Review* 43, no. 3 (2006): 743; Jennifer Koshan, "Disclosure and Production in Sexual Violence Cases: Situating *Stinchcombe*," *Alberta Law Review* 40, no. 3 (2002): 655; Sheehy, "Judges and the Reasonable Steps Requirement," 483; David Tanovich, "An Equality-Oriented Approach to the Admissibility of Similar Fact Evidence in Sexual Assault Prosecutions," in *Sexual Assault in Canada: Law, Legal Practice and Women's Activism*, edited by Elizabeth Sheehy (Ottawa: University of Ottawa Press, 2012), 541; Lucinda Vandervort, "Lawful Subversion of the Criminal Justice Process? Judicial, Prosecutorial, and Police Discretion in *Edmondson*, *Kindrat*, and *Brown*," in *Sexual Assault in Canada: Law, Legal Practice and Women's Activism*, edited by Elizabeth Sheehy (Ottawa: University of Ottawa Press, 2012), 111.

83 *Ewanchuk* SCC at para. 95.

84 See generally Barbara Krahé et al., "Prospective Lawyers' Rape Stereotypes and Schematic Decision Making About Rape Cases," *Psychology, Crime & Law* 14, no. 5 (2008): 461.

85 Citing Nancy Levit, "Confronting Conventional Thinking: The Heuristics Problem in Feminist Legal Theory," *Cardozo Law Review* 28, no. 1 (2006): 391.

86 *R v Rhodes*, Sentencing Transcript (18 February 2011) Thompson (MBQB).

87 *R v Rhodes*, [2011] MJ No. 67 at para. 516 (unreported).

88 Ibid. at paras. 509, 512.

89 Ibid. at para. 519. Given his articulation of consent to sexual touching, it is surprising that Justice Dewar convicted Rhodes. Regardless, the Manitoba Court of Appeal overturned the conviction and ordered a new trial on the basis that he had failed to properly apply the burden of proof analysis. See *Rhodes* CA at para. 10.

90 Canadian Judicial Council, "Canadian Judicial Council Completes Its Review of Complaints Made against Justice Robert Dewar" (9 November 2011), https://www.cjc-ccm.gc.ca/english/ news_en.asp?selMenu=news_2011_1109_en.asp.

91 Canadian Judicial Council, "Judicial Education" (3 March 2011), https://www.cjc-ccm.gc.ca/english/news_en.asp?selMenu=news_ 2011_0303_en.asp.

92 Ibid.

93 Federation of Law Societies of Canada, *Model Code of Professional Conduct* (Ottawa: Federation of Law Societies of Canada, 2014), http:// flsc.ca/wp-content/uploads/2014/12/conduct1.pdf: "When acting as an advocate, a lawyer must not: (i) deliberately refrain from informing a tribunal of any binding authority that the lawyer considers to be directly on point and that has not been mentioned by another party," ch 5.1-2(i).

94 R. Blake Brown and Susan S. Jones, "A Collective Biography of the Supreme Court Judiciary of Nova Scotia, 1900–2000," in *The Supreme Court of Nova Scotia, 1754–2004: From Imperial Bastion to Provincial Oracle*, edited by Philip Girard, Jim Phillips, and Barry Cahill (Toronto: University of Toronto Press, 2004), 231; "Judge Profile: Gerald R.P. Moir, Q.C.," *Martindale-Hubbell*, http://www.martindale. com/Gerald-R-P-Moir-QC/1312012-lawyer.htm (accessed 23 July 2017).

95 Warren Sinclair LLP, "History," *Warren Sinclair* LLP, http://www. warrensinclair.com/about-us/history/ (accessed 23 July 2017).

96   Department of Justice, "Manitoba Judicial Appointments Announced"
      (9 September 2009) (on file with author).

97   Department of Justice, "Federal Court Judicial Appointments
      Announced" (26 June 2015), http://news.gc.ca/web/article-en.
      do?nid=992419.

98   Canadian Judicial Council, "Opening Submissions of Justice
      Camp," *Inquiry Committee Regarding the Honourable Robin
      Camp* (6 September 2016), https://www.cjcccm.gc.ca/english/
      conduct_en.asp?selMenu=conduct_inq_camp_en.asp.

99   See e.g. Global Integrity, "Global Integrity Report 2010: Canada," in
      Global Integrity Report 2010 (Washington, DC: Global Integrity, 2011),
      http://www.globalintegrity.org/research/reports/global-integrity-report/
      global-integrity-report-2010/gir-scorecard-2010-canada/: see "36. Are
      judges appointed fairly?" (under "3.3. Conflicts of Interest Safeguards &
      Checks and Balances: Judicial Branch"), receiving a score of 17 out of 100.

100 Richard Devlin, "Dirty Laundry: Judicial Appointments in Canada," in
      *Securing Judicial Independence: The Role of Commissions in Selecting
      Judges in the Commonwealth*, edited by Hugh Corder and Jan Van Zyl
      Smit (Cape Town: Siber Ink, forthcoming). Devlin cites several studies
      that have arrived at this conclusion.

101 Newfoundland, Department of Justice, *The Lamer Commission of
      Inquiry Pertaining to the Cases of: Ronald Dalton, Gregory Parsons,
      Randy Druken* (2004) (The Right Honourable Antonio Lamer), 164,
      http://www.justice.gov.nl.ca/just/publications/lamerreport.pdf.

102 David Staples, "Who's Best for the Bench?" *Edmonton Journal* (12
      August 2007) (archive on file with author).

103 Ibid.

104 Ibid.

105 Canada, "Government of Canada Announces Judicial Appointments
      and Reforms the Appointments Process to Increase Openness and
      Transparency" (20 October 2016), http://news.gc.ca/web/article-en.
      do?nid=1140619.

106 Canada, Canadian Judicial Council, *Judicial Education Guidelines for
      Canadian Superior Courts*, September 2009 update (Ottawa: Canadian
      Judicial Council, 2008), https://www.cjc-ccm.gc.ca/cmslib/general/JEC-
      edu-guidelines-2008-04-finalE-revised-2009-09-final-E.pdf.

107 Canada, Office of the Commissioner for Federal Judicial Affairs
      Canada, "Considerations which Apply to Application for Appointment"

(Ottawa, 1 April 2016), http://www.fja-cmf.gc.ca/appointments-nominations/considerations-eng.html#Professional (accessed 6 September 2016).

108 Adam Dodek and Richard Devlin, "'Fighting Words': Regulating Judges in Canada" (2015), 12, http://www.icpublicpolicy.org/conference/file/reponse/1433471752.pdf.

109 There has been an extraordinary degree of public criticism of the judiciary, in response to high-profile cases such as Justice Camp's conduct of the case in *Wagar* and Judge Lenehan's decision in *R v Al-Rawi*, Audio Trial Transcript: Oral Decision (1 March 2017) Halifax 2866665 (NSPC) (unreported). See e.g. Cristin Schmitz, "CJC Considers Imposing Mandatory Professional Development on Federal Judges" (21 March 2017), https://www.thelawyersdaily.ca/criminal/articles/2743/cjc-considers-imposing-mandatory-professional-development-on-federal-judges-. In March 2017, Leader of the Opposition Rona Ambrose introduced a private member's bill – Bill C-337, *Judicial Accountability through Sexual Assault Law Training Act: An Act to amend the Judges Act and the Criminal Code (sexual assault)* – which if passed would require sexual assault training of all potential federal appointees as a criteria of eligibility. The House of Commons unanimously agreed to fast-track the bill to committee level. Shortly after this occurred, the CJC changed its policy to make sexual assault training for new federally appointed judges mandatory. At the time of writing, the Bill had passed in the House of Commons and was awaiting consideration by the Senate.

110 Canadian Judicial Council, "Training for New Federally Appointed Judges," https://www.cjc-ccm.gc.ca/cmslib/general/Judicial%20Training/Training%20for%20New%20Federally-Appointed%20Judges.pdf (accessed 23 July 2017).

111 Philip Rumney and Rachel Fenton, "Comment: Judicial Training and Rape," *Journal of Criminal Law* 75 (2011): 473.

112 Ibid., 474.

113 Allison Jones, "Sexual Assault Education Now Required for New Ontario Judges," *The Globe and Mail* (18 May 2017), https://www.google.ca/search?q=Sexual-assault+education+now+required+for+new+Ontario+judges&sourceid=ie7&rls=com.microsoft:en-US:IE-Address&ie=&oe=&rlz=1I7SKPT_en&gfe_rd=cr&ei=ugofWa_cINHOXsjNvLAB&gws_rd=ssl (reporting on a May 2017 move by

the Ontario Court of Justice to require sexual assault training for new provincial judges); Slav Kornik, "Retired Justice Weighs In on Training for Judges amid Alberta Justice Robin Camp Hearing," *Global* (9 September 2016), http://globalnews.ca/news/2930485/retired-justice-weighs-in-on-training-for-judges-amid-alberta-justice-robin-camp-hearing/ (discussing training and mentoring of Alberta provincial court judges).

114 In Ontario, for example, newly appointed provincial court judges are "encouraged" to attend a one-week intensive program devoted largely to substantive criminal law. Anecdotal evidence suggests the large majority of new appointees do attend. Ontario Court of Justice, "Continuing Education Plan" (2012–13), *Judicial Conduct*, http://www.ontariocourts.ca/ocj/ojc/education-plan/.

115 For other recent cases in which trial judges were overturned because of their stereotypical thinking, in addition to *Adepoju, Wagar, B(IE)*, and *R(J)*, see *R v G(AD)*, 2015 ABCA, [2016] 2 WWR 40; *G(CM)*; *R v G(J)*, 2015 ONSC 5482 at para. 5, 124 WCB (2d) 413 [*G(J)*].

116 Canadian Judicial Council, "Opening Submissions of Justice Camp."

117 Sean Fine, "Judge Apologizes for 'Unforgiveable' Rape Comments at Inquiry," *The Globe and Mail* (9 September 2016), http://www.theglobeandmail.com/news/national/judge-who-made-rape-comments-says-he-held-unconscious-bias/article31794361/.

118 Standing Committee on the Status of Women, "Taking Action to End Violence Against Young Girls and Women in Canada" (20 March 2017), http://www.parl.gc.ca/HousePublications/Publication.aspx?Language=e&Mode=1&Parl=42&Ses=1&DocId=8823562&File=216.

119 This list of topics was provided to me by the executive director of the NJI, Justice Adèle Kent (personal email, 10 October 2016).

120 National Judicial Institute, "The Social Context Education Program: Summary," 1, http://web.law.columbia.edu/sites/default/files/microsites/clinics/sexuality-gender/files/SG13.pdf (accessed 23 July 2017).

121 National Judicial Institute, "Social Context Education: Integration Protocol for Social Context" (October 2009), http://www.iojt-dc2013.org/~/media/Microsites/Files/IOJT/11042013-Integration-Protocol-for-Social-Context.ashx.

122 Canadian Judicial Council, "Opening Submissions of Justice Camp."

123 Bill Graveland, "Alberta Justice Robin Camp in 'Knees Together' Case Admits 'Non-existent' Knowledge of Criminal Law," *Canadian Press* (10

September 2016), http://globalnews.ca/news/2932207/alberta-justice-
robin-camp-in-knees-together-case-admits-non-existent-knowledge-of-
criminal-law/.

124 Ibid.

125 Dodek and Devlin, "'Fighting Words,'" 12.

126 The concern over judicial independence has not precluded jurisdictions
such as the United Kingdom from imposing mandatory training for
judges before they are assigned to rape trials. See Jennifer Temkin
and Barbara Krahé, *Sexual Assault and the Justice Gap: A Question of
Attitude* (Oxford, UK: Hart Publishing, 2008), 191. See also Rumney and
Fenton, "Comment: Judicial Training and Rape."

127 Dodek and Devlin, "'Fighting Words,'" 18–19.

128 Sean Fine, "Third Alberta Judge Faces Review over Handling of Sex-
Assault Case," *The Globe and Mail* (14 September 2016), http://www.
theglobeandmail.com/news/national/third-alberta-judge-
faces-review-over-handling-of-sex-assault-case/article31892370/.

129 Ibid.

130 Vandervort, "Lawful Subversion of the Criminal Justice Process?" 141.

131 [2008] 3 SCR 3, 2008 SCC 51.

132 Canada, "Considerations which Apply."

133 Canadian Judicial Council, *In the Matter of S 63 of the Judges Act,
RS c J-1: Canadian Judicial Council Inquiry into the Conduct of the
Honourable Robin Camp: Report to the Minister of Justice* (Ottawa:
Canadian Judicial Council, 8 March 2017).

Chapter Eight

1 The most detailed report on sexual assault in Canada is from the 1993
National Violence Against Women Survey. In that survey, 39% of adult
Canadian women reported having been a victim of at least one sexual
assault since the age of 16: Statistics Canada, *Measuring Violence
Against Women: Statistical Trends 2006*, Catalogue No. 85-570-XIE
(Ottawa: Statistics Canada, 2006), 24, http://www.statcan.gc.ca/pub/85-
570-x/85-570-x2006001-eng.pdf. In the 2011 National Household
Survey, 25.9% of adults in Canada had a university degree; see Statistics
Canada, "Education in Canada: Attainment, Field of Study and Location
of Study," Catalogue No. 99-012-X2011001 (Ottawa: Statistics Canada,

2011), 7, http://www12.statcan.gc.ca/nhs-enm/2011/as-sa/99-012-x/99-012-x2011001-eng.pdf. The most recent data on the gender wage gap is from the annual Survey on Labour and Income Dynamics, 2011 (now discontinued), which found that on average a woman earns 72 cents for every dollar a man earns: Statistics Canada, "Average Earnings by Sex and Work Pattern (Full-time Workers)" (27 June 2013), http://www.statcan.gc.ca/tables-tableaux/sum-som/l01/cst01/labor01b-eng.htm.

2 Youth Women's Christian Association, "Violence Against Women," *Advocacy & Policy*, http://ywcacanada.ca/en/pages/advocacy/priorities/vaw (accessed 23 July 2017), citing Holly Johnson, "Limits of a Criminal Justice Response: Trends in Police and Court Processing of Sexual Assault," in *Sexual Assault in Canada: Law, Legal Practice and Women's Activism*, edited by Elizabeth Sheehy (Ottawa: University of Ottawa Press, 2012), 613, at 631; Blair Crew, Daphne Gilbert, and Elizabeth Sheehy, "The Ghomeshi Verdict: This Is No Time for Complacency," *Policy Options* (12 April 2016), http://policyoptions.irpp.org/magazines/april-2016/the-ghomeshi-verdict-this-is-no-time-for-complacency/ ("997 of 1,000 men who commit this crime can expect to be unsanctioned").

3 Statistics Canada, "Sexual Assault in Canada: 2004 and 2007," by Shannon Brennan and Andrea Taylor-Butts, Catalogue No. 85F0033M – No. 19 (Ottawa: Canadian Centre for Justice Statistics, 2008), 6, http://www.statcan.gc.ca/pub/85f0033m/85f0033m2008019-eng.pdf.

4 Canada, Department of Justice, *A Survey of Survivors of Sexual Violence in Three Canadian Cities*, by Melissa Lindsay, Catalogue No. J2-403/2014E (Ottawa: Research and Statistics Division, 2014), 13, 23; Larry C. Wilson, "Independent Legal Representation for Victims of Sexual Assault: A Model for Delivery of Legal Services," *Windsor Yearbook of Access to Justice* 23, no. 2 (2005): 249, at 254.

5 See e.g. Jody Berkes, "The Role of Criminal Defence Counsel in Sexual Assault Trials," JUST (17 March 2016), https://www.oba.org/JUST/Archives_List/2016/March-2016/The-Role-of-Criminal-Defence-Counsel-in-Sexual-Ass (responding to criticism of criminal defence lawyers by pointing to the adversarial system); Sean Robichaud, "Sexual Assault Trials in Canada: Assumptions and Misinformation Clarified," *Robichaud Law*, https://robichaudlaw.ca/what-happens-at-trial-sexual-assault-cases/ (accessed 23 July 2017) (arguing that most victims do not seek further protections and that the criminal

justice system in its present form delivers fairness for both victims and accused); Reid Rusonick, "In Defence of Rigorous Sexual Assault Defences," *Toronto Star* (21 February 2016), https://www.thestar.com/opinion/commentary/2016/02/21/in-defence-of-rigorous-sexual-assault-defences.html (implying an arguably false dichotomy between the right of the accused to be presumed innocence and assessments of the complainant's credibility); The Canadian Press, "Ghomeshi Verdict a Vindication of Canada's Justice System: Hicks," *Advocate Daily*, http://www.advocatedaily.com/ghomeshi-verdict-a-vindication-of-canadas-justice-system-hicks.html (accessed 23 July 2017) (summarizing aspects of Justice Hicks's decision in *R v Ghomeshi*, which linked criticisms of the treatment of complainants with changes to the rules of evidence or burden and standard of proof).

6 See e.g. Solomon Friedman, "The Numbers Contradict Ghomeshi Case Rhetoric," *Ottawa Sun* (7 February 2016), http://www.ottawasun.com/2016/02/07/friedman-the-numbers-contradict-ghomeshi-case-rhetoric.

7 For discussions of the 'second rape,' 'second assault,' or 'secondary victimization,' see e.g. Lee Madigan and Nancy C. Gamble, *The Second Rape: Society's Continued Betrayal of the Victim* (New York: Lexington Books, 1991); Patricia Yancy Martin and R. Marlene Powell, "Accounting for the 'Second Assault': Legal Organizations' Framing of Rape Victims," *Law & Social Inquiry* 19, no. 4 (1994): 853; Cassis C. Spencer, "Sexual Assault: The Second Victimization," in *Women, The Courts, and Equality*, edited by Laura L. Crites and Winifred L. Hepperle (Beverly Hills, CA: Sage, 1987); J.E. Williams and K.A. Holmes, *The Second Assault* (Westport, CT: Greenwood Press, 1981); Rebecca Campbell and Sheela Raja, "Secondary Victimization of Rape Victims: Insights from Mental Health Professionals Who Treat Survivors of Violence," *Violence and Victims* 14, no. 3 (1999): 261; Rebecca Campbell et al., "Preventing the 'Second Rape': Rape Survivors' Experiences with Community Service Providers," *Journal of Interpersonal Violence* 16, no. 12 (2001): 1239.

8 See Jennifer Temkin and Barbara Krahé, *Sexual Assault and the Justice Gap: A Question of Attitude* (Oxford, UK: Hart Publishing, 2008).

9 See David Tanovich, "'Whack' No More: Infusing Equality into the Ethics of Defence Lawyering in Sexual Assault Cases," *Ottawa Law Review* 45, no. 3 (2014): 495; Elizabeth Comack and Tracey Peter, "How

the Criminal Justice System Responds to Sexual Assault Survivors:
The Slippage between 'Responsibilization' and 'Blaming the Victim,'"
Canadian Journal of Women and the Law 17 (2005): 282, at 297, citing
Cristin Schmitz, "Whack Sexual Assault Complainant at Preliminary
Hearing," *Lawyer's Weekly* 8 (1998): 22: "Whack the complainant hard
at the preliminary hearing. Generally, if you destroy the complainant
in a prosecution, you destroy the head ... You've got to attack the
complainant with all you've got"; Lise Gotell, "The Ideal Victim, the
Hysterical Complainant, and the Disclosure of Confidential Records:
The Implications of the *Charter* for Sexual Assault Law," *Osgoode Hall
Law Journal* 40, no. 3 (2002): 251; Lorenne Clark and Debra Lewis, *Rape:
The Price of Coercive Sexuality* (Toronto: Women's Press, 1977).

10 One of the best-known examples of this type of vilification involved
public statements by then Alberta cabinet minister Stockwell Day. In
a public letter to the *Red Deer Advocate*, Day asserted that defence
lawyer Lorne Goddard must himself believe in the right to possess
child pornography because he made *Charter* arguments in defence
of an individual accused of possessing child pornography; see Jill
Mahoney, "Day Defamation Trial Postponed in Alberta," *The Globe
and Mail* (27 October 2000), http://www.theglobeandmail.com/news/
national/day-defamation-trial-postponed-in-alberta/article4168500/;
Goddard v Day, 2000 ABQB 942; 194 DLR (4th) 559). Day eventually
settled a defamation suit brought by Goddard as a result of the letter:
Judy Aldous, "Stockwell Day Settles Defamation Suit out of Court,"
CBC *News* (23 December 2000), http://www.cbc.ca/news/canada/
stockwell-day-settles-defamation-suit-out-of-court-1.211675.

11 See generally David Luban, *Legal Ethics and Human Dignity* (New
York: Cambridge University Press, 2007); Alice Woolley, "Not Only in
America: The Necessity of Representing 'Those People' in a Free and
Democratic Society," in *How Can You Represent Those People?* edited
by Abbe Smith and Monroe Freedman (New York: Palgrave Macmillan,
2013), 199.

12 *R v Finney*, Trial Transcript, Volume II (30 September 2011) Lindsay
C55780 (ONSC) at 548:4–549:2 (discussed in ch. 2).

13 *R v B(IE)*, Trial Transcript (8 November 2011) Kentville 343759 (NSSC)
at 32:3–17 (discussed in ch. 2).

14 *R v Wright*, Trial Transcript, Volume 1 (28 May 2012) Winnipeg CR11-
01-31550 (MBQB) at 35:13–29, 65:30–66:9 (discussed in ch. 2).

15 Bill Graveland, "He Made Me Hate Myself: Sex Assault Complainant Testifies at Judge's Hearing," *Toronto Star* (6 Sept 2016), https://www.thestar.com/news/canada/2016/09/06/alleged-sex-assault-victim-to-testify-at-hearing-of-knees-together-judge.html.

16 *R v Wagar*, Trial Transcript (9 September 2014) Calgary 130288731P1 (ABPC) at 119:10–11, 119:14–15 (discussed in ch. 7).

17 *R v Wagar*, 2015 ABCA 327, 125 WCB (2d) 471. The accused in *Wagar* was acquitted a second time.

18 *R v Schmaltz*, Trial Transcript (12 December 2013), Medicine Hat 081056319P1 (ABPC) at 85:15–35 (discussed in ch. 2).

19 *R v L(G)*, 2014 ONSC 3403, 114 WCB (2d) 108; *R v Luceno*, Trial Transcript, Volume I (19 March 2014) Toronto C59248 (ONSC) (discussed in ch. 3).

20 Canada, Justice Department, "Ontario Judicial Appointments Announced" (1 June 2012), http://www.justice.gc.ca/eng/news-nouv/ja-nj/2012/doc_32748.html.

21 *R v L(G)* at para. 24.

22 *R v Adepoju*, Trial Transcript, Volume I (30 April 2013) Red Deer 120580485Q1 (ABQB) at 87, 89–90 (discussed in ch. 2).

23 *R v Adepoju*, 2014 ABCA 100, 8 Alta LR (6th) at para. 8 (quoting the trial judge, Justice Sisson; discussed in ch. 7).

24 For an eloquent examination of the resilience and resistance of sexual assault survivors see Alison Young, "The Wasteland of the Law: The Wordless Song of the Rape Victim," *Melbourne University Law Review* 22, no. 2 (1998): 442. See also Australia, New South Wales, Department for Women, *Heroines of Fortitude: The Experiences of Women in Court as Victims of Sexual Assault* (Woolloomooloo, NSW: Department for Women, 1996).

25 *R v B(S)*, Trial Transcript, Volume VI (6 June 2014) St John's 201301G4957 (NLTD) at 138:19–139:6 (discussed in ch. 3 and 6).

26 *R v Griffen*, 2016 ONSC 2448 at para. 143, [2016] OJ No 1916.

27 *R v Johnson*, Trial Transcript, (21 June 2016) Windsor CR-14-00003172-0000 (ONCJ) at 85:9.

28 *R v Luceno*, Trial Transcript, Volume I (19 March 2014) Toronto C59248 (ONSC) at 176:26. See also ibid. at 181:1 ("Q. So that's your new story. MS. NEDELKOPOULOS: Objection, Your Honour. Whether it's new or not, perhaps that's saved for submissions.").

29   *R v Al-Rawi*, Audio Trial Transcript: Testimony of the Complainant (9 February 2017) Halifax 2866665 (NSPC).

30   *R v Ghomeshi*, Trial Transcript, Volume IV (1 February 2016) Toronto 4817 998 15-75006437 (ONCJ) at 48:24.

31   *R v Johnson*, Trial Transcript, (20 June 2016) Windsor CR-14-00003172-0000 (ONCJ) at 90:30.

32   *R v B(S)*, Trial Transcript, Volume I (16 May 2014) St John's 201301G4957 (NLTD) at 32:7, 35:5, 39, 41:5.

Index

Aboriginal women. *See* Indigenous
complainants
accountability, 216
accused, rights of, 11, 112–14, 117–18,
120, 124, 140, 181–2, 220
Adepoju, R v, 36–7, 196–9, 225,
241nn64–6, 287nn26–33,
287nn32–5, 288nn37–40,
288nn42–4, 290n74, 290n76,
294n115, 299nn22–3
A(J), R v, 246nn138–9, 283n74
Al-Rawi, R v, 37–8, 142, 227, 241n67,
242nn68–74, 271n24, 293n109,
300n29
American College of Trial Lawyers,
85
apologies, 69, 207, 212
arrest of sexual assault
complainants. *See under* sexual
assault complainants

Backhouse, Constance, 59, 63, 97–8,
127
Baillot, Helen, 96
Barbara Schlifer Clinic (Toronto), 163
barriers to reporting sexual assaults:

fear of criminal justice system,
3, 10–11, 21, 190, 219. *See also* self-
blame and shame of sexual assault
complainants
Beilhartz, R v, 244n115
Bernardo, Paul, 109–10
"Best Lawyers in Canada," 65, 76,
83–4
B(IE), R v, 45–6, 141, 168, 192–6, 224,
244n106, 244nn108–11, 271n22,
280n4, 286nn2–8, 286nn10–11,
286nn14–16, 287nn23–5, 289n71,
290n76, 294n115, 298n13
Blanchard, R v, 6, 231n15
Boesveld, Sarah, 248n21
Boucher, R v, 269n1, 276n98
Bryant, Michael, 62
B(S), R v, 51–2, 76–83, 169–74, 225–
6, 227, 245nn127–32, 252nn109–11,
253nn112–36, 280nn11–14,
280nn16–25, 281nn26–30, 281n32,
299n25, 300n32

Cain, Joshua, 38–9
Cain, R v, 38–9, 178–80, 242nn75–9,
282nn52–7

Camp, Mabel Van, 188

Canadian Judicial Council (CJC), 191, 202, 204, 207, 209–12, 215, 217

Cardinal, Angela, 6, 231n15

Chambers, Marilyn, 84–5

Charter of Rights and Freedoms, 113, 298n10

CJC. *See* Canadian Judicial Council

Clarke, Allyson, 5

"clumsy Don Juan." *See Rhodes, R v*

CMG, R v, 203

colonialism, 187

consent: affirmative required, 33, 193–4, 195, 231n16; age of, 248–9n29; defence of, 31, 48, 49, 194; definition of, 125, 202–4, 219; judges' knowledge of legal definition, 191–218; must be contemporaneous, 54–5, 183–4; must be given voluntarily, 196–9; must be awake, 54–6. *See also Criminal Code*; judges, harm to sexual assault complainants; section 276 of the *Criminal Code*

"The Consequences of an Allegation of Sexual Assault" (Bayliss), 25

Cook, R v, 276nn98–9, 276n101

Courts of Appeal: Alberta, 37, 39, 176, 183, 198–9, 201–2; Newfoundland, 79–80, 169, 173, 245n131, 253n122; Nova Scotia, 195–6; Ontario, 28, 30, 31, 176, 240–1nn40–1

Cowan, Sharon, 96

Criminal Code: about, 120–1, 184; section 273.2(b), 193, 195, 201, 205; section 276 (*see* section 276 of the *Criminal Code*); section 277, 48–9,

141, 168–9, 244n116; section 278 and 278.2, 163, 168

criminal justice system: adversarial nature of, 7, 11, 101, 106–12, 166, 220–1; harm to sexual assault complainants, 4, 6–7, 108–9, 139–40, 220–1; role-based nature of trial process, 106–8, 109–12; sexual assault complainants' fear of, 3, 10–11, 21, 190, 219

Criminal Lawyers' Association (Ontario), 26

cross-examinations: audio recording of, 240n39; demonstrating minor inconsistencies, 181–2; in good faith, 116–17, 142, 219

Crown attorneys: duty to protect the process, 135–7, 140–1; training of, 161–2, 278n132. *See also* Crown attorneys, potential harm to sexual assault complainants

Crown attorneys, potential harm to sexual assault complainants: through lack of challenge to defence lawyer, 46–9, 137–47; through lack of witness preparation, 151–66

Cunliffe, Emma, 18

D, R v, 257n176

Darrach, R v, 264n47, 267n66

Dauvergne, Mia, 238–9n16

Day, Stockwell, 298n10

death threats, 38–9

defence lawyers: aggression as laudable/heroic, 64, 92–4, 98, 127; "Best Lawyers in Canada," 65, 76, 83–4; Crown attorneys' observations of, 57–8; disciplinary action against, 131–2, 269n87, 282n51; ethical duty or behaviour, 52–3, 61, 101, 103, 117, 124–34, 142, 219; feminist values of, 113–14; marketing/websites, 20, 85–6, 92–3, 118, 236n42, 255n168; mentorship, 92; myths held by, 24–60; notion of the hired gun, 101–6, 115–17; professional identity, 106–12; socialization in law school, 98–9, 258n187, 259nn188–90; work as important, 133, 233. *See also* defence lawyers, potential harm to sexual assault complainants; legality/rule of the law

defence lawyers, potential harm to sexual assault complainants: denial of, 25–6, 62, 125–6; use of arguably bullying/aggressive techniques (including repetition, interruptions, lengthy), 11–12, 28–32, 42, 53–4, 63–76, 150, 177–80, 249–50nn52–3, 251n78; use of intimidation (to discourage the complainant from proceeding), 105, 118–20, 125, 128–30, 269n87; use of stereotypes (including not applying for or misusing applications under sections 276–8), 34–51, 55, 63, 76–83, 86–92, 118–19, 122, 125, 127–9, 168–74, 184. *See also* whacking the complainant

Devlin, Richard, 214–15

dignity of accused. *See* accused, rights of

disclosure, delayed, 34–5, 42, 231n16

Dodek, Adam, 214–15

domestic violence, 95, 257n178

Donagan, Alan, 112

"Drunk Jane," 37–8, 242n70

ethical duty or behaviour, 52–3, 61, 101, 103, 117, 124–34, 142, 219

Ethical Principles for Judges (Canadian Judicial Council), 191

Ewanchuk, R v, 27, 33, 54–6, 196, 238n14, 241n55, 246n137, 246n144, 267n67, 283n75, 286n12, 286n17, 287n20, 288n36, 288n53, 288n54, 290n79, 290n83

Facebook, 70

false allegations, 94–7, 256n173, 257n174, 257nn176–8

feminism, 26–7, 113–14, 120, 126

Finlayson, George D., 64, 248n18

Finney, R v, 8, 30–2, 147, 152, 175–6, 224, 232n23, 241nn43–54, 241nn56–7, 272–3nn52–5, 274nn74–5, 274nn80–1, 281n36, 281nn38–9, 281nn42–4, 298n12

Franklin, John, 96

Freedman, Karyn, 7–8

G(A), R v, 240n22

G(AD), R v, 294n115

G(CM), R v, 289nn67–8, 289n70, 294n115

Ghomeshi, Jian, 3, 61, 124

Ghomeshi, R v, 4, 12, 62–3, 227, 247n8, 300n30

Gill, R v, 240n24

G(J), R v, 294n115

G(PG), R v, 150, 226, 240nn27–33, 273nn66–7, 273–4nn69–73

Graveline, R v, 281n31

Grey, Mandi, 4, 230n6

Griffin, R v, 240n29, 240nn34–9, 268n79, 273n67, 282n58, 299n26

Groia, Joseph, 131–2, 282n51

Groia v Law Society of Upper Canada, 269nn84–5, 281n33, 281–2n45

Halifax taxi driver. *See Al-Rawi, R v*

Hamilton, R v, 283n59, 283n73

heuristics, 123–4, 130

H(JJ), R v, 28, 240nn20–1

I(D), R v, 240n26

Indigenous complainants, 5–6, 21, 75, 187–8, 204, 237n44, 252n102, 284n87

Jaffe, Peter G., 96, 258n182

JK, R v, 144–5, 271n40, 272n42

Johnson, Ben, 86–9

Johnson, R v, 86–92, 226–7, 254nn151–5, 255nn156–67, 299n27, 300n31

Jonas, George, 24

judges: appointment, training, and assessment, 206–18, 285n91, 293n109, 295n126; expectation of basic legal knowledge, 191–218; inappropriate comments by, 240–1n41. *See also* judges, potential harm to sexual assault complainants

judges, potential harm to sexual assault complainants: from failure to intervene in cross-examinations, 46–9, 80, 168–74, 176–83, 283n72; from failure to make courtroom setting comfortable, 184–190; from seeming lack of knowledge of the law, 76–83, 146–9, 168–74, 191–218, 225, 272n44

Kaufman Report, 158

Kelln, R v, 240n26

Kench, R v, 283n63

Khaery, Mohamed, 72

Khaery, R v, 5–6, 72–5, 139, 152–3, 185–6, 231n13, 251nn76–89, 252nn90–100, 271nn17–18, 274n82, 284nn80–2

Kimber, Stephen, 63, 247n15

Konradi, Amanda, 138, 155, 177

Koshan, Jennifer, 49, 245n122

Krahé, Barbara, 222

language/names, 15–17, 234n34

law reforms, 6–7, 25, 27–8, 52–3, 59, 120–1, 125, 205, 222, 231n16

law school culture, 98–9, 258n187, 259nn188–90

law societies, 131–2, 282n51

Law Society of Upper Canada, 131–2, 174

lawyers. *See* defence lawyers

Lazar, Ruthy, 123, 138

legality/rule of the law, 112, 113, 115, 120, 124, 133

legal representation, state-funded, 162–4, 278n137

Levit, Nancy, 123

L(G), R v. See Luceno, R v

Luban, David, 111–12, 117

Luceno, Giuseppe, 65, 248–9n29

Luceno, R v, 29, 65–71, 177–8, 181, 224–5, 227, 248n28, 248–9n29, 249nn30–51, 249–250n52, 250nn53–68, 251nn69–73, 282nn48–50, 299n28.

Lyons, R v, 268nn68–9

Lyttle, R v, 125, 268nn70–1, 272n51, 283nn60–1

male sexual entitlement, 192–6

marital rape cases, 141, 245n122

medical records of complainant, 118–19, 163–4, 168

methodology, 20, 235n39, 235–6n40, 236n42

Miller, Karen-Lee, 5

Mills, R v, 243n92, 268n68, 268n72

M(L), R v, 240n26

Morin, Guy Paul, 158

Muise, R v, 277n119

Mundle, Dr, 255n165

Munro, Vanessa E., 96

myths, defence lawyers', 24–60; feminism, political correctness, and fair trial rights, 32–40; insulation of sexual assault complainants, 41–60; law reforms and cross-examinations, 28–32

names/language, 15–17, 234n34

National Judicial Institute (NJI), 211–14

National Post: "Regan a Victim of Matriarchal Justice" (Jonas), 24

New Judges School, 210

Nicholson, R v, 252n111

O'Heron, Rhyannon, 137

Osolin, R v, 16, 182–3, 272n50, 283n66

Parrott, R v, 233n29

Peterson, R v, 240n26

policy manuals, 17, 20, 136, 157–61

Practice Note on Sexual Offences (Nova Scotia), 160

preliminary inquiries: inconsistencies from, 68, 157, 181; review of statements from, 152, 159; use of intimidation (to discourage complainant from proceeding), 42–3, 52–3, 94, 105–6, 119, 129, 133

pre-trial applications, 51, 76–80, 169–71

provincial policies on sexual offences, 135–6

Queen's Counsel, 64, 76

rape, 30–1, 138, 140–1, 245n122

rape mythology, 10, 52, 56, 120–4, 128, 138, 173, 204–6, 265n59. *See also* rape; rape shield law; twin myth stereotypes

rape shield law, 41, 43, 46, 48, 142. *See also* section 276 of the *Criminal Code*

recommendations for change, 23, 184–90, 214–17, 279n147

Regan, Gerald, 24, 63

Regan, R v, 24, 63, 237n3, 238n7, 247n12, 277n115

"Regan a Victim of Matriarchal Justice" (Jonas), 24

Regehr, Cheryl, 154, 165
REM, R v, 216
Rhodes, R v, 206–7, 290n76,
    291nn86–9
R(J), R v, 203, 289nn65–6, 290n75,
    294n115
Robson, Ruthann, 235n38
rule of the law/legality, 112, 113, 115,
    120, 124, 133

S, R v, 257n176
Sabourin, Norman, 207
Schecter, Barbara, 248n21
Schmaltz, Joshua, 183
Schmaltz, R v, 40, 146, 175–6, 183–4,
    224, 243nn85–6, 272nn46–9,
    273n56, 274nn74–5, 281n37,
    281nn40–2, 283nn67–72,
    283nn76–7, 299n18
Seaboyer, R v, 244n116, 264n43,
    264n45, 268n68
Seamone, Evan R., 96
section 276 of the *Criminal Code*:
    about, 41, 44–5, 49, 121–2, 128,
    169, 244n115, 245n119, 272n44;
    application as intimidation,
    55–6; applications denied, 43–4;
    effectiveness of, 141, 224; failure to
    apply, 45–46, 48–9, 86–92, 142–6,
    168–73; failure to understand, 144,
    199–203; improper application of,
    50–2; misuse of, 76–83, 122
self-blame and shame of sexual
    assault complainants, 7–10, 127,
    155, 162, 204–205, 232–233n25,
    275–276n96
sexual assault complainants: arrest
    of, 5–6, 72–3, 231n15; coping
    strategies, 139, 152–3, 232–3n25;
    dignity/resilience of, 120, 225–6;
    suicide attempts, 29–30, 73–4,
    150, 226, 273n68; term usage,
    15–17, 234n34; testimonial aids,
    136–7, 154; vulnerability of,
    135–6, 151, 155. *See also* barriers
    to reporting sexual assaults;
    Indigenous complainants; self-
    blame and shame of sexual assault
    complainants; sexual assault
    complainants, harms to
sexual assault complainants, harms
    to. *See* criminal justice system;
    Crown attorneys, potential harm
    to sexual assault complainants;
    defence lawyers, potential harm
    to sexual assault complainants;
    judges, potential harm to sexual
    assault complainants
Sexual Assault Response Team, 72
sexual assaults/cases, statistics, 3,
    16, 21, 219, 232n24, 233–4n32,
    238–9n16, 295n1
sexual entitlement, male, 192–6
Shearing, R v, 180, 243n92, 283n62
Sheehy, Elizabeth, 18, 151
S(JS), R v, 49–51, 245nn123–126
Slater, R v, 240n26
Small, Peter, 248n26
Smith, Abbe, 126–7
Social Context Education Project
    (NJI), 213
Spence, R v, 277n126
Standing Committee on the Status
    of Women, 212–13
stereotypes. *See* consent; rape
    mythology; section 276 of the

Criminal Code; sexual assault complainants, harms to; twin myth stereotypes

suicide attempts. *See under* sexual assault complainants

Supreme Court of Canada, 121, 125, 132, 173–4, 180–3, 195, 216, 253n122

Tanovich, David, 42, 58

Taslitz, Andrew, 86

T(B), R v, 240n23

Temkin, Jennifer, 123, 138, 222

testimonial aids, 136–7, 154

"Thoughts of an Advocate," 84–5

T(J), R v, 43, 118, 243nn94–100, 243n103, 263n39

trauma: to legal professionals, ix, 96, 107–8, 165, 258nn182–4, 262n18; to sexual assault complainants, ix, 140, 226. *See also* barriers to reporting sexual assaults; sexual assault complainants, harms to

Traynor, R v, 254n145

T(SG), R v, 268n79, 268n81

twin myth stereotypes, 41–2, 46, 51, 82, 121–3. *See also* consent; section 276 of the *Criminal Code*

Ururyar, R v, 34–5, 142–3, 230n6, 241nn58–63, 271nn26–39, 272n42

Vandervort, Lucinda, 149, 165, 279n147

Vrklevski, Lila Petar, 96

Wagar, R v, 39–40, 143–4, 146, 147–9, 199–203, 224, 243nn80–4,

272nn42–3, 272n45, 273nn57–61, 273nn63–5, 288nn45–52, 288nn55–7, 288n59, 289n72, 290nn76–7, 293n109, 294n115, 299n16–17

Warnica, Richard, 248n21

Weiss, Karen, 232–3n25

whacking the complainant: denial of, 41–2, 61, 220; example of, 169; lawyers not disciplined for, 174; legal limits to, 124–5; as strategy, 52, 58, 93, 97, 125–6, 141, 234–5n35

Wilson, Larry, 163

Windsor Star (Ontario), 21–2

Woolley, Alice, 101, 111–12, 128, 138, 151, 156, 157

Wright, R v, 47–9, 142, 168–9, 224, 244nn112–13, 245n120, 271n23, 280nn5–8, 298n14

Zachariou, R v, 244–5n117

Zadeh, R v, 240n26